TOMORROW'S TOURIST: SCENARIOS & TRENDS

BY

IAN YEOMAN

Futurologist
With the Future Foundation

ELSEVIER

Amsterdam • Boston • Heidelberg • London • New York • Oxford
Paris • San Diego • San Francisco • Singapore • Sydney • Tokyo

Elsevier
Linacre House, Jordan Hill, Oxford OX2 8DP, UK
Radarweg 29, PO Box 211, 1000 AE Amsterdam, The Netherlands

First edition 2008

British Library Cataloguing in Publication Data
A catalogue record for this book is available from the British Library

Library of Congress Cataloging-in-Publication Data
A catalog record for this book is available from the Library of Congress

ISBN: 978-0-08-045339-2
ISSN: 1572-560X

For information on all Elsevier publications
visit our website at books.elsevier.com

Printed and bound in Hungary

08 09 10 11 12   10 9 8 7 6 5 4 3 2 1

To Mam and Dad

Contents

Acknowledgements

I owe a big debt to the Future Foundation, which allowed me to use the content and data from their *Changing Lives*' Survey. In particular, I appreciate the patience of Jamie Allsopp and Ed Greggs, who put up with constant harassment from me and who handled my many specific and unusual requests with much forbearance.

All the analysts at the Future Foundation who wrote the consumer reports which I adapted for this book.

Una McMahon-Beattie, Senior Lecturer in Marketing at Ulster University, for her assistance with Chapters 12 and 14.

Paul Flatters and Jim Murphy at the Future Foundation for their advice on the 'Assault on Pleasure' trend in Chapter 23.

Chris Greenwood, Research Analyst at VisitScotland, who provided the data-analysis and forecasts in Chapter 5. Chris also wrote papers which were the foundations for Chapters 3, 4 and 14.

Professor Brain Hay of Strathclyde University, who provided assistance and advice with Chapter 19, based upon previous work done by the Future Foundation.

Rob Davidson of Westminster University for his advice about tourism in China and the conference markets which are covered in Chapter 20.

Dr Alastair Durie of Stirling University, who assisted with Chapter 2 on the history of world tourism.

Judith Sleigh for proof-reading many drafts of the chapters.

Lori Pennington of the University of Florida for access to her unpublished research on Grand Travellers.

VisitScotland for allowing me to write this book.

Professor Stephen Page of Stirling University for supporting this proposal.

Sally North of Elsevier for her patience.

Rosie, my cat, who listened silently to all my readings and did not criticise me once!

Foreword

Knowing what will happen ahead is a wish as old as mankind. Anticipation of future developments helped always to be better prepared and more successful, whether for travelling, protection, hunting, pilgrimage or for choosing the site of a settlement, for instance.

Nowadays, it has become a standard to refer to the complexity of the environment when analysing and explaining actual or past developments. The reasons are manifold and have to do with the increasing degrees of freedom of choice, flexibility and economic wealth. However, for those who plan, invest and manage the infrastructure, the frameworks and the human resources it is fundamental and, there is no other alternative but to understand to the largest extent possible what will or might happen tomorrow.

Prof. Ian Yeoman has been working for more than a decade in the field of scenario planning for the tourism industry. His thinking outside the goldfish bowl, combined with a sound understanding of the many different areas of the tourism sector, brings new and key contributions to this analysis. This new book presents new insights on how to be better prepared for the future ahead, to be more successful and above all to successfully face the enormous challenges ahead, including climate change, new tourists and the millennium development goals. These challenges will not be only solved through the activities from inside the tourism sector. But the constantly growing economic and social importance of the sector, the enormous sensitiveness to external shocks and the importance for more and more peoples well-being, give us a special reason to focus intensively on what lays ahead of us. It is our responsibility and our contribution towards a better and more sustainable tourism development.

I hope that reading this book will bring you thoughts and ideas on how to better achieve this aim.

Dr. Dirk Glaesser
Chief, Risk and Crisis Management
World Tourism Organization (UNWTO)

Understanding and anticipating your customer.

Being customer focused is, today, universally accepted as being good for business and public sector organisations. Developing products and services that fit existing, and emerging, customer needs, creating communications that are resonant with your target audience – few would deny these as their aim. However, it is easier said than done in an era where lives are more complicated than ever, the pace of change is faster than ever, and society is more diverse than ever.

The Future Foundation works to help you understand the increasingly complex lives—the stresses and strains, the hopes and fears, the underlying needs of your customer. Our analysis and forecasts are there to explain how the different forces—social, economic, technological, cultural and political— are shaping society, markets and the lives of individuals themselves.

Our work recognises the intricacy and interconnectedness of the issues that you face, our role is to provide solutions that are dynamic and practical using thinking that is both vibrant and challenging.

The Future Foundation has clients ranging from Coors and Visa to Electrolux and Nissan. FMCG brands, media owners, agencies, financial services, retailers charities and government departments across 24 countries. Wherever we work the aim is the same; robust, intelligent analysis of the changing world and the opportunities that it affords for you.

"nVision is now a key pillar of account planning and new business activity within the advertising industry. Having access to it these days puts you on a level playing field. You have to use it to keep up with your competitors and the way you use it can give you the edge." *Madonna Deverson*, Head of Leo IQ, Leo Burnett.

"Our client needed a strong creative input, one that would generate a media agenda outside the personal finance pages...the award winning campaign this resulted in a high profile 'news' presence, driven by a landmark piece of research from the Future Foundation." *Band & Brown Communications* quoted in — Marketing magazine.

"The Future Foundation has shown how the right insight, prepared and presented in the right way, can inspire management and help generate real commercial value...a first class product from first class people."

Alan McWalter (Alan now has a portfolio of business interests having previously been Group Marketing Director at Marks & Spencer, and a Director of Woolworths and Comet)

For more information please contact:
E: info@futurefoundation.net
W: www.futurefoundation.net
p: +44(0)203 042 4747

future foundation
An Experian company

The Future Foundation 6th Floor, Cardinal Place, 80 Victoria Street, London, SW1E 5JL, UK

SECTION I

Chapter 1

Introduction: World Tourism and the Tourist in 2030

I wanted to write this book in order to set out where I think world tourism will be in 2030. As the world's only dedicated scenario-planner and futurologist in the tourism field I am in privileged position. I could have been controversial and predicted the end of the world because of high oil prices, war in the Middle East, demographic time bombs, pandemics and terrorism. I do not, however, believe that the world is coming to an end in the next 25 years — but I do believe that tourism is changing and that markets are shifting.

This book is about where world tourism will be in 2030 and what the tourist will be doing in 2030. I believe that tourism is about experiences, not about virtual worlds — so Captain Kirk's virtual tourism experience is not included (however, a weekend break in outer space will be possible). This book is not about technology, because technologies are not places but are simply information channels and enablers. I do, however, discuss how technologies and the new media are drivers of the tourist's choice of destination. This book is not about the future of terrorism, war, diseases and disasters, as these have always been part of our lives and will continue to influence what we do. This book is about *you*, where *you* will go on holiday and what *you* will do when you get there. All the chapters set out to explain why changes are occurring and this is done through a comprehensive analysis of trends — along with a little bit of blue skies thinking.

The writing of this book has been supported by the Future Foundation, a leading London-based consumer think-tank, with which VisitScotland has worked since 2004. The book has drawn heavily on the Future Foundation's *Changing Lives* Survey, which is a comprehensive omnibus survey of European households. The book, therefore, is a collaborative effort between myself, my colleagues at VisitScotland, my academic partners and the team of analysts at the Future Foundation.

I believe the world economy is strong and will continue to grow, even given the present debate about global warming and climate change. The book is *supported* by a website www.tomorrowstourist.com, where you will find a range of materials about everything that is not mentioned in this book and more.

Prof. Ian Yeoman
Futurologist
5th November 2007

The Future

History tells us that war affects tourism. Durie (2003) established that the first tourists came to Scotland because of war in Europe. The first Grand Tours of Scotland, for example, were enjoyed by European tourists who were avoiding France and Germany during the Napoleonic Wars, and tourists chose Scotland rather than Ireland in early Victorian times because Ireland was regarded as barbaric and unsafe for travellers.

The 9/11 attack on targets in New York and Washington in 2001 sent the world into a panic, and the resulting legislation has impacted on US tourism, making it harder for tourists to visit the country because of higher barriers to entry, such as visas, biometric passports and extra security checks at airports. There is also a perception within potential markets that if people say something negative about the United States then they could face detention (Yeoman, 2007).

As Durie (2003) points out, wars have always happened and will continue to happen. The same can be said about the present debate about global warming. People often forget that the climate has been undergoing change since the beginning of time — in the twenty-first century, we tend to believe that climate change is a new phenomenon and the world may be coming to an end.

Taking the Long View

If people's time horizon encompasses only 1 day in the past and 1 day in the future — then their perception of the future will be the same as their understanding of the present. If we cannot see beyond tomorrow, then we shall not have the ability to anticipate change, nor take relevant action in response. If our time horizon is only yesterday and we do not consider circumstances of long ago, then we cannot understand the cycle of events when they re-occur. The long view is about 'picturing' what the world could look like as a consequence of change. Taking the long view is important because the consequences of unfolding trends can be 'pictured' only over a time period of 10, 20, or 30 years, whether it be the impact of demographics or technologies.

Taking the long view is the secret ingredient of success, because without doing that the business world cannot prepare for the future. Today, the pace of change in the modern world is frightening as the line between fact and science fiction becomes blurred. If you want to understand the future of technology, you have to take a science-fiction approach in order to imagine the imaginable — such is the pace of change. The nature of work, consumer expectations and the environment are all shifting radically, making it difficult for society and businesses to plan ahead and to prepare adequately for future challenges. Indeed, in our age of hyper-change, many people have no notion of what sort of world they should prepare for. Taking the well-considered long view or having sufficient foresight, in contrast to accepting fatalistically what will happen, gives us increased power to shape our future, even in the most turbulent times. People who can think ahead will be prepared for the rapid social and technological progress that is affecting every aspect of our lives.

Many of the best-known techniques for long-term planning were developed by US military planners, because the post-World War II nuclear age made it critical to 'think about the unthinkable' and prepare for whatever might happen. Pioneering futurists at the RAND Corporation (the first think-tank) began to seriously consider what new technologies might emerge in the future and how these might affect the security of the United States. The RAND futurists, along with others, refined a number of ways of thinking about the future. Futurists recognise that the future is continuous with the present, so we can learn a great deal about what may happen in the future by looking systematically at what is happening now and what has taken place in the past. The key is not simply looking at events but rather scrutinising trends, such as long-term shifts in population or the increase in the processing power of technology. Futurists develop these trends into scenarios, as a way of thinking about the future. Scenarios are not predictions but are a way of setting the scene (or scenes) so as to state in a credible way what could happen in the future. Scenarios help us think about what the future may bring and help us react or adapt to circumstances in a relevant way.

A useful technique is trend analysis, which is an examination of the causes, the speed of developments and the impact they may have. This is one of the techniques that has been used throughout this book; for example, a longer lifespan is one of the key drivers of change in a number of chapters:

- As society ages, medical discoveries extend people's lifespan and consumers also become more interested in well-being therapies.
- As society ages, people become interested in sporting activities in order to stay healthy and live longer.
- As the population ages, people's attitudes and outlooks change, and they desire earlier retirement or second/holiday homes or more time with grandchildren.

This book is based on a combination of different disciplines and methodologies. The thinking about scenarios has required an appreciation of history in order to understand the future; it means recognising the macro drivers that are shaping the world and what impact they may have on tourism. The thinking has also necessitated a comprehensive understanding of economics and demographics in order to envisage future purchasing power and the impact on tourist flows and destination choice. We have used the application of psychology and sociology in order to understand what the future tourist will do on holiday. Scenarios also consider barriers to growth, such as people's need for security and the impact of climate change. The strength of argument in this book lies in the methodology and analysis behind it, which seek to explain through trends where the tourist will go on holiday in 2030 and what they will be doing with the use of a little bit of creativity and imagination. As well as providing scenarios for the future, this book gives an insight into *how* change is occurring, by using data from the Future Foundations *Changing Lives* Survey.

Changing Lives is a comprehensive survey of European households, which since 1980 allows futurists or researchers to understand how change has taken place over a period of time. In addition, the data which comes from such a survey allows futurists to put forward projections of trends in order to find out what the impact of those trends would be.

Some of the chapters vary in size depending on the complexity of the subject. They can be read in whichever order you prefer, but I would recommend that the first section is read first — it just reads better that way.

What Will World Tourism Look Like in 2030?

According to some history books, with the invention of money by the Babylonians and the development of trade round about 4000 BC, travel and tourism was invented! Chapter 2 discusses the development of world tourism and the tourist, and whether the tourist is travelling for business or for pleasure. Chapter 3 begins with a forecast that the world GDP will rise by 129% by 2030, but the world in 2030 will be different from that in 2005, whether in terms of changing demographics or the impact of energy supply. The chapter looks at 17 mega drivers that will shape the world in the years leading up to 2030 and their consequences for world tourism. Chapter 4 examines the macro conditions that will shape destinations and the consumer trends that will influence the tourist's choice of destination and activity.

Chapter 5 is one of the most important chapters in the book, because it gives forecasts of who the winners and the losers will be in 2030. By 2030, there will be 1.9 billion international arrivals and world tourism receipts will grow to US $2 trillion. China will be the world's largest receiver of international tourists and the United States will be the largest economy in terms of international receipts. The winners in 2030 will be Turkey, the United States, Macao, Australia, Malaysia and China, whereas Europe will be the biggest loser, losing 13% of market-share between 2005 and 2030.

What Will the Tourist Do on Holiday in 2030?

The opening chapter in this section explores how an affluent and ageing society searches for the foundation of youth and the perfect body in *Incredible India*, whether it be medical enhancement of their body or a holistic well-being approach. The chapter provides an in-depth analysis of the trends which are shaping an ageing society and, from a tourism perspective, how India has positioned itself as medical tourism destination for plastic surgery. An elderly population will be more frequent users of health-related goods and services in the future, making tourism and health the world's largest industries by 2022. Look out for waiters as your nutritional advisor and fashionable pampering holidays for tourists with pets.

Chapter 7 looks at how the family structures will change in the United States, moving from a traditional, horizontal to a vertical model with more aunties and uncles. In 2030, the world will have fewer children and grandparents living longer; children will become more important in 2030 because adults will want to spend more time with — and money on — them. The niche market of grand-travellers will emerge, where grandparents and grandchildren will take holidays together, especially during school holidays when many parents have to work. In Chapter 8, we show how the mountainous country of Albania on the Adriatic Sea known as *Shqiperia*, or the land of eagles, once a shadowy Communist prison state, will emerge as a leading Southern European destination by 2030 because of its low cost of living, sunny climate, sandy beaches, stunning landscape and proximity to the European markets. One of the key factors to drive this growth will be the second-home tourist. We also explore how the increasing number of second homes could be the economic facilitator for the development of golf courses and resorts along the Adriatic coast.

In Chapter 9, we look at how, at a time when many futurists are talking about the 'greening' of tourism and about sustainable development, Las Vegas, the Disneyland for adults, provides an example of the opposite end of the spectrum. Las Vegas is the place where anything can happen, where anything goes and wives will never find out! Its naughty, raunchy marketing slogan, 'What happens in Vegas, stays in Vegas', represents the sinful side of tourism. Vegas is about conspicuous consumption and lavishness. Why will it be so successful in 2030? Simply because of sex and sin. Vegas is a sinful city where tourists take vacations for adult, undiluted erotica; this is where their fantasies are played out. At the same time, however, Las Vegas has a dark side of exploitation and modern-day slavery.

Chapter 10 explores shopping as a leisure activity and Dubai as the world's most ostentatious, luxurious retail destination in 2030. Dubai is about conspicuous consumption where themed environments act as attractors, catering for adults — it is the bourgeois Disneyfication of destinations. Shopping in Dubai is the symbol of luxury, of play and of pleasure, all associated with lifestyle and consumerism. This chapter provides an analysis of shopping trends and an examination of Dubai and the Middle East as retail-shopping destinations. Chapter 11 explores the world of Bridget Jones because by 2030 single females who live alone could represent 19% of UK households. For them holidays in 2030 will be meeting places for singletons and the opportunity for romance and sex!

In Chapter 12, we explore several themes that will shape the future of tourism in Africa. Our scenario follows Siubhan, a wildlife enthusiast, who is taking a career break, doing volunteer work and searching for new and meaningful experiences. She stays longer and goes 'deeper' than most tourists — seeking a truly authentic experience. The Middle East is the centre for the Islamic religion and in Chapter 13, pilgrimage and tourism are discussed — we look especially at the consequences of the rise of Islam and the decline of Christianity, along with the rise of spirituality.

Observers of Scotland's food have contrasting opinions. For some observers, the Scots have the worst of diets and the highest obesity rates in Europe; others consider Scotland as the producer of the finest smoked salmon, game and shellfish in the world. Food is an important feature of Scotland's tourism landscape and living culture. Chapter 14 explores how the concept of the food tourism will develop and what the food tourist to Scotland will look for in 2015.

Extreme sports, particularly those such as skateboarding, surfing, bugging, base-jumping and extreme ironing, evoke a lifestyle choice resulting from a certain mindset associated with the adrenalin rush which people seek in order to break through the boundaries of normality and everyday life. Chapter 15 explores why the tourist of the future will be interested in sport and how destinations are being shaped by sporting events, in this case London as the venue for the Urban Rat Race. In 2030, the Gleneagles Lunar Space Station will be the world's most exclusive resort. On entering the Virgin Galactic spaceship at Auchterarder, space tourists will fasten their seat belt, hear the rockets roar and feel the sudden power of 4G acceleration. As the spaceship reaches the stratosphere they will gaze down on Planet Earth for the most exclusive view in the world. During their stay at the Gleneagles Space Station tourists will enjoy a round of golf, take the lunar buggy out for a spin and float around the leisure complex. Chapter 16 discusses space tourism as a metaphor for the changing concept of luxury and the tourist's desire for new experiences, whether it be space travel or something rather more down to earth.

Chapter 17 looks at the future of Macao and the emerging middle classes of China's burgeoning population. By 2030, Macao will outstrip Las Vegas as the world's most important gambling and entertainment resort. Much of this growth will be driven by the Chinese people's love of gambling and the lack of opportunity to indulge their passion on mainland China. Chapter 18 focuses on the cultural capital through participating in festivals, with the Rio Carnival used as the leading example of a spectacular extravaganza of costumes, parades and parties. There is nothing conformist about participating in the Carnival — it is a parade of self-expression and creativity that encourages non-conformity. The reference point for the tourist who takes part is individuality and innovation, and of being different, because being at the Carnival is a self-expression of escapism from the norm and of becoming the kind of person one cannot be at home.

What will the tourist to Scotland look like in 2025? In Chapter 19, three scenarios are developed, looking at how different generations perceive Scotland and what they would do on holiday. These three global clans in 2025 are designated as: 'Freedom Fighters' — those aged 65 +; 'Millennial Sophisticates' — those aged 40–45 years and 'Shanghai Virtual Social Network' — those aged 20–25. These generational scenarios bring different perspectives of the future, some good and some not so good! The final chapter in this section explores the feminisation of travel and business in China as a result of urbanisation, educational attainment and the changing roles of women in society.

What If?

In this section we explore how circumstances could influence or impact on the growth of world tourism in the future, whether climate change or the tourists' lack of trust in governments and their need for personal security. In Chapter 21, we look at how, post-9/11, the United States has found itself cornered by the dual crisis of security and lack of trust, which has fundamentally challenged the visions of the world because companies and individuals are seriously concerned for their physical security and anxious about the future. Consequently, tourists to the United States now have to prove beyond any reasonable doubt that they are who they say they are before entering the country. These precautions, in turn, have made potential tourists wary of travelling to the States and have impacted upon the destination's branding. This chapter explores in detail how this could seriously damage America's image abroad and lead to the failure of tourism in the United States.

In Chapter 22, I explored the impact of global warming and climate change and how it will change the tourism products in several destinations; just imagine the French Alps without snow and skiing! Countries such as the Seychelles will not exist because they will have been submerged by the sea and the desertification of Crete will make it a harsh and unattractive land. What we are saying is that destinations cannot ignore climate change, because tourists' choices will be shaped by the environment in 2030.

In Chapter 23, we explore the trend of the *Assault on Pleasure* and the end of world tourism by 2030 because it will be deemed immoral by society, bad for the environment and too dangerous for individuals to participate in. At present, there is an ongoing debate about tourism and sustainability and any outcomes from this discussion could curtail the growth of world tourism in the years leading up to 2030. If the New Puritans have their way, then the world may be driven by a fear of the future and the myth of decline.

And Finally...

In Chapter 24, I have advised how to make the trends and drivers that are explored in this book come alive by using the Future Foundation's future-proofing technique. By incorporating such techniques you can adapt what you do and how you market your product to encompass future trends.

Concluding Remarks

In 1950, 25 million people took an international holiday; by 2030, we predict that 1.9 billion people will take an international holiday. How the world will have changed in this period! But holidays are about experiences as well as places, whether horse-riding in the Wild West or skiing down a mountain in Afghanistan. The places may change but the experiences will be fundamentally the same. But there will be more tourists from different countries who want to enjoy themselves. The only difference between 2005 and 2030 is that holidays in Outer Space will be more accessible!

Remember to visit www.tomorrowstourist.com for further details, trends and scenarios related to this book.

Chapter 2

History of World Tourism

The Early Beginnings

Tourism is one of the world's major economic success stories, a story that, like time, has no beginning or end. It is a phenomenon that has been created and is difficult to define because of the complexity. To summarise, when time began so did tourism.

With the Babylonian invention of money and the development of trade in 4000 BC, travel and tourism were invented. Not only were the Babylonians the first to grasp the idea of money and use it in business transactions, but according to Goeldner and Brent Ritchie (2006), they founded the travel business. *People* could now pay for transportation and accommodation with money or barter. Beginning in 2700 BC, the Egyptians started building pyramids as elaborate burial tombs, including the Step Pyramid of Djoser, the Sphinx and pyramid complexes at Giza and Abusir. So wonderful were these tombs that they attracted large numbers of visitors. In the words of Casson (1974, p. 32):

> As each monument was a hallowed spot, so the visitors always spent some moments in prayer, yet their prime motivation was curiosity or disinterested enjoyment, not religion.

Around 1500 BC, Queen Hatshepsut took a cruise from Egypt to Punt (on the east coast of Africa); the journey is recorded in the temples of Deir el-Bahri at Luxor. Another Egyptian, Harkhuf, was an envoy of the pharaoh to Sudan. He brought home a pygmy trained in native dances as a present for his ruler — the first recorded souvenir. Early Egyptians also purchased bargains or specialties abroad for their friends and relatives. In 1800 BC, a young Uzalum received this request:

> I have never before written to you for something precious I wanted. But if you want to be like a father to me, get me a fine string full of beads, to be worn around the head.
>
> Casson (1974, p. 34)

Further evidence of Egyptian travellers is reported by Herodotus:

> The Egyptians meet to celebrate festivals not once a year but a number of times. The biggest and most popular is at Bubastis ... , the next at

Busiris ... , the third at Sais ... , the fourth at Heliopolis ... , the fifth
at Buto ... , the sixth at Papremis. ... They go there on the river, men
and women together, a big crowd of each in the boat. As they sail,
some of the women keep clicking castanets and some of the men play
on the pipes, and the rest, both men and women, sing and beat time
with their hands. ... And when they arrive at Bubastis, they celebrate
the occasion with great sacrifices, and more wine is consumed at this
one festival than during the whole rest of the year.

Casson (1974, p. 31)

The same stories, as mentioned above, are repeated in Ancient Greece, the Roman
Empire, Persia and the Silk Road. In Ancient Greece, according to tradition, in
776 BC the citizens of city-states honoured the god Zeus by organising an athletic
competition that led to the Olympic Games. The Phoenicians carried paying
passengers around the Mediterranean. People of the Qing dynasty paid homage to
gods and goddess in sacred sites throughout China. As countries, civilisations and
economies developed, travel and tourism grew for business and pleasure. Hence it is
difficult to say when tourism actually began.

The Foundations of a Modern Industry

One of the best-documented roots of today's tourism industry is found in many
religious traditions, such as making a pilgrimage to Benares for Hindus or to Mecca
for Muslims. The French guidebook *The Travels of Sir John Mandeville* (Mandeville,
1375) provided the travellers with information about the Holy Land, including
itineraries. This early guidebook was translated into many languages for international tourists. In the fifteenth century, the Venetian government assigned two galleys
to carry pilgrims across the Mediterranean to Palestine.

Shrines such as Compostela in Spain and healing wells throughout Europe
attracted growing numbers of tourists; and spa treatment — with classical origins
traceable back to the Romans (present-day Budapest's baths are heir to the hot
springs of the spa settlement that they called *Aquincum*) — bridged the gap into the
post-Reformation world. Although in places the older Catholic tradition of healing
continued; notably at Lourdes, by the 1860s cures were scientific rather than
miraculous and under the direction of physicians rather than priests. Treatments
took time, which meant that spa resorts had to provide accommodation and
entertainment for invalids and their companions; for example at Bath, promenades,
reading rooms and theatres were added to the pools and pump rooms.

The business of health was to remain an important component in tourism. Resorts
such as Vichy in France, Baden-Baden in Germany, Saratoga Springs in America
and Buxton in Britain catered for invalids and convalescents, and often specialized in
the treatment of particular conditions. Some areas, of which the Riviera is an
example, became popular as winter retreats for consumptives; the grim contemporary saying was that 'Cannes is for living, Monte Carlo for gambling and Mentone

for dying'. Many health resorts were inland, as well as remote, and at high altitude in clean mountain air, away from the smog and filth of the industrialised cities.

New Dimensions and Developments

From the later eighteenth century onwards, there was a growing fascination in Europe with salt water and the seaside from which evolved, in England, mass resorts such as Blackpool and Scarborough. It started with a medical enthusiasm: salt-water *dipping* (rather than swimming) at Brighton, as endorsed by the prince regent, came to be regarded as both fashionable and health-giving. Where the upper classes led, other sections of society were to follow; gradually, the beach became a source of entertainment and amusement for all ages and classes. The English showed a particular appetite for the seaside; the Lancashire resort of Blackpool, which was developed after the coming of the railways in 1846, had no rival in the Western world. Sunday trains left Manchester at 6 a.m. and returned at 8 or 9 p.m., providing people ample time at Blackpool to bathe, play and refresh themselves, and also — or so the railways optimistically suggested — attend a place of worship. Where England led, the rest of the United Kingdom followed; then mainland Europe: Arcachon in France, San Sebastian in Spain, Bad Doberan close to the Baltic coast and even Heligoland were noted European sea-bathing stations. What had started as a health fashion for the aristocratic few became a must for the many.

But not all tourists were sickly. Some, nearly all of them male, travelled for sport. The Highlands of Scotland, thanks to grouse, deer and salmon, became a playground for the very rich or well connected. Big-game hunting in India or Africa attracted enthusiasts, though most of them followed their exploits only in print, from the safety of an armchair. Golf was to exercise a much wider appeal across the classes, and was exported from Scotland to England and to the Continent.

Sport interested mostly men, but a much larger tourist constituency was drawn to travel by scenery; travellers set out in search of the picturesque in nature and ruin fascinated by history, literature, architecture and antiquities, especially those of the Classical world. In many respects, this began with the Grand Tour of the Continent, primarily France and Italy, which was developed in the eighteenth century as an essential part of the education of those in Britain who could afford it. Under the supervision of a tutor or a 'bear-leader' — Adam Smith gave up his post at Glasgow University to conduct the sons of the Duke of Buccleuch — the tour might last months or even longer and take in a period of study at a Continental university. There was even an informal agenda for many boys away from home which looked to their sexual education. The numbers fluctuated but were considerable; by the later eighteenth century it was in thousands rather than handfuls and travellers' taking a Grand Tour. Indeed, a Scottish banker, Robert Herries, pioneered the creation of a network of agencies on the Continent from the Channel ports to the Mediterranean where travellers' notes could be cashed.

An important shift occurred when the Napoleonic Wars led to the closing of the Continent to visitors for nearly 20 years. The closure of the Continent turned British attention towards the discovery of their own country, the Lakes, Mid Wales and of course Scotland. Another influence was that of romanticism, which converted remote localities — the Swiss Alps, the Scottish Highlands — into places of fascination rather than of fear. Romantic literature peopled these places with invented or embellished heroes and ruffians. The cult of Ossian fascinated Europeans (Napoleon is said to have carried a copy of the poems in his travelling bags), and the legend of William Tell rather than John Calvin drew many to visit Switzerland. Walter Scott was to turn this change in taste to the great advantage of himself, his publisher and his country, particularly the Trossachs. So great was the tourist interest that his poem *The Lady of the Lake* (Scott, 1810) aroused, that a local landowner was rumoured to be looking for the prettiest girl in Edinburgh so that she could play the part of the lady for the summer visitors to Loch Katrine.

The Influence of Transport

Tourism, once the preserve of the monied and leisured, was to change radically during the nineteenth century. Of central importance to broadening the flow of tourism were new forms of transport that allowed greater numbers of tourists to travel at lower cost and on more predictable schedules, both reinforcing existing flows and penetrating new areas. Eighteenth-century transport was not as hopeless as it is often portrayed: the grand chausées had made travel in France by private coach or public diligence quite tolerable, and the turnpikes had done likewise in Britain. In Britain the paddle-steamer, which made its appearance in the Clyde and on the Thames ca. 1812, made travel possible for the middle orders, and made popular within a few years the river or estuary 'pleasure excursion'. In addition, buffeting of the Channel crossing was mercifully shortened by better, faster ships.

The railways took tourism to new levels, first in Britain then throughout the Continent. British railways catered for every class of society. Well-off passengers travelled first class with their servants and luggage to select resorts; professional families from the larger cities migrated to the seaside for the summer (often with father returning to his work during the week). At weekends and fair holidays, the trains filled with working-class day-trippers, sometimes rowdy and liable to ruffle social convention with their lack of respect for separate-sex bathing, the Sabbath or sobriety. Excursions, whether organised by Sunday school workers, charities or political groups, became a part of summer life for many.

Transport change and tourism have always been closely intertwined: the coming of motor transport and air services exercised an equally profound effect on the direction, scale and degree of tourism, at the expense sometimes of domestic resorts. The advent of the charter flight in the 1960s led to an exodus of British holidaymakers to Mediterranean resorts, where the sun could be guaranteed. In the late 1990s, a remarkable expansion of cheap air flights opened up short-stay possibilities throughout Europe. Just as the inhabitants of select Brighton and snooty Torquay had once complained about the behaviour of the urban masses that the railway brought, now it became the turn of the citizens of Riga and Prague to tut-tut at the antics of the hen and stag parties.

In Canada, the Canadian Pacific Railway (Pole, 1991) desperately needed to improve its cashflow to help offset the debt incurred in the construction of a railway. William Cornelius Van Horne, general manager of the railway company, hits upon the idea of creating a tourism industry in the mountains of western Canada by bringing the tourists to the scenery. In Banff Springs, the Canadian Pacific Railway built what was to be the first of a fleet of mountain hotels. The 250-bedroom hotel, with sulphur water piped from Upper Hot Springs, opened on 1 June 1888. It was the largest hotel in the world at the time. Room rates started at $3.50 a day. The Banff Springs Hotel turned a tiny community into a destination. More than 5000 visitors arrived in the year following its opening. The hotel's nightly capacity was increased to 500 bedrooms in 1903. During 1904, almost 10,000 guests registered and others were turned away to sleep in railway cars at the train station. Banff rapidly became famous as a resort where one's health could be restored by clean mountain air and healing hot springs — all made accessible by the railways.

As the tourism industry grew and diversified in the nineteenth century, the level of competition between areas increased, unrestrained by the cartel arrangements or price collusion common in other industries. By 1900, new resorts and regions had emerged in Europe, including San Sebastian, Biarritz and the Riviera, and new activities started. The most notable of these was the development of winter sports in Switzerland, for which much credit goes to British visitors.

There were some resorts and localities that remained relatively select and could count on a steady clientele, loyal from year to year. Literary tourism, to the land of Scott, the home of Burns or Shakespeare's birthplace, was anchored and relatively durable. But elsewhere the provision of facilities tailored to the tastes and incomes of visitors became increasingly important, or else a resort could slip back. There had to be good hotels and clean lodgings rather than grubby inns; museums and aquaria; reading rooms and concert halls; casinos and racetracks; piers and promenades; golf courses and swimming pools.

Continental and American resorts tended to be noticeably different from British resorts in their provision, and gay rather than respectable, with casinos and racetracks. Atlantic City and Las Vegas had their counterparts in Europe, but not in Britain. The demimondaines and grand horizontales of the European spas shocked respectable society in Britain, although, as ever, public disapproval did not prevent private patronage.

There was no master plan for tourism: private capital put up most of the necessary financing, and development was piecemeal, although some individuals did design comprehensive schemes, not always successfully. The attempt in the early 1860s by the speculator Leopold Lewis to create a 'Brighton of Ireland' at Youghal, which he had bought from the Duke of Devonshire, served only to push him into spectacular business failure. Local administrations in the tourist resorts became increasingly involved in shaping development, though they were often caught between those enthusiastic for growth, such as local hoteliers and shopkeepers and those who disliked the cost and disturbance, especially retired incomers. There was social tension everywhere; for example, at Arcachon, the 'Bournemouth of France', where, thanks again to the railways and cheap fares, working class visitors from Boudreaux disregarded polite rules about beach dress and decorum.

Government and Tourism

It can be argued that the British pioneered modern tourism and developed key forms: the seaside experience, the package holiday and event tourism. The Great Exhibition of 1851, prompted by Queen Victoria's spouse Prince Albert, was one of the watershed moments for tourism, attracting millions of visitors of all classes to London. The model was copied and repeated throughout Europe and America, for example in the Chicago Exhibition of 1893. Static displays eventually gave way to sporting and cultural events, Olympic Games and the like, but the template was set in 1851. The extent of national governments' interest and involvement varied, but in Britain the attitude was, and remained one of almost complete disinterest until 1929 when the Treasury provided a modest subsidy to the *Travel Association of Great Britain*. By contrast, in Germany, the State Kraft durch Freude handled over 9 million holidaymakers in 1937. Italy created its Commissariat of Tourism in 1931; in Switzerland, a national association was formed for the promotion of tourist traffic; and in Canada, a state-funded travel bureau was created in 1934 to co-ordinate the promotion of tourism at provincial and national levels. Even Japan set up a network of agencies, including the Publicity Association and the Board of Tourist Industry. There was a radical reappraisal in Britain of the state's role after the Second World War, although amidst many other demands, spending on the renovation of tourist attractions did not receive much priority despite the desperate need for American dollars. In the late 1960s, however, comprehensive legislation created the British Tourist Authority, which was given responsibility for marketing tourism in Britain.

The Role of Private Enterprise

In the nineteenth century, the promotion of resorts and localities was left either to the resorts themselves through their advertising committees or to the railway and steamship companies serving them. These commissioned an ever-increasing range of attractive guidebooks and posters. Impartial advice was offered by publishers such as Murray and Baedecker, whose handbooks both reflected and shaped tourist flows supplemented by private travelogues and journals. Travel firms, themselves a new feature, produced their own literature. Thomas Cook was described in 1865 by Lydia Fowler, who had travelled with one of his tours, as the 'King and Father of excursions'. The particular niche that Cook exploited with consummate success was the provision of supervised tours run to a very tight schedule for a preset cost, matters of real concern to those for whom holiday travel was a new experience, and whose time and income alike were limited. His first venture in July 1841 was a temperance day trip from Leicester to Loughborough. But soon he was ranging further afield to Wales and the Lakes, to Scotland with his Tartan Tours, on the Continent, and eventually to Palestine and Egypt, where the firm was to operate a fleet of tourist steamers on the Nile. Even 'round the world' was a Cook tour! Cook and his son had an eye on the growing American market; a partnership with an American who was a fellow temperance enthusiast foundered, but the firm continued its presence. By 1914, the firm had agents in every major American city, from Baltimore to Worcester (MA); in Europe; in the Middle East and in India, and even one in Japan at Yokohama (Durie, 2000).

The flow of Americans to Europe was of growing significance in the later nineteenth century, parallel to the surge of Japanese in the 1980s. America itself was opening up with resorts such as Coney Island for the masses, Florida or Newport for the elite, Gettysburg and other Civil War sites for the history-minded. But Europe drew many Americans. The wealthy travelled first class, but the steamship companies found ever-increasing numbers willing to travel in less luxurious conditions in second-class or steerage (later renamed 'tourist') accommodation. In 1913, 250,000 American tourists, many of whom were women, crossed the Atlantic, as against 50,000 in 1880, 'doing Europe' for educational and cultural purposes. Colleges organised study tours, and ethnic groups — Swedes, Irish and Scots, for example — explored the lands from which their families had emigrated. American millionaires were renowned for their spending, amongst whom was the notorious Gordon Bennett who sponsored the first-ever international motoring competition. A motoring competition organised in July 1903 in Ireland, contested by 12 drivers, was won by a Belgian driving a German Mercedes tourer at the then enormous average speed of 49 mph, and was a huge boost to Irish tourism: 1500 visitors brought their cars to tour the country after the race.

War and Its Aftermath

This transatlantic flow was brought to an abrupt end by the outbreak of the European war in August 1914; emergency rescue operations had to be mounted for the tens of thousands of tourists stranded on the Continent. Not until 1919 did transatlantic tourism resume, a period of drought which had serious effects on Europe and even on neutral countries like Switzerland, a nation of hotelkeepers whose clientele were else wise engaged or stayed away.

There was some limited compensation to Europe after the war in the form of battlefield tours of France and Belgium. But long-distance tourism in the interwar years had a hard time: it was buffeted by the economic difficulty, depression and exchange rates, especially in the 1930s. Domestic tourism in Britain held up surprisingly well: the established resorts attracted large numbers — Blackpool had 7 million visitors a year — and new forms of holidaymaking such as caravanning became popular. Holiday camps made their appearance, thanks to Billy Butlin, at Skegness and Clacton. The passing in 1937 of the Holidays with Pay Act should have been beneficial in Britain, but it appears that many of those who benefited were too poor to convert time off with pay into time away.

Tourism Since 1945

Since the Second World War, tourism, for all its problems of unpredictable fluctuation and seasonality, has grown exponentially. There have been several driving forces. The first is the rise in disposable income in the developed world, with Asian economies moving into the consumer era. The rise, of course, has not been evenly distributed; early retirees and seniors have especially benefited, as have 'twinks' (two incomes, no kids), and the tourist product (and its marketing) has become ever more sophisticated at tapping into their needs.

Long-distance travel has also transformed tourism, thanks to jet aircraft, cut-price airlines, and new national and regional airports. The modest departure boards of the 1950s have lengthened into packed screens as many once obscure locations have come within the travelling range of people of all income groups. To reach Crete, for example, in 1970 required a sea voyage.

Governments of virtually every political complexion have become proactive; the fall of communism in Eastern Europe led a country like Bulgaria to open up its Black Sea resorts to Western tourists rather than reserve them for the workers (or, more often, the party elite). Two key policy objectives of developed countries have been to persuade more people to explore their own country and to attract foreign visitors at the same time because air travel has brought new destinations into reach. The balance between public and private finance has varied from place to place, and country to country, but travel firms have done much to develop the industry through specific packages and holiday offerings.

Advertising budgets have grown ever larger and their offerings more and more sophisticated. It is remarkable that when TV advertising in Britain made a start in 1955, one firm (Global Tours) thought it was not a suitable medium. Newspapers began to carry travel supplements, and television followed suit with travel programmes — *Holiday* with Cliff Michelmore on BBC (then in black and white) led the way in 1969, and the first colour advertising was taken out by Clarkson in 1970. Brochures abounded, and guides of every kind and for every location proliferated, some of which (e.g. the Rough Guides) were less respectful than had been the custom. The consumer had an immense range of information to marry to more and more choice.

The Foundations for Today

It is staggering to remember how undeveloped a place like Benidorm was in the 1950s. It was just a quiet fishing village, which once discovered became a mass resort catering for more visitors than some entire countries. But while the rise of Spain, the

North African Mediterranean countries and the Far East were tied to sand and guaranteed sun, that was not the only formula: southern Ireland, where tourism had been minor, grew as a cultural destination and because of easy access.

Today, you can take a holiday at the North Pole, South Pole and everywhere in between. Tourism today is more than sand and sea — it can include business, sport, heritage and scenery. You can even take a skiing holiday in Dubai, and space travel is becoming a reality. Tourism is now a specialist experience, from the graveyards of Highgate Cemetery in London to Pere Lachaise in Paris. Other forms have enjoyed a revival: luxury cruising and spa treatments, to name but two. Some forms renew themselves; Sir Walter Scott may be dead, but literary tourism is not. There are new writers on the scene: Peter Mayne for Provence, Ian Rankin and Edinburgh, and Dan Brown with his Da Vinci Code. Film has played a significant role in promoting places as well, as with *The Lord of the Rings* and New Zealand; and it is not just adults who are influenced, as the Harry Potter films have shown.

The competition in global tourism is intense. New countries and destinations appear, and there have been losers as well as winners, of which the seaside resorts of Britain in the 1960s were an example. Thrusting entrepreneurship has been a hallmark of Western tourism, but the growth has been littered with failures; the bankruptcy of British Eagle in 1968 and that of the Court line in 1974, taking Clarkson with it. Freddie Laker went bust in 1982, and in 1991 the sudden collapse of International Leisure Group/Air Europe left 35,000 customers stranded abroad. At a domestic level, the hotel business has always had a high level of uncertainty.

But, for all the problems, short of a breakdown in the world economy tourism is here to stay, and it is an industry which cannot be outsourced. Tourism today is no longer the privilege of the few but the basic need of a modern mass society.

Chapter 3

What Will the World Look Like in 2030?

Introduction

It is very easy to paint a picture of doom and gloom with events such as pandemics, floods in South East Asia, war in Iraq, oil depletion and stock market collapse. To a certain extent, we live in a world of fear and uncertainty. However, according to forecasts by Oxford Forecasting (2006) for VisitScotland, world GDP will rise by 129% by 2030 and in general consumers get richer rather than poorer year on year. Today we are observing significant shifts in the tectonic plates of world power; the old Soviet Union is no more and China is a superpower in its own right (NIC, 2004). The world is moving eastwards, with the European Union expanding through an accession of countries like, Poland, Latvia and Turkey hopefully joining the EU in 2015. This eastward movement is not without fear: if the tectonic plates touch, a rise of Islamic fundamentalism could drive protectionism and instability, especially over the issue of energy supply. The West's ageing populations could significantly reduce the economic power of Europe in the long term. Either European countries adapt their work forces, reform their social welfare, education and tax systems and accommodate growing immigrant populations or they will face protracted economic sclerosis. Technology is making the world a smaller place and accelerating the pace of globalisation. Science brings us new inventions, whether this is a cure for AIDS or the emergence of the hydrogen economy in the next decade. The world will see a new generation of middle-class consumers, emerging from the economies of Brazil, China and India. The United States of America will still be the world's largest economy and superpower in 2030 — and those that live in the east will have a propensity for Western lifestyles and want to live the Western dream.

Mega Drivers

Susan Greenfield (2003) in her book *Tomorrows People* images people's lives in the future, a world free of pain and disease, where they can manipulate their bodies with machinery, their moods with smart drugs and innate nature with gene therapy. This is the world portrayed in the film *I, Robot* (Asimov, 1968), in which we all have mechanical servants (robots) who begin to think for themselves or *The Manchurian*

Table 3.1: Mega drivers.

Mega drivers	Name
Mega driver 1	A world of changing values
Mega driver 2	Living with uncertainty and fear
Mega driver 3	The dichotomy between rich and poor
Mega driver 4	The power of USA in the world
Mega driver 5	The power of the Asian block in the world
Mega driver 6	The power of the EU in the world
Mega driver 7	A changing business world
Mega driver 8	The global/local society
Mega driver 9	The relationship between people and governments
Mega driver 10	AIDS
Mega driver 11	Physical access: Transport of people and goods
Mega driver 12	Access to knowledge
Mega driver 13	Changing labour and demographics
Mega driver 14	Energy/oil
Mega driver 15	The environment, natural resources and climate
Mega driver 16	Food
Mega driver 17	New technologies

Candidate (Condon, 2004), where the corporation controls the President. Whatever you think, there is no map of the future because it is uncharted. All we can do is use the evidence around us and make a number of rational and creative assumptions that describe possible futures. Seventeen mega drivers have been identified based on VisitScotland's scenario-planning research (Table 3.1).

Mega Driver 1: A World of Changing Values

Increasing evidence of a conflict between consumerism and a wider concern with societal impacts is emerging, which is reflected in our concern for the environment. Politics has shifted from a red to a green agenda since the fall of communism and the Berlin Wall. The word 'socialism' has disappeared from the political conversations in many countries as politicians and consumers focus on single issues. It is as if the environment is the new anti-capitalism focusing demonstrations across the world at many G8 government conferences. Faith and a concern with moral certainties is juxtaposed with the immediacy of news and information that can transport suffering, war and famine into real time to a developed nation instilling an individual or community-based reaction whether to famine (as in the case of Live Aid response) or destruction (as is the case with the Tsunami crisis). Cultural changes towards an experience driven culture are generating awareness in morals; supported by an ever-developing information network, people's opinion may be determined more rapidly as a result.

Mega Driver 2: Living with Uncertainty and Fear

In an increasingly unsafe world humans will become more aware of crime and terrorism. Uncertainty becomes more of the norm, driving the phenomena of fear, such as an uncomfortable feeling of suspicion when travelling with a person of Middle Eastern appearance carrying a briefcase (Coughlan, 2005). Disruption to everyday life as a consequence of geopolitical tensions, environmental disasters and rising costs will be mirrored by government's increasing attempts to monitor, manage and combat such shocks (Masciandaro, 2004).

Mega Driver 3: Education, Wealth and Choice

Increasing extremes of wealth and poverty in our societies will create more challenges and uncertainty about our future (Corrigan, 1997). The size and rate of population growth in developing economies will fuel this divide and create increasing pressures on economies in China, India and many other parts of the world. The polarisation of wealth is reflected in increasing polarisation in the fields such as education. As wealthy countries seek to increase graduate-level qualified employees, many developing countries continue to struggle to commit resources to basic primary education. India and China both show high percentage of population without education. This is projected to decline over time with an extension in the provision of education duration fuelling economic growth. Higher education may increase tax revenue, savings and investment, and lead to a more entrepreneurial and civic society. It can also improve a nation's health, contribute to reduced population growth, improve technology and strengthen governance. With regard to the benefits of higher education for a country's economy, many observers attribute India's leap onto the world economic stage as stemming from its decades-long successful efforts to provide high-quality, technically oriented tertiary education to a significant number of its citizens (Bloom, Canning, & Chan, 2006).

Mega Driver 4: The Power of USA in the World

There is no doubt that US politics and policy is impacting on the world stage (Everest, 2004). Against a backdrop of difficult economic conditions at home the United States continues extensive, interventionist foreign policy that will impact on global economics and security (Tisdall, 2004; Cederwell, 2004). The consequence of a single dominant voice in an uncertain world impacts on many aspects of society (Roberts, 2004). These consequences range from the environment, the US non-compliance with Kyoto to the increasingly unacceptable face of US corporate brands.

With the dollar established as a global reserve currency, the power of the US government is considerable. Whilst the United States retains military and economic strength to influence global politics, the increased possibility of a rising resentment of anti-US politics may ensue. With redistribution of dwindling energy reserves, a swing in power away from the United States to hydrocarbon rich regions in the mid-term

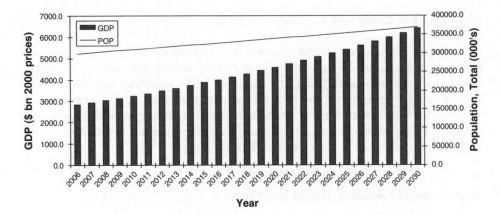

Figure 3.1: The wealth of the United States from 2006 to 2030. *Source*: Oxford Forecasting (2006).

future is possible. A change in the US political climate towards a non-interventionist foreign policy may turn opinion back to viewing the United States as the home of freedom and democracy, therefore rebuilding its economic strength and contributing towards global economic stability. However, in 2030 the USA will be without doubt the worlds largest and most powerful economy (Figure 3.1).

Mega Driver 5: The Power of the Asian Block in the World

The expansion of the economies of India and China (Figure 3.2) is seen by many respected commentators as one of the major factors in how the world's geopolitical economy will alter in the next decade (Scase, 2000; Pender, 2004). The consequences are vast, ranging from the need to feed the exponential growth in these nations' consumer populations to the alteration in world economic power from north to south (Burgess, 2004; Lutz, 2001). At a conservationist level, the consequences of such growth will be noticeable. Energy requirements of Asian nations and the environmental impact of their economic growth will be significant.

China represents 20% of the world population and currently has the largest currency reserve in the world, recently surpassing Japan in February 2006 (Anon, 2006). Extensive purchasing of resources outstrips the consumption capacity of many other nations as China's economic growth continues. As economic growth and improvements in income occur, demands for resources will grow. The fiscal strength of China is developing, and it is well placed to control future trade agreements with its ability to influence markets and out-purchase other countries.

Mega Driver 6: The Power of the European Union in the World

A larger, integrated and more powerful Europe will become an important element of the world economy. The relationship of the United Kingdom with the EU will be an

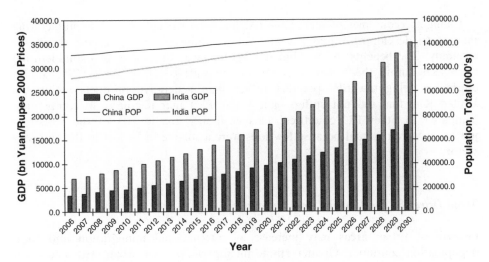

Figure 3.2: Projected growth in Chinese and Indian GDP and population from 2006 to 2030. *Source*: OEF.

increasingly important driver towards 2030. Already the idea of borderless travel via the Schengen Treaty has created greater mobility for Europeans. This trend is likely to continue, as political and economic union becomes a greater reality amongst the majority of the EU countries (Wagstyl, 2004; Strauss-Khan, 2004).

The expansion of the EU to encompass nations with weaker economies (compared to founding EU nations), the commitments to social and fiscal reform impact EU budgets. According to the European Central Bank, a standardised fiscal policy has drawbacks and benefits. Larger economies such as Germany have shown declining manufacturing and employment levels, against a backdrop of an ageing population. The emerging economies of the EU are thriving, such as Ireland and Spain, with a future projected younger demographic and mobile workforce. The blurring of trade barriers and movement of labour across EU states shows the potential force of the EU. The strengthening EU provides an alternative to the Far Eastern and US economies as a reserve currency, which provides another focal point for dominance in political power.

Mega Driver 7: A Changing Business World

As a consequence of the power shift in economies, employment patterns will change and manufacturing and service employment will move to developing economies. New lessons on wealth generation will have to be learnt in the Western economies as their traditional dominance is eroded. New consumer markets will contribute to transition economies (Central and Eastern Europe) and in developing economies (Asia and South Asia).

Changing economies of scale have redefined the workplace with manufacturing moving to developing economies and service industry growth in the developed economy. The benefits to the United Kingdom with the move of manufacturing were seen during the recent recession at the start of 2000. With UK manufacturing evolving towards specialist rather than generalist, products within the United Kingdom did not suffer against Far East manufacturers in competition compared to other EU countries. This cushioned the impact of the recession; job losses were minimal because few jobs were available to be lost in this industry sector.

Mega Driver 8: The Global/Local Society

Growth of urban areas may increase as international immigration and rural depopulation continues. Greater ethnic mixing within vast urban settlements will blur the boundaries between the global and local society. Half the world's population will be living in urban areas by 2007, with almost all of the increase in world population expected during 2000–2030 to be absorbed by the urban areas of developing regions (Anon, 2002). The ethnicity of countries and cities will change because immigration changes the characteristics of countries' population. At the same time, distances will be perceived as shorter as international connectivity becomes the norm. The Internet means the world is only a click away.

Mega Driver 9: The Relationship between People and Governments

People are becoming increasingly sceptical of politicians, governments and corporations. At an international level, hostility to the United States is matched by concern with the sustainability of growth and impacts on the environment (Travis, 2004). Countries that have democracy are seeing less and less engagement with the electorate whereas in many countries democracy is an alien concept, that is the Middle East. Increasing access to greater amounts of information and the ability to form subjective opinions makes the electorate able to question the decisions an elected body makes. The converse viewpoint is that with the influence of media to present information biased in a particular direction, they can therefore guide the attitude of the electorate to a particular decision.

Mega Driver 10: AIDS

AIDS will impact on world labour supply and has the potential to impact on emergent economies. HIV affects the economy, and the economic system affects the level of distribution of HIV (Cohen, 2002). The output of a country where AIDS is occurring in significant levels will be impacted upon. GDP will be slowed and national output is likely to decline, GDP per capita will fall as will the standard of living by

- Decline in life expectancy
- Reduced school enrolment
- Higher infant mortality

The effects are already being seen in the United States with the rise of anti-immigration legislation meant to forbid entrance by HIV-positive individuals. In the United States, HIV infection has already occurred in stigmatised populations (homosexual men, prostitutes, street youth, drug users, etc.) and this fact is likely to amplify the tendency to discriminate against immigrants with HIV. With the recent advent of greater cooperation between developed and emergent economies for funding and distribution of antivirals, short-term trends show declining AIDS deaths. The World Health Organisation (WHO) researchers (Mathers & Loncar, 2005) forecast increases in AIDS mortality in the mid to long term due to increasing complacency and reliance in pharmacological rather than educational intervention. WHO estimates that at least 117 million people will die from AIDS by 2030.

Mega Driver 11: Physical Access: Transport of People and Goods

The availability and widespread access to travel and communications has connected our society as never before, yet the transport network is far from integrated and is vulnerable to shortages in fuels, particularly oil. Air transport as a global industry will alter in the years to 2030 and although the debate is significant in respect of reserves and medium-term supply, oil remains a finite commodity that will continue to impact on the world economy. The United Kingdom and much of the developed world remains vulnerable to shortages, price rises and evaluation of stocks. Invariably this will cause consumers to consider other, more sustainable transport forms in the medium term and the connectivity and linkage to Europe may well be crucial to the United Kingdom as an economic power.

Mega Driver 12: Access to Knowledge

The scale of communication and the immediacy of knowledge are global phenomena. This may help the way populations and people attempt to understand their societies and the dynamics within them. Yet such access is linked to wealth and availability and this is not yet uniform.

Table 3.2 shows the correlation between a nation's wealth and its access to knowledge. Based on world rankings the correlation between wealth ranking and Internet users is almost the same, with a few minor exceptions. These differences relate to economic, demographic and cultural influences. For example, South Korea

Table 3.2: Comparison of world rank in GDP and Internet users in 2030.

GDP rank	Country	GDP (purchasing power parity)	Internet user rank	Internet users
1	USA	$ 12,980,000,000,000	2	205,327,000
2	EU	$ 12,820,000,000,000	1	247,000,000
3	China	$ 10,000,000,000,000	3	123,000,000
4	Japan	$ 4,220,000,000,000	4	86,300,000
5	India	$ 4,042,000,000,000	5	60,000,000
6	Germany	$ 2,585,000,000,000	6	50,616,000
7	UK	$ 1,903,000,000,000	7	37,600,000
8	France	$ 1,871,000,000,000	9	29,945,000
9	Italy	$ 1,727,000,000,000	10	28,870,000
10	Russia	$ 1,723,000,000,000	12	23,700,000
11	Brazil	$ 1,616,000,000,000	11	25,900,000
12	South Korea	$ 1,180,000,000,000	8	33,900,000
13	Canada	$ 1,165,000,000,000	13	21,900,000
14	Mexico	$ 1,134,000,000,000	15	18,622,000
15	Spain	$ 1,070,000,000,000	14	19,205,000

Source: CIA World Factbook.

is one of the most technologically advanced nations in the world, with a vast amount of money spent on technology infrastructure; however, it is ranked twelfth in GDP.

Mega Driver 13: Changing Labour and Demographics

The ageing of Western society will create labour and skills shortages. As production moves to new destinations, patterns of migration and immigration will be influenced by sources of employment. This will create further geopolitical shifts in power and resource bases as we see increased connectivity contrasted with vulnerable transport infrastructure. Further, the degree of economic inactivity of the older population is by no means certain. With the UK government actively looking at long-term plans for health care and pension provision, it has been suggested that individuals will work longer before retirement thereby extending the available workforce.

Mega Driver 14: Energy/Oil

One of the major economic issues in the world is the inevitable rise in the price of oil and the consequent impact this has on economies. Uncertainty over future availability of oil and the availability of reserves will occupy many governments and pan national corporations. Alternative sources of energy and concern about carbon emissions are major items on the world agenda and there is a much greater public awareness of fuel/energy issues.

Rising oil prices are becoming a factor of everyday life in most global economies. With declining supplies and increasing demand, countries with reserves that were previously unattainable are now investing in technology to access these resources. The future without oil will see further development in sustainable, alternative energy and transportation systems; however, changes to lifestyle, work and domestic setup are also likely.

A growing debate on alternative energies has shown confusion in government policy. Sustainable technologies are promoted, however implementation is hampered by the ecological and societal impacts they may cause (e.g. Wind farms). A proposed tidal barrage power scheme in the Severn Estuary could generate 6% of England and Wales's power by 2017, the opposition to the £15bn scheme is the destruction of ecological habitat that is unique to the area (BBC, 2006a). Nuclear power has the potential to provide mid- to long-term supplies; however opposition by the public and non-government parties is delaying implementation. With up to 15 years construction time the buffer between losing a hydrocarbon economy and reliance on alternatives is decreasing.

Mega Driver 15: The Environment, Natural Resources and Climate

The trend of growing attention to the effects of environmental issues is now clearly on the political agenda. Countering the environmental impacts, damage and climate change vary regionally subject to the stage of economic development and availability of technology and resources. The decline in biodiversity has become a major concern, climatic change is regularly on the agenda of global summits and our use of earth's natural resources is regularly called into question. These issues create a range of assumptions about our environment that can no longer be taken for granted. Tragically, the Kyoto Protocol, Agenda 21 and attempts for industry and society to govern its own activities have been little more than token gestures. Yet increasingly we have indications of a growing awareness and a concern amongst society that these issues are raised at national and international levels.

Following Kyoto, the nations of Europe actively sought to improve manufacturing methods to ensure that environmental impacts were minimised. Nations, such as the United States have not acknowledged the protocol, as it was perceived to impact on the industrial economic stability. At the same time, although countries like India and China have signed up to Kyoto they have not implemented change due to their poorer status, as sustainability is seen as a barrier to poverty evolution.

Mega Driver 16: Food

Food and health and the quality of the food we eat have become a major driver and concern. Food is politicised over issues such as genetic modification or via resistance to brands, which represent nations and unacceptable corporations. Food and farming remain political and societal issues that can impact on the environment whether it is through land closure (as in the case of a diseases such as Foot and Mouth Disease) or through remarks about food quality in destinations. A growing world population and increasing wealth will demand food with higher quality and variety. UN forecasts suggest that demand can be fulfilled; however increasing factors from declining energy to climate change may cause issues in the long term.

Mega Driver 17: New Technologies

Eric Moore in 1965 made the prediction that number of transistors on a chip could double every 2 years, this observation has shaped the present digital era. The intended consequences of this law, when applied to other areas of technology or science mean exponential growth and discovery across a range of fields, whether it is AIDS, the emergence of nanotechnologies or our ability to put a man on Mars. This pervasive growth of technology and alternative technologies across all sectors of society is causing far-reaching changes in communication, work, wealth creation and society. Challenges such as the digitisation of information are upon us and regulation and monitoring of people will increasingly be reliant on technology in advanced societies. This creates new ethical questions about freedoms in our societies and other societies. Technologies, which have been forecast to be commonplace by 2030, are found to be in NBIC (Pearson, 2004):

- (N) Nanotechnology — Manipulation of matter down to molecular level, this will enable better electronics, fuel cells, sensors and displays.
- (B) Biotechnology — Utilising nanotechnology to manipulate at a molecular level will improve medicines, increase longevity and allow the ability to synthesise materials using biological processes.
- (I) Information Technology — Continuous development will produce low-cost faster computers with better storage, improved communication, artificial intelligence and interfaces that will ubiquitously and pervasively interact with all aspects of our lives.
- (C) Cognitive Science — A greater understanding of our nervous system and consciousness will allow the means to manipulate and enhance minds and create synthetic ones.

What Does This Mean for World Tourism?

Tourism in the world is a reflection of rising prosperity amongst consumers. Today, according to the Future Foundations *Changing Lives* Survey, travel is perceived as the consumer's number one desire amongst Western consumers. As disposal income levels rise in emerging economies, travel is also booming especially amongst the upper middle classes which means destinations across the world are seeing new tourists with new languages. These new tourists will shape the landscape, which benefits some and renders others obsolete.

Analysing the mega drivers, what are the implications for world tourism in 2030?

- Concern for the environment and the rise of cultural awareness means the tourist becomes more of a traveller, going deeper and staying longer.
- The world in the future will be based upon the paradigm of 'freedom to' rather than 'freedom from' as countries adopt big brother practices through the introduction of biometric passports and visa restrictions.
- Western destinations may be accused of pandering to discrimination as countries become uncomfortable with the unknown because of the rise of fear in society. We will see some countries introduce barriers to entry and tourists from Asian countries feeling uncomfortable in this security world.
- We will see more deluxe and gated communities as the bipolarity between rich and poor continues.
- The United States of America will be both the world's largest economy and tourism economy by 2030. However, this position is threatened depending on how politics shapes the country. In the short term the destination will be attractive to tourists due to the rising fiscal deficit and current account making the US $ weak and therefore favourable for inbound tourists.
- We will see significant shifts in world tourism to Eastern and Asian markets due to the low-cost base and rising prosperity. Asia's growth will be fuelled by more inter-regional travel up to 2015, and then further growth from out bound travel as the economies grow. China will replace Japan as the regional powerhouse.
- Europe's economic prospects will be dampened by demographics and high costs of production. Europe's populations face strategic challenges on who will pay for the future. The baby boomer generation, which has driven the growth of Europe's short break market, will slow down as generations X and Y are constrained by rising pension costs, working longer, caring for parents and paying for higher education, which the baby boomer generation was not straddled with.
- The ethnic mix of countries is changing with Polish being the second language of the United Kingdom and Spanish the first language of California. Countries that encourage immigration also encourage competition and product innovation, but at the same time may lose destination authenticity.
- AIDS will have a big impact on labour supply in Africa, as generations are lost to the disease.
- What has happened in the past in the business world is no longer a model for the future as exponential pace of change in technology transformed business models.
- Technology media channels moves from corporations as individuals create their own media channels through www.facebook.com making consumer destination reviews more accessible and immediate.
- Based on present known oil supplies, 86% of the world's oil supply will be in the hands of Middle Eastern countries; however, the higher the oil price, the more economical the opportunity alternatives become. As transport is the key driver of

tourism, destinations that do not have a substantial sustainable infrastructure investment programme will fall behind. Transport and competitiveness will be key drivers to 2030.
- New technologies and the advancement of science means the era of space tourism is upon us.
- In 2030, tourism will be here but the tourists will be different.

Chapter 4

What Will the Tourist Be Doing in 2030?

Tourism began when time began. Babylonian money-traders travelled for business, the Egyptian Queen Hatshesput took a cruise along the east coast of Africa and the British aristocracy took Grand Tour of Europe with Thomas Cook in the nineteenth century. Tourism is about experiences, whether exploring an unfamiliar culture, shopping, lying on a beach or enjoying sport in far-flung places — or a little nearer home.

What has changed is the massive growth in tourism, including both the choice of destinations and the number of tourists. In Chapter 3, many world megatrends were discussed; this chapter places them in the context of consumer behaviour in the first decades of the twenty-first century. What are the drivers and trends that will shape world tourism and the tourist of the future? Two main areas have been identified: Megadrivers, the macro conditions that will shape international tourism, and trends, which shape individuals' thought processes when they make choices about destination or activity.

Mega Drivers — Economic and Political

A range of factors determines the scale of tourism. Some continue to exert influence decade after decade; others have an effect for a much shorter period. According to the UN World Tourism Organisation (2001), the principal determinants and influences that will impinge on the development and growth of tourism in the future, affecting and creating the tourism economies, are prosperity and affordability, accessibility, events, culture, globalization, competition, and climate.

Prosperity and Affordability

According to research by the Future Foundation, consumers perceive holidays as the number-one luxury product. They desire holidays over houses, fast cars, expensive perfumes and designer clothes (Allsopp, 2004). This desire for holidays has been driven by consumer prosperity and product affordability (Silverstein, Fiske, & Butman, 2005). Prosperity has resulted from rising incomes, which in real terms have doubled over the past 20 years; and affordability has resulted from falling prices.

This is exemplified by consumers who stay in luxury hotels but travel by budget carrier. Consumers are making their money go further, as incomes rise, prices fall. This pattern of economic behaviour is happening all over the world, and over the next two decades the number of people in the middle classes in China, India, and Eastern Europe will grow — and these will be the tourists of tomorrow.

Accessibility

The tourists' world is shrinking because of technological advances. The ability of the Internet to inform and to break boundaries allows consumers to choose a tourist destination anywhere in the world — and beyond. With an improvement in the economies of scale brought about by the online economy, travel and tourism are becoming a buyers' market. In recent years, low-cost airlines have come to represent the pinnacle in the adoption of technology. Travel is much easier today, with more direct flights between destinations, and the cost in real terms — yield per passenger per airline kilometre — is the lowest since statistics have been recorded (Kuhlmann, 2004). The world is opening up to the tourist. Even just a few years ago, many citizens of China and Russia could not imagine travelling outside their village — international travel was more a dream than reality. Today, visa restrictions are less onerous and the world is accessible to nearly everyone.

Events

With the worldwide expansion of accessible tourism destinations, people are increasingly exposed to and influenced by events, whether sporting occasions or environmental disasters. Arbitrary acts of violence by terrorist organisations, increasing occurrences of extreme weather in popular tourist destinations and the role of government policies in all areas of society determine how safe people feel in a particular situation. A lot depends on how specific negative events are dealt with. It has been shown that US tourists are increasingly suffering from "American Angst", preferring to stay at home or to go to only foreign destinations which are perceived as being pro-American (World Travel Market, 2005). On the positive side, events such as the Olympic Games and the football World Cup increase the number of international visitors to the host countries. Cultural events such as the Edinburgh International Festival and the Hajj in Saudi Arabia shape destinations' social cachet through event-based strategies.

Cultural Capital

As wealth and educational attainment increase, culture becomes more important as a destination driver. The cultural capital of a destination is a measure of the total stock of knowledge, attitudes, perception, skills and tastes that are encompassed within the arts, sports and heritage of a nation. Anholt (2006) sees culture and heritage as one of the six components of a nation's brand, a key measurement of tourism and the propensity to travel to a destination.

Globalisation and Competition

Globalisation and localisation are two concurrent but apparently conflicting developments: The world is increasingly polarised between the 'macro' and the 'micro'. All countries are integrally locked into the global economy and no country can succeed without operating in all the major established and emerging markets. People respond to globalisation of economies and cultures by looking to their own identities. The openness of the world economy means that the tourist has more choices and increased competition means better value.

Climate

That climate shapes a destination's tourism product is obvious: What would Switzerland be like without snow and skiing or the Caribbean without sun and beach holidays? Figure 4.1 shows how consumer's perception of the climate of a destination influences luxury travellers' choices across all age groups.

Consumer Trends Which Will Shape the Tourist's Choice

How consumers make decisions about their choice of destination is the next consideration. Individual trends shape the tourism proposition and influence the motivation to travel. The trends identified are anxiety about health and safety, demographics, image and brand, technology, environment, individualism, time pressures, movement from an experience economy to authenticity, hedonism and erotica, and perceptions of luxury.

Anxiety about Health and Safety

Since 9/11 and the London bombing, terrorism has come to influence and shape tourism flows and destination choice (Yeoman, Galt, & McMahon-Beattie, 2005). This backdrop of anxiety forces the consumer to decide between two courses of action. Fear leads to risk-minimisation so that perceived dangers will be avoided. However, over time, a sense of complacency develops and people think that "whatever will happen, will happen", so a wider choice opens up again. Associated with this is the events mega driver, where specific events affect tourism in the short term but the resilience of the consumer invariably returns within a short time.

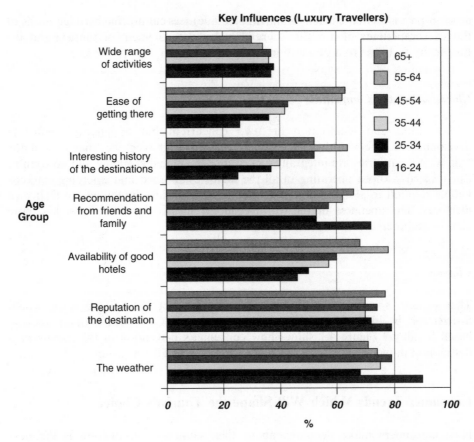

Figure 4.1: Determinants of destination choice amongst luxury travellers.

Demographics

In the established economies the population is ageing, and with an ageing population comes a shrinking workforce and the economic restraints of relying on a pension. Society is changing demographically in other ways as well: higher divorce rates, starting families later in life, and second marriages are altering the make-up of households. In the future greater emphasis will be on multi-generational holidays where destinations have to cater for everyone, from grandparents to grandchildren.

Image and Brand

Destinations will become increasingly fashionable in the future. Tourism products will need to offer something that the consumer can associate with (such as heritage or celebrity endorsement), and new destinations perceived as being 'untouched' will develop an associated cachet. Brand will be a marketing tool increasingly used to distinguish between destinations when the market is saturated with messages. Furthermore, brands and images will become more important, because the choice of destination will be shaped by the values held by the consumer. Destination brands will, in the future, have to be trustworthy, ethical, and sustainable (Yeoman, Munro, & McMahon-Beattie, 2006).

Technology

The tourist of tomorrow will be better informed, have wider choice and be able to purchase holidays on demand, helped by technology such as the Internet, video on demand and online booking.

Environment

Tourists' growing awareness of social and environmental issues leads to a conflict between conscience and the desire to travel. The provision of sustainable travel products (i.e. carbon offsetting) aims to bridge the gap between these two states of mind, but the consumer will ultimately have to decide whether the environment or freedom to travel is of greater importance.

Individualism

A main challenge to the marketing of tourist destinations will be consumers' increasing diversification of interests, tastes, and demands. According to the Future Foundation's *Changing Lives* survey, today's consumers change their hairstyle every 18 months, make a new friend every year and select a new holiday destination every year. Therefore, in this world of constant change and diversification, destinations need to be increasingly innovative in product development, specifically offering tailored experiences to meet changing attitudes and beliefs.

Time Pressures

With changing work practices and traditional work-leisure boundaries blurring, the trend is increasingly towards escapism and indulgence. Several shorter breaks are replacing the established long break as consumers adopt a snacking culture towards holidays, i.e. sampling lots of experiences rather than one main holiday. Increasingly, people want to capture the experience of a place through relaxation or by overloading their senses with adrenaline-charging activities. Tourists want holidays that offer physical and mental recharging in a short time, before they must return to normal life.

Movement from an Experience Economy to Authenticity

From a tourism perspective, as the experience economy matures consumers desire more authentic and real experiences rather than false and manufactured experiences we associate with theme parks and resorts. Driving this trend is higher education attainment, ageing populations, a knowledgable consumer and concern for how we lead our lives.

Hedonism and Erotica

Hedonism is the philosophy that pleasure is the most important pursuit of humans. The word derives from the Greek 'hëdonë', 'pleasure'. One of the basic tenets of tourism is having fun, whether lying on the beach, sky diving in Namibia or gambling in Macau — it's all about pleasure, entertainment and fun. One of the genres of hedonism is erotica — the pursuit of sexual desire, whether pursued through romance or a lap-dancing experience.

Perceptions of Luxury

Luxury is becoming less about materialism and increasingly about self-enrichment and time. The consumer is increasingly aware of the importance of luxury as a concept of fulfilment. Destinations are adapting to this demand by diversifying into niche areas where the traditional perceptions of luxury and opulence share the market with wellness and self-fulfilment. At the same time, a polarised society of 'haves' and 'have nots' increases the propensity for gated communities, the second homes' debate and the importance of materialism in societies where wealth is just beginning. As consumers in the East gain wealth, they will focus on opulence and 'bling' when on holiday, compared to Western Europeans who already have comparatively high standards of living and who can, therefore, focus on holidays which offer an experience.

What Do People Do on a Holiday?

It has been shown that many factors determine the choices made by tourists. Because of direct and indirect forces, the consumer is making greater demands of the tourist industry. Since the mid-1980s the consumers' view of what a holiday should be has evolved from the traditional fortnight beach holiday into a multiplicity of new experiences, such as short adventure breaks or a 6-month trip round the world.

Studies carried out by Mintel (2005a) discovered that the content of holidays is changing. Families are spending more time on activities, although the pool-based holiday is still high on the list of priorities because it provides entertainment for children, whilst allowing parents to relax. However, holidays are now perceived as prime family quality time, something that is on the wane at home. Activity-based breaks as a means of bonding for families are becoming increasingly popular. Culture-based holidays are also on the increase, with their popularity highest amongst the active-retired generation. The recently retired, or 'empty-nesters', have gone against trends by taking more adventurous holiday breaks than people of similar demographics in the past. The baby-boomer generation is living longer, is more affluent and is undertaking more holidays than comparable generations in the past. With the world experiencing an ageing demographic over the next few decades, plus financial issues associated with pensions and long-term care, this trend, however, may be short lived.

Other areas of the traditional tourism industry are also changing. Business travellers' habits are evolving in the face of uncertain global economic conditions. Digital communication and teleconferencing allow virtual face-to-face meetings without the expense and inconvenience of travelling round the world. For companies tightening their budgets this is seen as a benefit. However, with the market becoming globalised, cultural differences between countries mean that some business dealings are best handled by personal meetings, and this may lead to the development of some travel routes and a decline in others.

Eco-tourism and issues of sustainability are gaining importance with consumers. Although the negative ecological impact of air travel is widely accepted, people's desire to travel to remote areas to experience an unspoiled natural environment continues unabated. Tour operators are quickly beginning to understand the relationship the consumer has with the environment and are providing packages which meet those needs. Ongoing factors which may deter tourists from travelling to certain destinations are fluctuating fuel prices and fear of terrorist attacks. Such factors move the focus of tourism clusters, depending on the current activity in these areas.

Conclusions

Tomorrow's tourists lead complicated lives and have a fluid identity. On one hand they desire eco-stress-free experiences but at the same time they play the tables at Las Vegas. New experiences, luxury, culture and authenticity are some of the trends that will shape the future of world tourism. The tourist wants to sample the ethnicity of the destination, increasingly interests in culture, food and sport are shaping the way people approach their choice of holiday. As a society, our leisure time and disposable wealth are increasing and are primary catalysts within a growing tourism industry. However, the consumers' perception is one of blurring between increasing stress at work and a desire to rejuvenate through experience. In contrast, consumers have a wealth of choice, which means that they search for value for money. The challenge for destinations will be how to offer a heterogeneous product when tourism is becoming homogeneous. Throughout the rest of the book, many of the trends mentioned above will be elaborated on in order to show how they are shaping tourist experiences and products.

Chapter 5

World Tourism in 2030

Introduction

Once upon a time, overseas holidays were only for the rich and famous. In 1939, it cost US $79,000 in today's money to fly across the Atlantic on the world's first scheduled crossing with Trans Atlantic Airways. By 2015, Virgin Galactic will be following flights into outer space for less than US $50,000 (Whitehorn, 2006). In 1950, 25 million tourists took an overseas holiday; by 2005 this had risen to 803 million, representing an annual growth rate of just over 6% (Mintel, 2006a). By 2030, we expect this figure to reach 1.9 billion international arrivals, spending US $2 trillion. By 2030, markets will have shifted eastwards based upon cost, travellers' desire for new experiences in far-flung destinations and the rising level of disposal incomes in Asia. By 2030, every part of the globe will have been visited by tourists, new destinations will have emerged which had not even been considered in 1950 and pioneer tourists will be taking adventure holidays in outer space as the ultimate luxury experience. Looking into the future, we expect a considerable slowdown in the world tourism growth rates as a result of shrinking and ageing populations; therefore, the average growth rate will be 3.4% by 2030. By 2030, more than US $5 billion will be spent by international tourists every day across the world, from US $2 billion in Europe to US $1.5 billion in Asia. This will mean more revenue spread across the world generated by the new tourists from today's emerging economies.

World Tourism in 2030: Winners and Losers

Forecasting, by its very nature, is a hazardous exercise. Projecting future international tourism flows has become more difficult over time, because, on the one hand, events such as wars cause only a temporary disruption but, on the other hand, political regimes and restrictive legislation cause more permanent change. The forecasts that appear in this chapter have been prepared based on economic prosperity and a correlation with propensity to travel (Mintel, 2006a; UN World Tourism Organisation, 2001; Oxford Forecasting, 2006).

By examining Tables 5.1 and 5.2, we can see that, over the next 25 years, international arrivals will grow by 3.4% per annum and receipts by 4.4%, with

Table 5.1: International tourist arrivals by tourist-receiving region (million).

Arrivals	Base year (millions)	Forecast (millions)		Average annual growth rate (%)	Market share (%)	
	2005	2015	2030	2005–2030	2005	2030
Total	802.9	1156.2	1897.0	3.4	100.0	100.0
Europe	438.7	555.1	779.9	2.3	54.6	41.1
Asia and the Pacific	155.3	287.6	546.5	5.0	19.3	28.8
Americas	133.2	184.1	309.8	3.4	16.6	16.3
Africa	37.3	57.9	101.8	4.0	4.6	5.4
Middle East	38.4	71.5	158.9	5.7	4.8	8.4

Table 5.2: International tourist receipts by tourist-receiving region (US $ million).

Receipts	Base year (US $ billion)	Forecast (US $ billion)		Average annual growth rate (%)	Market share (%)	
	2005	2015	2030	2005–2030	2005	2030
Total	677.5	1275	2016.2	4.4	100.0	100.0
Europe	349.7	535	787.1	3.2	51.6	39.0
Asia and the Pacific	134.6	335	568.5	5.8	19.9	28.2
Americas	145.2	280	412.7	4.2	21.4	20.5
Africa	21.8	50	98.2	6.0	3.2	4.9
Middle East	26.3	75	149.7	7.0	3.9	7.4

Europe being the world's dominant region. However, a shift will take place, with Europe losing market share to Asia and the Middle East by 2030. Europe's share of international arrivals will fall from 54.6% to 41.1%, whereas the Asia and Pacific region will enjoy a rise in market share of 19.3% to 28.8%, with a similar increase in receipts. The Americas' market share will remain stable and Africa will experience a significant growth but from a small base. The changes in market share reflect different growth rates for different regions. Europe will grow at 2.3% per annum, whereas Asia will grow at 5%. From an analysis of expenditure, it seems that receipts in the Middle East will rise from US $26.3 billion to US $149.7 billion, a staggering growth rate of 7% per annum, capturing 7.4% of all tourism expenditure. Africa will follow a similar pattern, with receipts rising from US $21 billion in 2005 to US $98 billion by 2030, a growth rate of 6% per annum.

Europe

Europe faces ever-increasing levels of competition from other destinations, from both within and outside the Continent. This competition comes from both the west and east and from both countries as a whole and from cities. By 2030, Europe's share of international arrivals will be 41.1%, falling from 54.6% in 2005, with an annual growth rate of 2.3%. Over the same period, international receipts will fall from 51.6% to 39%, with an annual growth rate of 3.2%. Europe's growth rate will be constant. However, the growth rate in receipts of 8.2% between 2000 and 2005 will not be repeated, with growth rate falling to levels that are more modest (Tables 5.1 and 5.3).

France

France has long had the most varied tourist offerings in the world, from skiing and beaches to fashion, food and wine. Paris is described as the cultural capital of the world, with its world-famous attractions of the Eiffel Tower and the Mona Lisa. It even has its own beach on the Seine (UN World Tourism Organisation, 2001)! However, looking to 2030, we forecast that the rate of growth for international arrivals will be a full 1% below Europe's overall rate of growth. According to the forecast, arrivals will grow from 76 million in 2005 to 102 million by 2030. This low growth rate can be attributed to the fact that France is a very 'mature' destination, so no major surprises or new products are expected. However, receipts will grow at a faster pace as a result of the trend towards the higher end of the market, with tourists choosing more luxurious accommodation and an emphasis on fine dining, leading to a higher spend per head.

Spain

Spain will remain the leading sun-and-sand destination in Europe in terms of receipts — but not arrivals. An expanding city-based product makes Spain an all-year-round destination. During the 1990s and the early part of the twenty-first century, the expansion of Spain as a second-home destination took place at an accelerated pace, but future growth is threatened by the uncertainty of the second-homes' market because of the problems arising from legislation and planning and a query on the adequacy of water supply. Therefore, given the maturity of the market, we expect international arrivals to increase from 55.9 million in 2005 to 84.7 million by 2030. The rate of growth is expected to slow down between 2015 and 2030 to 1% per annum, but tourism receipts are expected to double over the next 25 years, rising from US $48 billion to US $107.6 billion by 2030.

Table 5.3: International arrivals and receipts: Europe.

International arrivals	International tourist arrivals (millions)					Market share (%)	Change (%)			Average annual growth (%)		
	1990	2000	2005	2015	2030	2005	05/00	15/05	30/15	00/05	05/15	15/30
Europe	264.7	393.6	438.7	555.1	779.9	54.6	11.5	26.5	40.5	2.2	2.4	2.3
France	52.5	77.2	75.9	88.2	102.4	17.3	-1.7	16.2	16.1	-0.3	1.5	1.0
Spain	34.1	47.9	55.9	67.8	84.7	12.7	16.7	21.3	24.9	3.1	1.9	1.5
Italy	26.7	41.2	36.5	45.4	56.7	8.3	-11.3	24.3	24.9	-2.4	2.2	1.5
United Kingdom	17.2	23.2	28.0	42.3	65.9	6.4	20.8	50.9	55.8	3.8	4.1	3.0
Germany	17.0	19.0	21.5	28.9	38.9	4.9	13.2	34.4	34.6	2.5	3.0	2.0
Turkey	4.8	9.6	20.3	32.9	90.8	4.6	111.5	62.3	176.0	15.0	4.8	6.8
Austria	19.0	18.0	20.0	23.2	26.9	4.5	11.0	16.3	15.9	2.1	1.5	1.0
Russian Fed.	–	–	19.9	26.2	43.3	4.5	–	31.4	65.3	–	2.7	3.3
Poland	–	17.4	15.2	17.6	23.7	3.5	-12.6	15.8	34.7	-2.7	1.5	2.0
Greece	8.9	13.1	14.3	18.1	25.1	3.3	9.0	26.8	38.7	1.7	2.4	2.2
Other	82.2	127.1	131.2	164.5	221.5	29.9	3.2	25.4	34.7	0.6	2.3	2.0

International receipts	International tourism receipts (US $ billions)					Share (%)	Change (%)			Average annual growth (%)		
	1990	2000	2005	2015	2030	2005	05/00	15/05	30/15	00/05	05/15	15/30
Europe	142.9	232.4	349.7	535.0	787.1	51.6	50.4	53.0	47.1	8.2	4.3	2.6
Spain	18.5	30.0	48.0	76.5	107.6	13.7	60.1	59.5	40.7	9.4	4.7	2.3
France	20.2	30.8	42.3	59.6	92.9	12.1	37.5	41.0	55.9	6.4	3.4	3.0
Italy	16.5	27.5	35.4	53.2	73.7	10.1	28.8	50.3	38.5	5.1	4.1	2.2
United Kingdom	15.4	21.9	30.7	43.3	63.6	8.8	40.3	41.2	46.9	6.8	3.4	2.6
Germany	14.2	18.7	29.7	47.4	77.1	8.5	58.7	59.8	62.7	9.2	4.7	3.2
Turkey	3.2	7.6	18.2	29.3	78.6	5.2	137.7	61.4	168.3	17.3	4.8	6.6
Austria	13.4	9.9	16.0	24.1	32.0	4.6	61.2	50.5	32.8	9.6	4.1	1.9
Greece	2.6	9.2	13.7	21.5	33.5	3.9	48.9	56.6	55.8	8.0	4.5	3.0
Switzerland	7.4	7.8	11.0	16.0	21.6	3.2	42.0	44.9	35.0	7.0	3.7	2.0
Netherlands	4.2	7.2	10.5	16.0	21.6	3.0	45.1	52.7	35.0	7.5	4.2	2.0
Other	27.3	61.9	94.3	148.1	184.9	27.0	52.4	57.0	24.8	8.4	4.5	1.5

Germany

German inbound traffic is heavily orientated towards the business and conference markets; its success, therefore, is closely aligned to the overall world economy. Germany's success in hosting the football (soccer) World Cup in 2006 has also boosted the country's image as a short-break/city-break destination. By 2015, the country is expected to have fully recovered from the costs of reunification in the 1990s, making Germany the economic powerhouse in mainland Europe. However, on the downside an ageing population will create labour shortages and stifle GDP growth by 2030. International arrivals are expected to increase from 21.5 million in 2005 to 38.9 billion in 2030. International receipts will grow at one of the highest rates in Europe due to the higher spend from business tourists and therefore revenues will be more than double from US $29 billion to US $77 billion.

United Kingdom

Most of the United Kingdom's inbound tourism is focused on London, which offers a diversity of both leisure experiences and strong corporate business performance (Mintel, 2006). With the Olympics coming to London in 2012, the capital city will gain from massive investment in terms of infrastructure, hotels and sporting venues. London will, therefore, do very well in the long term as well as the short term, that is during the Games and beyond; the city will also gain immeasurably from the publicity generated. In addition, Scotland could emerge as an independent nation, fuelling an interest in the destination. Scotland's strong business tourism products, perception of being a safe country and connectivity to Europe should also facilitate growth. Over the next 25 years, arrivals and receipts are expected to double to 65.9 million and US $63.6 billion, respectively.

Russia

Gone are the days of Soviet-style hotels renowned for poor service, inedible food and bedroom bugs courtesy of the KGB! In 2007, St. Petersburg is a famous cultural capital with the Hermitage and the Kirov Ballet, whereas Moscow is a thriving business centre, achieving Europe's highest revenue per available room (RevPAR) in 2006 (Kuhn, 2006). It is expected that Russia will loosen visa controls and red tape, making it easier for tourists to visit, in particular Europeans. Because of the vastness of the country and Asian connections, Russia can also expect exponential arrivals from China and India. International arrivals will increase from 26 million to 43.3 million by 2030, an increase of 3.1% per annum.

Turkey

By 2030, Turkey will be the jewel in the crown of European tourism, sitting as it does at the crossroads of Christianity and Islam, with international arrivals growing at 6%

per annum and arrivals trebling from 20.3 million to 90.8 million. At the same time, receipts will rise from US $18.2 billion to US $78.6 billion, an annual increase of 5.9%. Over the next 25 years, restructuring of the tourism sector from predominately all-inclusive resorts to a broader appeal will transform the industry, whether it be Istanbul as a vibrant, cosmopolitan capital city or rural tourism's authenticity and the sports products such as hiking and water skiing. The country's location will also make it a focal point between Europe and the Middle East. With Turkey expected to join the EU in 2015, the country should benefit from a thriving short-break market from Europe. However, Turkey may not achieve EU membership and its secular position could change with the rise of radical Islamic political parties, which have a strong following in poorer parts of the country.

Italy

The Italian market is very mature, which leaves little prospect for significant growth. However, Italy's diversity of cultural product, whether fine art or excellent food, cathedrals or beautiful cities give it the opportunity for growth in specific niche markets. We expect Italy to lose market share to other Mediterranean countries such as Albania, Croatia and Morocco in the sun-and-sand holiday market, as it will not be able to compete on price. Further, growth is expected from the US and UK inbound markets, driving international arrivals from 36.5 million in 2005 to 56.7 million by 2030, an average growth of 1.8% per annum. In the same period, international receipts will grow from US $35.4 billion to US $73.7 billion in 2030, a growth rate of 2.9% per annum. The achievement of this growth is dependent on Italy maintaining its luxury tourism position.

Greece

The Greek inbound market is essentially comprised of those seeking sun and sand, and this market is mature. Greece faces intensive competition from Albania and Morocco over the next decade, as both can offer a better quality of product at a lower price (particularly Morocco). International arrivals will rise from 14.3 million to 25.1 million by 2030, an annual increase of approximately 2.3%.

The Asia and Pacific Region

Rising levels of disposal income mean that the Asia and Pacific region will experience exponential growth by 2030, stealing market share from Europe. With Western European tourists wanting to explore new destinations plus a growth of travellers from within the region; the region's lower cost base and high standards of hotel accommodation services will make it one of the most competitive in the world. In 2030, the region will have 28.8% of world international arrivals and 28.2% of world receipts, an annual growth rate of 5% and 5.8%, respectively. China will be the dominant player by 2030, offering a diversity of experiences, from Disneyland to ski resorts and from beach holidays to adventure treks. Cities like Shanghai will lead in the world of conference destinations, whereas Macao will be a gambler's paradise (Table 5.4).

China

With China showcasing the Beijing Olympics in 2008, the world's eyes are on the destination. There can be no doubt that China will be the regional dragon in tourism, attracting major investment and large number of tourists. Boeing estimates that China's airline industry will be operating a fleet of 22,000 passenger aircraft by 2019, which would constitute 10% of the world's total stock. China has an open-skies policy, which is facilitating direct connections to the rest of the world, whether it is Manchester, Istanbul or Baltimore. The Chinese government's policy of investing in Africa guarantees the country oil and minerals to fuel its economic growth and also its place in the world as a superpower. Tourism in China is not the low end of the market, with hotel room rates comparable to those in Moscow, London and New York. According to Howarth Asia Pacific's China Hotel Study (Mintel, 2006), the average room rate in five star hotels has risen by 9% from 2003 to 2005. The budget end of the sector is expanding rapidly, whether bed and breakfast or branded accommodation such as Travelodge or Holiday Inn Express. Therefore, taking all these factors into account, we expect the arrivals to grow upto 167 million by 2030, an annual growth rate of 5.1% and international receipts will rise to US $114 billion by 2030, making China the world's most popular destination with an 8.8% market share. On the downside, another SARs or similar new pandemic originating in the region would severely affect tourist flows.

Malaysia

Malaysia offers a wide variety of experiences, from long sandy beaches to medical tourism and an expanding conference product. The country is currently — in 2005 — ranked 14th in the world for international arrivals and will rise to 6th by 2030. It is expected that this will nearly double by 2015, reaching 29.9 million, and quadruple by 2030, with 70.7 million international arrivals; receipts will rise from US $8.5 billion to US $41.8 billion in the same period.

Macao Region

Macao (China) is outstripping Las Vegas as the world's gambling and entertainment resort. Since the liberalisation of concessions for the industry between 2000 and 2004, revenue from gaming has surpassed that of Las Vegas, totalling US $5.3 billion

Table 5.4: International arrivals and receipts: Asia & the Pacific.

International arrivals	International tourist arrivals (millions)					Market share (%)	Change (%)			Average annual growth (%)		
	1990	2000	2005	2015	2030	2005	05/00	15/05	30/15	00/05	05/15	15/30
Asia and the Pacific	56.2	110.6	155.3	287.6	546.5	19.3	40.5	85.2	90.0	6.8	6.2	4.3
China	10.5	31.2	46.8	92.9	167.4	30.1	49.9	98.5	80.2	8.1	6.9	3.9
Malaysia	7.4	10.2	16.4	29.9	70.7	10.6	60.7	82.0	136.5	9.5	6.0	5.7
Hong Kong	–	8.8	14.8	20.9	37.6	9.5	67.6	41.5	79.9	10.3	3.5	3.9
Thailand	5.3	9.6	11.6	18.9	39.3	7.4	20.8	63.4	107.9	3.8	4.9	4.9
Macao region	2.5	5.2	9.0	29.5	45.9	5.8	73.4	227.3	55.6	11.0	11.9	2.9
Singapore	4.8	6.1	7.1	11.6	24.0	4.6	16.8	63.8	106.9	3.1	4.9	4.8
Japan	3.2	4.8	6.7	11.9	18.5	4.3	41.4	76.9	55.5	6.9	5.7	2.9
Korea (Rep)	3.0	5.3	6.0	8.5	15.2	3.9	13.2	41.1	78.8	2.5	3.4	3.9
Australia	2.2	4.5	5.0	8.1	12.7	3.2	10.8	61.4	56.8	2.1	4.8	3.0
Indonesia	2.2	5.1	5.0	10.5	21.8	3.2	-1.2	109.9	107.6	-0.2	7.4	4.9
India	1.7	2.6	3.9	7.3	15.1	2.5	47.9	86.3	106.8	7.8	6.2	4.8
Other	13.3	17.1	22.9	37.6	78.3	14.8	33.7	63.9	108.2	5.8	4.9	4.9

International receipts	International tourism receipts (US $ billions)					Share (%)	Change (%)			Average annual growth (%)		
	1990	2000	2005	2015	2030	2005	05/00	15/05	30/15	00/05	05/15	15/30
Asia and the Pacific	41.1	85.2	134.6	335.0	568.4	20.0	57.9	148.9	69.7	9.1	9.1	3.5
China	2.2	16.2	29.3	61.5	114.0	21.8	80.5	109.9	85.4	11.8	7.4	4.1
Australia	4.2	9.3	16.9	29.4	52.3	12.5	81.8	74.3	77.9	12.0	5.6	3.8
Japan	3.6	3.4	6.6	24.4	35.4	4.9	96.6	268.0	45.1	13.5	13.0	2.5
Hong Kong	4.7	5.9	10.3	18.2	32.9	7.6	74.2	76.8	80.8	11.1	5.7	3.9
Thailand	4.3	7.5	9.6	21.7	40.3	7.1	28.4	126.3	85.7	5.0	8.2	4.1
Malaysia	1.7	5.0	8.5	20.1	41.8	6.3	70.5	135.3	108.0	10.7	8.6	4.9
Macao region	1.5	3.2	8.0	18.4	28.6	5.9	148.8	130.6	55.4	18.2	8.4	2.9
India	1.5	3.5	7.5	17.9	49.4	5.6	117.5	137.9	176.0	15.5	8.7	6.8
Singapore	4.9	5.1	5.9	12.3	25.6	4.4	14.9	108.2	108.1	2.8	7.3	4.9
Korea (Rep)	3.6	6.8	5.8	12.9	31.1	4.3	-15.0	122.2	141.1	-3.3	8.0	5.9
Other	8.9	19.3	26.2	98.2	117.0	19.4	35.5	275.3	19.1	6.1	13.2	1.2

according to the World Travel and Tourism Council (Mintel, 2006a). The estimated total supply of gaming tables in Macao in 2008 will be approximately 4000, rising from 1092 at the end of 2004 (Mintel, 2006a). Such exponential growth is driven by the Chinese people's love of gambling and the lack of opportunity on mainland China to indulge their passion for it. Growth, however, depends on the continuation of these trends. In addition, Macao's growth will be hindered by the availability of land and there are already plans to take all non-gambling tourism activity out of the country, thus maximising revenues. Due to capacity constraints we expect the Macao region to be redefined to incorporate land from nearby mainland China. Therefore, tourism receipts will rise from US $8 billion in 2005 to US $28.6 billion, an annual growth rate of 8.4% per annum to 2015; however, capacity constraints could well reduce this growth rate to 2.9% per annum thereafter.

Japan

The incoming market is heavily weighted towards business-related travel, which reflects its science and knowledge economy. Key markets are South Korea and Taiwan. Japan will face strategic challenges in the future, potentially losing market share to China, with its ageing population, which will means that economic growth is stifled. It is expected that international arrivals to Japan will slow down considerably post-2015, compared to other countries in Asia. However, the growth will still be considerable, with arrivals increasing from 6.7 million in 2005 to 18.5 million by 2030 — a trebling of arrivals.

India

At present there are more four and five star hotels in New York than there are in the whole of India (Morgan, 2007), and therefore capacity constraint is the biggest hurdle to tourism growth rather than demand. India has been positioned, along with China, as the tiger of the Asian economy. India's many cultural and historic sites and that the fact that English is the official business language makes the country an ideal destination for growth. Air travel to India is booming, with major restructuring of the country's major airports, notably Mumbai and Delhi, which, together, handle two-thirds of India's air traffic. The International Air Transport Association (IATA) has warned India that it must increase capacity quickly if it is to meet future demand (Mintel, 2006). Another concern for Western travellers is the perception of food hygiene and the sustainability of economic growth, which will have an impact on water supply and sanitary conditions. If India can overcome these difficulties, international receipts are expected to rise to US $49.4 billion, at an annual growth rate of 7.5%.

Australia

On the one hand, Australia is a mature destination but, on the other hand, it is close enough to Asia to benefit from her neighbours' growth. The Australian inbound market is essentially orientated towards leisure, with the country having an excellent brand and a positive currency outlook against the yen. On the negative side, Japan's failing economy will continue to impact on inbound markets, but this will be replaced by new opportunities from India and China. Forecasts show higher growth from receipts because of tourists' expenditure on accommodation and their length of stay. International arrivals will increase from 5 million in 2005 to 12.7 million by 2030, with receipts increasing from US $16.9 billion to US $52 billion, respectively.

The Americas

The Americas' market share of world tourism in 2030 will be virtually the same as in 2005 because of the continent's proximity to Asia and the Pacific. As the United States is also the world's largest economy, the country will be the key driver in the region, thus North America will be the senior partner in the region. Expect strong performances from Cuba, Brazil and Argentina in region over the next decades. The Americas' rate of growth per annum will be 3.4% for arrivals and 4.2% for receipts, with international arrivals reaching 309.8 million and receipts US $412 billion, respectively (Table 5.5).

United States

In 2030, the United States of America will be the world's largest economy and receive the highest tourist receipts. The country offers the most extensive range of products and experiences, from remote national parks to island paradises and vibrant cities. Many of the experiences are iconic brands in their own right such as Disneyland and Las Vegas. In itself, in fact, the United States is the world's most powerful tourist attraction. Favourable exchange rates make the United States an attractive choice for many visitors. The fiscal and current-account deficit in the United States is driving the currency markets and this is not expected to change before 2012. Increased expenditure on advertising, promoting an iconic national brand and an improved destination website are all expected to help reposition the United States of America in the world tourism market in the next couple of years (Morgan, 2007). Therefore, international receipts are forecasted to grow from US $81.7 billion in 2005 to US $223 billion by 2030, an increase of 4% per annum, giving the United States an 11.1% share of world tourism receipts.

Table 5.5: International arrivals and receipts: Americas.

International arrivals	International tourist arrivals (millions)					Market share (%)	Change (%)			Average annual growth (%)		
	1990	2000	2005	2015	2030	2005	05/00	15/05	30/15	00/05	05/15	15/30
Americas	92.8	128.2	133.2	184.1	309.8	16.6	3.9	38.2	68.3	0.8	3.2	3.5
United States	39.4	51.2	49.2	69.7	116.7	36.9	-4.0	41.6	67.4	-0.8	3.5	3.4
Mexico	17.2	20.6	21.9	25.4	34.2	16.5	6.2	15.9	34.6	1.2	1.5	2.0
Canada	15.2	19.6	18.8	23.3	33.8	14.1	-4.4	24.1	45.1	-0.9	2.2	2.5
Brazil	1.1	5.3	5.4	8.5	15.9	4.0	0.8	58.6	87.1	0.2	4.6	4.2
Argentina	1.9	2.9	3.8	6.1	11.0	2.9	31.4	59.6	80.3	5.5	4.7	3.9
Dominican Rep.	1.3	3.0	3.5	5.9	11.3	2.6	15.8	71.0	91.5	2.9	5.4	4.3
Puerto Rico	2.6	3.3	3.7	5.4	13.0	2.8	10.3	46.5	140.7	2.0	3.8	5.9
Cuba	0.3	1.7	2.3	5.0	13.7	1.7	29.9	121.1	174.0	5.2	7.9	6.7
Chile	0.9	1.7	2.0	3.1	6.0	1.5	16.4	52.9	93.5	3.0	4.2	4.4
Uruguay	–	2.0	1.8	2.6	4.8	1.4	-8.1	43.8	84.6	-1.7	3.6	4.1
Other	12.9	16.7	20.9	29.1	49.4	15.7	25.2	39.3	69.8	4.5	3.3	3.5

International receipts	International tourism receipts (US $ billions)					Share (%)	Change (%)			Average annual growth (%)		
	1990	2000	2005	2015	2030	2005	05/00	15/05	30/15	00/05	05/15	15/30
Americas	69.2	130.8	145.2	280.0	412.6	21.4	11.0	92.8	47.4	2.1	6.6	2.6
United States	43.0	82.4	81.7	143.2	223.2	56.3	-0.9	75.3	55.9	-0.2	5.6	3.0
Canada	6.3	10.8	13.6	21.5	34.6	9.4	26.0	58.3	60.9	4.6	4.6	3.2
Mexico	5.5	8.3	11.8	19.2	34.7	8.1	42.3	62.7	80.7	7.1	4.9	3.9
Brazil	1.5	1.8	3.9	6.0	12.5	2.7	113.3	55.4	108.3	15.2	4.4	4.9
Dominican Rep.	0.8	2.9	3.5	5.5	10.7	2.4	23.0	56.3	94.5	4.1	4.5	4.4
Puerto Rico	1.4	2.4	3.2	4.7	11.7	2.2	35.6	45.1	149.1	6.1	3.7	6.1
Argentina	1.1	2.9	2.7	4.3	7.7	1.9	-6.0	57.6	79.1	-1.2	4.5	3.9
Bahamas	1.3	1.7	2.1	3.2	5.7	1.4	19.5	54.4	78.1	3.6	4.3	3.8
Cuba	0.2	1.7	1.9	4.1	7.4	1.3	10.5	113.5	80.5	2.0	7.6	3.9
Costa Rica	0.3	1.3	1.6	2.4	4.1	1.1	20.6	52.9	70.8	3.7	4.2	3.6
Other	7.7	14.6	19.2	65.9	60.3	13.2	31.7	242.8	-8.5	5.5	12.3	-0.6

Mexico

Beach tourism from the US market accounts for 90% of incoming traffic to Mexico, with Acapulco the major tourist honeypot. Mexico's proximity to the United States makes the destination a cheap alternative for many US visitors, both for a holiday and a second-home destination. However, Mexico faces stiff competition from the Caribbean, especially with the opening up of Cuba to US tourists in the next decade. We are, therefore, forecasting a slow growth of 1.5% to 2% over the next 25 years, with arrivals increasing from 21.9 million to 34.2 million.

Canada

Canada's wide-open spaces and natural authenticity has been a magnet for tourists over the last decade. However, the Canadian dollar's strength has been a barrier to growth, making the destination expensive for US visitors. The future outlook really depends on what happens to timber and energy prices, as these influences the strength of the dollar. We are, therefore, forecasting slow growth for Canada over the next decade, well below the average for the Americas as a whole. Arrivals will increase from 18.8 million to 33.8 million by 2030, a 2.4% increase compared to the region's 3.4%.

Brazil

Growth in tourism to Brazil has been largely driven by marketing undertaken by the private sector. The key issue limiting Brazil's tourism growth is the government's lack of focused marketing in Europe and North America. The lack of reciprocal visa arrangements limits the number of high-spending arrivals from the United States. However, this should change in the short term with the election of a new US president and subsequent policy changes. International arrivals, therefore, are forecasted to grow from 5.4 million in 2005 to 15.9 million by 2030 at a rate of approximately 4.4% per annum.

Argentina

In 2005, Argentina restructured its massive debt and tourism has played a large part in restoring the country to economic stability. As democracy grows, the economy strengthens and new tourism investments come on stream, arrivals will increase. In 2005, there was a record number of visitors — 3.9 million. With a record of direct investment of above US $2.7 billion in the sector, the country's tourism now accounts for 8% of GDP and is encouraging decentralisation and the spread of wealth in Argentina. Therefore, the prospects are good, with international arrivals growing to 11 million by 2030.

Cuba

Cuba is the largest of the Caribbean islands, situated in it's the westernmost Caribbean, just south of Florida. The capital, Havana, projects the familiar Cuban images of elegant colonial streets, patrolled by 1950s finned Cadillacs, to the beat of a bustling nightlife. The relaxation of American trade and tourism barriers is on the horizon, drawing inexorably closer. This will radically energise the coffers of an already lucrative tourism business. The forecast is that international arrivals will grow from 2.3 million in 2005 to 13.7 million by 2030, contributing US $7.4 billion to the economy. Cuba will be one of the fastest growing tourism economies in the Americas in the next decade.

Africa

Africa has always been the smallest tourism region in the world, mainly because of ongoing civil wars, political instability and the subsequent lack of wealth. However, as more and more tourists seek new destinations and if political stability becomes widespread, the prospects for Africa are good and receipts are forecast to grow by 6% per annum, which means that revenues will double in 25 years, from US $50 billion to US $98 billion by 2030. The strong growth will be driven by the length of stay of tourists who opt for luxury accommodation (Table 5.6).

South Africa

South Africa offers a variety of activities, from wine tourism to safaris. Record arrivals' figures for 2004, however, disguise a number of problems facing her tourist industry, including losing market share of visitors from a number of countries to competing destinations. Attracting new and repeat business has become harder in the face of a strong rand, which has resulted in a reduction in the time and money that tourists spend in the country. However, with South Africa hosting the Soccer World Cup in 2010 and the expected subsequent increase in the quality and capacity of accommodation, the prospects are good. However, crime is very much an issue and could become a barrier to growth. The forecast is that international arrivals will grow from 7.4 million in 2005 to 22.6 million by 2030, at a growth rate of 4.5% per annum.

Morocco

In 2003, Morocco set out to double the number of tourists by 2010 from 4.5 million to 10 million visitors. In order to achieve this it has invested substantially in infrastructure. Morocco has 14 commercial airports, the annual total activity of which reached about 7.6 million passengers in 2004, making it one of the more advanced African countries in transport terms. Its road network is approximately

Table 5.6: International arrivals and receipts: Africa.

International arrivals	International tourist arrivals (millions)					Market share (%)	Change (%)			Average annual growth (%)		
	1990	2000	2005	2015	2030	2005	05/00	15/05	30/15	00/05	05/15	15/30
Africa	15.2	27.9	37.3	57.9	101.8	4.6	33.7	55.2	75.8	5.8	4.4	3.8
South Africa	–	5.9	7.4	11.5	22.6	19.8	25.5	56.1	96.5	4.5	4.5	4.5
Tunisia	3.2	5.1	6.4	9.0	15.1	17.1	26.1	41.1	67.8	4.6	3.4	3.4
Morocco	4.0	4.3	5.8	9.2	15.4	15.7	36.6	57.5	67.4	6.2	4.5	3.4
Zimbabwe	0.6	2.0	1.6	2.5	6.0	4.2	–20.7	60.4	140.0	–4.6	4.7	5.8
Algeria	1.1	0.9	1.4	2.3	4.9	3.9	66.6	59.4	113.0	10.2	4.7	5.0
Swaziland	0.3	0.3	0.8	1.3	2.8	2.2	198.6	54.9	115.4	21.9	4.4	5.1
Senegal	0.2	0.4	0.8	1.3	2.1	2.1	97.7	69.1	61.5	13.6	5.3	3.2
Mauritius	0.3	0.7	0.8	1.2	1.8	2.0	16.0	57.7	50.0	3.0	4.6	2.7
Uganda	0.1	0.2	0.5	0.8	1.3	1.3	187.1	70.9	62.5	21.1	5.4	3.2
Reunion	0.2	0.4	0.4	0.7	1.0	1.1	–4.9	71.1	42.9	–1.0	5.4	2.4
Other	5.1	7.9	11.5	18.1	28.8	30.7	44.5	57.9	59.1	7.4	4.6	3.1

International receipts	International tourism receipts (US $ billions)					Share (%)	Change (%)			Average annual growth (%)		
	1990	2000	2005	2015	2030	2005	05/00	15/05	30/15	00/05	05/15	15/30
Africa	6.4	10.4	21.8	50.0	98.2	3.2	109.5	129.4	96.4	14.8	8.3	4.5
South Africa	1.8	2.7	7.3	16.2	38.9	33.6	173.9	121.1	140.1	20.2	7.9	5.8
Morocco	1.3	2.0	4.6	7.3	14.9	21.2	126.6	58.0	104.1	16.4	4.6	4.8
Tunisia	0.9	1.7	2.1	3.0	5.9	9.7	26.3	41.2	96.7	4.7	3.5	4.5
Mauritius	0.2	0.5	0.9	1.5	3.6	4.0	60.7	72.2	140.0	9.5	5.4	5.8
Tanzania	0.1	0.4	0.8	1.4	4.0	3.8	118.6	69.9	185.7	15.6	5.3	7.0
Kenya	0.4	0.3	0.6	1.1	3.1	2.7	104.6	90.0	181.8	14.3	6.4	6.9
Botswana	0.1	0.2	0.6	1.1	2.9	2.6	153.2	95.7	163.6	18.6	6.7	6.5
Reunion	–	0.3	0.4	0.7	1.8	2.0	49.3	58.4	157.1	8.0	4.6	6.3
Namibia	0.1	0.2	0.3	0.7	1.9	1.6	117.5	101.1	171.4	15.5	7.0	6.7
Seychelles	0.1	0.1	0.2	0.3	0.6	0.9	38.1	45.8	96.4	6.5	3.8	4.5
Other	1.3	2.0	3.9	16.7	20.7	17.9	96.6	327.6	23.5	13.5	14.5	1.4

60,000 km, varying from all-weather highways around the major population centres to unpaved mountain roads in the more remote Western Sahara and Atlas region. The train network is hailed as one of the best in Africa with *trains rapides clematises* (fast, modern, air-conditioned trains) linking the major cities and reliable European-standard regional trains for commuter areas. Fares in Morocco are extremely good value, with the longest train journey (the 510 miles from Oujda to Marrakech) costing £25 for first class (Mintel, 2004a). International arrivals are forecast to grow from 6.4 million in 2005 to 15.1 million by 2030, approximately tripling the visitor numbers.

Tunisia

Tourism is forecast to grow by 3.4% over the next decade, with international arrivals increasing from 6.4 million to 15.1 million by 2030. However, in order to achieve this growth, the country will have to compete against Libya which is now opening up to tourism after decades of inaccessibility.

Uganda

With Uganda experiencing strong growth in total tourist arrivals over the last 5 years, the inbound holiday market is still characterised by the overland and back-packer market. The number of high-spending holiday/leisure visitors is still relatively small compared, for example to Kenya, Tanzania and Botswana. Tourism to Uganda did not develop as expected in the mid-1990s and this has in part been due to the significant setback it received in 1999, when rebels killed eight tourists who had been tracking silverback gorillas. Various other security issues, in particular in the Murchison Falls National Park, have also constrained growth. As a result of this, investors in tourism facilities have suffered considerable losses and some establishments have gone into liquidation. The forecast is that international arrivals to Uganda will rise from 0.5 million in 2005 to 1.3 million by 2030, if the country maintains a stable political economy and preserves its eco-tourism products (Mintel, 2006b).

The Middle East

The Middle East is expected to increase its world market share by approximately 75% and double the value and volume by 2030, with growth rates of 5.7% for international arrivals and 7% for international receipts. These growth rates will be the strongest of all the regions of the world and will reflect the wealth and the creation of a strong brand identity, such as Emirates emerging as a truly international airline, with Dubai as a hub, or an increase in pilgrimage to Saudi

Arabia. Political turmoil, civil war and radical Islamic agitation could, however, hamper the growth of tourism in the region (Table 5.7).

Saudi Arabia

Saudi Arabia is the destination for Islamic pilgrims, and tourism is growing at an immense pace. Consequently, there is considerable scope for tour operators to establish upmarket packages for middle and upper-income travellers to visit Mecca and Medina to perform Umrah. In addition to this, there are opportunities to offer add-on packages for further travel within the country and indeed to other destinations within the region. In a world where societies increasingly resemble one another, 'different' is an attractive commodity. As a tourist destination, Saudi Arabia has that difference, because it is one of the few countries not yet overpopulated with tourists (Mintel, 2005b). The prospects are good, with international arrivals expected to grow from 8 million to 35.2 million by 2030 and receipts growing from US $5.2 billion in 2005 to US $35.4 billion by 2030. Saudi Arabia will be the number one destination in the Middle East by 2030.

United Arab Emirates

Dubai, the heartbeat of the Emirates' tourism, has declared its intention to welcome 15 million visitors annually by 2010. For this to be achieved, it seems certain that Dubai will have to establish itself both as a city-break destination and as a staging point for further exploration of the UAE and the Middle East in general. The UAE is tourism success story, whilst other Middle Eastern countries have struggled to maintain the rapid growth rates of the 1990s, dragged down by association with security issues and fear of terrorism.

Despite being in what has sometimes been a no-go region for many Western tourists, Dubai seems to have positioned itself as an urbanised, Westernised, luxurious, home-from-home, beach-and-shopping destination with spectacular success. However, the political turmoil found in the Middle East could yet impact on Dubai, along with the over-development of property, which some experts predict could be Dubai's undoing. Overall, international receipts to the UAE are expected to quadruple to US $8.8 billion by 2030.

Egypt

Egypt is almost entirely a leisure destination and Europe its primary market. Located right on the Mediterranean, Egypt has been one of the greatest stories of tourism over the last decade even given the terrorism incidents, which have occurred there. Emerging inbound markets have included Russia, based upon a no-visa entry policy. Tourism arrivals are forecast to grow from 8.2 million in 2005 to 26 million by 2030.

Table 5.7: International arrivals and receipts: Middle East.

International arrivals	International tourist arrivals (millions)					Market share (%)	Change (%)			Average annual growth (%)		
	1990	2000	2005	2015	2030	2005	05/00	15/05	30/15	00/05	05/15	15/30
Middle East	9.6	24.5	38.4	71.5	158.9	4.8	56.9	86.4	122.2	9.0	6.2	5.3
Saudi Arabia	2.2	6.6	8.0	14.7	35.2	21.0	22.1	82.9	139.5	4.0	6.0	5.8
Egypt	2.4	5.1	8.2	14.4	26.0	21.5	61.1	74.7	80.6	9.5	5.6	3.9
Syrian Arab Rep.	0.6	1.7	3.4	6.6	13.6	8.8	99.9	96.0	106.1	13.9	6.7	4.8
Jordan	0.6	1.6	3.0	6.0	12.4	7.8	89.1	100.9	106.7	12.7	7.0	4.8
Lebanon	–	0.7	1.1	2.3	5.5	3.0	53.6	101.8	139.1	8.6	7.0	5.8
Other	3.9	8.7	14.6	27.5	66.2	38.0	66.8	88.6	140.7	10.2	6.3	5.9

International receipts	International tourism receipts (US $ billions)					Share (%)	Change (%)			Average annual growth (%)		
	1990	2000	2005	2015	2030	2005	05/00	15/05	30/15	00/05	05/15	15/30
Middle East	4.3	15.2	26.3	75.0	149.0	4.1	72.2	185.7	98.7	10.9	10.5	4.6
Egypt	1.1	4.3	6.9	12.3	30.3	26.1	57.7	79.5	146.3	9.1	5.9	6.0
Saudi Arabia	–	–	5.2	13.1	35.4	19.7	–	153.0	170.2	–	9.3	6.6
United Arab Emirates	0.3	1.1	2.2	3.9	8.8	8.4	107.0	77.3	125.6	14.5	5.7	5.4
Syrian Arab Rep.	0.3	1.1	2.2	4.1	9.7	8.3	101.0	88.5	136.6	14.0	6.3	5.7
Jordan	0.5	0.7	1.4	2.9	7.1	5.5	99.3	101.2	144.8	13.8	7.0	6.0
Oman	0.1	0.2	0.5	0.9	1.7	1.8	117.6	78.8	97.7	15.6	5.8	4.5
Other	2.0	7.8	7.9	37.8	56.0	30.2	1.5	377.2	48.0	0.3	15.6	2.6

Table 5.8: Top 10 countries by arrivals.

	Arrivals	Base year (millions)	Forecast (millions)		Average annual growth rate (%)	Market share (%)	
	Country	2005	2015	2030	2005–2030	2005	2030
1	China	46.8	92.9	167.4	5.1	5.8	8.8
2	United States	49.2	69.7	116.7	3.5	6.1	6.2
3	France	75.9	88.2	102.4	1.2	9.5	5.4
4	Turkey	20.3	32.9	90.8	6.0	2.5	4.8
5	Spain	55.9	67.8	84.7	1.7	7.0	4.5
6	Malaysia	16.4	29.9	70.7	5.8	2.0	3.7
7	United Kingdom	28.0	42.3	65.9	3.4	3.5	3.5
8	Italy	36.5	45.4	56.7	1.8	4.5	3.0
9	Macao region	9.0	29.5	45.9	6.5	1.1	2.4
10	Russian Fed.	19.9	26.2	43.3	3.1	2.5	2.3
	Total	358.0	524.8	844.6	3.4	44.6	44.5

Table 5.9: Top 10 countries by receipts.

	Receipts	Base year (US $ billion)	Forecast (US $ billion)		Average annual growth rate (%)	Market share (%)	
	Country	2005	2015	2030	2005–2030	2005	2030
1	United States	81.8	143.3	223.2	4.0	12.1	11.1
2	China	29.3	61.5	114.0	5.4	4.3	5.7
3	Spain	48.0	76.5	107.6	3.2	7.1	5.3
4	France	44.0	59.7	93.0	3.0	6.5	4.6
5	Turkey	18.2	29.3	78.6	5.9	2.7	3.9
6	Germany	29.2	47.4	77.2	3.9	4.3	3.8
7	Italy	35.4	53.2	73.7	2.9	5.2	3.7
8	United Kingdom	30.7	43.3	63.6	2.9	4.5	3.2
9	Australia	16.9	29.5	52.4	4.5	2.5	2.6
10	India	7.5	17.9	49.5	7.5	1.1	2.5
	Total	340.9	561.7	932.9	4.0	50.3	46.3

So...

By 2030, nearly all the souvenirs in the world will be 'Made in China' and, at the same time, Chinese tourists will be travelling the world and buying those souvenirs! How the world has changed since 1950 when tourism statistics were first recorded, with just 25 million tourists. The big winners by 2030 will be China, India, Malaysia,

Macao, Turkey and the United States of America. In this chapter, we have shown how Western Europe will lose market share but France, Spain, United Kingdom and Italy will still be in the top 10 destinations in the world, along with Turkey as the rising star. Although the US international arrivals dropped post-9/11 and a wave of anti-Americanism spread across the world, it is still the world's favourite and strongest brand. Fundamentally, the prospects for world tourism are good, but tourist flows have changed as the world has moved east (Tables 5.8 and 5.9).

SECTION II

Chapter 6

The Health Tourist — Searching for the Fountain of Youth in Incredible India

'If you're looking for plastic surgery, correction of congenital malformation, teeth-whitening services and other beauty-enhancing cosmetic surgery, Kerala offers highly specialised departments and expert surgeons to take care of your needs' reads the Joan Collins' advertisement on the official Indian Tourist Board website. Michelle Harris is one of those consumers who are looking for first-class medical services at a third-world cost and wants to combine it with a holiday. Kerala in Southern India with its secluded hotels, relaxing backwaters, coconut groves and majestic beaches seems the perfect choice. Michelle, a recently retired teacher, wants to enhance her figure and feel young again. Friends have tried it, so she wants to do it. So, let the story begin.

This is Michelle's story in 2022

Introduction

An affluent and ageing society allows consumers to refine their approach to health because they now have the choice of striving for perfect health, as opposed to merely living disease-free. The elderly are the most frequent users of health-related goods and services. Consumers have begun to realise their capacity for longevity and to demand a fit and active lifestyle in their golden years. This means that consumers are searching for ways through which to slow down the ageing process or even discover the fountain of youth. It is not surprising, therefore, to note the rise of medical tourism holidays in South Africa or the greater use of alternative approaches to health, such as yoga, Chinese herbal medicines and spas.

This chapter sets out to

- Show why health and beauty tourism is important for the future
- Analyse the trends and drivers which shape health in society
- Demonstrate how a country's tourism product is using this trend, with India as an example
- Study the prospects for health and beauty tourism

Travel to enhance one's health is not new; Durie (2006) writes about 'taking the waters' in the 1800s in the hydro towns of Scotland or German spas such as Baden-Baden. In the late nineteenth century, the emerging urban middle class sought the healthy benefits of fresh sea water or mountain air as an antidote to the overcrowding and pollution caused by industrialisation. Many flocked to spas in pristine mountain locations or by the sea, particularly in Europe and the United Kingdom. In the early twentieth century, 'health farms' or 'fat farms' emerged, with an emphasis on fitness and a healthy diet. According to a report by Mintel on Health and Wellness (Mintel, 2004b), the modern era of health tourism is considered to have begun in 1939 when Deborah and Edmond Szekely opened a US $17.50-a-week, bring-your-tent spa and healthy-living retreat, which became the renowned Rancho La Puerta fitness resort in Mexico. In the same vein, Mel and Enid Zuckerman opened the Canyon Ranch, Tucson, Arizona, in 1979. Today, both locations still provide pampering, fitness activities and medically supervised wellness programmes to their high-paying clientele. They have established important models which have been copied and modified around the world. Today, health and travel have become global phenomena, to the extent that a trend has emerged, giving new meaning to the idea of going on holiday and returning 'a new person'. Whether this is a nip and tuck in a Beverley Hills' clinic or accruing a new set of teeth in Costa Rica for US $6000, health and beauty as the main reason for travel is a burgeoning market because travellers like Michelle search for the fountain of youth.

What Are the Key Trends Shaping This Phenomenon?

Over the past two decades, society has witnessed a steady growth in disposable income and further growth is anticipated over the next 20 years.

Figure 6.1 shows that staying fit and healthy has been consumers' top priority since 1983, according to the Future Foundation's *Changing Lives* Survey, and it will continue to be so in the future. The World Health Organisation predicts that 'health' will be the world's number-one industry by 2022 (Lister, 1999). Today's society is aligned between the consumers' strong interest in health and the rising affluence, resulting in a plethora of consumer products, whether anti-ageing creams or medical procedures.

Two of the measures of society's well-being are life expectancy and rates of infant mortality; when combined, these measures paint a picture of the age structure of society as it will be in the years to come (Figure 6.2). Living longer means that consumers have more time to do the things that they want to do. Part of this is as a result of advances in medicine, but it also has to do with affluence and looking after one's health. These health-related trends affect the demographic composition of UK society. Declining infant mortality, increased life expectancy and couples deciding to have children later in life have led to a shift in the age composition of society at large — fewer young people and more old people.

Between 2005 and 2030, the proportion of the UK population aged 50+ will increase by more than 40% whilst there will be negligible, and perhaps even negative,

Concern about staying fit and healthy, by gender, age and social grade

Proportion of adults who say they are concerned about trying to stay fit and healthy

"Some of the things people have told us they are concerned about are listed here. For each item, please tell me whether you find you are concerned about it at all...Trying to stay fit and healthy"

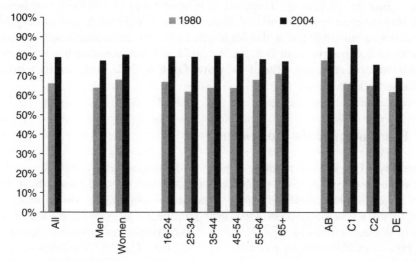

Source: nVision Research/Taylor Nelson Sofres
Base: 1000 adults aged 16+, UK

nVision

8576: Growing Consumerism in the UK Healthcare Market

Figure 6.1: Concern for staying fit.

By gender
2002 based forecast

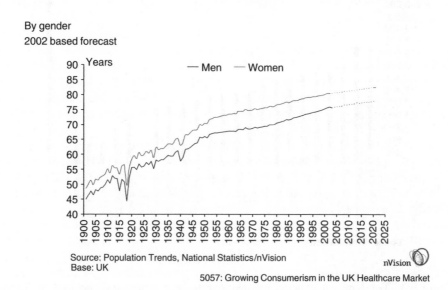

Source: Population Trends, National Statistics/nVision
Base: UK

nVision

5057: Growing Consumerism in the UK Healthcare Market

Figure 6.2: Life expectancy at birth in the United Kingdom.

growth in the population aged under 50. It can be anticipated that advances in science will play a greater role in shaping the demographic structure of UK society through the increased success of IVF treatments, new treatments for cancer, the role of genetic engineering and, potentially, an HIV vaccine. All of these point in the same direction — increased longevity. Therefore, it is anticipated that in the future health care will become even more dominated by the needs of the elderly and also by the people's desire to remain fit and active for longer in life. By 2030, health will be a core driver of tourism experiences. In fact, the World Health Organisation has forecasted that health care will represent 12% of the world GDP by 2022, followed by tourism at 11% (Lister, 1999).

Health Behaviour and the Consumer

The centrality of health in modern society is demonstrated by the progressive increase in expenditure in both public and private sectors, and rising insurance premiums. Across the developed world, healthcare spending is rising and will continue to do so as population ages, new treatments are demanded and price inflation in the sector remains high. Since 1970, the average real growth in spend in rich countries outside America has been 4.0% a year. The OECD (2006) data in Figure 6.3 show the annual, per person healthcare spend in purchasing power parities (PPP) varies from around US $700 in Poland and Slovakia to above US $3500 in

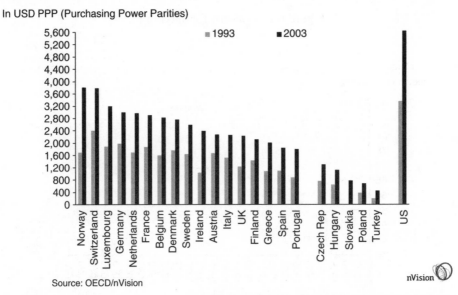

Source: OECD/nVision

nVision

22414: Healthcare and Key Future Health issues in Europe

Figure 6.3: Total health expenditure per capita in Europe and the United States, by country.

Switzerland and Norway. Continental Western Europe and the Nordic countries fall between US $2300 and US $2800. Spain and Portugal rank at the bottom of the EU 15 countries, with figures around US $2000. In America, expenditure has now reached almost 15% of the GDP, by far the highest share anywhere.

Our Perception of Our Own Health

Are we satisfied with our own health? Figure 6.4 shows that women are less satisfied with their health than men are. Moreover, satisfaction with health naturally declines across the age groups, with older Britons being less satisfied than younger ones. Bodies fail as people get older and, as a result, satisfaction with health declines. Accordingly, as expectations of perfect health increase in society, people perceive that their bodies are failing to conform to this standard. Therefore, consumers will search for the fountain of youth and the resultant consumer trend is that healthcare expenditure will exponentially rise.

Incidence of illness increases significantly as people get older. The conditions that account for the majority of the diseases in Europe are primarily related to age, such as cancer and cardiovascular diseases. Success with preventive measures and advances in treatment for hypertension, cardiovascular diseases and diabetes have had the effect of blunting mortality from these diseases. Yet these same

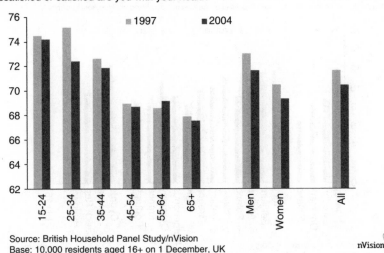

Satisfaction with own health, by age and gender

Mean levels of satisfaction on a 100 point scale, with 100 being completely satisfied and 1 being completely unsatisfied

"How dissatisfied or satisfied are you with your health"

Source: British Household Panel Study/nVision
Base: 10,000 residents aged 16+ on 1 December, UK

nVision

11241: Growing Consumerism in the UK Healthcare Market

Figure 6.4: Satisfaction with own health.

advancements may leave more elderly people — by virtue of the longevity which has been created by medicine — experiencing increased disability and dependency.

Living Longer

People are living longer. However, do people live longer and better or only gain years of life in poor health? Figure 6.5 shows the healthy life years' expectancy (HLYE) indicator. It measures the number of remaining years that a person is expected to live in a healthy condition. Data show that as time passes and society gets wealthier, the number of healthy life years tends to increase. This means that although one may live longer, most of this incremental time will be spent in active health. Yet the period of ill health at the end of an active life will remain the same length. This phenomenon is sometimes discussed under the term 'compressed morbidity'. Currently, in Europe, at the age of 65, one can expect to have another 18 years left, of which, on average, around 10 should be disability-free. By 2030, this is forecast to rise to 25 extra years of life for 65 year olds.

Over the past decade, substantial lifestyle changes have led to variations in causes of death. Mortality rates from heart disease, strokes and cancer have declined, while behavioural changes have led to an increased prevalence of obesity and diabetes. In 2006, 22% of the British, 20% of the German, 13% of the Spanish and 10% of the French populations were considered to be clinically obese. This is defined as the proportion of people with a body mass index (BMI) of over 30. Childhood obesity is

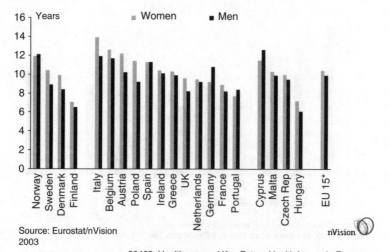

Healthy life expectancy at 65 across Europe, by gender within country

The indicator 'healthy life years' measures the number of remaining years that a person of a specific age is still expected to live in a healthy condition. A healthy condition is defined by the absence of limitations in functioning/disability

Source: Eurostat/nVision
2003

nVision

20463: Healthcare and Key Future Health issues in Europe

Figure 6.5: Healthy life years' expectancy.

of most concern looking at the socio-demographics of obesity across Europe; observations can be made about obesity amongst people in the lower social classes and those who have terminated their education at an earlier age, that is, below 18 years. In some cases obesity is due to genetic defects, yet the stresses and strains associated with economic disadvantage have the potential for creating food dependency as a type of addiction. It is important to remember that mass affluence, knowledge of health issues and interest in being healthy can be unevenly distributed, leading to a polarisation of health within European societies. Those who can afford better healthcare are likely to pay for it.

Lifestyles

The growth of sedentary jobs from physically demanding occupations to more desk-based ones means a shift to less physical activity for many people, leading to a more sedentary lifestyle overall, which partly explains the rise in obesity over recent years. A healthy body craves physical movement and consumers, who now have a less active working life, are actively searching for new outlets for that urge, such as visit to the gym, alternative medicine or diet.

Whilst diet, nutrition and alternative medicine seem to be the domain of women, physical activity through sport remains a solid interest for men. Still, since 1970, women have made notable gains, with women's participation in sports doubling (Figure 6.6). However, for women regular participation in organised sports clubs is less frequent than taking part in sports as individuals. This suggests that the qualitative nature of physical activity is changing, which seems to mirror the transformation of the health and fitness industry in the past few years. Participation in sports club activities is just one of many leisure pursuits from which to choose.

Smoking is both expensive and physically damaging. It has been estimated that, at today's prices, a 20-a-day smoker will spend more than $120,000 over the next 20 years. In the European Union alone, smoking-related illness causes 500,000 deaths per year, 10% of them are non-smokers killed by passive smoking (Future Foundation, 2006b). Hence, the governments of several Western countries have launched initiatives to ban smoking in public places. One thing that is certain — there will be fewer smokers in the future.

Over the last decade we have witnessed heightened public concern about alcohol consumption levels. There has been particular anxiety in many countries about the phenomenon of binge drinking associated with anti-social behaviour, to the extent that the Scottish Parliament has passed legislation to curb this problem (PA, 2005). Growing health worries about the effects of alcohol, combined with an increased interest in 'staying fit and healthy', are clearly going to have an impact on the consumption levels of alcoholic drinks in the future. Some of these health concerns have been driven by government communications, pressure groups and the media, all trying to do something to alleviate the health and social problems caused by alcohol abuse and binge drinking.

Figure 6.7 shows data on overall levels of alcohol consumption, measured in litres per person per capita by year. At an EU level, data indicate stable levels of

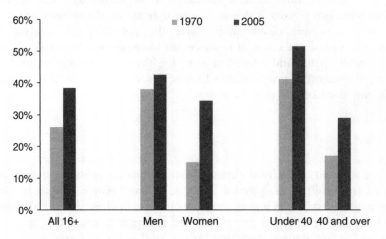

Figure 6.6: Sports participation in the United Kingdom since 1970.

consumption over the last 15 years. Remarkable variations can be noted between countries. In some countries, such as France, Germany and Portugal, consumption levels have fallen. The trend has been stable in other countries, such as Denmark, Netherlands and Poland, whilst in some — Ireland, Latvia and Lithuania — people have increased their alcohol intake in recent years. There does not seem to be any geographical pattern to explain these trends.

Basic health care is available to all who live in the United Kingdom. However, this does not mean that there is no consumer activity in the area of healthcare and maintenance. The health of society is paradoxical — despite being healthier, we are less happy with our image and are likely to report more health problems than in the past. This paradox seems to encourage us towards preventing ill health through better nutrition and more exercise, whilst at the same time opting for alternative treatments which are unlikely to be covered by either private medical insurance or the NHS (e.g. acupuncture, homeopathy) and other Eastern medical practices.

Searching for an Alternative?

More and more people are choosing alternative medicines as a way of augmenting conventional medicines or as an alternative to mainstream healthcare, as shown in Figure 6.8.

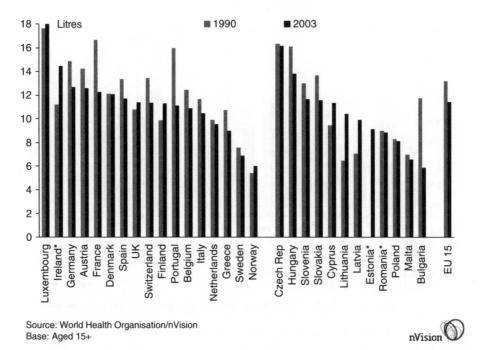

Alcohol consumption trend, by country
Litres of pure alcohol per person per year

Source: World Health Organisation/nVision
Base: Aged 15+

nVision

18621: Healthcare and Key Future Health issues in Europe

Figure 6.7: Alcohol consumption trends in Europe.

Considering that women report more health problems than men, are more likely to be clinically obese or overweight and are more likely to report the conditions, it is not surprising that key health behaviours show a gendered pattern. Women are more likely than men to try alternative medicine and treatments, including acupuncture, homeopathy, osteopathy and Chinese medicine. Furthermore, a higher proportion of women have used alternative medicine in the recent past than women did before. Also, increasing use of alternative medicine is more noticeable among younger Britons. For example, in 1992 about 2% of Britons aged 20 to 24 used alternative medicine. By the time this group reached the age of 25 to 29 in 1997, about 5% of them used alternative medicine. Seven years later, in 2004, over 5% of those aged 35 to 39 — the same cohort — used alternative medicine. Examining cohorts in this way across time, we are able to note that, within cohorts, younger Britons tend to be more likely to turn to alternative medicine and treatments. Those aged 50 to 54 and older in 1992 tended not to turn to alternative medicine over time as they moved through this time span. Since the trend in trying alternative medicine indicates that youthful adopters are the most likely to do so, this implies a further social diffusion of alternative health ideas in the United Kingdom over the next 10–20 years.

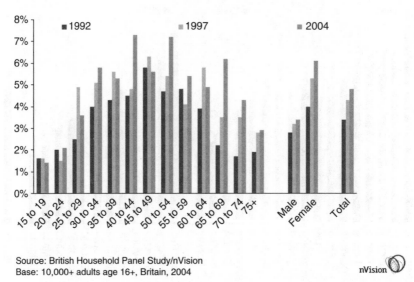

Increasing use of alternative medicine

Proportion reporting that they have used alternative medicine in the prior year

Source: British Household Panel Study/nVision
Base: 10,000+ adults age 16+, Britain, 2004

nVision

18256: Growing Consumerism in the UK Healthcare Market

Figure 6.8: Increasing use of alternative medicines.

As a rough indication of growing cultural interest, Figure 6.9 shows the number of newspaper articles in the UK press mentioning 'Eastern Medicine'. A clear historical jump occurs between 1997 and 1998. Eastern and alternative medicines, with their holistic way of preventing disease and ill health, will likely see a flowering in the West. Growing affluence and dissatisfaction with current health services could motivate people to try alternative approaches. In other words, basic health via Western sources will be taken for granted, while the pursuit of perfect health will lead a greater number to alternative medicine.

Consumers have the ability to increase their own life expectancy through their everyday behaviour. Improvements in diet and exercise regimes, reductions in stress and the judicious exclusion of alcohol and cigarettes can add years to people's lives. Improved education — in schools, by the media and by government — means that consumers are better informed about health matters than previous generations were, and therefore are more able and willing to make important and life-extending changes to their lifestyles.

According to the Future Foundation (2006b), 'being in good health' is found to contribute most to the quality of life. It is the wish that people place at the top of their list of priorities. For today's consumers, the concept of well-being has become a key factor contributing to their satisfaction with life. This happens as a direct consequence of affluence; as consumers get wealthier, the number of aspirations in all

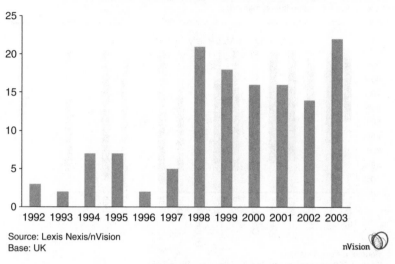

Figure 6.9: Increased public interest in medical alternatives.

areas of life tends to rise. The average consumer has come to expect a lot from life — indeed, much dissatisfaction in modern society comes when those expectations are not met. Thus, people expect to have successful careers, live in nice houses, be great parents, feel energetic and keep in good shape, among other aspirations. The message here is that people seek fulfilment in every aspect of life; they want to get the most from everything they do or buy. The search of well-being is likely to have huge consequences on the way consumers behave; as people become more health conscious, they tend to change their lifestyles accordingly.

European consumers can be segmented according to different combinations of healthy and unhealthy behaviour (Figure 6.10). The Future Foundation's *Changing Lives* Survey research asked consumers for two indications of a healthy lifestyle (e.g. eat a good balanced diet and exercise at least twice a week) and for three indications of an unhealthy lifestyle (e.g. regularly drink alcohol, smoke and feel stressed). They also asked for a health self-assessment of the respondent's lifestyle. The Future Foundation (2006a) has identified three broad categories. First is the 'ultra-healthy' cluster: this category includes people who claim to eat a healthy and balanced diet, to exercise twice a week, to not drink alcohol regularly and not to smoke. We observe that, according to this measure, the proportion of people who actively pursue an almost 'monastic' lifestyle are indeed a minority, approximately just 15% of the European population.

The second category is that of the 'moderately healthy'. This group is difficult to categorise as they combine unhealthy and healthy lifestyles, such as eating well and

Healthy lifestyle segmentation in Europe, by country

% who combine different types of healthy and unhealthy
behaviours (see notes for segmentation method)

"Now let's talk about your lifestyle do you or don't you..."Eat a good balanced diet... Exercise at least twice a week... Regularly drink alcohol... Smoke?"

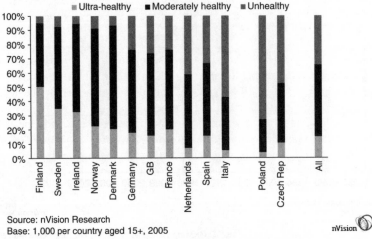

Source: nVision Research
Base: 1,000 per country aged 15+, 2005

nVision

20612: Healthcare and Key Future Health issues in Europe

Figure 6.10: Healthy lifestyle segmentation.

exercising, but also drinking and smoking — or a combination of both sides of the fence. Half of European consumers fall into this category.

The third category is the 'unhealthy' group, which, approximately, accounts for 35% of European consumers. These are the people who do not think they eat a healthy diet, do not exercise, and some also smoke or drink or both.

There are very significant differences to take into account between countries, with Finland and Sweden, for example, having a much higher proportion of people in the ultra-healthy segment. This is probably because of the low levels of smoking and the very high proportion of people exercising on a regular basis. On the other hand, Italy displays the highest proportion of people in the unhealthy segment. This seems to conflict with the fact that Italy has the highest level of life expectancy in Europe and very good health outcomes in general. Therefore, this good health could be the result of good weather, the Mediterranean diet and relaxed lifestyles, or simply that, culturally, people may be less prone to describe their diet as healthy, compared to people in other countries.

Health in an advanced consumer society is riddled with cultural paradoxes. Despite being healthier, people are more demanding of their health and more likely to report problems than people would have done in the past. Consumers feel more empowered to choose alternative cures and with proliferation of information on the Internet and in other media sources, it is raising people's knowledge of, and interest in, the field.

In the context of growing reported stress levels, the use of natural remedies and the practice of yoga and meditation — all self-motivated health activities — have risen in popularity in most European countries. Figure 6.11 shows that a remarkable proportion of consumers already use herbal medicines quite often; for instance, 36% of people in Switzerland, 28% in Austria and 26% in Hungary claim to use herbal medicines 'always or almost always' when they have a health problem.

All this shows an increased awareness and understanding of health-related issues as well as a willingness by people to take responsibility for achieving their own health aspirations. No longer happy to be viewed as bodies that occasionally need fixing, more and more people are demanding to be viewed as a 'whole person'. The popularity of holistic (literally meaning 'the complete person') medicine is a direct consequence of this. Hence the trend seems to point towards consumers taking more and more responsibility for their well-being and acting accordingly.

It seems that modern society and its stresses have together provoked a broad range of mental anxieties and phobias. Probably depression is the most common. The number of people with depression is hard to estimate. Epidemiologists (Weissman et al., 1996) have found that rates of major depression throughout the world range between 4% and 10% of the population. Anxiety or depression is

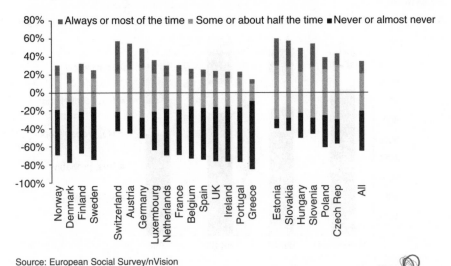

Use of herbal remedies, by country

% who use herbal remedies always, sometimes or never

"When you have a health problem, how often do you use herbal remedies?"

Source: European Social Survey/nVision
Base: 2,000 per country aged 15+, 2005

nVision

22672: Healthcare and Key Future Health issues in Europe

Figure 6.11: Use of herbal remedies.

linked to pressures in everyday life as over half of us report feeling under pressure in our daily lives, with over two-thirds of those between the ages of 25 and 34. Only the retired, those over the age of 65, report low levels of time pressure in everyday life (Future Foundation, 2006).

Technology and Science

European citizens seem to be more informed about and more trusting of biotechnology (Future Foundation, 2006b). The European public is not risk-averse about technological innovations which seem to promise tangible benefits; for instance, people generally perceive that the development of nanotechnology, pharmacogenetics (analysing a person's genetic code in order to create drugs which are tailored to him/her and are therefore more effective) and gene therapy is useful to society and morally acceptable. Interestingly, the analysis in Figure 6.12 reveals that the youngest respondents (those under 25) are more willing to take a genetic test in order to detect any serious disease, compared to people in the older age groups. Therefore, current public opinion seems to support the uptake of self-enhancement and the progress of science — as long as people perceive the benefits.

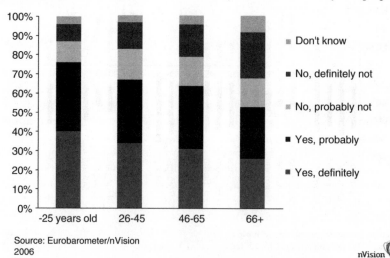

Figure 6.12: Willingness to take a genetic test.

What Does All This Mean?

- An ageing population implies a growing demand for goods and services catering to the elderly, who seek to remain fit and active.
- Demand has increased for healthier foods and for better access to a variety of physical activities as a way of combating growing anxiety problems and depression — as well as growing waist lines.
- There is an increasing interest in Eastern medicine and health-related activities such as yoga, meditation and herbal remedies. Growth in this area may be most closely linked to affluence because they will remain an alternative to the staunchly supported public health service, of western societies.
- At present, women make up a significant majority of 'health' consumers, but we anticipate a steady growth in participation by males in the market.
- Disparities between the self-reporting of conditions and the actual treatment of conditions suggest a demand for non-medically prescribed remedies or treatments, particularly in areas of the greatest discrepancies between condition and treatment, for example, heart and circulation problems, as well as alcohol and drug problems.
- An increasing use of beauty aids, combined with continued growth in disposable income, suggests a bright future for cosmetic treatments and for those searching for the fountain of youth.

All the above indicates that health tourism will become even more important in the future. According to the study by Lister (1999), health and tourism will be the world's top industries by 2022.

Beauty and Appearance

It's Always Been Like This!

Sociologists tell us that humans, as animals, are programmed to appreciate a youthful, healthy appearance because this signals fitness for reproduction. But consumers are vain and cultural definitions of beauty also encapsulate a youthful appearance. It is no surprise, therefore, that health concerns encompass physical appearance (Morris, 1994).

It goes without saying that, since time immemorial, women's appearance has been influenced by the ideal of feminine beauty prevalent at the time — from the voluptuous curvaceousness of the early Greeks to the waif-like frailty of the 1990s supermodels, which has led to the contemporary emphasis on looking thin. Generally speaking, women's attitudes towards their looks have been conditioned by the prevailing stereotypes, which are reinforced by the media and by society as a whole.

But there is a growing awareness regarding the pressure which men and boys are under to fit the male stereotype of beauty and how the media also construct, inform and reinforce prevalent ideas about men and masculinity. The pressure to look good has intensified for both sexes over the years, leading to an age of the image, where visual appearance is prized above all else. Yet a subtle shift has occurred in recent years. Post-feminist empowerment in the 1970s heralded a new era of 'women doing it for themselves', that is, looking good for their own satisfaction, not for men. Now we are seeing an emphasis on health and youthful vigour alongside an alternative ideal that values internal as well as external beauty. The conventional standards of beauty are evolving ever so slightly and the next section reveals how.

A Woman's Search for the Fountain of Youth

Women's fascination with beauty and appearance is a universal development that seems to have intensified in the past few decades. In contemporary Western society the standard of female beauty is normally unattainable for the majority of women — an ideal has been set of being young, slender and highly attractive. It is a fact that beauty fascinates and there is a strong desire for the body beautiful in contemporary society. This is partly fuelled by consumers' aspiration to look like the supermodels they see in the media. These portrayals of the 'ideal' body have a profound impact on women's self-perception, their self-esteem and how they rate their own attractiveness.

Many women feel intense additional pressure to look good because modern culture increasingly equates internal and external characteristics, that is, slim = success and self-discipline, obese = laziness and a lack of will-power. According to the Future Foundation's *Changing Lives* Survey (Figure 6.13), the key concern among European women is staying fit and healthy (80%), closely followed by three-quarters of women agreeing that their appearance is important to them. It is impossible to look at any of these statements in isolation and the results may indicate that well-being among women is primarily derived from feeling fit and healthy in general. But agreement with the statement 'My appearance is important to me' is also high. Despite the ambiguity of this statement, the fact that 71% of women agree that 'successful twenty-first century women can be concerned about looking feminine' shows that conventions of what constitutes feminine beauty still guide opinion.

Figure 6.13 shows that 38% of female respondents agreed that they are 'more concerned about having an attractive body shape rather than about their weight'. This might indicate that there is a significant minority of women who are open to deconstructing those deeply ingrained perceptions. However, it must be said that, even if body weight is taken out of the equation, the conventional definition of what then constitutes 'an attractive body shape' still dominates.

Body Shape

In a survey conducted by Harvard University for Unilever (Etcoft, Orbach, Scott, & D'Agostino, 2004) women in ten countries were asked to choose from a list of terms those which best described their view of the way they look. The results show that women tend towards modesty when asked to reflect on their own looks and also that women in the different countries have very different ideas about their appearance.

Women's attitudes to personal appearance in Western Europe

% who agree with these statements

"Please indicate how much you agree or disagree with each of the statements that I read out? Remember, we are interested in your attitudes, opinions and views alone, not those of others"

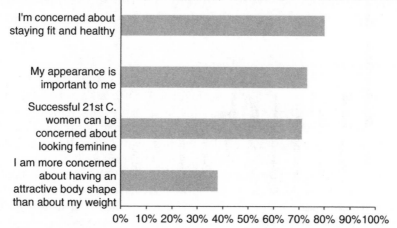

Source: nVision Research
Base: 500 women per country in France, UK, Germany, Italy, Spain and Sweden, 2004

nVision

20728: Beauty and Appearance in Europe

Figure 6.13: Women's attitudes towards personal appearance in Western Europe.

Figure 6.14 shows the scores from the four European countries surveyed. French (43%) and Italian (37%) women were more likely to have chosen 'natural', while most British women (31%) described themselves as 'average'. In the Netherlands an equal share (28%) chose one of the two terms. Neither of the two terms can be said to indicate that the women questioned ooze self-confidence. In Britain, 20% chose rather more positively the term 'attractive'. By contrast, only 9% of women in the Netherlands, 6% of women in France and 4% of women in Italy did so. Italians were more likely to choose 'pretty' (17%)', whilst 19% of the Dutch chose 'feminine'. The third most popular term in France was 'good-looking', but chosen by only a minority of 11%. In all the countries only a minority of 1–2% would agree to use terms such as 'beautiful', 'sophisticated', 'sexy' or 'gorgeous' when describing their appearance. This survey, therefore, points to a certain disinclination by women to describe their own appearance in positive terms.

Physical appearance is integral to women's lives and well-being. There is simply no denying that physical attractiveness is still upheld as a great measure of success in life and that women feel pressure to work on attaining this ideal, which often has implications on their self-esteem and eating habits. Data from the Future Foundation's *Changing Lives* Survey show that the top concern for women is staying fit and healthy. Certainly there is an increased emphasis on healthy living in

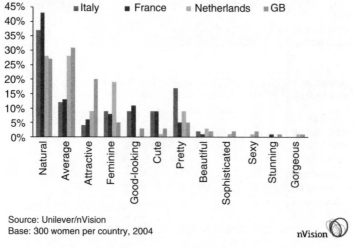

Women's self-descriptors for their looks in selected EU 15 countries

% who strongly agree (those who selected 8,9,10 on a scale where 1 is 'completely disagree' and 10 is 'completely agree')

"Which ONE of the following words, if any, would you be most comfortable using to describe the way you look?"

Source: Unilever/nVision
Base: 300 women per country, 2004

nVision

20740: Beauty and Appearance in Europe

Figure 6.14: European women's self-descriptors for their looks.

contemporary Europe and women are at the forefront of a trend towards a healthier lifestyle. This is driven largely by an ageing population, but also because of the desire for well-being and inner development which we are witnessing as a result of a backlash to our 24-h, 'have-it-all' lifestyles.

Figure 6.15 shows that the proportion of men and women who claim to take part in 'alternative' leisure activities, such as yoga or meditation, is clearly dominated by women. Whilst men are more likely to take part in sports, women find that alternative leisure activities are more compatible with their lifestyle. Part of this appeal is the 'promise' of alternative activities to improve both inner and outer health — benefiting the mind as well as the body (Figure 6.16).

Research by the Future Foundation's *Changing Lives* Survey on dietary changes reveals that more than a third of women say that they have made changes to their diet in the last 3 years, whilst only 25% of men say they have. In the United Kingdom, about 30% of all adults who have tried to lose weight within the last 12 months have used a slimming product. The number of women using slimming products is twice that of men, but men seem to be just as likely to prepare themselves for public appreciation. In addition, women more than men, say they do so out of a concern to 'stay healthy'. Whilst the trend towards alternative lifestyles is driven by a number of factors outside the scope of this chapter, the link between alternative physical lifestyles and the changing perceptions of beauty should be noted.

Taking part in 'alternative' leisure activities, by gender within country

% who practice yoga, meditation or alternative therapies at least once a month

"Please say which of the activities on this list, if any, you do on average at least once a month…. Do one of the following –yoga or meditation or alternative therapies"

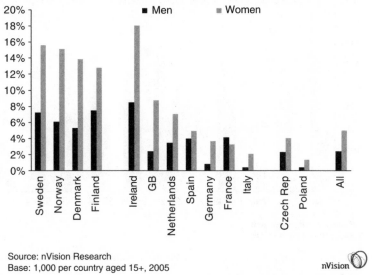

Source: nVision Research
Base: 1,000 per country aged 15+, 2005

nVision

14712: Beauty and Appearance in Europe

Figure 6.15: Taking part in alternative leisure activities.

Data from the Future Foundation's *Changing Lives* Survey (Figure 6.17) show that an average of only 10% of working women's time is spent on meals and personal care. This is just a fraction compared to the time that goes into working (whether paid or housework), sleeping and socialising. This research reveals that an average of 40% of European women say that 'I never have as much time as I would like to spend on my appearance', pointing to a balancing act for women, who have to juggle family and working life and, therefore, lack the time they would ideally like to invest in looking after themselves.

Most modern definitions of 'beauty' are nearly always constructed in terms of outward appearance and physical attractiveness. But 'beauty' can also include intangible personal qualities. Baker (1984) writes in *The Beauty Trap*, 'A truly beautiful woman makes the best of her physical assets but, more importantly, she also radiates a personal quality which is attractive'.

In *Beauty in History*, Marwick (1998) defines human physical beauty in more direct terms: 'The beautiful are those who are immediately exciting to almost all of the opposite sex'.

These alternative views of beauty, ranging from the skin deep to beauty from within, still undoubtedly prevail. Perhaps today there is one dominant camp

Proportion of adults who have consumed slimming

products in last twelve months, by gender and age

"Have you eaten slimming products at all in the last twelve months?"

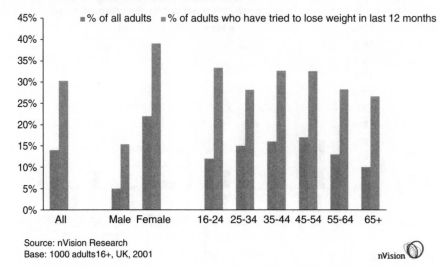

Source: nVision Research
Base: 1000 adults16+, UK, 2001

nVision

8452: Growing Consumerism in the UK Healthcare Market

Figure 6.16: Use of slimming aids in the United Kingdom.

operating in terms of physical perfection where beauty is only skin deep, whilst another is about beauty from within, about being natural and healthy and one's radiance being the embodiment of life and character.

What Does This All Mean?

It is, however, unlikely that we will witness a move away from the emphasis on youth and physical attractiveness for a very long time. And yet certain trends are changing and broadening the definitions of beauty:

- *Old beauty*: In an ageing society are we going to start accepting our looks and seeing old age as beautiful? Are there not already calls for older women to be more interested in looking good for their age rather than trying to look a different age?
- *The changing role of women*: As women become stronger and more independent in various spheres of life, the view that appearance is a measure of success seems dated. Yet in an image-dominated society the pressures to conform still prevails.

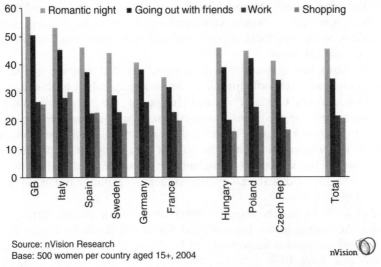

Women: time spent getting ready before going out, by country

In minutes

"Roughly how long does it take you to get ready on each of the following occasions... Before going out on a Saturday evening with a group of friends / Before going out on a Saturday evening for a romantic night out / Before going to work / Before going shopping?"

■ Romantic night   ■ Going out with friends   ■ Work   ■ Shopping

Source: nVision Research
Base: 500 women per country aged 15+, 2004

nVision

19640: Beauty and Appearance in Europe

Figure 6.17: Time spent on getting ready before going out.

- *Beauty from within*: With the growing emphasis on healthy living and physical as well as psychological well-being, perhaps the notion of inner health and beauty will contribute to 'beauty from within' becoming more highly regarded.
- *Multi-culturalism*: This is another contributing driver to expanding the ideal of beauty. Representations of non-whites in the fashion world were until recently almost non-existent. To a certain extent a woman's beauty is still determined by her ethnicity and black women are encouraged to follow the same standards as white women. But in a successful multi-cultural society diversity and differences are celebrated and, although we are far away from equal representation, things are beginning to change.

The Unilever study (Etcoft et al., 2004) tells us that there is clearly a desire amongst women for a letting go of conventional and stereotypical representations, into which only a small minority of women fit — would the beauty industry perhaps act wisely to talk about 'making the best of who you are' rather than trying to make you become someone different? ... who knows.

Plastic Surgery

Many people today are prepared to go under the knife to improve their appearance. There are countless examples of people who have endured great suffering in the name of beauty and physical appearance — either voluntarily, as with modern-day cosmetic surgery where the tip of the surgeon's knife promises to hold an elixir to immortality, or because of societal pressures and habits, as with China's foot-binding practices or Victorian corsets. Although modern techniques have removed much of the 'pain' from the 'gain', beauty enhancers, such as body-piercing, tattoos, chemically enhanced hair products, waxing and acid skin treatments, mean that the cliché still rings true for many.

Figure 6.18 shows that a minority of Europeans say that they are 'prepared to suffer physical discomfort to look attractive'. More women admit to this than men: 28% versus 18%. Italians, Czechs, Poles and Hungarians are more likely to say that they are willing to suffer in the name of attractiveness, but the numbers are low and we suspect that — across Europe — there is a degree of resistance to openly declaring a willingness to suffer discomfort, either because of pure vanity or simply because of the taboo nature of the subject. It is undeniable, however, that one of the most extreme forms of body modification — plastic surgery — is on the rise in many parts of the world (Figure 6.19).

At a global level, by far the largest market for aesthetic plastic surgery is the United States. According to the International Society of Aesthetic Plastic Surgery (2006), the American market accounted for 16.4% of the global market in 2003. However, this was down from 21% in 2001. Add in Mexico, Brazil, Canada and

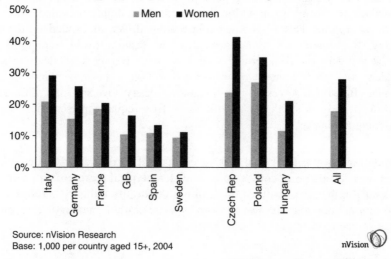

Figure 6.18: Physical discomfort and attractiveness.

Type of most popular plastic surgery procedures performed worldwide, by gender

As a % of all procedures performed on women and % of all procedures performed on men

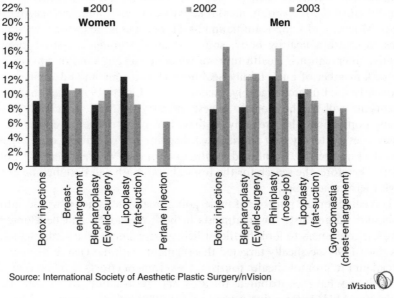

Source: International Society of Aesthetic Plastic Surgery/nVision

nVision

20746: Beauty and Appearance in Europe

Figure 6.19: Most popular types of plastic surgery.

Argentina and the five countries together account for nearly 50% of procedures worldwide. But the European market for plastic surgery is expanding. Procedures in the three biggest countries — Spain, France and Germany — total 14% of all global cosmetic surgery operations.

Currently, the most popular procedure for both men and women is Botox treatment — a muscle-relaxing injection which softens wrinkles and gives a more youthful appearance. Part of its popularity is that it is a non-surgical treatment which means that its users can pop out for lunch and return looking years younger! According to the British Association of Cosmetic Doctors (Mathews, 2004), 40,000 vials of Botox-enough to treat 150,000 patients-were sold in 2004 in the United Kingdom. On a worldwide scale, Botox treatments grew in popularity from 9% of total procedures in 2001 to 14% in 2003.

For men the second most popular treatment is eyelid lifts, whereas for women it is breast enlargement. Breast augmentation apart, it is clear that the growth in the market is driven by an ageing population — most treatments are sought by the middle-aged, but an increasing percentage is being carried out on under-21s. The gender division is also clear; 89% of procedures are carried out on women.

Tourism and the Search for the Fountain of Youth

Wellness can be defined as a balanced state of body, spirit and mind, with fundamental elements such as self-responsibility, physical fitness, beauty care, healthy nutrition, relaxation, mental activity and environmental sensitivity. According to Mueller and Lanz-Kaufmann (2001), wellness is viewed as a way of life, which aims to create a healthy body, soul and mind through acquired knowledge and positive interventions. Health tourism is defined as any kind of travel to make oneself or a member of one's family healthier. Health tourism and wellness tourism are frequently used interchangeably. According to Lister (1999), healthcare and health treatments will be the world's largest industry in 2022, principally driven by an ageing population who are active rather than passive when it comes to healthcare. Lister goes on to say that tourism will become the world's second largest industry over the same period. Combined, health and tourism will represent 22% of the world GDP. Therefore, the search for the fountain of youth will become one of the world's largest leisure activities.

Travelling for the purpose of undergoing treatment is not new; escalating medical costs and waiting lists for treatments in both developed and developing countries have led consumers to look further a field. For example, the Malaysian government has since 1998 specifically targeted this segment, with the Health Ministry forming a special unit to promote health tourism. Government efforts to fill beds in 35 hospitals in Malaysia have contributed towards the Association of Private Hospitals in Malaysia (APHM) reporting a total of 191,000 foreign patients in 2002, generating revenue of RM150 million. The main markets for Malaysia's health tourism products are the rising middle classes of China and India and the medical tourists of the Middle East (Mintel, 2004b).

According to Mintel (2005c), spa holidays in the Far East and on the islands of the Indian Ocean are flourishing. This is attributed to the 'spa-savvy', that is, those who are seeking more 'authentic' experiences in exotic destinations. With the expansion of the European Union, destinations such as Hungary and Bulgaria offer value-for-money packages. Mid-haul destinations such as Lebanon and Dubai continue to grow in the extended short-break market. Spa holidays in destinations such as India will grow because of improved facilities and investment by international hotel chains. India offers great value for money and provides a spa experience in an unspoilt, spiritual and scenic setting.

The term *spa* comes from the Latin *sanitas per aqua* — health through water — and according to Mintel (2005) is broadly defined as water-based and non-water facilities offering a range of health/medical/beauty/relaxation treatments. Otherwise, spa treatments are classified as

- *A Day Spa*: A facility that offers a variety of spa services on a day-use basis only.
- *Mineral Spa Springs*: A spa offering an on-site source of natural mineral, thermal or sea water used in hydrotherapy treatments.
- *Resort/Hotel Spa*: A spa located in a resort/hotel providing spa services, fitness and wellness components and spa-cuisine menu choices.

A Case Study of Medical Tourism in India — Will Michelle Find the Fountain of Youth?

From India's exotic destinations in the high mountains of the Himalayas to Goa's sun-drenched beaches, wellness abounds. The destination resorts, wellness retreats and spas offer the body, mind and spiritual wellness, traditions of yoga, ayurveda and numerous other healing practices, all in the name of Michelle searching for the fountain of youth.

India has several areas of excellence in its healthcare industry which appeal to potential medical tourists. High-demand areas for international patients include

- Breast implants
- Orthopaedics
- Non-trauma disease treatment
- Replacement/corrective surgery
- Urology
- Dental surgery

In these specialisations, India has the advantage of cost savings and expertise, as well as minimal waiting times for treatment. Many non-resident Indians who have been educated and trained abroad and have worked abroad are now returning to India with their expertise and expanding these capabilities, skills or products. Healthcare costs are considerably lower in India compared to those in the Western Hemisphere; for example, costs for open-heart surgery in the United Kingdom run from $40,000 to $100,000, whereas in the United States such surgery can cost up to $200,000. In comparison, the average cost of open-heart surgery in India is closer to $10,000. Therefore, price becomes a key driver in the choice of destination.

A report by the Confederation of Indian Industry (Connell, 2006) projected that medical tourism in India will be worth $1 billion by 2012 and is expected to contribute 3–5% to India's healthcare sector. It is now typical for the UK residents to travel to India for medical care, whether for a hip replacement or a breast implant (Wright, 2004). In 2004, 80,000 non-resident Indians and foreign nationals travelled to undergo medical treatment which was worth $300 million (Mintel, 2004b).

In order to target this market of international medical tourists, the Indian government is cultivating the need for medical facilities to be developed throughout the states. Kerala, in the south west of India, already receives patients from the Gulf countries, Canada and the Maldives. Mumbai attracts patients from European countries. Gujarat, in the north west of India, has quickly emerged as a preferred destination for tourists with cardiology problems because of its specialised centres. To leverage this trend, serious promotional efforts have been initiated. For example, a group of Indian tourism officials recently visited Dubai to promote their 'Greet and Treat' packages which include treatment options, plus visits to holiday resorts and rejuvenation centres. The state of Karnataka has also promoted its offerings in Bahrain at the International Health Tourism and Holidays Exhibition. The tourism staff and hospital representatives from this state are working with the Bahrain government to send its patients to Bangalore for specialised treatments. Sri Lankan tour operators have also developed specific tour packages for medical tourists to Karnataka.

The India Healthcare Federation, an association of the healthcare delivery sector that includes Apollo Hospitals Group, Mumbai's Hinduja Hospital, Max Healthcare and the Fortis Heart Institute, has announced a co-operative promotion between members to help promote India as an attractive healthcare destination (Connell, 2006). In 2005, the Apollo group alone treated 95,000 international patients, many of whom were of Indian origin. Apollo has been a forerunner in medical tourism in India and attracts patients from South East Asia, Africa and the Middle East. The group has established links with hospitals in Mauritius, Tanzania, Bangladesh and Yemen as well as has been running a hospital in Sri Lanka and managing a hospital in Dubai. The Ruby Hospital in Kolkata has signed a contract with the British insurance company, BUPA, to treat British patients who are in the queue for National Health Services.

The market is growing; for example, the Escorts Heart Institute and the Research Centre in New Delhi has seen a large exponential growth in the number of patients, from 89 in 1988 to 5533 in 2004 (EHRIC, 2004). It is estimated that foreigners account for 10–12% of all patients in the top Mumbai hospitals, despite obstacles such as poor road infrastructure and the absence of uniform quality standards. Price is the key driver shaping this trend.

Health Tourism India is a company established by SAMI World Travels and medical professionals to help people with medical needs to schedule medical treatments in India, as well as making the necessary travel arrangements on their behalf. The company will

- Suggest hospitals/clinics as per the treatment required and budget
- Organise world-class treatment by UK/US-trained doctors
- Arrange appointments, prior to arrival, with chief doctors as a top priority
- Arrange consultations with doctors
- Arrange accommodation for family members and/or carers
- Organise package tours at very reasonable cost to various places of interest, such as Delhi, Chennai, Bangalore, Hyderabad, Mumbai and Agra

For further details see http://www.health-torism-india.com/introduction.htm Whether for breast enhancement combined with a beach holiday in Goa or that elusive search for the fountain of youth which Michelle craves for, India appears to be well placed to satisfy both needs and desires.

Prospects for Health and Beauty Tourism

With the rising cost of healthcare in the Western world, the trend of medical tourism in India and other emerging destinations is likely to continue because price is a core demand driver. India, with its exotic climate, combined with the merging of the concepts of medical, health and beauty into one concept called 'wellness', will lead to the prosperity of resort-style destinations offering a range of services, from breast enhancement to safari excursions, from hip replacement to holistic experiences. Furthermore, hospitals will resemble resort hotels, with golf courses and a pampering service. In the foreseeable future, branded spas will be set up in hospitals and resorts for seniors will emerge.

Many other destinations also follow these trends, mainly driven by the world's ageing population seeking the fountain of youth. Middle-class consumers will travel anywhere in the world to seek out the best services and the most competitive prices. As better health in later life reinforces the consumers' focus on appearance and physical condition, cosmetic surgery and beauty treatments will become more important. Concepts such as Healthcare City in Dubai will appear in destinations with a lower cost of living, especially in India and Eastern Europe. These concepts will combine the best of Dubai's Healthcare City and McCarthy Retirement homes.

At the same time, healthcare insurance providers will focus on preventive measures to improve people's health, such as checking on body mass indexes, lifestyles and alcohol consumption levels and the results will shape the cost of premiums.

By 2030, new markets will emerge, based on specific consumer segments; for example, spas are expanding and in the near future every destination in the world, a rural or an urban location, will have some sort of health proposition, similar to the Bliss spa in New York, operated by the luxury conglomerate, Moet Hennessy Louis Vuitton, or the brand extension of chocolate as seen in the Hershey's spa and chocolate treatments in the United States.

Beauty bars will open up in leisure centres and hotels will offer these products as part of the room-service menus. Watch out for the mobile beauty bar, part of a home-delivery service brought to you by Tesco or Wal-Mart (ASDA). Hotels will extend the range of health-style services, such as 'the waiter as nutritionist' who can advise on the right balance of food, water and the calorie count of meals.

Indian and Chinese medicine spas will appear in resorts all over the world, combining herbal medicine and yoga with spa treatments. Even Chinese restaurants will offer a herbal fusion of ingredients at a premium price. Indian spa centres will offer a range of cultural health products, such as dance, meditation, yoga, readings and drumming workshops as well as selling organic products from India and Asia.

Wellness products will focus on men, teenagers, children and the family pet! The metrosexual man will seek feminine-like treatments, such as manicures and facials. Metrosexual-man centres will combine physical, emotional and medical products, whether climbing mountains, camping out, massage services or cosmetic surgery.

Rising obesity in children will lead to fitness camps and lifestyle gurus for teenagers, and spa days for groups of female children aged 7+ will become mainstream. Parent-and-baby packages will become more popular, both for fathers and mothers, as offered at Evian Spa in France. These packages will focus on the concept of good parenting and healthy lifestyles. The rising number of singletons in society means that money will be spent on pets rather than on children. Spa centres will also offer grooming and massage services for pets and their owners. Every major health and spa centre will have a resident behavioural therapist available for both owners and pets in order that they can understand each other. Cats and dogs will even be hired out to consumers as therapeutic products. Relaxation music for pets will also be available.

Tour operators will offer Chinese medicine tours and spa tours to the Far East, combining expert lectures with visits to the local herbal doctor for the latest treatments. Exclusive retreats, associated with religious orders, will be set up in Bhutan and Nepal. Operators will combine and promote a number of themes; for example, wine tours in South Africa will be based on the assertions that drinking red wine in moderation is good for one's health. Even Amsterdam will promote itself as a health destination, based on the availability of cannabis, specifically focusing on people suffering from acute pain or a debilitating disease. At the same time, rural destinations, such as the Highlands of Scotland, which are accessible but still remote, will emerge as premium destinations because of their tranquillity, authenticity and the closeness to good, public-sector healthcare. Sport will become an important well-being and life-improvement tool of the future, whether participating in fat-busting camps or hill-walking in the Scottish Highlands. It can be expected that consumers will employ lifestyle gurus to help them achieve a balanced lifestyle of enjoyment and well-being.

In the future, the state will regulate the health of its people as a way of improving the quality of life and reducing the burden on front-line medical services that deal with diseases such as obesity and liver damage. Governments will use supply-side regulations to improve consumers' well-being, for example by imposing taxes on unhealthy living choices such as the over-consumption of fast food; banning fizzy drinks in schools; or limiting the provision of calorie allowances for all consumers.

As price becomes more important to the consumer, revenue management and Internet models, as used by the airline industry and online providers such as www.expedia.com or www.lastminute.com will become mainstream. As health and beauty becomes more of a commodity rather than an experience, the consumer will use only price as a distinguishing factor. Such Internet pricing models will be used to search for last-minute deals or to make advance bookings. Buying a spa treatment on www.easyjet.com in Bulgaria, along with the flight, will become the norm-all part of the trend of dynamic packaging and pricing.

Conclusion

As health and beauty becomes even more mainstream, *yet* highly fragmented, global and destination brands will emerge. India will become a leading medical destination, highly regulated and offering first-class products. At the same time, because of their close proximity to Western Europe, countries in Eastern Europe will grow more popular as both health and beauty destinations. Demand for wellness will sore as the consumer's perception of health changes into a concept of a combination of mind, body and spirit. Whether travelling to 'no-food' Japanese hotels for the weekend, having a spa treatment in Thailand or hill-walking in Scotland, the prospects are excellent. According to Lister (1999), tourism and health will become the world's two biggest industries by 2022. Together they will be an unbeatable consumer force. Somehow, she hopes, Michelle will find the elusive fountain of youth. But in the meantime, world tourism will grow richer as it follows demand to help those travellers who, like Michelle, are seeking health and beauty treatment. First-class standards will be combined with price competitiveness — and a holiday in an exotic destination.

Chapter 7

The US Grand-Traveller: The Changing Roles of Families and Travel

Spending time with the family has always constituted one of society's strongest bonds and in an era when both parents work, it is natural that grandparents should spend more time with their grandchildren, whether assuming the role of child-carers or taking them on holiday. Our story begins with Mr and Mrs Jeff Smith from New York, who are taking their grandchildren on holiday at half term. The family have flown from JFK to Orlando and are staying in Elderhostels family centre in Key West. On arrival, they are greeted by 'Florida Orange' and checked into their condo. Highlights during the holiday will include milking the goats, story-telling by local children's authors and skydiving for both children and grandparents. There is even a trip planned to see Mickey, Donald and friends at Disneyland World. The best part of the trip will be in the SeaDisney Experience, when Grandad Smith puts on his diving suit to swim with the Little Mermaids through all the hoops and jet streams. All-in-all, a wonderful experience awaits!

Mr & Mrs Smith's holiday in 2030

In the United States, a noticeable trend is occurring. Fewer babies are being born and people are living longer. In today's modern family often both parents work and children spend more time with their extended family. Today, families are more mobile and grandparents live more active and independent lives than any previous generation of seniors. As a result, many grandparents and grandchildren often live too far apart to see each other regularly, so grandparents are always looking for ways to draw their families together and strengthen the relationship with their grandchildren. Characteristics of the senior population include lots of free time, willingness to travel and a desire to spend time with their family, especially grandchildren. The baby-boomer generation, in particular, is better off than any other generation has been and, consequently, are spending more money on grandchildren. Together these factors have resulted in the establishment of a new niche travel market called 'grand-travellers' in which grandparents holiday with grandchildren, especially during school holidays when parents may have to work. *So, why are trips for Mr and Mrs Smith becoming more popular?*

This chapter looks at the combined trends of an ageing population and the increasing importance of children in society, which together have resulted in the emergence of the grand-traveller trend.

Population Changes

The United States, the third most populous country in the world, accounts for about 4.6% of the world's population, at just over 300 million people; in 2008 the population is expected to reach twice its 1950 level of 152 million. Basically, the US population is increasing and is becoming older and more diverse. The doubling of the US population over this period is remarkable when compared to other industrialised countries. Germany and Italy, for instance, grew by 20% and 22%, respectively, over the same period, and a number of countries, most notably in Eastern Europe, have experienced reductions in population size. Despite the growth in population, the States' share of the world's population has been declining because the populations of less-developed countries, which have higher fertility rates, have grown more rapidly. Bangladesh and Nigeria, for instance, now rank eighth and ninth in population, surpassing more developed countries, such as Germany, France, the United Kingdom and Italy, which are no longer in the world's 10 most populous countries (Shapner, 2007).

In the first half of the twentieth century the population of the United States was relatively young, a consequence of three demographic trends acting in concert — relatively high fertility, declining infant and childhood mortality, and high rates of immigration to the United States by young and therefore fertile workers and their families. Since 1950, the United States has undergone a profound demographic change, with the rapid ageing of the population, a phenomenon that has resulted in an older population replacing what used to be a young-age sex demographic.

By 2030, the population of the United States will be 363 million, but the age profile will be very different to that of 1950, when 33.9% of the population was under 19, compared to 26% in 2030. In 1950 8.1% of the population was over 65, whereas in 2030 it will be 19%. Figures 7.1 and 7.2 show that the baby-boom generation, that is, those born between 1946 and 1964, is represented by the ages of 35 to 54 in 2000. After 1964, the birth rate moved downwards until the late 1970s. As the last members of the baby-boomer generation approached their child-rearing years in the 1980s, the number of births rose again, peaking in 1990. In 2005, the number of births per woman is near an all-time low, although the population continues to grow, partly because of the children and grandchildren of the baby-boomers. At the same time, the number of people aged 65 and older has steadily increased and is now 35.1 million, representing 12.4% of the American population. The fact that female survival rates in 2000 exceeded those of men, especially at the older ages, means about 4.3% of the total female population was aged 80 and above in 2000, compared to only 2.2% of men (Shapner, 2007).

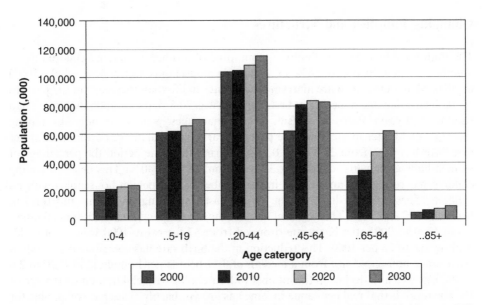

Figure 7.1: Projected population of the United States by age 2000–2030 (*Source*: US Bureau of Census).

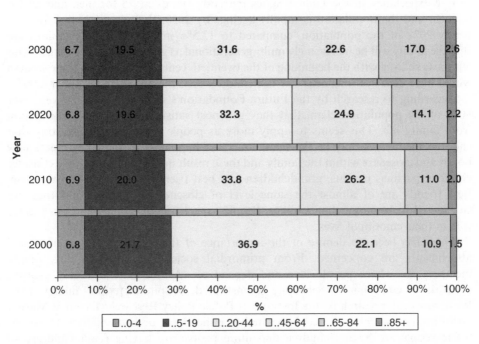

Figure 7.2: US population age distribution: 2000–2030 (*Source*: US Bureau of Census).

Changing Families and Structures

The traditional image of the family — composed of mother, father and children living together — described just 24% of American households (Silverstein et al., 2005) in 2000. Men and women are marrying much later in life than they have in the past. In 1970, the median age of people at first marriage was 20.8 years; by 2005 that figure had risen to 27.0 years. Partly as a result of later marriages, women are now also having their first child later in life. Over the past 30 years, the median age of a mother at her first birth has risen from 22.5 to 27.0 years; during the same period the percentage of women having their first child after 30 rose from 18% to 40%. This delay in having children has resulted in an increase in the number of two-person households with no children. These couples have driven the increased spending on leisure and tourism between 1990 and 2005. This segment has had money to spend and few responsibilities. From 1970 to 2005, the birth rate dropped from 87 for every 1000 women of child-bearing age to 65 per 1000. This reduction in the birth rate has contributed to a fall in the average household size from a median of 3.11 people per household in 1970 to 2.6 in 2000, as well as a decline in the number of households with children under the age of 18. The result is that real per capita income has grown sharply. The share of income for each household was US $12,400 in 1970 and had risen to $30,000 in 2005, a rise of over 100%. This means there has been more disposable income for the average family, and this has fuelled a growth in expenditure on tourism and leisure.

Life expectancy in the United States currently stands at 75 for men and 80 for women, and the population is rapidly ageing. By 2030, the over-65s will constitute nearly 20% of the population, compared to 12.5% in 2000. The implications are that the family will be increasingly multi-generational as grandparents live longer. This contrasts sharply with the beginning of the twentieth century when the average woman would have died not long after her last child reached the age of 15 (Shapner, 2007).

According to research by the Future Foundation's *Changing Lives* Survey, over 90% of the population claim that they get most satisfaction or equal satisfaction from family life. This seems to apply more as people grow older, suggesting that children themselves may be the main source of happiness or that they create new bonds and closeness within the family and these result in satisfaction. People consider children, partner, parents, grandchildren and best friends as being extremely close. Best friends are of almost the same level of closeness as parents and they are considered to be closer than siblings. People expect friends to play an even greater role in their emotional lives.

There has been no demise of the importance *of* the family as far as emotional attachments are concerned. From primordial societies to modern day, family members are whom people love and depend on. As the nuclear family evolves, networks of emotional closeness are reconstituted. In spite of fertility falling in the Western world, research by the Institute of Public Policy Research (Dixon & Margo, 2006) found that 90% of people wanted to either have or had children. However, fewer people are having children and more people are having fewer children, so perhaps what we are seeing in this apparent contradiction is actually less of an aspiration to remain childless and more of a by-product of life choices and the prioritising of other choices. In spite of the falling birth rate, nothing has changed in that there is still an inherent assumption that children will add happiness and fulfilment to our lives. People who have children within marriage tend to be the happiest. The Pew Research Centre (2006) found that in the United States 43% of married people tended to be 'very happy', in comparison to 24% of unmarried people.

Even with rising divorce rates, the emotional attachment people have to the family is still strong. Therefore, it could be concluded that the emotional attachment to the family is still as important as ever. The family is not in decline, as commentators such as Giddens (2006) and Beck and Beck-Gernsheim (2002) have suggested; rather, as Castells (1996) suggests, 'it is the psychological lynchpin of people's lives'.

The family is changing not only in structure but also in the attitudes which govern relationships within it. Family members are becoming more open with each other than before. Parents are increasingly including children in major decision-making and giving them more autonomy over their personal consumption choices. Additionally, traditional domestic roles, such as women being the primary carer for children, are becoming slightly less rigid. This phenomenon is referred to as the 'democratic family'. The Future Foundation suggests the majority of parents believe that they have a more open relationship with their children than they had with their parents and that they include their children in major decisions.

Families also provide a system of support and reciprocity to the extent that there is an inter-dependent network — grandparents are baby-sitters; teenagers are carers; and parents are increasingly offering financial support when their children buy their first home. Indeed, in spite of the changing composition of households, kinship ties appear to be very much alive in everyday life. Families of the future will be egalitarian, democratic and flexible, and effectively operate as a partnership or team where each member has an equal voice and acts as an individual consumer with his or her own demands and expectations — for example, more and more children have a significant degree of influence on purchase decisions within the household, including holidays.

The Vertical Families

Longevity and smaller core families have led to the family structure becoming more vertical rather than statically horizontal in form (Figure 7.3). Because there are more, longer-lived grandparents and fewer children, grandparents are enjoying more time with their grandchildren.

Consider the following: in 1900, the life expectancy of a woman in the United States was 47 years; today it is 80 (Shapner, 2007). Today, grandparents can expect to enjoy several more years with their grandchildren than could grandparents of the 1960s. The term multi-generational family, also known as the 'vertical family', is a term first coined by sociologist Michael Young (Briggs, 2001). It refers to the fact that because of increased longevity, there has been a gradual shift towards there being more generations in a family. Because people live longer and lead healthier lives it is more common now for a family to consist of three, four or even five

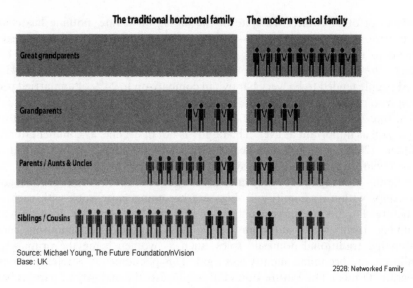

Source: Michael Young, The Future Foundation/nVision
Base: UK

2928: Networked Family

Figure 7.3: The multi-generational family.

generations. Supporting this trend is the phenomenon of falling birth rates, which leads to fewer siblings, cousins, aunts and uncles compared to previous generations. Thus, the structure of the family is more vertical and less horizontal than in the past. The implications of this 'stretching' are manifold for family life and for the relationship between generations at a societal level.

Longevity means that grandparents are more likely to assume supervisory childcare. At present, more and more people in the age group 45 to 55 are finding themselves with dual care responsibilities, namely teenage children and elderly parents. But it is probable that in the future this age group could find themselves at the centre of a five-generation family, with great-grandparents in their nineties, grandparents in their seventies, parents in their forties, their children in their thirties, and grandchildren at primary school etc. (Figure 7.4 illustrates the increased frequency of grandparents looking after grandchildren).

Grand-Travellers

As grandparents have more leisure time and parents lead increasingly complicated lives, a new trend is emerging — that of grandparents and grandchildren holidaying together. This is called grand-travel, which, according to Curry (2000), is one of the fastest growing trends in the twenty-first century society. According to the Travel Industry Association of America, 30% of US leisure travellers who are grandparents have taken at least one vacation with their grandchildren, and a survey conducted by Yesawich, Pepperdine, Brown & Russell, a marketing agency in the United States,

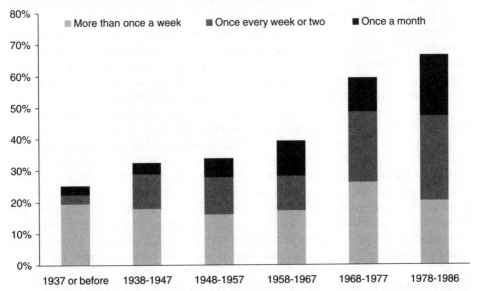

Frequency of grandparents looking after grandchildren
% who were looked after by their grandparents, by year of birth and frequency
'When you were a child how often did your grandparents look after you?'

Source: 'Complicated Lives', The Future Foundation/nVision
Base: 1010 adults 16+,2002

nVision

15638: Graphics from nVision for Ian Yeoman

Figure 7.4: Grandparents and grandchildren.

revealed that 56% of children aged 6 to 17 would 'really like to' vacation with their grandparents (O'Brien, 2007).

The growing demand for grand-travel is indicated by the fact that the business in this sector has increased 60% since 1996 (Jeffrey & Collins, 2001). The concept of grand-travel was first put into practice by Helena Koenig, who set up the tour operator *Grandtravel* in 1989 in Maryland; *Grandtravel* runs escorted tours for grandparents and grandchildren and has received over 15,000 enquiries without any advertising (Schlosberg, 1990). Schlosberg hypothesised that if 15,000 sought out *Grandtravel* when no promotion had been done, then thousands more would respond to advertising. Tours range from 7 to 15 days and include the United States, Europe, Africa and Australia. Koenig believes the grand-travel experience draws grand-parents and grandchildren closer together and helps them relate to each other in remarkable ways. Grand-travel is an innovative way to expand the scope of grandparent/grandchild relationships (Koenig, 2004). Recognising a lucrative market niche, companies other than *Grandtravel* are also now developing special grand-parent/grandchild packages.

The Walt Disney Corporation was another pioneer of the idea of grandparents travelling with their grandchildren. In 1998, Disney recognised opportunities to attract grandparents and grandchildren to Disney theme parks for vacations, and they offered special packages and travel arrangements specifically arranged for grandparents with grandchildren. These packages are still on the market today (Walt Disney World, 2005).

While grand-travel trips take travellers all over the world, there is a particular interest in Florida. An independent telephone survey conducted in February 1998 asked 521 grandparents what their first, second and third choices would be in the United States as a destination to take their grandchildren on vacation. Consistently, respondents mentioned Orlando: 45% put Orlando in their top three choices and 34% gave Orlando as their number-one choice. Other popular cities included Washington D.C., San Francisco and New York (Palmieri, 2006).

In a survey by Palmieri (2006), 29% of the respondents had participated in grand-travel, with the top destination being Orlando and its surrounding attractions (Orlando/Orange County Convention and Visitors Bureau, 2001; cf. Palmieri, 2006). The grand-travel trend is catching on. This type of travel now appears in the brochures of many American tour operators, including Elderhostel, a company well known for its educational travel programmes (Gardyn, 2001). The grand-travel business may be one of the most lucrative travel niches in tourism. Jerry Mallett, head of Adventure Travel Society Inc, researches travel trends and remarks that

> Grand-travel is the new cutting edge; for the first time in history we're going to see grandparents taking the grandkids along as the next level of leisure activities.
>
> (Maxwell, 1998, p. 18)

Grandparents who like to spoil their grandchildren without interference from the parents have discovered that the safest bet is trips to theme parks and historical sites and on vacation (Palmieri, 2006). One of the keys to the popularity of grand-travel may be that it offers something for everyone, even the parents who are not involved in the actual trip — grandparents and grandchildren are able to spend quality time together away from the parents and parents are able to relax, knowing that their children are with someone they trust. Grand-travel traffic has increased by 60% since 1996 and now accounts for at least one-fifth of all trips taken with children in the United States. Grandparents are democratic with the kids. Although the grand-parents are most likely to decide when and where to travel, how much money to spend and where to stay, the study (Palmieri, 2006) found that they share with their grandchildren decisions about what to do once they arrive at their destination, as well as what food to eat.

Palmieri identified some grandparents who travelled with a different grandchild every year or arranged to take each child on a trip when they reached the age of 12 or 13. Some grandparents liked the idea of grand-travel but were unable to do it because they had to care for an ailing spouse or the children were busy with school activities or the parents were divorced and one parent would not agree to the arrangement. In 2000, 60 million grandparents in the United States spent $36.6 billion on their grandchildren (Curry, 2000), including $6.5 billion on vacations.

So, why is grand travelling proving to be popular? One of the keys to the popularity of the grand-travel experience is that it offers something for everyone involved, even the parents who are not involved. Grandparents are able to spend quality time with their grandchildren without interference from the parents. The parents are able to relax, knowing their children are away with someone they trust (Maxwell, 1998).

Maxwell reported that the most difficult part for the grandparents may be remembering how to deal with young children and being prepared for problems (carsickness, homesickness, etc.). However, many trips are pre-arranged in order to alleviate these problems. Often in group travel, grandparents are offered breaks with separate arranged activities for the grandchildren; for example, in Hong Kong, grandparents get a day off for shopping and sightseeing, while grandchildren are taken on a tram tour.

The Palmieri (2006) study found that the main motivation for grand-travellers was the strong emotional attachment to the family, similar to the findings of the Future Foundation's *Changing Lives* Survey. Grandparents tend to favour daughters' children over sons' children. Results indicated that almost two-thirds of respondents stated that their favourite grandchild was a daughter's child. There may be several reasons for this; first of all, in American society when sons marry, they tend to be emotionally pulled towards their wife's family. This may mean that when couples have to choose between spending a vacation with the husband's or the wife's parents, they are most likely to choose the wife's parents. This could mean that grandparents with both sons and daughters might be more likely to spend time with the children of daughters than with those of sons. Therefore, grandparents may feel closer to the former, not necessarily because they consider them 'favourites' but because they are able to see them and interact with them more than with sons' children.

The findings on decision-making indicate that grandparents want to be, or at least think that they are, in control of all decisions. There is no way to measure how much subconscious influence a child has on a grandparent. For example, a child may influence the grandparents to travel to Disney World. Even though the child is not making the decision him/herself, there is a definite influence. Grandparents, however, may or may not be aware of the influence in this and other travel-related decisions. In the Palmieri study, grandparents were asked how much of the decision-making lay with them as against the level of decision-making they allow their grandchildren. Grandchildren being 'allowed' to make a decision and grandchildren influencing the decision-making of grandparents may be two different concepts. This study indicated that grandparents dominate the decision of where to go, when to go, how much to spend and where to stay. They are evenly split on the decisions on where to go and what to eat.

Conclusion

In 2030, there will be fewer children in the world and more relatives and grandparents. As a result, children will become more important, they will be showered with more gifts, and relatives will spend more time with them. Therefore, the grand-travel concept will grow in importance. The close bonding of families is important now and will be more so in the future. To a certain extent, time spent with grandchildren will become the new luxury, as there will be fewer children and grandparents will place more value uon them — just as the Smiths are doing by taking their children on vacation in Florida.

Chapter 8

My Life in Pogradeci — The Phenomena of Second-Home Living

Pete and Mandy, like many people in 2030, spurred on by the prospect of a long life, the attraction of year-round sunlight, the plethora of direct flights, rising disposable income, and the low cost of living abroad, spend their summers in their second home in Albania. Pogradeci is one of the country's most charming tourist resorts and is located on Lake Ohrid, with its clear, blue waters and mountains all around. Having bought a 200-year-old farmhouse for only US $70,000, Pete and Mandy are in heaven because they simply couldn't afford such a property and lifestyle back in Britain. A typical day is spent pottering around the village, taking in a gastronomic lunch and sampling local award-winning wines with friends, both expat's and Albanian. Afternoon activities include watercolour painting or a round of golf. In the evening, they enjoy a couple of glasses of beer and a stroll along Lake Ohrid or just watch the world go by.

Pete & Mandy's holiday home in 2030

Introduction

The mountainous country of Albania, known as the land of eagles or *Shqiperia*, on the Adriatic Sea, once a shadowy Communist prison state, will emerge as a leading Southern European destination by 2030 because of its low cost of living, sunny climate, sandy beaches, stunning landscape and proximity to European markets. One of the key factors to drive this growth will be the second-home tourist.

Over the past decade, second-home tourism has emerged as an important part of the of the tourism industries in many countries, especially Eastern European ones. Second homes are often located in attractive and popular tourism destinations and are often bought and used by city dwellers, whether for a weekend retreat or to spend the whole season. In 2005, 26% of the Finnish population owned a second home whereas in the United Kingdom it was 4%. The overall rate of home-ownership within the EU15 is 15%. Although, traditionally, second-home tourism is driven predominately by nationals seeking regions with better climatic conditions, today other factors, such as a lack of confidence in conventional pension provision, has led many people to invest in property as their retirement nest egg. Television programmes such as *Pay Off Your Property In A Year* or *Location, Location, Location* have fuelled people's interest in owning property abroad, including behind the former Iron Curtain. Property speculation is now a key tourism driver; resorts such as *The World Islands* in Dubai or the new expansion at Gleneagles in Scotland would not be financially viable without second-home developments. Today, High Street travel agents such as Thomson's will sell a property in Albania along with your airline tickets.

What are the key drivers shaping this phenomenon?

Drivers

The eight drivers, which are shaping second-home tourism, are mentioned in Table 8.1 and discussed below.

Driver 1: Affluent Societies

Between 1980 and 2000, disposable income for UK consumers of all generations doubled in real terms as a result of low inflation, low unemployment, low interest rates, rising house prices and a buoyant stock market (see Figure 8.1). In 2005, consumers had more discretionary income than ever before and their spending patterns were different from previous generations because, according to the Office of National Statistics (BBC, 2007c), more money was being spent on fun and holidays than at any other time.

Driver 2: An Englishman's Home Is his Castle — The Cult of the Home

The Englishman's obsession with home-ownership is not driven just by macro-economic factors, but is also a product of political and ideological factors

Table 8.1: Drivers shaping second-home tourism.

	Driver
1	Affluent societies
2	An Englishman's home is his castle — the cult of the home
3	A low-cost world and Eastern Europe
4	Access — the Internet and budget carriers
5	Pension provision and property development
6	Leisure-time use and holidays
7	Climate
8	Longevity

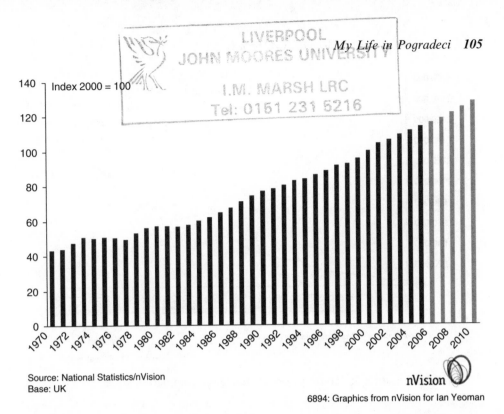

Source: National Statistics/nVision
Base: UK

nVision

6894: Graphics from nVision for Ian Yeoman

Figure 8.1: Household disposable income. Index of real household disposable income — nVision/Experian forecast (August 2006-based projection).

which result in home-ownership being perceived in terms of security and of being in control of one's destiny. This notion of security is a prime motivating factor for people wanting to own their own home, based upon a sense — whether real or perceived — that they then have control over their resources and the physical space around them and this results in a sense of greater control of and security for their future. This sense of ownership is different from that in other countries; for example, home-ownership in Germany is associated more with settling down and raising a family. As Figure 8.2 shows, house prices have risen exponentially in the past decade, with the average price of a UK home in 2005 being £200,000 (US $400,000) and in Greater London that price is £300,000 (US $600,000). Research by the Halifax Bank revealed that in 2005 the total value of all private housing in the United Kingdom was £3.2 trillion (US $6.4 trillion), which is three times economic output of the United Kingdom (Future Foundation, 2006c).

Driver 3: A Low-Cost World and Eastern Europe

Today, we live in a low-cost world, which is being driven by mass-market retailers such as Wal-Mart, Costo and Stelios Haji-Ioannou's easyWorld of easyJet,

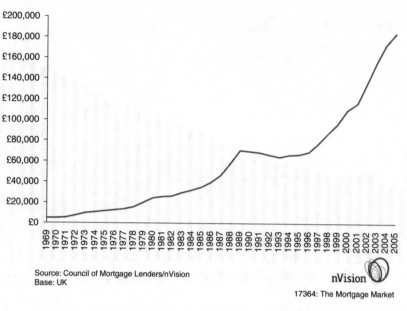

Source: Council of Mortgage Lenders/nVision
Base: UK

nVision

17364: The Mortgage Market

Figure 8.2: House prices at mortgage completion stage.

easyCinema, easyMusic, easy4men. This is a world where these and other providers have reduced prices on a wide variety of goods, and this has resulted in consumers having more disposal income to spend on other, more discretionary and even luxurious products. With the opening up of Eastern Europe, UK travellers now visit destinations such as Prague, Slovenia and Budapest as a matter of course. One of the observations made by many visitors is the strength of their purchasing power — their holiday pound goes so much further compared to what it buys the United Kingdom. That, combined with the fact that UK property has become very expensive for the first-time buyer (with house price to salary ration now 8:1) means that buying a property in the United Kingdom is well out of the reach of the first-time buyer. This means, that the number of people purchasing properties in Eastern Europe is rising exponentially.

Driver 4: Access — The Internet and the Budget Carrier

Eastern Europe is now readily accessible as a result of the increasing use by budget carriers of secondary airports such as Doncaster, Liverpool and Luton. Over 100 low cost and low fare airlines now operate across the European continent alone and Ryanair is now the world's most popular airline for international passengers. According to the International Air Transport Association (Future Foundation, 2008), Ryanair carried more international passengers in 2006 than any other airline – 40 million passengers over the course of 2006, ahead of Lufthansa (38 million), Air France (30 million) and British Airways (29 million). This continuous rise has been driven by low fares and a route network, which continues to grow. New destinations that have been added in 2007 so far include Dalmatia and Pula in Croatia, Warsaw and Katowice in Poland and Maribor in Slovenia. EasyJet, Ryanair's main low cost rival, was 6th on the list carrying 22 million cross-border passengers in 2006.

The spending by UK residents abroad has increased from £24.3 billion (US $48.6 billion) to £30.3 billion (US $60.6 billion) between 2000 and 2004, an annual growth rate of 5.7%; the average spend per visit rose from £426 (US $852) in 2000 to £500 (US $1000) in 2005. This increase shows no signs of slowing down partly because the number of new destinations offered by budget airlines continues to grow. European destinations remain the most popular for UK holidaymakers, with Spain and France the most favoured, according to the Office of National Statistics. However, Eastern European countries have experienced enormous growth in the number of UK visitors, with, in 2004, year-on-year growth resulting in increases of 62% in Bulgaria, 78% in Croatia, 10% in Turkey and 11% in Slovenia.

According to the Future Foundation's *Changing Lives* Survey in 2006, 95% of flights are purchased on the Internet and by 2030 it is expected that 80% of all holidays will be purchased online. The Internet has become the channel of mass consumer choice for the travel industry and this has had the effect of introducing transparency, allowing the consumer to book holidays, source information and compare prices. The consumer has, in fact, become his own travel agent.

Driver 5: Pension Provision and Property Development

With the first of the baby-boomers having retired in 2006 (those born between 1945 and 1960) the UK pension industry is at a crossroads, because the number of people retiring will rise dramatically over the next 20 years. This, combined with the fact that many people are living longer, means that final-salary schemes of many companies have closed to new entrants because companies are unable to finance the required level of pension — and this has had the knock-on effect that retirees can no longer rely on a guaranteed high level of income on retirement. This, in turn, has had the result that consumers are asking themselves, 'Where shall I put my money to pay for my pension?' and a significant number have turned to property development as a means of securing their future. Figure 8.3 highlights the sharp rise in the number of people who have re-mortgaged in order to fund home improvements or to buy a second property, which, in turn, has driven the buy-to-let market.

One of the consequences of this trend has been the rise of property entrepreneurs, people who buy a rundown property, renovate it and sell it on at profit. This

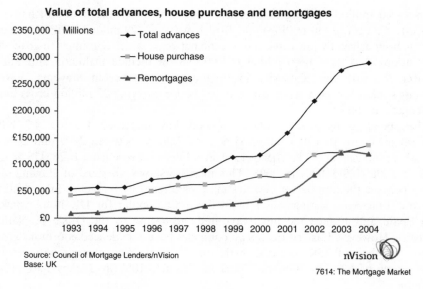

Value of total advances, house purchase and remortgages

Source: Council of Mortgage Lenders/nVision
Base: UK

nVision

7614: The Mortgage Market

Figure 8.3: Mortgage advances.

phenomenon is highlighted by dedicated television channels, such as the Over-seas Property Channel which was launched in September 2006 by Sky, featuring would-be developers, offering advice and giving viewers the chance 'to see how it is done'.

Driver 6: Leisure-Time Use and Holidays

According to Yeoman and McMahon-Beattie (2006), increases in affluence and educational attainment have meant that today's consumer is more 'travelled, cultured and liberal' compared to previous generations. Changing gender roles, a decline in the importance of religion, increased sexual freedom and a more liberal outlook has resulted in a greater focus on experiencing new worlds. People are enjoying much more material comfort in comparison to their parents and grandparents, in the trend of a cultural shift towards personal fulfilment and aspiration through experience. Therefore, it could be argued that luxury is increasingly about enrichment and time, as well materialism. This has had the result that holidays are now perceived as the number one item of luxury and therefore the UK consumer is taking more holidays than ever before, both short breaks and long-haul trips (Figure 8.4).

The growth in time spent outside the home is fuelled by the growing number of the older generation, those who have lots of time, and in many cases, high disposable

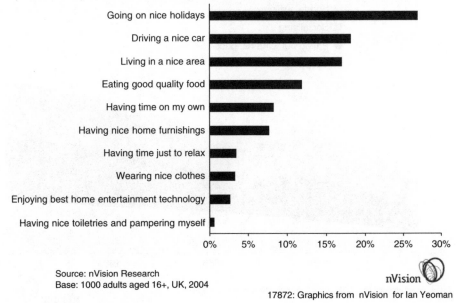

Perceptions of luxury - best description
Proportion of adults who choose various aspects of life to be the best description of luxury to them
"Can you tell me, for you, which of the following things would be the best description of 'luxury' in your life?"

Source: nVision Research
Base: 1000 adults aged 16+, UK, 2004

nVision

17872: Graphics from nVision for Ian Yeoman

Figure 8.4: Perception of luxury.

incomes. As a result, the United Kingdom has become more of a leisure society in the sense that expenditure on leisure activities plays an increasingly significant role in the economy and accounts for a growing share of consumer spending, and, therefore, a resultant rise in employment in this sector. Increased leisure time has also made consumers more demanding. People have come to expect a lot from life — but at the same time are being dissatisfied with the lack of work like balance. Thus, if people are dissatisfied with work, then leisure time and the chance to escape from their daily life become more important — hence the significance of holidays and second homes.

The growth in the number of leisure trips is increasingly associated with the baby-boomers who have retired early and are wealthier than previous generations of retired people. In addition, society's use of leisure time has changed; time spent out of the home has doubled since 1960 (as shown in Figure 8.5).

Driver 7: Climate

The climate is the No 2 reason why Brits choose a particular holiday destination, after the accommodation and facilities which are available, according to Mintel

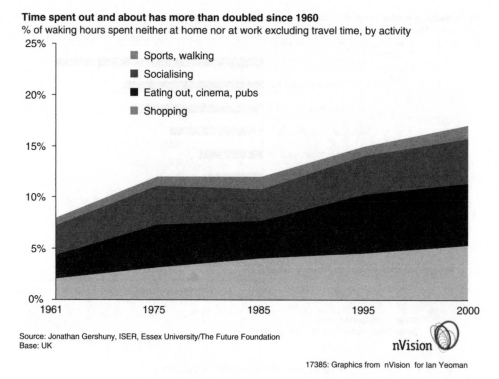

Time spent out and about has more than doubled since 1960
% of waking hours spent neither at home nor at work excluding travel time, by activity

- Sports, walking
- Socialising
- Eating out, cinema, pubs
- Shopping

Source: Jonathan Gershuny, ISER, Essex University/The Future Foundation
Base: UK

nVision

17385: Graphics from nVision for Ian Yeoman

Figure 8.5: Time spent out of the home.

(2006f). Britain's unpredictable climate is a reason not to holiday in the United Kingdom, whereas Albania's all-year-round sunshine acts as the key draw for the destination. Climate is one of the main reasons why the British have bought holiday homes in Spain and France, especially the baby-boomer generation (Figure 8.6).

Driver 8: Longevity

What was the most important demographic development of the twentieth century? According to the Future Foundation, it was the increase in longevity — a near doubling of life expectancy over the course of four generations. The two main factors that drove this were the massive decline in infant morality, particularly during the first part of the century; and mortality rates across all ages because of improvements in medicine improvement in the mortality rates for the elderly but across all age groups'. Figure 8.7 demonstrates a significant shift in consumer spending by people

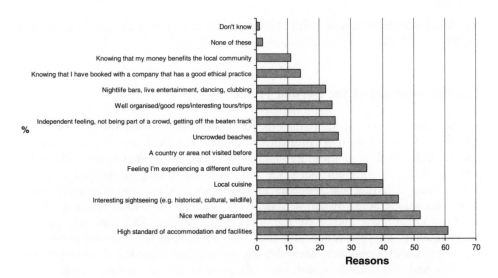

Figure 8.6: Brit's reasons for holidays abroad. *Source*: Mintel (2006f).

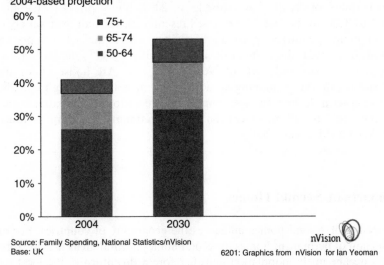

Figure 8.7: Share of spending on leisure goods and services by those over 50.

over fifties and those in retirement. This market will become increasingly active and wealthy, which will mean a cultural change in attitudes.

The Phenomenon of the Second Home

Second homes are an integral part of the future of world tourism and they will make a significant contribution to tourism economies, but they are also the focus of resentment by local populations and politicians because they are perceived as putting pressure on the existing housing stock and, therefore forcing an increase in prices, thus making it harder for residents to buy homes. Many commentators would argue that second-home owners also deprive communities of local facilities such as schools, post offices and even the local pub, because they are not part of the community all year round and thus they exacerbate the seasonal patterns of the destinations' economies. Second-home owners are regarded as outsiders and invaders and this creates resentment and, in extreme cases, may result in the vandalism of their property (Hall & Muller, 2004). But whatever the negative side of the phenomenon, second homes are a key driver for future growth in world tourism.

What if, Second Homes Prices Fall?

The price of second homes in Eastern Europe could fall as a result of the present credit crisis in the world, as price rises in recent years are based on speculation and easy availability of credit. For example, in 2007, house prices in Estonia have dropped by 10% in the last 12 months. Presently, there is an over supply of real estate in many countries, particularly Dubai where the sell on market has collapsed. In Florida, the number of sales has fallen by 47% in 2007 with similar figures in Las Vegas and parts of New York State. Are house prices are over priced and the market is making an adjustment or is the housing cycle about to enter a long-term decline due over supply and recession. If the latter is the case; expect the world to fall into recession and discretionary spending on tourism to fall (Pickard & Mulligan, 2007).

The Impacts of Second Homes

The ownership of second homes influences the geography of countries. For example, the conversion of permanent homes to second homes in rural areas usually arises in the wake of a decline in the population and therefore a downturn in the local economy. Whereas the construction of purpose-built second homes in addition to existing housing stock usually means a temporary increase in the population and an increasing inflow of economic resources into the area. The development of second homes usually occurs after a period of economic decline and loss of the sustainability of traditional 'industries' such as agriculture, which means that second homes fill a void once decline has set in. Local councils often regard second homes as a means to repopulate areas and to increase expenditure where this decline has occurred (Bohlin, 1982; Nordin, 1993).

Studies by Shucksmith (1983) identified how second-home tourism contributed towards the maintenance of local services by generating a marginal income that enabled local shop-keepers and tradesmen to continue in business. For example, the Finnish Islands Committee identified the importance of second-home tourism for the rural economy by comparing figures between the resident population and the second-home owners. Between 1980 and 2000, the population living permanently in the countryside had declined by 31% to about 900,000. At the same time, the number of persons using second homes had increased by 79% to more than 1.8 million second-home owners' using their second homes between 80 and 109 days per year. Mullur (1999) established that four German second-home owners in Sweden spent as much in the local community as one permanent Swedish household. Similarly, a study by Marcouiller, Green, Deller, Sumathi, and Erikkila (1998) demonstrated that second-home owners played an important role in generating local business activity, mainly because they use their properties at periods throughout the year (albeit with greater use in the summer).

Fundamentally, the consumer loves the concept of owning a second home. According to Mintel, (2006f) with relatively few bargains to be found in the United Kingdom, thousands of Brits are looking abroad to invest in a cheap holiday home both for holidays and as an idyllic spot for retirement and, as a result, they are fuelling a boom in house prices in many countries such Slovenia and Spain. Today the boom destinations for housing demand are mostly in Eastern Europe and Scandinavia, according to a survey of international house-price inflation by estate agents Knight Frank. Cheaper air travel is bringing more distant destinations within easier reach for Brits considering buying a home abroad. There is also a growing demand for second homes in countries such as Canada and South Africa, but Eastern European countries are experiencing the real boom in this sector. For example, in Latvia, annual property inflation in 2005 was 45%, driven mainly by UK people buying property; Mintel's (2006f) survey revealed that Latvia actually topped the league.

The Eldorado Effect

The debate about second homes is nothing new; Jordan (1980) discussed the phenomenon in the 1960s and 1970s. Coppock's (1977) classic work 'Second Homes: Curse or Blessing' reviewed two decades of growth in the number of second homes in north west Europe, which reflected the increase in disposable income and the accessibility to coastal and rural areas.

Since the 1990s property ownership by Brits has been encapsulated in the BBC television programme *Eldorado* — a fictional portrayal of the British expatriate community in southern Spain. Although retirement migration represents a small (but significant) percentage of migration flows within Europe, it has become very important since the early 1980s, particularly in countries such as Spain, Italy and Portugal. During the past decade international retirement migration has experienced a rapid growth as a result of increased life expectancy and changing lifestyles. In Spain, regions such as the Costa Blanca, the Costa Del Sol, the Balearic and the Canary Islands have become favourite destinations for both permanent and temporary British residences (Casado-Diaz, 2004) to the extent that in some regions second homes account for 80% of all new developments.

Product Development

The development of second homes in Spain is tied to the development of the tourism product — golf in particular. According to Pedro (2006), golf tourism is one of the most important segments to drive the second-home market for several reasons, including:

- Golfers tend to belong to affluent socio-economic segments and to spend considerable time on golf courses.
- Golf tourism is related to high-expenditure tourism, because the average spend is greater that in conventional tourism.

There has been an enormous expansion of the golf market in Europe. The number of golf courses has increased from 2914 in 1995 to just over 6000 in 2005 (Mintel, 2006g); for example in Spain there were 290 golf courses in 2005, a figure which had more than trebled over the past 20 years, and a further 300 are in the planning stages. But even taking into account this projected increase, the golf-course capacity will be insufficient to fulfil the growing demand for the sport, according to Aymerich Golf Management (Mintel, 2006g), which has 19 golf courses in Spain and Portugal and is involved in 50 new projects.

Spanish golf courses are at present concentrated in the southern resort region of Andalusia in Catalonia and around Madrid. Much of the new development is also found in these regions, a prime example being Sotogrande, a large golf and resort complex between Gibraltar and Malaga (Mintel, 2006g). In Spain, golf provides an important contribution to both the local and the national economies and in 2004 it generated a turnover of £1353 (US $2707 billion), representing a rise of 252% since 1997. Furthermore, incoming golf holidaymakers spent an average of £846 per person (US $1692) and stayed in the country from seven to nine days and a comparison with the overall average spend for foreign tourists illustrates the high, value-added nature of golf tourism; the average tourist spent only £489 (US $979) and stayed 5.7 days. Spain is the number one foreign destination for three out of the four leading, outbound golf tourism markets in Europe (the United Kingdom, Germany and Sweden) and is ranked the second most popular by the French market. As well as foreign tourists, the number of registered Spanish golfers has grown rapidly in recent years, more than quadrupling since 1990 to reach its current level of almost 235,000. This adds up to a participation rate of 0.6% of the population, which is similar to that in France and Germany (Mintel, 2006g). Second homes and golf together provide the financial model for resort development in many countries.

Resort Real Estate Trends

The model for second-home expansion in Eastern European countries in the future will evolve and will be based on resort enclave developments. Resorts provide a place for escape, relaxation and recreation and are spacious. They are popular and perceived as safe by tourists.

Resorts usually consist of both hotel accommodation and leisure products, for example golf, tennis, swimming pool, spa, health and beauty treatments, etc. Resorts fulfil a growing, diverse set of consumer needs and, therefore, they aim to balance core amenities with lifestyle trends. One of the key business models for resort development is real estate. Why? The baby-boomers are now retiring and have significant purchasing power. In Europe, there has been a shift towards single-family, detached homes in preference to smaller apartments, located in resort-style communities that include golf, fitness centres and other facilities, such as hiking trails These baby-boomers will maintain both an urban residence as well as a property in a resort. Resort-orientated retirement developments are driven by the following key prerequisites:

- Low crime rate
- Good hospitals nearby
- Low overall cost of living
- Mild climate
- Low taxes
- Low housing costs
- Expatriate neighbours
- Major city nearby
- Active social/cultural environment

The baby-boomer generation has a tremendous hunger for self-improvement classes, and learning courses. Health and wellness facilities, fitness centres and sports activities are also key factors in their decision-making on where to buy. Another noticeable trend in the United States is the movement of major hotel companies, such

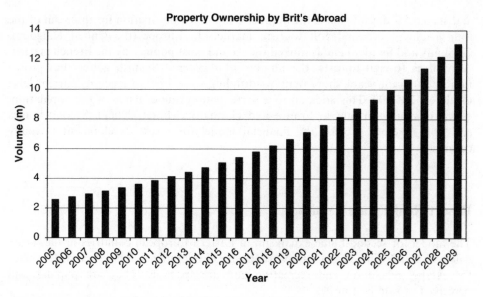

Figure 8.8: Forecast of UK residents ownership abroad. *Source*: Mintel (2006g).

as Hyatt and Marriott, into the assisted-living sector, targeted at elderly people who require extra facilities.

Forecast for Brits Owning Property Abroad

In 2005, 4% of the British population (or 2.41 million) owned property abroad and forecast is that it will increase to 12.8 million by 2030, an exponential increase of 7% per annum. This is a realistic assessment of the present market, given the rises in disposable income, the uncertainty of pension provision and the affordability of second homes. However, as this forecast is based on a purchasing power index, the growth may come under pressure from rises in interest rates and the sub prime mortgage market. Also, as the economies of Eastern Europe develop, government regulation in these countries may become a barrier to further ownership. (Figure 8.8)

Concluding Remarks

Second-home tourism should be viewed as a positive trend for the future. Destinations that set out to restrict land-use and therefore second-home tourism will miss out on a good opportunity. We should not underestimate the force of the drivers that will shape this phenomenon; wealth creation is difficult to restrict in capitalist economies. Destinations will need to adapt to this kind of tourism and embrace the change rather than try to curtail development. Second homes have to be considered in the wider context of leisure-time usage and changing lifestyles, and the allocation of land usage for this purpose (Mintel, 2006f) is something which many destinations should consider.

Chapter 9

The Sex Tourist — What Happens in Vegas, Stays in Vegas

> It is modern and gleaming, with about a hundred scantily clad blondes and brunettes in G-strings parading around and lots of Silicon Valley executives at the tables. This is Spearmint Rhino's, the world's brand leader in lap dancing. I watch Chastity, one of the girls, approach three different customers to offer a lap dance, but they act as though there are fish hooks in their pockets, so she is out of luck. When the fourth prospect, a portly man in his thirties, accepts her offer, she spends nearly an hour with him. After she has performed several dances and left him glassy-eyed and devoid of reason, Chastity is $1000 better off. Even in 2030, the lure of sex is as powerful as it was in 2005.
>
> The Sex Tourist in 2030

Las Vegas is the Disneyland fantasy destination for adults, where anything can happen, where anything goes, and where wives will never find out. Its naughty, raunchy marketing slogan, 'What happens in Vegas, stays in Vegas', represents the sinful side of tourism. It is about sex and sin, not authenticity, green pastures and great mountain views. Vegas is a destination that offers the opposite of ethical consumption, caring for the planet and worrying about climate change. It is about conspicuous consumption and lavishness rather than communities and humanity. So why, when so many policymakers talk about the 'greening of tourism', is Vegas so successful? The answer is simply sex and sin. Vegas is a sinful city where tourists take a vacation for adult, undiluted erotica.

Sex

Once upon a time, sex was a taboo subject; today it is used to sell everything from shampoo to holidays. All over the world, sex has been commodified and is supplied in various forms for a variety of different markets. In Vegas tourists can hire an escort (although it is illegal, nobody cares), watch topless showgirls at a Crazy Horse revue, be body surfed at Spearmint Rhino's, and admire the Pussy Cat Dolls at Caesar's Palace. Sex in Vegas is an affair of the groin, sometimes shallow and perfunctory, but at other times glamorous and romantic, for example, when lovers opt to get married in Vegas.

Tourism and sex have always gone together for various reasons. It is theorized that Columbus brought syphilis from America to Spain in 1492 (Clift & Carter, 2000). Soon after, epidemics of syphilis spread across Europe, mainly associated with the movement of men. In 1494, the 50,000 troops dispatched to the Alps by Charles VIII were handicapped by syphilis and the troops were withdrawn to France. Between 1495 and 1496, cases of syphilis were reported in several countries, from England to Hungary, and throughout Germany and Russia.

More recently, the scale and character of Thai prostitution has changed significantly following the appearance of US forces in the region during 1960s and 1970s. Thailand served as a rest and relaxation area for American servicemen and, in addition to the 50,000 men stationed in the country, some 70,000 men were flown in each year to recover from the stress of the Vietnam War. It is estimated that 700,000 American servicemen visited Thailand between 1963 and 1976 and their spending in restaurants and brothels over this period exceeded 40% of Thailand's export earnings (Clift & Carter, 2000).

Tourism, romance, love and sexual relations have always been linked and will continue to be so in 2030 and beyond. For as long as people have travelled, they have engaged in romantic and sexual encounters of various kinds. Sometimes sex or the prospect of sexual encounters in the destination or along the way plays a central role in the decision to travel and the choice of destination. At other times, sex represents an incidental aspect of a trip or plays no role whatsoever in the decision-making. Sometimes sexual activity is regarded as being a socially acceptable and mutually beneficial reason to travel, as in the case of honeymoons or romantic getaways. But sexual encounters are regarded as illegal when child prostitution is involved and sordid in the case of extra-marital affairs (Bauer & McKercher, 2003).

Sex tourism is one of the most emotive and sensational issues in tourism. It is an extremely problematic area to define. Opperman (1999) defines sex tourism within the context of purpose of travel, length of time, relationships, sexual encounters, and travel. Opperman argues that combining these variables constitutes a debate on sex tourism. However, as we have already noted, sex tourism is more than red-light districts, lap dancers, prostitution and exploitation. It is a vast subject and, therefore, for the purpose of simplicity, in this chapter the sex tourist is defined as 'a tourist whose primary or secondary motive is to travel for sexual encounters'.

Las Vegas: Explicit Images and Thoughts

Ever since Las Vegas became a gambling oasis in the Nevada desert, sex has played an important role in its entertainment scene. When Bugsy Siegel first opened his Tropicana Casino in this sleepy desert town, in 1957, he featured beautiful female hostesses and lavish shows with scantily clad women. That formula is still prevalent in Las Vegas casinos today. In nearly every casino, beautiful cocktail waitresses dressed in ultra-short skirts and low-cut tops float around the gaming tables, dispensing smiles and free drinks. The entertainment venues present topless reviews and risqué entertainment. Just walking along the sidewalks of Las Vegas Boulevard, visitors pass numerous newspapers and posters flaunting revealing photographs of female escorts and nude models. In the streets men thrust flyers advertising sexual services into the hands of passers-by. Vegas certainly gives the appearance of living up to its reputation as 'sin city' (Leco, 2006).

Sheehan (2006) describes an advertisement in Vegas showing an attractive woman crawling into the back of a limousine, letting her hair down from its neatly tied bun, fondling the leather interior, flirting with the driver, changing clothes en route to the airport, and caressing the driver as he drops her off. The message couldn't be clearer:

> Vegas is a place where you totally relax your inhibitions and indulge in behaviours you would never have dreamed back home in Walla Walla.
>
> Sheehan (2006, p. 9)

This is the basis for the Las Vegas marketing campaign, 'What happens ... .', that is, letting visitors know they can do whatever they want in Las Vegas, whether gambling or having sex with a complete stranger or doing other things they would never dare do in their home town. The marketing concept is 'freedom', people leaving their woes behind, going right to the edge and having adult fun.

Sheehan (2006) invites us to imagine a shot of a woman from the waist up. She is sitting at a desk and is wearing a pinstripe suit, and a shirt and a tie, all Armani. Her hair is pulled back. She is blonde (just like Catherine Deneuve in 'Belle du Jour') and she's wearing horn-rimmed glasses. She says in a refined voice, 'Research shows that people of every description, no matter their cultural, ethic or economic background, all need to cut loose and explore their wildest fantasies'. Then she leans forward, unclips her hair, shakes it, looks up, pulls down the tie, takes off the glasses and says 'In Las Vegas, we are the world's greatest experts in that!' In a competitive world, sex is used to sell Las Vegas.

Sex is everywhere — on the Strip, on the Boulevard, in numerous men's clubs, in the yellow pages and in hotel lobbies, where well-dressed, young-looking women sit patiently. Sex and Vegas go together; they are inseparable — the marketing image presented by 'What happens in Vegas, stays in Vegas' is known all over the world.

The Dark Side

> Each year an estimated 800,000–900,000 human beings are bought, sold or forced across the world's borders [2003 US State Department estimate]. Among them are hundreds of thousands of teenage girls, and others as young as 5, who fall victim to the sex trade. There's a special evil in the abuse and exploitation of the most innocent and vulnerable. The victims of [the] sex trade see little of life before they see the very

worst of life, an underground of brutality and lonely fear. Those who create these victims and profit from their suffering must be severely punished. Those who patronize this industry debase themselves and deepen the misery of others.

President Bush, addressing the U.N. General Assembly
September 23, 2003
(*Source:* Shared Hope International, 2007)

Wherever there is tourism there are sex tourists. However, the dark side of this is that, increasingly, people under the age of 18 are being recruited into the commercial sex markets to service the demand resulting from the normalisation of and the promotion of commercial sex across America (Shared Hope International, 2007). These young victims join the adult women who have also been deceived about the kind of work they were being offered and have been coerced into prostitution, becoming victims of human trafficking as defined by the US Trafficking Victims Protection Act of 2000.

The commercial sex trade flourishes in the United States, in part, because the media bombards all age groups with explicit sexual imagery. On the one hand many American policymakers and citizens condemn the immoral and unethical nature of the commercial sex trade; on the other hand, American culture promotes commercial sex. Religious and educational institutions advocate abstinence and fidelity, yet many businesses blatantly and pervasively market sexuality and sex acts to all Americans. Simultaneously, in a culture that takes pride in women's rights and professional achievement, females are commonly portrayed as sexual commodities.

In the midst of — and in part owing to — these contradictory yet powerful cultural cues, the sexual exploitation of children in the United States appears to be growing. Each year, an estimated 14,500–17,500 foreign nationals are transported into the States (Ashcroft, 2006). The number of US citizens trafficked within the country each year is even higher, with an estimated 100,000–300,000 American children at risk of becoming victims of commercial sexual exploitation (Estes & Weiner, 2002). Evidence suggests that children under the age of 18 now constitute the largest group of victims. According to authoritative estimates, the average age of entry to prostitution and the commercial sex industry is 11–14 years old (Nadon, Koverola, & Schludermann, 1998) and the gender is overwhelmingly female. In Clark County, Nevada, for example, 181 cases of prostituted juveniles were pending between August 2005 and December 2006, only one of which involved a male victim. While 38% of these girls were from Nevada, the remaining 62% were from 28 other states, as far away as Alaska and New York.

Running away from home was a common characteristic of over 60% of prostituted juveniles in a data collection project in Las Vegas that spanned the years 1997–2006 (Shared Hope International, 2007). Indeed, 90% of all runaways become part of the commercial sex industry (Estes & Weiner, 2002). A runaway is defined as a child of 14 years or younger who chooses not to return home and stays away overnight or a child of 15 years or older who chooses not to return home and stays away for two nights. A 'throwaway' child is told to leave home by a parent/guardian/

adult and stays away overnight or is prevented from returning home by a parent/guardian/adult (Shared Hope International, 2007).

Approximately 55% of street girls engage in formal prostitution; of these, about 75% work for a pimp. Pimp-controlled, commercial, sexual exploitation of children is linked to escort and massage services, private dancing, drinking and photographic clubs, major sporting and recreational events, important cultural events, conventions, and tourist destinations. About one-fifth of these children become entangled in nationally organised crime networks and they are transported around the States by a variety of means — cars, buses, vans, trucks and planes — and are often provided with counterfeit identification to use in the event of arrest (Estes & Weiner, 2002).

Escort services and massage parlours dominate the commercial sex market. The Internet and print media facilitate the selling of the 'products', especially the escort services, which can be found in the classified section of all the major newspapers and on electronic media. While massage parlours and brothels are relatively easy to investigate because of their fixed location, escort and call-out services form a market in which victims of all ages and nationalities can be hidden and exploited at little cost to the exploiter (Shared Hope International, 2007). Higher prices can be charged for sexual services through escort services than in brothels and also a bigger buyer base can be accessed. Ethnic brothels have tapped into this advantage by expanding their marketing to offer escort-style services, which allow buyers from beyond the ethnic community to access the sexual services of the normally closed system. The trend toward trafficking victims through escort services mirrors the operations of the commercial sex markets in Japan, the Netherlands and Jamaica.

The Sex Trade in Vegas

> The problem has been made worse by Las Vegas' aggressive advertising promotions that encourage tourists to come here and sin all they like. We're basically giving a green light for people to come here and exploit women and children.
>
> Terri Miller, Co-ordinator of Anti-Trafficking
> League Against Slavery (ATLAS) of the
> Las Vegas Metropolitan Police Department
> (*Source:* Shared Hope International, 2007)

Many Americans believe that prostitution is legal throughout Nevada, including Las Vegas, a belief which is due in no small part to the highly visible, sexually based advertising. However, this is not the case; prostitution is not legal in Clark County where Las Vegas is located. The state law prohibits prostitution in counties with a population of 400,000 residents or more; Las Vegas, therefore, is excluded because its population is 1.1 million.

The sale of sex has deep historical and cultural roots dating back to America's westward expansion and the role of the mining and railway industries in the 1800s (Brents, 2000). Nevada drew large numbers of single men during the Gold Rush; this gave rise to a culture of tolerance for commercial sex that has persisted over time. The cycles of boom and bust in the industry were unpredictable. When times were good, a party mentality took root that included the purchase of sex, and the environment was conducive to prostitution because families seldom settled in these mining areas and men were on their own for lengthy periods. As a result, a different code of conduct evolved: 'Prostitution, if not prostitutes themselves, became an accepted part of the community from the perspective of working men. ... 'Good girls' on the frontier needed protection; 'bad girls' were sexually available and provided necessary services to frontiersmen' (Brents, 2000, p. 220).

Prostitution was almost legalised in Nevada in 1871 during a huge mining boom. Over the years, support for legalised brothels waxed and waned. Most brothels were closed by the federal government during World War II but re-opened their doors as soon as the war was over. In the 1970s, several county commissions passed licensing ordinances and dozens of brothels became legal. Ten counties together have 28 brothels that in 1999 collectively brought in $40 million in revenue (Brents, 2000, p. 222). In 2006, it was estimated that in Las Vegas alone the sex industry and related activities, both legal and illegal (including lap dancing, prostitution in strip clubs, commissions to taxi drivers, and tips to valets and bartenders for procuring women etc.) generate between US $1 billion and US $5 billion per year (Farley, 2007). Most women working in legal brothels were taken there by pimps or by other means of coercion and control, not because they freely chose to work as prostitutes. The lives of women at the Mustang Ranch (since closed) in Storey County, Nevada, were observed and related in a book by Albert (2001). She noted that the women at Mustang Ranch were forced by husbands, pimps or dire economic circumstances to become prostitutes — it was not their preference. Currently, one of the more popular brothels is Sheri's Ranch in Nye County, immediately adjacent to Clark County where Las Vegas is located; their website, www.sherisranch.com, is explicit and comprehensive. Prospective buyers can peruse photographs of available women and make a reservation online. 'Testimonials' from buyers are also available online.

Las Vegas has been described as America's 'Disneyland of Sex' (Frommer's, 2007). Its culture of tolerance promotes promiscuity more than anywhere else in the country. One encounters Las Vegas' sexualised culture even in the airport's baggage hall. Big-screen televisions show advertisements for seductive cabaret shows; big casinos vie for attention by featuring more risqué displays. Taxicabs display advertisements with female posteriors and little else promoting various shows. Billboards advertise 'shows' and outside their doors clubs advertise 'cabaret' shows that, in essence, are just glorified strip shows. The Internet features assorted advertisements, such as on www.hotspotsofnevada.com, a site which features legal brothels and other sex venues and depicts a man and woman engaged in sexual intercourse. In addition, the local yellow pages contain over 155 pages of advertisements for massage parlours and escort services, with suggestive phrases and photographs. Many are costly double-page advertisements and claim to 'bring the girls direct to you in your hotel room — 24 h'. Yellow page advertisements boast of college girls, student nurses, exotic beauties, wild teenagers of barely legal age, and Russian and Asian teen petites. Most advertisements claim to provide 'full service', implying that intercourse is available.

> Las Vegas offers no guarantees that you'll strike it rich at a slot machine or a blackjack table. However, it does promise that you'll get lucky under the sheets, quite possibly with one of the most beautiful girls you've ever seen ... presuming you have some extra cash in your pocket...Prices can range from $400 to $1000 and upwards. As the cop says, 'These women are like automobiles — the better looking and better built they are, the higher the price tag'.
>
> Sheehan (2006, p. 164)

Over 15,000 women dance topless or totally naked in licensed bars, and a female dancer earns between $200,000 and $400,000 per annum. According to Bianca Paris, who sold three hair salons in Susanville in order to pursue a career in exotic dancing,

> Las Vegas is the stripping capital of the world. There are more girls making good money here than any place else because the business is active from early in the afternoon until ten the next morning. It is amazing how much money walks into these clubs every night, and how much of it the girls manage to take home. A little quick arithmetic indicates just how important strip clubs are in the overall economy of Las Vegas. A place such as Jaguars, where Bianca works, employs over 500 dancers on any given day. It is one of the larger clubs in Clark County. If we estimate that the average number of dancers at a club is one hundred and they average $350 a day in tips, then $1.4 million in hard currency is slipped into G-strings in a single day. That equates to $430 million a year that's pumped or shall we say pumped into the economy.
>
> Sheehan (2006, p. 20)

In spite of the law prohibiting obscenity in advertising, on magazine racks, and on the streets of Las Vegas, there are free brochures and booklets explicitly advertising various sexual acts for sale, mostly escort services. Filipino, Korean, Thai, Russian, Chinese and Japanese women are advertised in these publications. Many of the brochures are published by Southwest Publishing Associates and include *Night Beat*, *Full Xxposure*, *Pussy Cat Magazine*, *Goodtime Girls*, *LV Heat* and *LV Nude Entertainment Guide*. In addition to these traditional means of advertising, picture cards are passed out every night on the streets, depicting different types and nationalities of women: Romanian, Asian, blondes, brunettes, and so on. The great majority of these offer services around the clock and advertise as 'full service'. Young

Latino men and women on the streets, especially on the Upper Strip, aggressively thrust the cards at passers-by, specifically targeting the men.

Advertising: Cards distributed to pedestrians on The Strip in Las Vegas

Source: Shared Hope International (2007)

Contrary to the public, idealised images of Las Vegas, reinforced by powerful advertising campaigns, the prostituted girls are typically not college students working their way through graduate school, although they may be advertised as such; rather, they are the runaways and homeless teenagers who arrive in droves by bus from nearly every state, especially nearby California. Predator pimps at bus stations, in arcades and in shopping malls quickly recruit a large number of these vulnerable youngsters; they groom them and force them out into the streets in and around the Fremont Street Experience — trafficking victims in the sex tourism market which is Las Vegas.

In recent years, Las Vegas has been identified as a major centre for Asian massage girls working in strip mall shops throughout Clark County (Smith, 2005). Clark County granted 39 massage establishment licences in 2005, while Las Vegas reported a jump from 52 in 2001 to 74 in 2005, but this does not reflect the true number of massage parlours in operation. Metro vice police point out that many illegal massage parlours are operating in Las Vegas (Smith, 2005). Precious resources and time are spent conducting background checks on applicants with questionable credentials and almost non-existent English. A massage industry source reports that an owner of two parlours commonly transfers his unlicensed girls from one location to the next just ahead of police visits.

Concluding Remarks

One thing is sure: all the talk about cyber sex is nonsensical when it comes to the real thing, and in Vegas sex sells. The use of sexual imagery and propositions is the backbone of 'What happens in Vegas, stays in Vegas'. Such a marketing message is based on secrets, the mystery of sex and doing something sinful well away from home.

Outside the world of sin, destinations also use sex as part of the romantic image they want to portray of themselves. As long as there is tourism, there will be sex tourists — and that will not change. The political correctness of destinations promoting authenticity and sustainability seems totally alien compared to what happens in Vegas, because tourists will still visit massage parlours and be fascinated by those silicon implants. However, as this chapter has demonstrated, there is a dark side to it all, which can be classified as modern-day slavery and exploitation.

Chapter 10

Ostentatiously Expensive Dubai: The Phenomenon of the Retail Tourist in the Middle East

> As my personal guide 'escorted' me around the Mall of Arabia, I saw ostentatious consumption at its best. This is the only place in the world where you can buy a gold-plated Ferrari, the latest Gucci handbag, exclusive designer clothes and the finest champagne — and all at duty-free prices! To me, shopping in Dubai is one big festival of pleasure and indulgence. It's even better than sex.
>
> A postcard from a retail tourist in 2030

Introduction

Interest in shopping as a leisure activity has emerged as a result of consumers' affluence, the economic dominance of the retail industry and the emergence of consumption by women (Harris, 2005). Shopping centres have become destinations in themselves, whether Las Vegas, Hong Kong, Dubai or Minnesota which are all examples of conspicuous consumption where themed environments act as attractors, catering for the adult, bourgeois Disneyfication of destinations. Shopping has become a symbol of luxury, of play and of pleasure, all associated with lifestyle and consumerism. In order to attract high-spending shoppers, destinations have added value to the experience they offer by providing exclusivity and/or pleasure. Vegas is all about pleasure, whereas Dubai is about exclusivity and luxury embodied by the designer transformations and experiences throughout the world. This chapter provides an analysis of shopping trends and an examination of how Dubai and the Middle East have shaped themselves into ostentatious, luxurious retail destinations.

Dubai is one of the seven states, which make up the United Arab Emirates (UAE). Dubai covers less than 4000 sq. km. and is sparsely populated outside the city. The economy is based on the oil industry but over the past decade, the government has diversified into financial services, tourism, retail and property, and developed its airport as a major international hub. Today, Dubai is an oasis in the desert, an oasis where dreams come true, with the most exclusive of hotels and the world's largest indoor ski resort. Dubai's duty-free shopping and its numerous arcades and markets (*souks*) are a major attraction and include Bur Dubai Souk, Deira Gold Souk, Deira Covered Souk, Perfume Souk, Spice Souk and the Electronics Souk. In 2008, the *Mall of Arabia* will become the world's largest shopping mall, covering 2 billion sq. ft. and catering for 35 million visitors every year. Dubai, by its very nature of exclusivity, has a reputation for shopping and luxury goods.

Tourists and Shopping

Tourists and shopping are not new, as Timothy (2005) observes. Some of earliest accounts of souvenirs date back to the ancient Egyptians, who brought mementos back to friends and family from their foreign trading expeditions. During the Middle Ages, as global exploration expanded into Africa and the Americas, voyagers came home with numerous examples of arts and crafts from the countries they had explored and the peoples they had conquered.

Colonialists and explorers, through their booty and tales of exotic places, introduced the crafts of unknown peoples to Europe. During the seventeenth and eighteenth centuries, young men undertook a Grand Tour through the cities of Italy and other countries, purchasing paintings, antiquities and bronze replicas of classical sculptures to take home. These tourists were primarily aristocrats and prosperous professionals, for whom wealth was part of life, whereas today wealth, consumerism and accessibility are what many consumers aspire to.

The emergence of malls can be traced back to the late nineteenth century, when multi-storey 'retail centres' started to appear alongside department stores, and by the mid-twentieth century they had become the standard feature of the ex-urban retail landscape. The most common location of retail services in cities was the High Street, but with limited space in the town centres and the emergence of the motor car, shopping malls appeared out of town or on the urban fringe. One of the earliest ex-urban centres was Brent Cross on the outskirts of London, which opened in 1873. Today, malls are part of the modern landscape throughout the developed world. The original idea of shopping malls was to provide consumers with a collection of shops indoors, which together would offer a variety of merchandise and prices so that consumers were not required to search through individual shops on different streets but could do all their shopping in one-stop locations. Whilst malls have continued to grow in number and size, they have also developed to become more intense recreational experiences, making them tourist destinations in their own right to the extent that Dubai promotes itself as a festival destination of shopping and exclusivity, and Las Vegas as an all-round destination for gambling, entertainment and shopping (Timothy, 2005).

Malls have become permanent recreational features, and they host a number of boat shows, vintage car fairs, fashion shows, craft shows and talent shows. Shopping malls now have hotels, airport terminals, restaurants, nightclubs, bars, spas and even roller coasters. The 'Mall of America' the largest mall in United States, even has its own tourism department. Malls can be themed; for example the El Mercado mall in San Antonio, Texas, is full of products from Mexico and South America (piñatas, sombreros and pottery) and the buildings are designed in stereotypical colonial style.

The Mexico-land theme is popular, because it allows Americans to 'visit' Mexico without actually going there.

There are specialist malls, which concentrate on sports, clothes, technology or discounted products. Malls may have festival themes, working with destinations as venues for comedy and music events and for food fairs. Malls such as Ocean Terminal in Edinburgh, Scotland, uses a major visitor attraction, The Former Royal Yacht *Britannia,* as a means to attract tourists to the Mall and thus shop. Airports have become shopping destinations in their own right, with Amsterdam's Schiphol Airport and Singapore's Changi Airport popular for gold, jewellery, perfumes, clothing and tobacco products. These airports also offer casinos, golf-ranges karaoke bars, swimming pools and even massage parlours. Airports are usually associated with duty-free shopping, but the concept of duty-free sales now extends beyond airports. Duty-free shopping is the purchase of items free of tax and import duty at the point where people depart a country. By purchasing merchandise after leaving the effective control of one paying country but before entering the next country, travellers can avoid paying import duties on highly taxed and deluxe items. Duty-free shopping is not about discounting but about giving consumers the opportunity to buy goods without paying what may be punitive duty in their own country. Nowadays, tax-free shopping is not limited to international gateways but can be found in shopping centres exclusively for tourists, for example in Johannesburg and Buenos Aires. Today, malls have broader community functions, with medical centres, churches, dental surgeries, launderettes and government offices all found in shopping malls. The malls have adopted multi-functional responsibilities, which are well outwith the retail sector.

Shopping Trends

Velben's (1994) analysis of the nineteenth century American 'leisure class' argued that fashion was invented by the upper classes in an attempt to distinguish themselves from their inferiors. The bourgeoisie dressed ostentatiously in order to symbolise their power and social status and to demonstrate their superiority. As society has become better off, the styles and practices of the upper classes have been adopted by others and ostentatious behaviour has become acceptable for all to embrace. At the same time, social class is no longer defined by where one is born or who one's parents are because wealth creates opportunities for upward mobility and new lifestyles. Modern societies have become more individualised and have eliminated the rigid codes of social stratification, which were based on categories such as wealth and class as existed when Velben developed his theories.

Today, the definition of 'social worth' has moved away from the status of one's class towards individualisation, where identity is no longer assumed from previous generations. In the contemporary consumer culture 'who you are' is something a person can actually create, partially through their consumption of goods and services. People increasingly use consumer goods, including clothes, to map their identities — whether to impress, to please, to rebel or to conform. In real terms today's consumer is twice as rich as the previous generation — and the leisure society which has been created through the accumulation of wealth likes to shop!

A direct consequence of shopping becoming more of a leisure activity rather than a necessary chore is that consumers are increasingly likely to expect a fun 'experience' from the retail environments they visit. As Prahalad and Ramaswamy (2000) famously put it in the Harvard Business Review:

> Managers also have to realise that the customer is no longer interested in buying a product. The product, in fact, is no more than an artefact around which customers have experiences. What's more, customers are not prepared to accept experiences fabricated by companies. Increasingly, they want to shape those experiences themselves, both individually and with experts and with other customers.

Rising affluence and the expectations that accompany it have broadened the meaning of 'having it all' and personal interests now extend beyond the sphere of just family and work. Plentiful and varied leisure pursuits are expected by today's consumers. Indeed, Pine and Gilmore (1999), in their book *The Experience Economy*, were already thinking about the possibility of some retailers charging customers admission to enter their stores.

> Think about a pure retailer that already borders on the experiential. The next time you go to a Sharper Image or a Brookstone — two retailers that provide a place where consumers can play with the latest high-tech devices — watch the customers as they wander around the store ... Could such an establishment charge admission? ... The retailer might very well sell more goods.
>
> Pine and Gilmore (1999, p. 28)

This raises the question: what, today and tomorrow, are bricks-and-mortar retailers actually selling? The word 'shoppertainment' has already entered the commercial language and we can be sure that the next decade will see the evolution of shops and malls into something more pleasant (or at least a diversification of their offer).

Figure 10.1 illustrates a well-established truth in the analysis of shopping behaviour — that so much of the activity and energy of the shopping experience are predominantly associated with women. In shopping, one of the biggest differences between women and men is that women constitute the overwhelming majority of consumers, making up to 80% of all consumer choices. Peters (2001), author of *Women Roar: The New Economy's Hidden Imperative,* claims that American women buy 80% of sit-on lawn mowers! That said, estimates vary widely and the proportion of choices made may well not equate to the economic value of choices made, because men still tend to dominate, or have a say in, the purchase of larger-value items. Figure 10.1 goes part of the way to explain why women buy more — women really like shopping! Women will shop for pleasure and relaxation, not just out of necessity (some would say).

% who go on a shopping trip at least once a month, by gender within country

"Please say which of the activities on this list, if any, you do on average at least once a month...Go on a shopping trip because you want to and not because you have to"

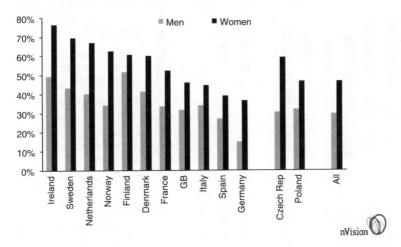

Source: nVision Research
Base: 1,000 per country aged 15+, 2005

14764: New Shopping Experiences

Figure 10.1: Shopping for pleasure.

As Figure 10.2 shows, women have an influential say in the clothes worn by their partners. Only around a third of men say that they have (voluntarily or not) complete autonomy over the clothes they wear. In a European context, there are geographical differences; Swedish, Polish and British men exercise most choice when buying clothes, although in these countries, in as much as 30–40% of the time, the woman has at least equal or more say than the man. At the other end of the scale, only 18% of Czech men say that they chose or mostly chose their clothes. In most cases where men are choosing their own clothes, women appear to have had at least a consulting role. It is worth noting that if the tables are turned almost no women reported that their partner has much influence over their day-to-day outfits. Many men say they lack sufficient time to look after themselves; more than 40% say 'I never have as much time as I would like to spend on my appearance'.

Women's greater involvement in consumption means that they are more sophisticated shoppers — research shows that women are more likely to spend time browsing and looking at different products in order to identify the best product at the best price, whereas men are more inclined to 'hunt' shop — they just go into a shop and buy!

According to the Future Foundation's *Changing Lives* survey, unplanned purchases are fairly common (Figure 10.3). One-fifth of the consumers surveyed, for example claimed that on their last shopping trip they bought something they had not planned to buy. If we also take into account those purchases made because of a special offer, the proportion of shopping trips involving impulse buying is closer to 40%. Growing affluence means that consumers do not have to maintain such tight

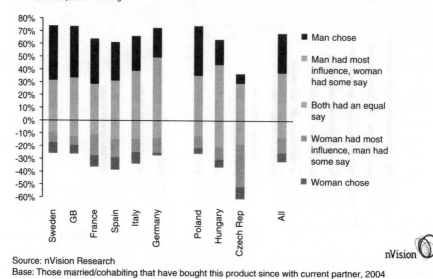

% men married/cohabiting who claim various degrees of control over the clothes they wear generally, by country
See notes for question wording

Source: nVision Research
Base: Those married/cohabiting that have bought this product since with current partner, 2004

19720: Consumer Trends Affecting the Fashion Industry

Figure 10.2: Female influence on males' choice of clothes.

control of shopping budgets as they did in the past. Therefore, there has been a continuing shift in the perceptions of what constitutes 'miserliness' or 'self-indulgence' — as affluence justifies impulsiveness in a wider range of markets.

One of the challenges for shopping malls is the impact of the Internet, as more and more people shop online, whether they are comparing prices or making a purchase and this trend will have an impact on the function of shops. According to the American academic, Sawhney (2002), consumers are likely to take this further. For example, someone may use the Internet to research digital cameras, but then visit a photographic shop for a hands-on demonstration. 'I'll think about it', they will tell the sales assistant, but back home they will use a search engine to find the lowest price and buy online. Michael Dell, the founder of Dell, has long said that many shops will turn into showrooms. There are already signs of change in the High Street; the latest Apple and Sony stores are designed to display products in the full expectation that many consumers will buy online. To some extent the online and offline worlds may merge. Multi-channel selling could involve a combination of traditional shops, a printed catalogue, a home-shopping channel and an e-commerce-enabled website. One of the biggest commercial advantages of the Internet is that it lowers transaction costs.

A driving force behind the growth of out-of-town malls has been the pressure on prices. Today's consumers are searching for bargains across all sectors of retailing — food, clothes and household and electrical goods.

A more impulsive consumer?
Frequency and justification

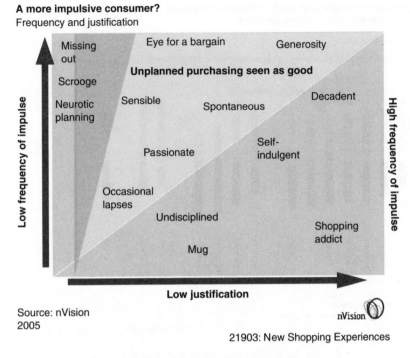

Figure 10.3: Impulsive consumers.

Understanding the consumer's relationship with individuality demonstrates to us that, for example what they wear is an expression of what they are, rather than clothes having just the function of covering the body. One of the reasons people buy particular clothes is that these clothes become an expression of their individual personality. Consumers' perception of their own individualism within society is no doubt seen by them in relation to the broader perceptions of liberalism within their society and the broader complexities of national identity. Figure 10.4 shows that the majority of respondents in most countries disagree that 'people should go along with the mainstream views of society rather than trying to be different', thereby demonstrating that consumers overall lean towards individualistic rather than the collectivist values of society.

In many senses, rising affluence, social mobility, the diversification of retail brands and consumer empowerment have all helped to democratise luxury, making it a key attribute of many branded products used to be the preserve of so-called 'high-net-worth individuals'. Now, however, the elements of exclusivity, expense, affluence, extravagance, hedonism and gratification inherent in the term 'luxury' are engrained in the marketing of many of the less expensive fast moving consumer goods (FMCG) (brands-fashion, beauty, personal care and clothing as well as these attributes finding their way into the consumer electronics, motoring, healthcare and leisure sectors).

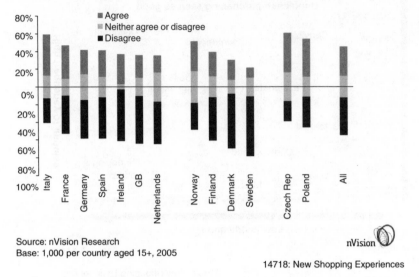

"People should go along with the mainstream views of society rather than trying to be different"

% who agree, by country

"Please indicate how much you agree or disagree with each of the statements I read out by using the scale on the card..."

Source: nVision Research
Base: 1,000 per country aged 15+, 2005

nVision

14718: New Shopping Experiences

Figure 10.4: The importance of individualism.

Although consumers, regardless of income group, can increasingly afford to 'splash out', but the consumer does not have a limitless pool of funds. As an alternative they selectively 'trade-up and trade down' to higher levels of quality and taste in products they are interested in and vice versa. Consumers still like to indulge in material goods (cars, clothes, etc.) but as preferences have changed, so personal possessions are now purchased with greater care; people search longer for the product that tells the right story about who they are. People are not looking for packaged solutions or complete outfits; it is more important to demonstrate their individual style. Many of the High Street fashion brands such as Zara, Bershka, H&M and Mango are successfully launching affordable copies of items hot off the fashion catwalk and are able to respond to changing consumer demands much more quickly than they used to. In 2004, H&M even teamed up with design legend, Karl Lagerfeld (aka Mr Chanel), to design a limited-edition line for the autumn/winter collection which went on sale at their typically very affordable prices. 'Designers at Debenhams', a 'sub-brand' within this UK department store chain, has existed since 1996 and its turnover for 2005 was in excess of US $200 million. As Silverstein et al. (2005) conclude, wealth has also come from trading down. This is the rise of 'low-price culture' and the search for a bargain. Across the world the value sector has grown dramatically; for example Tesco sells a pair of jeans for US $2. Low-cost stores such as Lidl and Aldi now have a presence on the UK High Street and tourists travel to New York or Dubai for duty-free shopping.

One of the reasons that consumers prefer shopping malls to the High Street is because they want the convenience of doing all their shopping under one roof. Convenience is so engrained in the consumer culture that it has been normalised and anything else is unacceptable. Today's consumers feel that their ever-more-complicated lives are constrained by an array of different demands, and women in particular feel time-pressured because of the dual demands of raising a family and handling their careers. In the same context, consumers also appear to be becoming more impatient. Wacker and Taylor (2000) noted that 'psychic' abuse can be endured. Financial abuse is unwelcome but bearable. It is time abuse that most strains loyalty to any organisation.

Schwartz (2004) contends that today's world is full of complicated choices which time-constrained consumers find frustrating. In markets which are more associated with leisure shopping, for example clothing, a greater choice may be welcomed. For many female consumers, the very attraction of shopping for clothing is the freedom to spend time browsing in a wide variety of stores and trying on various garments — the element of choice contributes greatly to the overall experience. However, where interest in the product is low, for example shopping for a new toothbrush or where the consumer may experience confusion or detachment, there is a sense that there is more choice than is actually necessary. Convenience, then, takes on a new aspect. In certain retail markets, consumers require help to navigate through the plethora of available alternatives across different sub-sectors in order to reach sensible and immediate solutions, hence the increasing presence of personal shoppers in many retail outlets.

In today's affluent society, consumers are able to enjoy a greater wealth of material possessions than previous generations did. Now everyday necessities getting relatively cheap for the majority of people to procure more, and consumers are interested in spending on traditional luxury products and brands. Luxury is, therefore, becoming increasingly accessible to the masses (though the average consumer's frequency of luxury purchases throughout the year may still be low). One no longer has to earn a six-figure sum to drive a Lotus or venture past H&M and Marks and Spencer to pick up the latest designer clothing in a high-fashion outlet. Indeed, just under 50% of consumers say they often or occasionally mix value clothing with designer wear — according to Future Foundation's *Changing Lives* Survey. However, while there is no question but that traditional, material symbols of status such as expensive suits and diamond-encrusted jewellery are still in demand, there has been a definite shift towards a more experience-based definition of luxury. People now attach more value to those areas of life which offer personal fulfilment, for example, free time, relaxation, tranquillity, adventure, knowledge and relationships. Luxury, therefore, takes on a wider, more complex meaning. It is no longer confined to champagne and caviar — it may also now appear in a multitude of different forms, depending on the individual. Luxury may continue to be mainly about status and exclusivity, but the concept is more fluid and can mean different things to different people. As a result, retailers are under pressure to provide unique and personalised luxury goods, services and experiences to meet the demand and to stimulate interest.

If luxury has been redefined to encompass experience and inner gratification, what now for the likes of Louis Vuitton, Rolex and Hermes, which founded their brands on simple, material prestige and opulence (and as such once commanded the unswerving loyalty of the elite)? Indeed, any brand, from Apple to Tesco, can offer luxury in its new form, if it effectively taps into what its target consumers want, as well as offering a sense of exclusivity. Traditional luxury brands are not likely to disappear — in fact, many such brands are busily working to create a new generation of luxury goods to target both old and new consumers in order to secure their custom in the future. For example, Chanel's Coco Mademoiselle fragrance (fronted by the young actress Keira Knightley) is targeted directly at young women, whilst Giorgio Armani's A/X Armani Exchange caters for what it terms 'the urban youth'.

However, realistically, in order to endure in the long term, discretionary brands must broaden not just their target markets but also the nature of their core offerings. They must provide the consumer with a unique and individual proposition or experience. It is a principle which Anderson (2007), in his book *The Long Tail*, dubs *micro-niche*. True luxury will lie in 'limited edition', 'authentic', 'customised' and 'one of a kind'. The challenge for luxury brands will be to create an illusion of acute personalisation when they have worked so hard up to now to become emblematic of affluence on a global scale.

General affluence has led not only to increased consumer demand but also to a shift in psychologies, affecting various aspects of the way people behave as consumers. This in turn has created a new set of complex attitudes and demands. To encourage people to shop for pleasure, retailers and shopping centres must create agreeable and stimulating environments in which consumers want to spend their time (and money). To conclude, consumers actually buy more than more than they need; otherwise why would Imelda Marcos have 3000 pairs of shoes (Danziger, 2004)?

Retail Tourism in Dubai and the Middle East

According to research by Mintel (2006h), the global luxury goods market was worth US $87.5 billion in 2005, with the Middle East and, in particular, Dubai, becoming the world's most ostentatious shopping destination. Dubai is the ultimate in conspicuous luxury, designer fashions, with the world's largest shopping mall, seven-star hotels and even festivals dedicated to shopping. The emirate is an example of the movement by a state government away from oil-dependency towards a diversified industry base, with retail and tourism being the sectors spearheading this development. According to Kuntze, Lindstaedt, and Lehmann (2007)

- Per capita, retail space in Dubai is already estimated to be four times that in the United States.
- In 2008, Dubai will have 3 of the 10 largest malls worldwide.
- By 2009, retail spending in Dubai's shopping malls alone is expected to exceed US $7.6 billion (for comparison mall-related retail spending in Saudi Arabia is US $6 billion and in Abu Dhabi it is US $1.9 billion).

- Dubai alone will benefit from more retail spend than Saudi Arabia, thanks to a forecasted 15 million tourists who are expected to visit by 2010.
- By 2010, Dubai will have 16 times more sales-floor space in malls per capita than the average for the 25 EU countries.

The Arab world — the member countries of the Arab League or the Gulf Cooperation Council (GCC) — has 330 million inhabitants, who live in 21 countries. It covers a huge area, from Morocco on the Atlantic to Oman on the Indian Ocean, representing a huge and rapidly growing market opportunity for these countries from Foreign Direct Investment (FDI). However, the countries of the Arab World are all very different — just as counties in Europe are — and these differences have implications for growth, economic development, political stability and business opportunities.

The Middle East region has excellent infrastructure projects, and well-developed free-trade zones, as well as industry clusters and long-term tax exemptions for both companies and individuals. Although its dramatic rise has been overshadowed in the media by other emerging markets — the so-called BRIC nations of Brazil, Russia, India and China — the Middle East region is now firmly on the globalisation agendas of companies throughout the world because of its booming economy and attractive, long-term growth prospects. Taken as a single entity, the Middle East would have ranked as the world's 16th largest economy in 2006, exceeding the GDP of the Netherlands and close to that of Australia. However, the real attraction of the Middle East as a market lies in the high per capita income of a growing middle class, which is comparable to that of many countries in the EU and much higher than those in the BRIC countries (Figure 10.5). The leading destinations in terms of international arrivals are Saudi Arabia (religious tourism) and Egypt (package holidays); however,

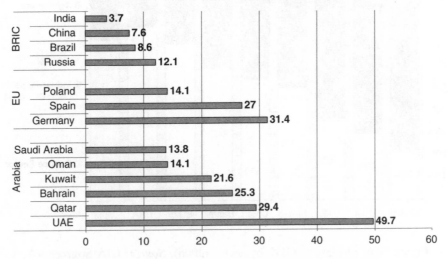

Figure 10.5: Purchasing power. *Source*: CIA Sourcebook.

the United Arab Emirates and, in particular, Dubai is the crème de la crème of luxury and revenue per tourist.

This favourable situation is a result of exceptional economic growth over the past two decades (4–8% per annum). The International Monetary Fund puts the 2006 growth rate of the UAE at 10.5%, one of the greatest worldwide, and the Dubai Strategic Plan announced by Sheik al Mahtoum, the ruler of Dubai in February 2007 projects 11% annual growth up to 2015 (tripling the current level of GDP). The major driver for growth is oil. However, because oil is a finite resource, the Middle East countries have embarked on a policy of diversifying their economies. Dubai is the best example, having been transformed from an oil-dependent into a diversified state, with strong travel and tourism, retail, real estate and financial sectors. Generous tax exemptions are granted for local and foreign companies setting up businesses in UAE.

The Middle East accounts for over 20% of the world's oil production and 42% of proven oil reserves. From Figure 10.6, oil is still the region's most important commodity. However, in order to diversify for future economic prosperity, countries in the Middle East are spearheading diversification by developing real estate, tourism and retail. In Dubai retail is the core tourism product, along with the development of financial centres in Dubai and Abu Dhabi, both of which attract banks, insurance and other financial institutional investment.

The construction and real estate sectors in the Middle East have experienced phenomenal growth since the early 1990s. While the first wave of construction was driven by building up a world-class infrastructure and the need to provide Western-standard accommodation for the local, expatriate and tourist population,

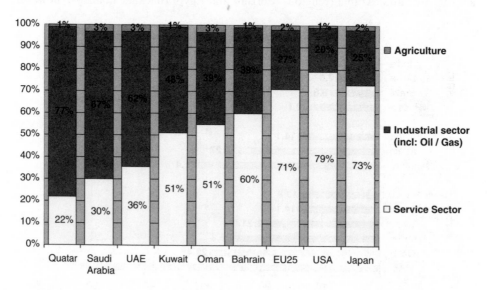

Figure 10.6: Origins of GDP by sector (2006). *Source*: CIA Sourcebook.

the New York's Twin Towers' disaster on 11th September 2001 resulted in a second real-estate boom in the UAE. Huge wealth was repatriated to the region and very often invested in real estate. The level of construction can be compared to the major growth which took place in Asian hot-spots such as Shanghai. One-fifth of all the world's cranes are now at work in Dubai alone. As of December 2006, projects worth over US $770 billion were either planned, put out to bid, or will be under construction during the period 2006–2011. This real-estate boom benefits the retail sector both directly through the construction of malls and supermarkets and indirectly through the boost which it gives to the economy. It also stimulates tourism and strengthens the Middle East's position as a transport hub for Asia, with many major airlines using it between Europe, Asia and Australasia.

How Tourism in the Middle East Is Changing Consumers' Perceptions of Service and Luxury?

Perceived as key ways to diversify the Middle East's economy, the travel, transport and tourism sectors have developed rapidly over the last decade, with Dubai as the largest transportation hub in the Middle East and Africa (Barbel, 2006). Tourism is something that the Middle East has embraced relatively recently. This has enabled countries in the region to specifically target higher-spending travellers, luring them with some of the world's most spectacular developments, such as its tallest building, the Burj Dubai in Dubai. One big challenge facing many Middle East destinations, however, is how to provide authentic experiences in cities where there are few well-preserved historic buildings, and where modern skyscrapers are the norm. In a region where aspiring luxury-travel destinations, like Qatar, are playing catch up with Dubai, countries also face the difficult task of differentiating themselves from competing destinations, which also offer waterfront living, vast air-conditioned malls and desert-base adventure activities (Mintel, 2007b).

According to its Department of Tourism, Commerce and Marketing (DTCM), Dubai's hotels attracted almost 6.4 million arrivals in 2006 and over 50% of the tourists stay in four- and five-star hotels. Tourism expansion in Dubai is both characterised and fuelled by the construction of ever more luxurious hotels (the emirate hopes to have 110,000 rooms by 2016) and equally elaborate projects. The emirate is one of the most inspirational destinations in the world, having attracted worldwide attention through its growing list of exciting superlatives, and having successfully established itself at the forefront of innovation. This has manifested itself in projects such as the first indoor ski slope to be constructed in the middle of the desert (Ski Dubai), the world's largest airport (Dubai World Central International Airport, which will have a capacity of 120 million passengers a year when it opens in 2008), and the Dubai Mall, which will be the world's largest shopping mall next year. Furthermore, Burj Dubai will most likely be the world's tallest building when it is completed in 2008. Dubai will be the world's largest theme park (opening in phases from 2010), and The Palm project — boasting the largest man-made islands in the world — will be visible from the moon (Mintel, 2007b). Dubai has raised the standards of service within the tourism market all over the world, to the extent that Peter Lederer, Managing Director of Gleneagles, once said that even his famous five-star resort could not compete with Dubai on service levels (Lederer, 2003).

Retail Tourism as the Catalyst for Growth

The Middle East has traditionally been a region of traders and merchants — including Arabs and Indians. Today, the retail sector is considered both dynamic and competitive, with local and international investors entering the market or expanding existing operations. Trade in the Middle East can be characterised by the contrast between traditional souks and small, independent stores on the one hand and ultra-modern shopping malls on the other. Customer behaviour has become more and more Westernised recently and it is only a matter of time until the thousands of small, independent stores and corner shops disappear. The Middle East is following much the same development as the retail sector has experienced in Europe since the mid-1970s. Organised retailers and large retail stores at one end of the spectrum and discounters at the other end are both increasing their market share at the expense of smaller, independent retailers and family businesses. This will lead to a situation similar to that in Europe, the difference being that the process in the Middle East started only in the late 1990s. It is, however, likely to evolve much faster.

The booming economy, a growing middle class with rising per capita incomes, and an increasing number of tourists provide fertile conditions in which retail can develop. The region has many migrant workers, but the resident population is increasing by approximately 2.8% per year, while the tourist influx is increasing by 7% per year. Another driver for future growth in retail turnover is the relatively low per capita spend on retail by the resident population. This is far below Western European benchmarks. During the 1970s, rich Arabs travelled to London or New York to spend their oil dollars, but now the retail shopping in the UAE is in many cases better than in London and New York, and the European middle classes are swapping Paris for Dubai. That fact is acknowledged by retailers who have recently moved into the region, such as the Swedish fashion giant H&M which opened its first two stores in Dubai in September 2006. CEO Rolf Eriksen said that his company was 'very proud to open our first stores in this fast-growing region with high fashion awareness and spending power' and that he sees 'huge market potential' for H&M in the Middle East (Kuntze et al., 2007).

Opportunities for Growth

The total Gross Leasable Area (GLA) in shopping centres has grown 20% on average over the past two decades in the Middle East and will continue to do so for the next 5 years (based on projects currently under construction). Even though this might suggest that the market is overheating, most industry experts agree that there is room for growth, especially in the mid-income market. European and American retailers targeting that segment are still very new to the market or are in the progress of planning their market entry. Examples include H&M, UK pharmacy and cosmetic chain Boots, French Hypermarket group LeMarché, Spanish fashion retailer Trucco, UK toy-seller Hamleys, the Danish home-fashion store BoConcept and US clothing retailer GAP. The Middle East region is one of the world's premier markets for luxury goods. With over 300,000 of the world's 8.7 million high-net-worth individuals living there, luxury products from cars to yachts, apparel to personal goods, and such exceptional services as space travel, are highly sought after. Personal goods such as cell phones also enjoy great popularity. UAE nationals are very keen on the latest technology and as Hassan Tavakoli, Vice President of Motorola for the Middle East and Africa, has learned from his distributors: 'A typical UAE national may change his cell phone up to six times per year'. Motorola reports very high demand for new, fashionable handsets.

Rich, Super-Rich or Just a Myth

Apart from money being spent increasingly locally by the rich and super-rich, the Middle East retail sector will also benefit from the growth of the middle class and their purchasing power. A common myth about the Middle East is that everybody is very rich and salaries are exorbitantly high, with virtually no taxes being imposed. The Middle East has the highest proportion worldwide of millionaires and billionaires — apart from Hong Kong — but at the same time, it has a huge expatriate workforce, most with very low spending power.

Uneven Population Structure

Apart from Oman and Saudi Arabia, the middle class in the Middle East is still underdeveloped. Oman has only very limited oil reserves and has thus put a lot of effort into getting nationals to take on regular jobs instead of relying on an expatriate workforce. Saudi Arabia, on the other hand, despite having the largest oil reserves worldwide, also has the biggest population in the Middle East, thus diluting the average per capita income. In general, the income groups are clustered along national lines, with 'locals' representing the highest income groups, Western and Arab expatriates the upper middle class, Asian 'white collar' workers the lower middle class and Asian 'blue collar' workers the lowest income groups (Figure 10.7).

The Malls of the Middle East

The future of retailing in the Middle East is clearly going to be shaped by organised retail formats (malls and mega-malls). Because of high summer temperatures, air-conditioned malls are hubs not only for shopping but also for meeting people

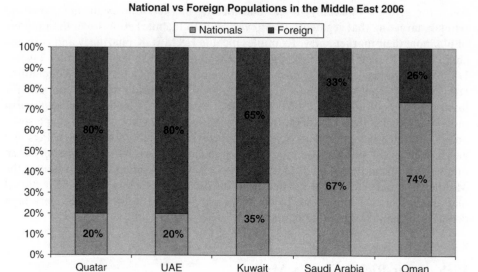

Figure 10.7: Nationals vs. foreign populations. *Source*: CIA Sourcebook.

socially. Aware of the retail industry's enormous potential, government and private companies are setting up new retail outlets at breath-taking speed. Dubai alone had 36 malls at the end of 2005 and this figure is expected to reach 50 by the end of 2008, when the city will have three of the 10 largest malls worldwide. By 2010, Dubai will have 30% of the total retail space in the Middle East. The second largest retail destination will be Saudi Arabia (specifically Jeddah and Riyadh). Of the top 20 malls, the Kingdom will add six new malls in the next 3 years, with a total GLA of approximately 630,000 sq. m. Per capita retail space in Dubai is already estimated to be four times that in the United States. More mega-malls are under construction and the forecast is that, by the end of the decade, Dubai will have 16 times more sales-floor space in malls per capita than the average for the EU25, and Doha, the capital of Qatar, will have about four times that of the EU25 (Kuntze et al., 2007).

Dubai Has Put the UAE on the Global Retail Map

Two local shopping events in particular attract a large number of regional and increasingly international crowds. These are the Dubai Summer Surprises (DSS) in August and the Dubai Shopping Festival (DSF) in December/January. What started as a retail project to boost sales in 1996 has turned into an unparalleled tourism initiative. Retailers make roughly 50% of their annual turnover during these festivals and tourists account for 65% of the retail business. DSF 2005 attracted 3.3 million visitors and generated business worth US $1.8 billion. This year's event is expected to generate US $2.18 billion in retail revenue. DSS — the smaller of the two events — attracted 1.5 million visitors in 2006, primarily from other Middle East countries. Clothing and fashion trends are very important in the Middle East, because the population is very young (over 50% are under the age of 20, the median age is 22 in Saudi Arabia and 28 in UAE, compared to 36 in the United States, 39 in the United Kingdom and 42 in Germany) and affluent, with a strong interest in brands. It is a common sight to see women in the traditional *abaya* (black gown) dress and headscarf, wearing Manolo Blahnik high heels and carrying Gucci or Louis Vuitton handbags, whilst men dressed in the traditional Arab white *dishdasha* complement their outfit with Boss or Prada shoes and the obligatory Montblanc fountain pen in their breast pocket. Most Middle East nationals also possess an impressive stock of Western-style apparel, which is worn underneath their native dress outside the home, in the privacy of their homes and while travelling abroad. The younger generation (those below 30) is also increasingly dressed in Western style. Satellite television and other Western influences are pervasive.

There appears to be little brand loyalty in the purchase of clothes and footwear, that is people buy high-prestige brands, but will also chose whatever is currently the newest and most fashionable item available, the price being secondary. As the Arabic saying puts it: 'Eat what you like, but wear what other people like'. Being well dressed reflects well on the bearer. Other cultural and regional aspects also need to be taken into account. Women's clothing, for example tends to be more modest. Local people will not wear 'indecent' apparel — short skirts and tank tops — for religious reasons and most expatriate residents avoid them out of respect for the culture of their host country.

Regional differences regarding what is tolerated are huge. Whilst the UAE and Bahrain are very liberal, Saudi Arabia is at the other end of the spectrum. Women have to wear an *abaya* in public and a black headscarf. In practice, Western women wear the scarf around their shoulders and put it on if the religious police (*matowa*), who routinely patrol public areas, spot them. In Saudi Arabia, many of the high-end department stores have segregated sections for women, which are staffed exclusively with female staff. The Kingdom Centre in Riyadh has a whole floor dedicated to women which men are not allowed to enter and shops close during prayer times. Yet items such as lingerie and swimwear can be presented as they would be in London and Paris. Some of the brands are quite 'risqué', for example La Senza or La Perla. Censorship is less about the item of clothing itself and more about the advertising/merchandising. Pictures of women in swimsuits are still not acceptable in the Kingdom, but are tolerated in the UAE and Bahrain. Most of the rules — or at least the way they are applied — are quite ambiguous and can differ from place to place. In general, practices have become less restrictive over the years and this trend will continue.

Weather-related shopping patterns are very different from those in Europe. While it is incredibly hot from May to September, with temperatures hitting 50°C during daytime and hardly falling below 30°C at night, the winter months are pleasant — 20 to 25°C during the day and hardly below 15°C at night. Nevertheless, clothing retailers follow the European sales pattern, offering winter garments during the winter season, which are readily bought by shopping tourists. Russians, in particular, go on a shopping frenzy when visiting the Middle East, shelling out over US $5000 in retail outlets per visit to Dubai, followed by tourists from other Middle Eastern countries, with US $2760 per trip. Visitors to Dubai from Germany, Switzerland and the United Kingdom, on the other hand, appear to be more interested in passing their time on the beach, spending only around US $750 on shopping per visit. During the summer months, business tends to be slower, because there are fewer tourists (it is simply too hot) and because many locals are away on holiday in more moderate climate zones.

The local religious calendar offers a chance for retailers to take advantage of both the Islamic and the Christian festivities. Whilst the most important Christian season in the retail calendar is Christmas, the Islamic calendar adds Ramadan and *Eid al fitr* celebrations. *Eid al fitr* marks the end of the fasting month of Ramadan and people give each other presents, thus boosting retail sales. Because of the moon-based Islamic calendar year, the Eid season moves forward 11 days each year. In 2007, *Eid al fitr* was in mid-October.

Overall, the apparel market is split between a luxury segment dominated by global brands and many Indian-style local independent stores. The expectation is that the luxury segment will continue to experience healthy growth rates, while small shops will massively lose market share. The most significant development, however, is expected to take place in the underdeveloped middle-market segment represented by brands such as GAP, H&M, Zara and Giordano (Kuntze et al., 2007).

Where Sex Does Not Sell

The Middle East consumer is different from the Western consumer; in the former society cultural and religious sensitivity are of paramount importance. Companies substitute 'sex sells' in their advertisements with other, more demure messages. However, as the Middle East opens up to Western consumerism, the communication is changing. Showing people praying as part of an advertising campaign would have been impossible some years ago. Foreign companies are nevertheless advised to be careful when considering what their message should be and how to communicate it. The Jewish/Arab distinction is also prevalent; Montblanc, a maker of high-quality pens and jewellery, experienced unexpected problems when entering the Middle East market. It was in 1910 when the three founders, while looking at the white cap of Europe's highest mountain, had the idea of calling the brand Montblanc. The logo with the white star was created in 1913, with a logo inspired by the snow-covered mountain, but when Montblanc started their market roll-out in the Middle East, they realised that many local customers hesitated to purchase their products, because they regarded the logo as representing the Jewish Star of David. In the Arab world, religion is of great importance and customers are unlikely to purchase any product with religious symbols — other than Islamic ones. Only when Montblanc's management understood this and started large-scale communication efforts to explain the origin of their logo did customers accept the brand.

High Levels of Service

As a result of the low wage structure and the availability of a large, mostly Asian, workforce, high-level service is affordable for retailers. For example, as BMW has learned, Middle East consumers expect a different level of service compared to what is available in Paris, New York or London. For example, in the West consumers might have to wait 3 days for their cars to be repaired. In the UAE, customers expect immediate service. As in most emerging markets, customer loyalty is still at a very low level.

BMW decided to set up a quick-service team for its top-end customers. Quick service would not only include immediate service of the vehicle, but also picking up the car and providing a replacement car for the time the service takes. BMW has been very successful with this approach. Sales volumes in the region rose steadily, especially in the top segment of their 7 Series, and BMW's performance in the UAE is very strong. Whilst the 7 Series accounts for 4.5% of BMW's global vehicle sales, it makes up roughly 30% of sales volume in the UAE. In addition, consumers in the Middle East do not buy cars to drive — they buy them to be chauffeured around in, which many cars top range BMW's are the 'stretched version'.

Concluding Remarks

The consumer of today is frequently time-constrained, female, looking for value, wanting an experience and with lots of choice — and this is likely to be the case up to 2030. Dubai is the destination consumers will visit to do their special leisure shopping — some shoppers would call it paradise. In this one city, people can shop the globe, trawling souks for Arabian products or exotic goods from around the region — Iranian caviar, Persian carpets or Aladdin slippers from Afghanistan (Carter & Dunston, 2006). Dubai is also where celebrities shop for clothes from the latest Stella McCartney collection and those of other international designers. Dubai is a place for gold, diamonds, caviar and the finest champagnes. It is the ultimate experience of luxury and ostentatious consumption. Strategic policies have made Dubai what it is today — an international, luxury-shopping destination, which is not only for the super-rich but also for the world's middle classes. Dubai is not about authenticity, sustainability and everything green — but about pure indulgence and conspicuous consumption.

Chapter 11

Bridget Jones Goes on Holiday

> Met this guy last night on a blind date. He is 34, single, tall, a lawyer in the city with a GSOH. I wish, I hope … he asks me out. Haven't had a decent s**g in ages. I hope he invites me away for the weekend. Haven't been on a romantic date since I can't remember when and even then, it was a disaster.
>
> Bridget Jones writing in her dairy on 31st January 2030

Being Single

There are lots of Bridget Joneses in society, so many, in fact, that by 2030 single females who live alone could represent 19% of UK households. Today, holidays can act as a meeting place for singles. For companies such as www.exploreworldwide.com the core market is the single traveller, while www.elenasmodels.com provides holidays for men looking for Russian wives. The main purchasers of 'Lonely Planet' guides (Yeoman & McMahon-Beattie, 2005) are single, middle-class females, and cities like New York are symbolised by Jessica in 'Sex in the City'. According to the 2000 US Census Bureau (Rogers, 2006), the number of people in the United States who live alone jumped from 17% of all households in 1970 to 26% in 2000.

There are 95.7 million single American adults according to the US Census Bureau (Rodgers, 2006), with New York having the highest population of unmarried adults. According to the Travel Industry Association (Rogers, 2006), nearly 25% of US travellers (34.8 million adults) take a vacation on their own. The average solo vacationer is 42 years of age, with an annual household income of $54,000. More than 25% have a professional or managerial occupation, 53% are male and 47% female, and 38% have graduated from university. Even married people sometimes prefer to holiday on their own; one in seven of the over-50s take holidays alone to escape the 'other half', according to research by Saga Holidays (2007). This research highlights the fact that going on holiday alone to meet new friends is a major driver for many and that 5% are searching for a new partner (whilst still married!).

In China there will be 10% more men than women by 2040 as a result of rising prosperity, the changing roles of women, new career options and the country's one-child policy. Across the world, the demographic shift away from married life and the subsequent rise in the number of independent singles have resulted in the *Bridget Jones* phenomena.[1]

In 2005, single-person households represented almost 30% of all households in the United Kingdom; over the past 25 years the average age of people at the time of their first marriage has increased significantly, rising in 2005 to 28 years for women and 30 years for men, a far cry from the 1980s when it was 22 for women and 24 for men. In the United Kingdom, the lifestyle of many single people aged between 25 and 40 is characterised by a focus on career and a busy social life. When it comes to holidays, therefore, many singles are looking for a wide variety of leisure services and activities that offer relaxation and a means by which to alleviate the stress created by day-to-day living. Furthermore, career-minded singles are more inclined to spend their higher-than-average disposable income on treating themselves, rather than on family life. This presents a potentially high return on investment for companies targeting this growing consumer group with their travel products and services. Without doubt, singles now represent a major consumer group in the United Kingdom.

Singleton is a term that is coming to represent a more important, durable life stage: the pre-family life stage is set to last longer and, therefore, become more important. Bridget Jones hasn't abandoned marriage; in fact, she still considers it to be a mystical, romantic and ideal state, while at the same time regarding it as a sullied, outdated institution. Many people are clearly die-hard optimists and retain the belief that marriage is still synonymous with true love, and there is unlikely to be a change in this attitude any time soon, so marriage is safeguarded for a few years yet!

Perhaps the most important point to remember is that the status of being single has changed dramatically since the 1950s. Once a stigma, being single is now largely considered exciting, a chance to experience personal development and opportunity before the responsibilities of marriage and parenthood crowd in. With this in mind, this chapter looks at the world of Bridget Jones and singletons on holiday.

The Changing Nature of Singletons

In order to pin down who we mean when we talk about singletons, it perhaps helps to begin by looking at how people's attitudes towards marriage and singleness have changed. In the 1950s, divorce was very rare, with only a tiny percentage of marriages ending that way. The expectation was that people would marry young and stay married. As the traditional marriage vows suggest, a woman was cared for by her father until such time as the husband took over the paternalistic role. There was only a short period of time in which a young woman could have sole responsibility for her life. Women also bore more children, with the mean number of

---

1. Bridget Jones is a column, serialised in UK newspapers, that chronicles the life of Bridget Jones, a thirty-something single woman living in London, surrounded by a surrogate 'urban family' of friends as she tries to make sense of life and love in the 1990s. The column was turned into a successful film 'Bridget Jones Diary' starring Renée Zellweger in 2001.

children per woman being about 2.5. In post-war Britain, being single was usually a momentary aberration between coming of age at 21 and being married. A 1958 US study (Silverstein et al., 2005) found that nearly all Americans assumed a woman would stay single only if she were ugly, immoral or neurotic.

By 2007, attitudes had obviously changed. In fact, a range of pop-cultural portrayals have turned that stereotype on its head: we no longer assume that single women are ugly and immoral. Single people are now standard-bearers for beauty, admired for their independence and self-reliance. People's lives are also very different from the 1950s. They marry later, often having lived outside the family 'independently' for a number of years, and many women expect to work until retirement age, including the period when they are bringing up a family. Critically, the fact that almost all women work for at least a part of their lives means that they are often economically independent and no longer need to rely on a man — father or husband — to take care of them and their offspring. These social and cultural shifts have created an environment where the meaning of marriage has shifted: marriage has become something people can now approach as a desirable living arrangement rather than as a social imperative.

It is a well-documented fact that the number of single-person households is on the rise — and has been for decades. In the 1960s, half of all households in the United Kingdom contained a couple with children — the traditional, nuclear model. A further 25% consisted of a couple either waiting to start a family or at the other end of the family stage (i.e. empty-nesters). The UK government forecasts indicate that by 2021 the proportion of homes containing nuclear families will have dropped to just a fifth of households — a massive decline since the 1960s. In place of model nuclear households, that is, a family with children, there will be a huge increase in single-person households from just 4% in 1961 to 20% in 2021 (Figure 11.1). This means that there will be equal numbers of single-person and family households. It could be predicted that by 2030 the number of single-person households containing a person under 35 will grow by about 70%.

Figure 11.2 shows the British Household Panel Survey (BHPS) data by lifestyle stage and age. Unlike most other surveys, the BHPS asked whether single people had a girlfriend or boyfriend, demonstrating a distinction between people with and those without partners of any kind. Unsurprisingly, the proportion of married people increases steeply between the ages of 25 and 35, at which point nearly two-thirds of the population are married. The proportion of married people peaks at almost 80% of 60 year olds then declines as the death of the husband or wife affects households. Cohabitation, on the other hand, follows the opposite trajectory. The proportion is highest amongst the under-thirties, but drops off as people marry — and represents just 5% of the over-fifties.

If married and cohabiting people are grouped together — those people in 'committed relationships' — this peak of 80% is reached much sooner, that is, at age 35. The BHPS also tells us that in 2004 the number of singletons in Britain had overtaken married couples — the Bridget Jones society had arrived! Further observations show that the number of people saying they have a boyfriend or girlfriend declines among older age groups to just 5% of the over-forties, presumably

Household composition as a proportion of all households

nVision forecast

2001 based forecast

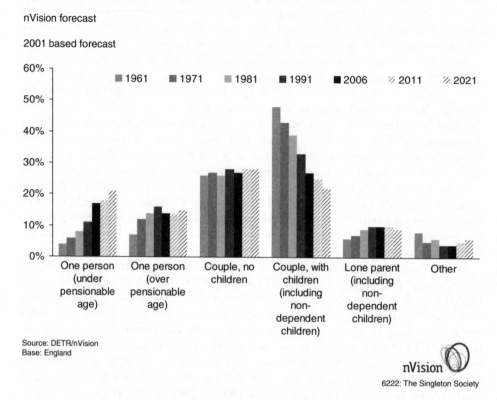

Source: DETR/nVision
Base: England

nVision

6222: The Singleton Society

Figure 11.1: Household composition in England.

because those relationships transfer into marriage or cohabitation. Just 13% of people in their early thirties are truly single, that is, without a partner of any kind. Between the ages of 30 and 60, at any one point 15% of people will be single: this is equivalent to one in every six or seven people, which, next to the 1950s' model, is high. When we divide the 'truly single' category by gender, then two interesting differences emerge. Typically, men marry later in life than women and marry women younger than them, with the result that they stay single for longer than women. However, men also die earlier, so at the other end of the age spectrum there are more widows than widowers.

Overall, then, today one in four 25- to 40-year-olds in Britain are truly singletons, which equals over 3 million people. This is undeniably an important life-stage which will become more important as a demographic grouping in the future.

In order to separate the widowed and divorced from the pre-married, Figures 11.3 through 11.6 isolate 25- to 40-year-olds. Figure 11.3 shows BHPS data on how much childfree individuals spend on leisure, segmented by relationship status. The data here is merged to group married and cohabiting people together into 'couples', while singletons are separated into those with or without a boyfriend or girlfriend, that is,

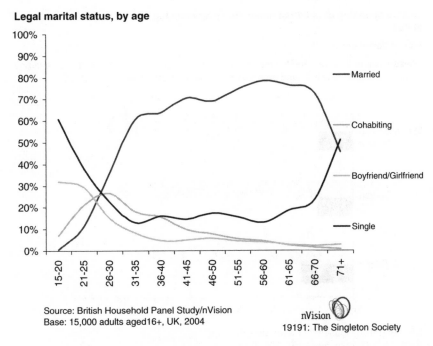

Legal marital status, by age

Source: British Household Panel Study/nVision
Base: 15,000 adults aged16+, UK, 2004

nVision
19191: The Singleton Society

Figure 11.2: Legal marital status in the United Kingdom.

'in a relationship' or truly single. Just 9% of people in relationships — whether live-in or not — spend less than £10 ($20) each month on leisure, versus 13% of singles. And the opposite is true: you are more likely to be a big spender — over £40 ($80) per month — if you have a partner with whom you do not live. This data suggests that leisure providers have to work harder to squeeze cash out of singletons than they might have thought.

It can sometimes be more revealing to consider attitudes towards money, rather than actual amounts spent since it may just be that singletons are younger than married/cohabiting couples and therefore are earning less. This attitudinal statement from the BHPS (Figure 11.4) asked respondents how well they thought they were managing financially. The findings show that if people are not in a live-in relationship, having a boyfriend or girlfriend does not seem to alter their perception of their financial stability (presumably because they continue to regard their finances as separate) (Figure 11.5).

The differences between cohabiting couples and singletons are negligible for the childfree, with over 70% of singletons managing fine. However, there is quite a disparity when children are added to the picture: again, being in a couple seems to offer more financial security to a family, but we see a considerable difference between those with children: three-quarters of all couples say they are coping fine, but less than half of single parents agree with this statement. This is not a huge surprise since single-parent families obviously have only one income and perhaps not even that if

Leisure spending of childfree under 40, by relationship status

Amount spent per month

"Please look at this card and tell me about how much you personally spend in an average month on leisure activities, and entertainment and hobbies, other than eating out?"

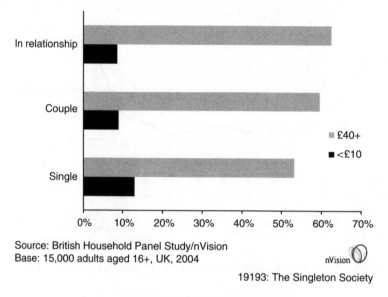

Source: British Household Panel Study/nVision
Base: 15,000 adults aged 16+, UK, 2004

nVision

19193: The Singleton Society

Figure 11.3: Leisure spending.

the parent has to take care of the children on a full-time basis. Looking more closely at the data from the Office of National Statistics (ONS), we can see that, because many singletons are just starting out, they have a much higher expenditure on the house compared to established families, but at the same time they also spend over half of what a couple together spend on alcohol and tobacco. They also spend more money and time in restaurants in groups, which Watters (2004) calls 'tribes'.

This assumption about eating out is borne out by the Future Foundation's *Changing Lives* Survey data on visiting restaurants. The Future Foundation asked several questions about people's leisure activities, two of which are broken down here by marital status so we can get a closer look at our singletons' lifestyles. Obviously, one of the key facts about a non-cohabiting couple is that they must routinely deal with the 'your place or mine' question, so perhaps it is no wonder that a higher proportion of them are likely to say they eat out once a month. An identical proportion of single people and cohabiting couples eat out once a month, but married couples are clearly missing out here. A singleton is more likely to go to a pub than a restaurant, with a greater proportion saying they go to a pub at least once a month. Three-quarters of people with a non-cohabiting lover are frequent pub visitors versus less than half of married couples. Similar statistics emerge from data on visits to the cinema; singletons with a boyfriend or girlfriend are more likely to

Proportion of under 40s who say they are "living comfortably/doing alright" financially

By relationship status

"How well would you say you yourself are managing financially these days? Would you say you are...."

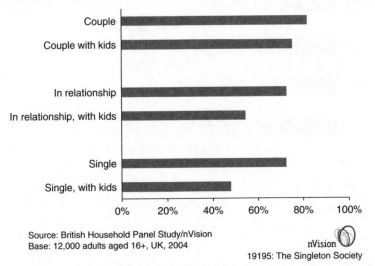

Source: British Household Panel Study/nVision
Base: 12,000 adults aged 16+, UK, 2004

nVision
19195: The Singleton Society

Figure 11.4: Financial management.

Eating out, by relationship status

Proportion of under 40s who eat out as an occasion at least once a month

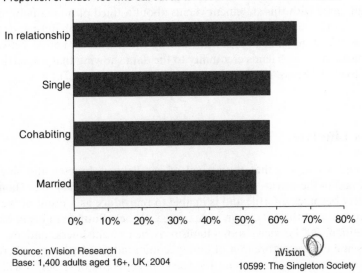

Source: nVision Research
Base: 1,400 adults aged 16+, UK, 2004

nVision
10599: The Singleton Society

Figure 11.5: Eating out.

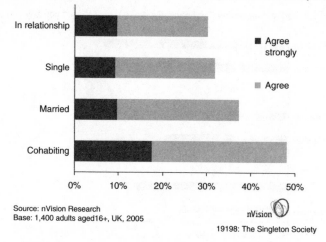

Proportion of who agree/strongly agree that they are under stress in their everyday lives, by relationship status

"Please say how much you agree or disagree with the following statements...I find my everyday life is very stressful"

Figure 11.6: Time pressures.

indulge in a range of leisure activities than the truly single person. Having a non-cohabiting lover is, therefore, a driver of a broader leisure portfolio.

Perhaps one of the reasons singletons spend so much time in the pub is that their lives are just that little bit less full of activity; not having someone else to worry about clearly takes off some of the time pressures. It is, however, somewhat surprising to see just how much more stressed cohabiting couples seem to be than married couples: almost half agree with this statement versus about a third of non-cohabiting couples (Figure 11.6). This may be indicative of the adjustments of cohabiting, or perhaps a sign of the difficulties that people have during the transition period between single life and marriage. It also lends credibility to the data showing that unmarried couples are more likely to break up than married couples (Figure 11.7).

Bridget's Lifestyle

Some people would say that the arrival of the Bridget Joneses and single society means the end of the world — as portrayed in the film *Children of Men* (James, 2006), when society becomes infertile and is unable to reproduce as a result of the changing roles of women and their rejection of marriage. Robert Putman in his book, *Bowling Alone* (Putman, 2001), views individualism as being selfishness, and putting one's own goals and desires before that of family, community and country, whereas Ethan Watters' commentary (2004) about the social phenomena of tribes in which friends become the new family, draws different conclusions. Watters argues that marriage — or, at least, the committed relationship — is still the key social unit in our society,

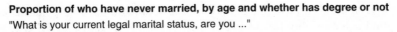

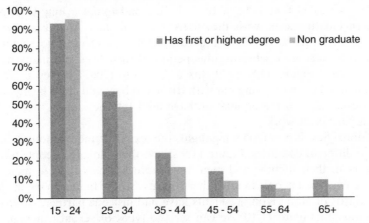

Source: British Household Panel Study/nVision
Base: 4,445 adults aged16+ who have never married, UK, 2004

nVision
19200: The Singleton Society

Figure 11.7: Education by marital status.

and something to which most of us aspire. Watters' research revealed that well-educated, ambitious young urbanites were those most likely to want to celebrate their wealth, independence and freedom by holding off on commitments and responsibilities for a few years. Having chosen to live outside a traditional family for a decade or more, they were forming new kinds of 'family' with their friends, replicating the networks of care that a nuclear family used to supply.

So, is delaying marriage a middle-class trend, as suggested by Watters (2004)? By examining the BHPS data, we can see that the level of education attained does have an impact on the speed with which people pair off. Having a degree means that a person is less likely to marry — perhaps because those with degrees often gravitate to urban areas in order to find work and then set up their own 'tribes', which make living outside a family more fun and less arduous. Further analysis suggests that the higher the social grade, the more sexual partners people have. For example, ABC1s are clocking up an average of fourteen partners before marriage versus nine for the lower social grades.

So, What about Bridget Jones' Love Life and Her Search for Mr Right?

In today's society, a host of companies are cashing in on the singleton's desire for a date: speed dating, slow dating, online dating, singles' holidays, singles' columns in newspapers and singles' clubs. The lonely hearts' columns once seemed like a last resort, but now busy young singletons have lots of socially acceptable options. There is arguably less fear and anxiety surrounding the dating process. Terms such as *spinster* and *on the shelf* have fallen out of our lexicon, and the dating market extends well beyond catering only for people in their twenties. A survey by GMI (2006) on Internet dating revealed that 10% of those polled had found a long-term partner through Internet dating sites, with Brazilians, Germans and Americans being the most active online when searching for partners. One might even go so far as to suggest that singletons are celebrating this period of their lives and many find that being single is fun. Figure 11.8 highlights a YouGov (2007) survey of methods employed to find a date, with going out with friends to bars and clubs being the most popular; however, 12% of the population have used Internet dating sites and 23% have found a partner at work.

Durex's Global Sex Survey (2005) highlights the sexual attitudes amongst different groups and in different countries. Figure 11.9 shows that, globally, people have nine sexual partners in their lifetime and men have more partners than women. Turks have more partners than people in any other country, whilst Indians have the fewest. Almost two-thirds of Hong Kong residents have had just one partner, compared to 12% in Norway. In Figure 11.10, we can see the types of sexual experiences UK people have had, with 44% of them having used a vibrator when having sex and 17% having had three in a bed.

Figure 11.11 shows that 50% of UK consumers have had sex in a car and 15% in public transport; however, only 3% are members of the mile-high club (having sex in an aeroplane). This insight raises a more general point — that British attitudes towards sex have changed; no longer is the long-running play 'No Sex, Please, We're British' a reflection of society. Today, the sex shop chain, Anne Summers, is found on many UK high streets. It has been a long time since pre-marital sex was taken off the moral blacklist, but as attitudes towards sex continue to become more and more relaxed, one could argue that marriage may become less and less relevant to people who are not yet planning to have a family.

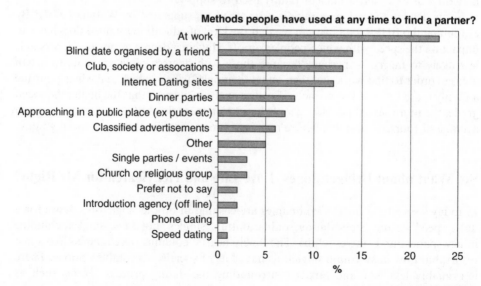

Figure 11.8: Dating methods people have used at any time (*Source*: YouGov, 2007).

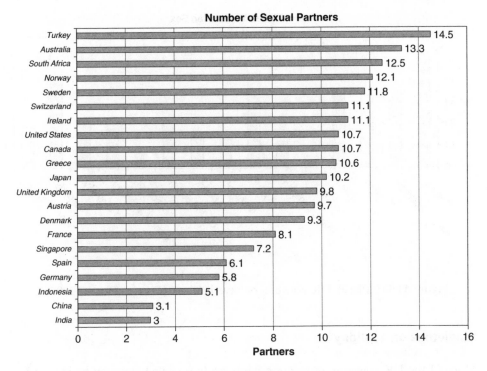

Figure 11.9: Selected sexual partners (*Source*: Durex, 2005).

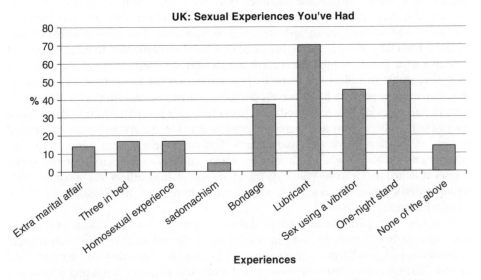

Figure 11.10: Sexual experiences you've had (*Source*: Durex, 2005).

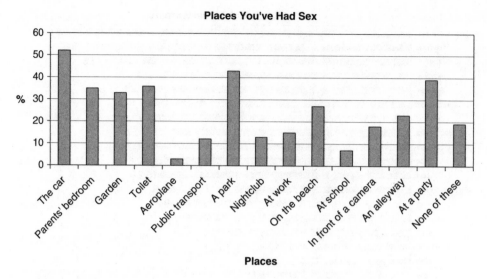

Figure 11.11: Places UK consumers have had sex (*Source*: Durex, 2005).

Singletons on Holiday

Much of the UK singleton population has already travelled alone on holiday, often during their gap year — or even earlier, that is, during their student years. This backpacker market remains well catered for and continues to flourish because of demand from travellers in their late teens or early twenties. However, career-focused singles, with higher disposable incomes plus an intense and work-filled life, are looking to indulge themselves more while on holiday and are willing to pay the price for higher-end service, unlike cash-strapped backpackers. The main drawback faced by those travelling alone is the higher price of a holiday, compared to going as part of a couple or a group. Whilst the airfare, meals and souvenir costs are the same for everyone, single travellers are made to pay surcharges for accommodation, making their trip more expensive. Most travel operators, whose packages are often affected by the surcharges levied by accommodation providers, also place an additional surcharge on single travellers, who are therefore penalised twice. Safety and security abroad is also of concern to singles, particularly female travellers who venture to new destinations on their own. Additionally, some singles feel conscious of the social stigma attached to 25- to 40-year-olds travelling solo, whilst others feel uncomfortable dining alone on holiday. Such issues currently impinge on the development of the sector (Euromonitor, 2006).

Very few tour operators have adapted their operations to offer packages for single, upwardly mobile consumers, and in consequence the industry remains surprisingly underdeveloped and disproportionately biased towards catering for couples and groups. Euromonitor (2006) believes that the tourism industry is missing a lucrative trick in not responding to the practical, cost-related and emotional restrictions which affect those holidaying alone. Indeed, the market for individual travel may be the next big thing for tour operators to focus on.

Singletons have different needs from those holidaying in couples or groups. In some ways they are more flexible, because they are not restricted to choosing a holiday which appeals to all members of their family or group. However, whilst this makes them open to a wider range of options, it also means that the needs of the single traveller are much higher in terms of specific requirements, safety issues and demand for more challenging and rewarding holidays. Presented with the freedom to choose a holiday to satisfy only themselves, single travellers often feel a strong urge to take part in activities which they could not do if they had to take into account another person's tastes. They are, for example, more inclined to consider adventure holidays and extreme sports. Themed holidays linked to hobbies, such as trekking, surfing, bird-watching, horse riding or yoga, as well as spa retreats and exotic city breaks, are also all niche-market products which operators would do well to offer single travellers.

More so than couples and groups, singletons also feel the need to take part in activities where they gain a sense of achievement. As such, themed holidays, educational holidays, volunteering tourism and ecotourism are all predicted to do well if correctly targeted at the singles' market. Holidays where new skills can be learned, such as courses on cookery, writing and massage, and sporting holidays, are also likely to be successful if marketed to singles. With young working singles willing to spend more on travel abroad or to achieve a lifetime ambition, a plethora of opportunities exist for travel specialists and niche travel agents to put together mid-to-luxury holidays. For single male travellers in particular, unique trips involving the latest technology, including trips on high-speed boats or other cutting-edge transport, are expected to be successful.

Has Bridget Ever Considered a Dating Holiday?

Bridget could always try a specialist 'singles' tour operator. With the rise in popularity of dating and online dating agencies, such as www.datingdirect.com, www.match.com and www.streetcupid.com, holidays marketed as spin-offs and tour operators offering a similar matchmaking service have begun to flourish. Thanks to the long-running television programme 'Blind Date', where the winning couple actually go on a holiday as their date, consumers are familiar with the concept of singles aged between 25 and 40 finding romance on a 'holiday date'. Tour operators now provide unattached travellers with a similar product, but without Cilla Black and her show as the middleman! Nevertheless, a significant proportion of single travellers remain uncomfortable with the social stigma associated with traditional 18–30 or Club-Med-type holidays and, as far as possible, prefer to avoid giving the impression that they are actively looking for a partner. Therefore, holidays which announce just that will be rejected by a large part of the single traveller market.

Whilst the 'going it alone' market remains small, some businesses in the United Kingdom have already forged ahead, recognising the potential of the independent singles' market. Established companies that help 'pair up' travelling companions, including www.thelmaandlouise.com and www.companions2travel.co.uk, have been in the market for some time and there is no emphasis in their holidays on travellers finding a partner for life. www.solosholidays.co.uk and www.friendshiptravel.com are amongst specialist operators cleverly catering for young and unattached single travellers who want to meet new people, whilst not actually highlighting the fact that they are full-blown dating agencies.

The rapidly developing online market has also stimulated a small, but growing, market for media content websites, where single travellers can exchange tips and ideas on travelling alone, as well as arrange to meet up somewhere en route. These chat sites provide a useful platform for singles to get advice and share experiences, and to exchange photos in case they meet a potential travel partner. There are also abundant opportunities for tour operators to develop spin-offs from travel services for singles, including holiday reunion events in the United Kingdom or abroad or reunion holiday packages for those who first met when holidaying alone. The potential growth of this product is made evident by the success of www.friendsreunited.co.uk, which is the leading reunion site in the United Kingdom and now boasts more than 1 million paying subscribers. This concept would also create a loyal consumer base of repeat purchasers, providing opportunities for singles to combine meeting up and socialising and travelling to new destinations.

The lucrative singles market will also provide opportunities for tie-ups between online dating agencies and travel retailers, where companies such as www.lastminute.com and www.match.com could potentially join forces to offer combined holiday/dating packages for those seeking to form partnerships whilst travelling. Such a concept is likely to be incredibly appealing to this generation of busy single people, who desire alternative and fun packages to counterbalance their hectic lifestyle, but are also on the look out for a partner for life (Euromonitor, 2006).

What about Mr Darcy; Where Will He Find His Bridget Jones?

It's getting harder for Mr Darcy to find a woman; according to research by Professor Wiseman of Hertfordshire University (Johnstone, 2006), Bridget Jones will make up her mind about a prospective partner within 30 s of meeting a man, whereas men take longer to reach a decision (see also Figure 11.12). No wonder Mr Darcy has turned to Eastern Europe for a prospective partner, through such sites as www.eastwestmatch.com, www.russian-rendezvous.co.uk and www.elenasmodels.com

According to the UK Home Office (Dudley, Roughton, Fidler, & Woollacot, 2006) 23,645 temporary visas were granted to wives and fiancées for up to 6 months prior to their forming a legal relationship. The biggest increase in the number of visas has been for Europe (outside the EU, namely Ukraine, Russia and Belarus) rising from 2645 in 2002 to 3223 in 2006. In the United States, according to the US Citizenship and Immigration Services, more than 200 mail-order-bride companies arrange between

Bridget Jones at the Husband Shop

A brand new store has just opened in London - and it sells husbands. When women go to choose a husband, they have to follow the instructions at the entrance:

"You may visit this store only once. There are 6 floors and the value of the products increase as you ascend the flights. You may choose any item from a particular floor, or may choose to go up to the next floor, but you can't go back down except to leave the building!"

So, a woman goes to the Husband Store to find a husband.

On the 1st floor the sign on the door reads:

Floor 1 - These men have jobs.

The 2nd floor sign reads:

Floor 2 - These men have jobs and love kids.

The 3rd floor sign reads:

Floor 3 - These men have jobs, love kids and are extremely good looking.

"Great," she thinks, but feels compelled to keep going.

She goes to the 4th floor and the sign reads:

Floor 4 - These men have jobs, love kids, are drop-dead good looking and help with housework.

"Fantastic" she exclaims, "I can hardly stand it!"

Still, she goes to the 5th floor and sign reads:

Floor 5 - These men have jobs, love kids, are drop-dead gorgeous, help with housework and have a strong romantic streak.

She is so tempted to stay, but she goes to the 6th floor and the sign reads:

Floor 6 - You are visitor 31,456,012 to this floor. There are no men on this floor. This floor exists solely as proof that women are impossible to please. Thank you for shopping at the Husband Store.

Supplied by an anonymous friend

Figure 11.12: Bridget Jones joke.

4000 and 6000 marriages every year. Googling mail-order brides on the Internet will bring up 4.5 million links.

For Mr Darcy, choosing the woman of his dreams from a catalogue of exotic Eastern European or Asian beauties has never been easier, nor has it ever been more popular among Western men — particularly since agencies such as Russian Rendezvous UK assure clients that most of their ladies speak English and that many 'prefer to meet a man 10 to 20 years older than themselves'. Foreign Affair, one of the largest providers of romantic tours to Eastern Europe, typically charges £2500 for a two-week tour of Russian cities, including several social events where the ratio of men to women is 1:35.

Concluding Remarks

Singletons in society are becoming more important as the pre-family life stage is set to last longer and, therefore, the value of singletons to the tourism industry can only become more valuable. Holidays for Bridget Jones become a meeting place for romance, social networking, activities or volunteering. Bridget Jones in 2030 will be aspirational and well educated, will have seen the world and will have read many Lonely Planet guides. With this in mind, we can see that tourism has many opportunities. Hopefully, Bridget Jones will get a decent s**g by 2030; the only problem according to social forecaster Richard Scase (2000) is that single women in their thirties and forties have the well-developed social networks and confidence that men lack. Men define themselves more by their work, and relax with too much unhealthy food and drink, a recipe for isolation and loneliness. Single women, by contrast, are more likely to see friends, explore their spiritual side and relax with yoga. Consequently Mr Darcy might not be up to Bridget Jones' standards by 2030!

Chapter 12

The Authentic Tourist: A Journey through Africa in 2030

Kilimanjaro and the African plains are icons of this fascinating continent and two of the main reasons for people to visit, but with the drawbacks of high temperatures, lack of a good transport infra- structure and uncertainty about security. Africa in 2005 was very different from the Africa of 2030. Siubhan Daly is a 28-year-old singleton from Northern Ireland taking a three-month sabbatical backpacking trip through Africa. Having watched programmes about the continent on the Discovery Channel, Siubhan became fascinated by Africa and had long wanted to visit. Her holiday began in Madagascar. The island has protected conservation status because of the low numbers of lemur monkeys and in 2015 the government introduced a US $2000 ecological tax to help pay for both tourism development and conservation measures in a balanced way. Siubhan was on the island for three weeks to help a local lemur sanctuary with the project, for which she paid a charity US $10,000 for the privilege.

Madagascar's strict policy on the ecology and sustainable tourism has meant that the island has maintained the viability of its local species and landscape compared with other countries in Africa, which have suffered from massive over-development as a result of allowing tourism to expand without putting ecological safeguards in place. The price of success in tourism has resulted in the despoliation of tourism icons, such as Kilimanjaro. Siubhan watched a television documentary about how the area around the mountain had been over-developed with pathways, souvenir shops and a funicular railway which spoiled the landscape and damaged irreversibly the fauna, flora and ecology of Africa's most famous mountain. The idea behind the scheme had been to make the mountain as accessible as Table Top Mountain near Cape Town. However, the magic of Kilimanjaro had been the remote wilderness and isolation, which was lost when the mountain became a mass tourism destination, accessible to everyone. The Government had thought that mass ecotourism was the answer to regeneration — but once you introduce the mass, the magic is lost.

Upon leaving Madagascar, Siubhan flew to Johannesburg to begin an overland South East Africa adventure covering South Africa, Mozambique, Malawi and Zambia with Southern African Drifters, one of Africa's leading, overland adventure tourism operators. The journey across the Mpumalanga region of the Blyde River Canyon was magical and in the South Africa Kruger Park Siubhan saw the 'big five'. She went snorkelling in the India Ocean off Mozambique and was bitten by lots of mosquitoes on Lake Malawi. The trip finished in Livingston, the adventure capital of the region, where Siubhan tried her hand at white-water rafting and bungee jumping. The trip with the drifters meant sleeping under canvas with like-minded travellers and sharing the cooking and daily chores. Overall, Siubhan wishes she could stay longer, but work beckons.

Siubhan's travels through Africa in 2030

Introduction — An Authentic Experience

Several themes occur within this scenario. Siubhan is a wildlife tourist, taking a career break, combining a tour in Africa with a search for new and meaningful experiences. She is staying longer and going 'deeper' than most tourists. This is what many tourism experts call authenticity!

As the experience economy matures, it evolves into authenticity because consumers search for real experiences rather than 'products' which are manufactured (Pine, 2004). There is a growing desire to find experiences and products that are original and real, not contaminated by being fake or impure. This trend away from impurity, the virtual, the spun, manufactured and the mass-produced in a world seemingly full of falseness needs further explanation.

The great writers, Plato (Guthrie, 1987), Dostoevsky (Stuchebrukhov, 2004), Freud (Gertner, 2000) and Baudrillard (1983) have all explored the concept of authenticity in order to understand its meaning in people's lives. Wilmott and Nelson (2003) have identified the complexity of consumerism, with consumers seeking new meaning, consistent with Maslow's self-actualisation concept. Initially, people are concerned about wider issues such as the environment, animal rights or Third World hunger. The movement to self-actualisation is a search for a deeper meaning and finding a sense of worth beyond material possessions. It is a fulfilment of self which moves beyond goods and services and on to experiences. At one level it results in increased spending on holidays, eating out, the theatre and so on. But it also includes special experiences such as white-water rafting or spending a weekend at a health spa. Thus, authenticity has emerged as a selection criterion for Siubhan when she made her decision on where to go on her holiday.

The desire for new experiences which are truly authentic and meaningful has resulted in more people — like Siubhan — taking a career break to travel through

Africa or to undertake a similar adventure; it has become a mainstream activity. Career breaks are gap years for adults, a chance to take life by the scruff of the neck and give it a shake, to take a pause for breath, to grab an opportunity to fulfil a lifelong dream. Whether they are young professionals or baby-boomers in their fifties, more and more people are taking time out to travel the world in an authentic way. Actor Ewan McGregor stepped off the Hollywood set to embark on a 20,000-mile tour around the world on a motorcycle. According to Mintel (2004c), the age groups that are more likely to undertake this kind of adventure are 25–34 year olds and 35–44 year olds, influenced largely by affluence and a desire for something more ambitious.

Today, career breaks or sabbaticals are seen as respectable. The Confederation of British Industry (CBI) survey of employment trends (Hindle, Bindloss, Hargreaves, Kirby, & Nystrom, 2006) showed that a quarter of firms offered their employees the opportunity to take a career break and over a third of Britain's high earners had considered or were actually taking a career break (amongst those under 34, the percentage was nearly half). Today, people no longer live to work, but rather work to live. Many adventure travel operators such as www.trailfinders.com or www.exploreworldwide.com offer trips of up to 28 weeks exploring continents, although these holidays can be broken down into shorter periods. People can spend months travelling through Africa or opt for just 3 weeks in one particular country. Another way to have a meaningful experience is to take part in a volunteering holiday and this sector has had a significant growth in the past few years. A number of organisations such as www.changingworlds.co.uk offer placements for 3 to 6 months, working in schools, orphanages or charities in countries such as Chile, India and Tanzania. Other organisations such as www.conservationafrica.net arrange for people to become involved in a wide range of conservation and research projects on game reserves in Southern Africa.

Trends that Will Influence the Authentic Tourist

What are the trends which will shape people's desire for an authentic experience? The tourist in 2030 is better educated, more sophisticated, has travelled the world, is concerned about the environment and wants a better quality of life. These facts lead to the conclusion that they have a desire for 'real' experiences rather than something false.

Nine trends which will shape the authentic tourist have been identified from the scenarios (Table 12.1) Let us look at the evidence, make assumptions and draw conclusions about the future.

Trend 1: A Global Network

'It is not what you know but whom you know' — that is the classic saying about how to get on in the world. Today, people, unlike previous generations, are free to choose connections and influences (whether the democratisation of the family, the phenomenon of blogging, the exponential rise of email or the establishment of personal

Table 12.1: Trends shaping the authentic tourist.

Trend 1	A global network
Trend 2	Ethical consumption and volunteering
Trend 3	The affluent consumer and the desire for new experiences in faraway places
Trend 4	The educated consumer
Trend 5	The role of the media
Trend 6	Individualism
Trend 7	Time pressures and authenticity
Trend 8	Busy lifestyles and getting away
Trend 9	Our affection for wildlife

contacts). Today there are fewer social boundaries. Technology has revolutionised personal communications and produced a global network knowledge society. Travel and the Internet have brought new tastes, interests, awareness of new ideas and destinations. Long-lost friendships are rekindled on www.friendsunited.com. Openness and transparency have become the norm. Technology has become an enabler. The desire for human contact is as strong as it has always been (Brass, 2005). The consumer is very much part of the global network society.

Trend 2: Ethical Consumption and Volunteering

There are very few markets in the United Kingdom not affected by the trend in ethical consumption. Wilmot (2003), in his book, *Citizen Brands,* recognises that the more affluent consumers (who are also better educated and more concerned about the environment) are turning to ethical consumption as a means of contributing to society, which results in the development of citizen brands, where the good of society is at the heart of the brand. One of the best examples of this has been the rise of Fair Trade over the past decade (Yeoman & McMahon-Beattie, 2006). Growth in the number of products under the Fair Trade label, which was launched in 1995, has stood at between 40 to 90% per annum. The brand has expanded from one kind of coffee to 250 foods, including fruit, juices, vegetables, snacks, wine, tea, sugar, honey and nuts, all sold at a premium price. By using the principles of ethical purchasing and citizen brands, individuals contribute to the society they live in. This movement towards ethical consumption is accompanied by a trend of inconspicuous consumption where consumers do not broadcast their personal success by ostentatious display. In line with this change in consumerism, volunteering is re emerging as a tourism experience, whether helping in a lemur sanctuary in Africa (as in Siubhan's scenario) or walking the Great Wall of China for AIDS research, or using a gap year to help build houses in Thailand. In this chapter, we observe the issues of sustainability and community involvement as a manifestation of ethical consumption.

Trend 3: The Affluent Consumer and the Desire for New Experiences in Faraway Places

According to the CIA, by 2020 the world GDP will grow by 50% (Hutchings, 2004). Such a forecast puts to bed the myth of economic decline, as hypothecated by a number of economists (Yeoman, 2004b). In the UK household disposable income has grown threefold in real terms between the early 1950s and 2000. This is an annual average increase of 2.5% per annum. This increase has had a major impact on the material aspects of people's lives; not only have televisions, telephones and washing machines become the norm, but now consumers have an increasingly large proportion of their discretionary income to spend on holidays, well being and leisure activities. Luxury, once for only the minority, is now a mainstream phenomenon. This accumulation of wealth means that consumers are constantly searching for self-esteem and self-actualisation because they perceive that they have all the material goods they need and their basic requirements have been met. The consumer focuses their expenditure on goods and services which will improve their quality of life and enhance their sense of self.

Therefore, as the experience economy grows, consumers devote their increasing wealth to travel and tourism products. According to research by the Future Foundation, expensive holidays in faraway places are now perceived by consumers as the No. 1 ultimate experience (Yeoman & McMahon-Beattie, 2006). As the experience economy matures, a trend is identified whereby consumers search for and buy a real experience rather than something that is false, fake or manufactured. And so the consumer, in choosing a holiday, searches for a destination that offers a sense of real place — hence Siubhan's journey through Africa.

Trend 4: The Educated Consumer

Across the world, levels of educational attainment are improving, especially in higher education. In 2004, 2.2 million of school-leavers in England and Wales went on to higher education, compared with 0.7 million in 1970 (Yeoman, 2004a). Education is a key driver in authenticity because the educated consumer is more discerning, affluent and sophisticated in the choices they make. In the scenario about Siubhan, it is shown that she is knowledgeable about Africa and wildlife.

Trend 5: The Role of the Media

The media has a substantial influence in determining holiday destination choice. As today's consumer is less influenced by overt marketing such as above-the-line advertising than previous generations, destination-marketing organisations have turned to other media to plug the gap, whether product placement in films or setting up information tours for journalists in the hope that they will write a positive story for a travel magazine or Sunday newspaper supplement.

Research by Thomson Holidays (Glover, 2004) suggests that 80% of UK consumers plan holidays to a particular destination after seeing a location on the screen. Films such as *Lord of the Rings, Harry Potter* and *Cold Mountain* act as virtual brochures, inspiring consumers to make a pilgrimage to the places featured. The opportunity to capture this market was exemplified by the See American campaign, which was based upon the promotion 'you've seen the film, now visit the set'. With the advent of a digital society, specialist television channels such as the Discovery Channel allow consumers to indulge their interest or hobby, such as wildlife or finding out more about a destination featured.

A digital society does not mean, however, that the guide book is dead; far from it, in fact, as our interest in culture, better-educated consumers and an increase in travel has resulted in a boost in sales of travel books over the past 5 years (Moss, 2005). Travel guides such as *Lonely Planet* are no longer about travel on a shoestring, but have become major influencers of destination choice. The typical reader of *Lonely Planet* is between the age group 18–34, educated to degree level, has strong opinions about social justice and world peace, and regards travel as a culturally valuable stage on life's way. 80% of *Lonely Planet* readers are single and 72% are female (hence Siubhan's profile). *Lonely Planet* travellers are ethical purchasers, who are savvy and knowledgeable about the world. However, they do not wear hippy-style clothing and ethnic jewellery of 1960s; they are more likely to be armed with an iPod, a photo mobile and a state-of-the-art digital camera.

Trend 6: Individualism

Linked to the trend of increased affluence and luxury has been a shift towards individualism in which the consumer searches for products and services which meet his or her individual needs. In addition, this is related to the trend of the diminishing role of social and mutual institutions, thus encouraging a decline in deference to authority and a growth in self-reliance. The impact of new media technologies and globalisation raises awareness of new communities and connections. The combination of these trends provides a melting pot from which people can draw their identity. This helps lower the barriers to people developing their potential and allows them to be exposed to a greater variety of options. As the consumer faces complexity of choice and markets become more fragmented and individualistic, so identity will still be derived from the family and place, as well as from lifestyle choices, specific brand affiliations and niche interests.

Authenticity becomes the expression of a person's individualism through the achievement of self-actualisation. This could express itself through participation in volunteering and contributing towards society. This trend of seeking self-actualisation is also illustrated in the scenario by Siubhan's undertaking work in the lemur sanctuary.

Trend 7: Time Pressures and Authenticity

Gazinta is a term coined by the American economist Burns (1993) to describe people's desire to maximise the efficient use of their time. He argues that time has become a more precious commodity as affluence has increased and as opportunities have increased and horizons have broadened. The law of *Gazinta* states that people are encouraged to sample a range of activities and to gain satisfaction from them rather than devote themselves to just one or two experiences. However, while in particular the portfolio of activities and leisure activities has grown, there are still only so many hours in the day. Many leisure venues have broadened their offer to the consumer so that a wider range of activities is presented under the one roof. For example, shopping centres have cinemas and cinemas contain cafes; pubs offer television viewing, food, quizzes and live music. On the other hand, according to a research by the Future Foundation and VisitScotland (2005), people will increasingly want more natural, authentic activities to operate as 'time spaces' in their lives. In effect, people's leisure portfolios will incorporate a wide range of 'short-burst', simultaneous or integrated activities alongside spells of, less hectic activity indulged in over a longer period of time, which can be described as 'time oasis leisure'. Climbing a mountain may be perceived as an example of a short-burst activity but once the climber reaches the summit the tranquillity of the authentic landscape becomes a person's time oasis.

Finally, there is the prediction by Naisbitt (1982) who said that 'the more our lives are steeped in technology, the more people will want to be with other people at movies, museums and book clubs'; hence the importance of authenticity as a means of escape.

Trend 8: Busy Lifestyles and Getting Away

Ulrich's (1983) stress reduction theory, a psycho-evolutionary model, emphasises the role of natural settings in generating psycho-physiological recovery from stressful experiences associated most often with contemporary urban environments and lifestyles. It has been found in studies that natural environments and areas such as national parks act as stress reduction models because participants in the studies viewed such environments as peaceful, tranquil and serene and as places for respite and relaxation. Hence, Siubhan's career break is an opportunity to de-stress in a natural environment away from a hectic lifestyle.

Trend 9: Our Affection for Wildlife

There seems to be a natural affinity between man and animals. Studies by Brodie and Biley (1999) found that the presence of animals instigate enhanced relaxation within their human companions, which explains why, for some wildlife tourists, just being in the presence of animals is sufficient to satisfy their needs. The great fascination of wildlife has for some tourists may reflect the influence of the interaction humans have with animals, especially when close up — touching, observing behaviour and even talking to them. Humans bond with animals through emotional attachment; animals are pets and companions in the home or they may have an aesthetic appeal — young animals in particular are often described as 'cute and cuddly'. People are always interested in attempts to save a whale marooned on a beach and stories about cruelty to animals frequently appear in newspapers, both tabloid and broadsheet. No wonder Siubhan is interested in caring for the lemurs.

Even politicians have used animals in order to connect with people. Consider Richard Nixon's use of his dog, Chequers, in his broadcast to the American people after being accused of corruption. It is reckoned that Chequers' presence helped sway people's opinion towards believing in Nixon (Woestendiek, 2002).

Why Is Authenticity an Important Tourism Concept?

Brass (2006) uses the term 'authenti-seeking' for consumers searching for authenticity in a range of products, services and experiences or looking for it within themselves. This trend presents an opportunity for tourism in Africa, because going on holiday is now perceived as the No. 1 luxury experience (Yeoman & McMahon-Beattie, 2006) and those who go holiday identify an authentic cultural experience as being the most important aspect of it — and this applies across all age, gender and socio-demographic groupings (Brass, 2006). This authentic experience is about avoiding areas and activities where there are many other tourists, indicating a desire to explore the untouched and unexposed. Authenticity is the enjoyment of the tranquil luxury of an unspoilt environment; the difference between the over-development of Kilimanjaro and the untouched beauty of Madagascar.

As we see in Figure 12.1, this trend is high amongst socio-economic grouping AB and the older generations, perhaps emphasising their world-weary cynicism about the unoriginal, which is less obvious in the not-yet-jaded younger generations. In terms of activities, the appeal of outdoor holidays and activities is on the rise, whether walking, camping or trekking. The phenomenal increase in the popularity of caravanning holidays over the last 5 years is a reflection of the lure of freedom and the open road. As a result of recent changes to the law regarding accessibility to land in the United Kingdom and a greater awareness of health issues, there has also been a rise in the popularity of outdoor holidays, as highlighted in Figure 12.2.

Additionally, hiking and nature-based activities are associated with the appeal of the outdoors. The Ramblers' Association is experiencing a rapid rise in its membership, especially amongst the 20–30 age group, and this suggests that singletons are looking for a social network to become involved, a network that is supportive and provides a community environment that counteracts the perceived negative affects of a networked society and globalisation. Extreme sports are also becoming mainstream activities because rising income levels have led to improved

Avoiding tourists on holiday by gender, age and social grade

Proportion of people who agree that when they go on holiday they try to avoid areas and activities where there are lots of other tourists

"How much do you agree or disagree with this statement … When I go on holiday, I try to avoid areas and activities where there are lots of other tourists?

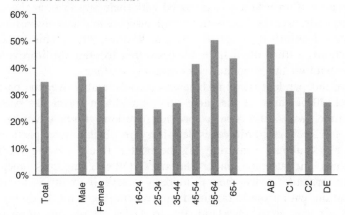

Source: 'Changing Lives'/nVision
Base: 1,414 adults aged16+, UK, 2005

Figure 12.1: Avoiding tourists.

Doing various leisure activities at least once a year

"Which of these best describes how often you do each of the following activities … take a long walk for pleasure / go camping /caravanning / go trekking, or cross country mountain biking?"
*Data is 2003-2005

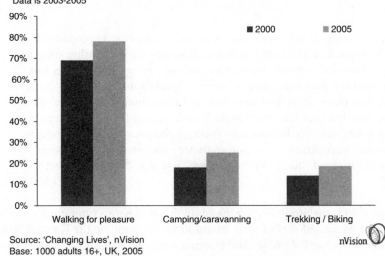

Source: 'Changing Lives', nVision
Base: 1000 adults 16+, UK, 2005

Figure 12.2: Activities on holiday.

accessibility to niche activities and driven tourism activity towards less-conventional experiences. This trend is pushing the boundaries of activity tourism to a stage where experiencing raw, unadulterated and unmediated thrills is the objective for the consumer. To a certain extent, this trend has a *carpe diem* about it; people are packing more in because of uncertainties associated with their lives. Yet, at the same time, people seem to undertake these activities within a secure and safe environment, hence the term 'safe adventurism' (Page, Bentley, & Walker, 2005). This certainly points to an opportunity within the market for operators to offer thrill-providing, original experiences without the attendant risks of going it alone.

The popularity of independent travel has increased considerably over the past 10 to 15 years (Mintel, 2005e) and, at the same time, expedition travel has become popular. For example, www.drifters.co.za provide overland tours covering the South East of Africa in a converted Mercedes Benz lorry, in which tourists participate in a holiday, just like Siubhan, venturing off the beaten track, viewing wildlife, sharing in the chores and sleeping under the stars. Other companies, such as www.greenforce.org, organise environmental holidays in several countries, focusing on wildlife conservation, with projects ranging from tracking elephants to diving for coral reef off the Tanzanian coast. Overland trips in Africa are proving popular at present, as result of the heightened profile of Africa and the rise of interest in ethical consumption.

Boyle's (2004) appraisal of authenticity indicates that tourists are searching for a connection with something that is real, unsullied and rooted within the destination. Authenticity has to connect to the destination and to be placed in the community, hence the importance of community-based tourism through which the benefits go back into the community. Carey (2006) of Tourism Concern notes that sustainable tourism is tied up with authenticity; he states that, when sustainably developed, tourism can create many social and economic opportunities for the destination community.

> 'Tourism can be a powerful tool of development, but its potential can also be wasted. Too often tourism enterprises see each other only as competitors and end up frustrating visitors. Every destination talks about quality and exceeding visitors' expectations, but what is the spark that transforms a destination into something remarkable? It is the destination that has pride in itself and its people and is passionate about celebrating its heritage, its food, its landscapes and its people. Of course, authenticity does not guarantee sustainability, but without the celebration of "local distinctiveness" it is just "another resort".
>
> Carey (2006)

Authenticity and sustainability go hand in hand where communities build a tourism product which belongs to their community; for example the Kawaza Village tourism project in central Zambia where tourists can stay in an authentic African village, learn about environmental issues, collect wild honey and find out about apiculturism (Schlesinger, 2006). Each evening, villagers and tourists gather round a campfire, tell stories and dance. The Kawaza tourism project allows tourists, who would normally stay in a nearby safari camp, to meet the real African people. Each tourist makes a minimum donation to the project of US $15 for a day visit or US $45 for an overnight stay. All the monies raised are used for a number of community projects, such as the employment of teachers in the local school or jobs for the village people. The village has everything from an entertainment manager to local dance troupes for the tourists. This concept is repeated all over the world, with specialist travel operators such as www.exploreworldwide.com or www.exodus.co.uk promoting themselves as sustainable tourism operators — where sustainability has become a key driving force in shaping tourism demand.

Sustainability, according to Brass (2006), is authenticity linked to goodness, and exploring one's inner potential is another aspect of authenti-seeking — that of searching for a non-material, authentic and deeper experience. According to research by the Future Foundation (Brass, 2006), an increasing number of people are undertaking activities which incorporate the creation of something new, for example learning new skills or even going back to traditional activities and putting a modern, techno-friendly twist on them. Learning new skills is evident in the rise of activity learning holidays, such as painting or bird-watching or attending a book festival to hear a reading by the author himself. Most important of all, holidays have become a means of escaping from everyday life (Figure 12.3) and getting in touch with one's true self.

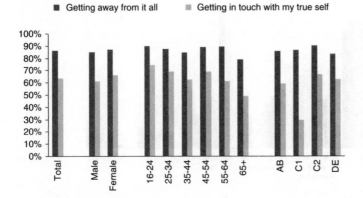

Figure 12.3: Getting away from it all.

Holidays provide the right environment for these kinds of unmediated experiences; the idea that 'it's just me and the mountain' and, of course, for some people, the great outdoors has that strong spiritual dimension which satisfies an inner need. The Future Foundation has, since 1983, been asking the question, *If you had just one wish, which of these would you choose?* This question was asked in 2005 just after the seventh July London bombings and over 35% of people still considered their greatest wish to be to fulfil themselves, up nearly 20% from 20 years ago.

As we can see in Figure 12.4, people seem respond to this inner desire in various ways, whether experimenting with yoga, climbing a mountain or trying a new sport such as bugging. For others it is simply a case of seeking spirituality or a religious meaning.

The desire for spirituality is a growing phenomenon in which people wish their lives to have more of a spiritual content, more of a sense of purpose. This seeking of a sense of purpose explains the spirituality through which we search for the opportunity to contribute to society.

In tourism terms this could be a trekking holiday, raising money for cancer research or helping out in a lemur sanctuary, as illustrated in the Siubhan scenario. Hence, as we have already observed, sustainability extends into 'volunteering', 'community' and 'ethical consumption'.

This search for a sense of purpose is explained in Maslow's hierarchical need for self-actualisation (Maslow & Lowry, 1999), which is associated with American

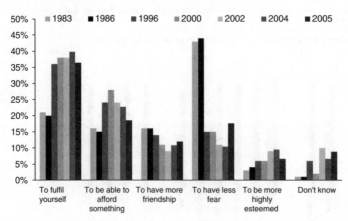

Choice of wishes

Proportion who chose a main wish from a list of five given options

"If you had just one wish, which one of these would you choose?"

Source: 'Changing Lives', nVision/Taylor Nelson Sofres
Base: 1288 adults 16+, UK, 2005

nVision

5016:

Figure 12.4: Choice of wishes.

television's Dr McGraw's (2004) definition of authenticity as: 'The authentic self is the YOU that can be found at the absolute core: it's the part of you that is not defined by your job, or your function, or your role. It is the composite of all your unique gifts, skills, abilities, interests, talents, insights and wisdom. It's all your strengths and values that are uniquely yours and need expression, versus what you have been programmed to believe that you are supposed to be and do'.

Concluding Remarks

The cornerstones of authenticity are quintessentially linked to Boyle's (2004) writing about authenticity. So, to conclude, authenticity should be:

- *Ethical* — An authentic experience should be founded on the principles of community involvement, sustainability and ethical consumption.
- *Natural* — Tourism should be a natural phenomenon, which is pure and not tainted nor manufactured. Natural tourism products are those which are quintessentially associated with the destination or region.
- *Honest* — Be honest with your visitors; the tourism industry should not promise something which can not be delivered or produce something tainted by falseness that will spoil the authentic proposition.
- *Simple* — An authentic experience should be simple to understand and something in which the visitor can see the benefits. The more complicated the experience, the more unbelievable it will be. As the world is full of complications, an authentic experience should be simple and pure and consumed in an inconspicuous manner.
- *Beautiful* — Authentic destinations have a beauty about them, whether a magnificent view which creates a sense or place, or the feeling that the experience cannot be copied because it belongs in that place and only there.
- *Rooted* — Authenticity has some sense of past which is rooted in the destination or community.
- *Human* — A human experience is something that is living and people-focused. This means that the tourist wants human contact which is local and real.

The important message in all of the above is for us to understand how this trend is developing and whether it will last. Some years ago the psychologist deGrandpre (2000) forecast that, as the world emptied of reality, we would see hyperactivity, depression and violence. As this analysis shows, this is far from the case. Rather, we are heading towards a vision outlined by Nozick (1989), who said; 'In a virtual word, we'll long for reality even more'.

This is surely an opportunity for Africa's tourism industry — especially for those providers who are trying to be authentic and appeal to visitors whilst also undertaking niche marketing. Will it last? It will! As long as technology and virtual life continues to develop at the pace they are maintaining at present, the need for human contact and for traditional activities will increase. As consumers become even more empowered and cynical about fake promises, they will continue to seek out the authentic in their own way.

For African countries to accurately position themselves with an authentic proposition, their tourism industries need to emphasise the attributes of honesty, natural, ethical, human and real, as Boyle (2004) discusses. This means that Africa must not patronise visitors with tokenism, for example when talking about green tourism and sustainability. Destinations must be seen to contribute some genuine benefit to the community and to make their offering personal and human. This means involving the tourist and community groups in promoting the destination and products through innovative methods that are seen as original and un-phoney.

A destination founded on authenticity needs community involvement and a strong brand proposition in which the brand equity of authenticity is positioned. Tapping into the visitor's desire for an authentic experience means harnessing the consumer's creativity to constantly enhance and refresh the experience and the product offering.

If all else fails, consider what the marketing guru Godwin (2005) said: 'Authenticity: If you can fake that, the rest will take care of itself'.

Chapter 13

From Birmingham to Mecca — The Ritual of Pilgrimage and the Desire for a Spiritual Existence

My pilgrimage to Mecca seems so far away when compared to Birmingham. Mecca and Birmingham are completely different places and seem to be in separate worlds. Birmingham is a busy, multi-cultured, metropolitan city, whereas on the first day of the Hajj, Mecca was a wild, incessant hooting of car horns. Day or night, it seemed to be one big traffic jam — completely different from Spaghetti Junction at home. More than three million pilgrims leave Mecca and head for the Mina Valley and getting around takes hours because of the hordes of people. The experience of the Hajj was the peak moment of my life, something that I had wanted to do for many years. It is amazing to see all these people praying and prostrating themselves at the holy places. It is one of the most moving experiences I have ever had, beautiful and unforgettable. Being there forces one to understand pilgrimages and to appreciate why this is such a momentous occasion for Muslims. We pray towards Kaba every day, five times a day. The Kaba is an object of worship although it is nothing more than a pile of bricks and mortar. Islamic scholars say that the Prophet Abraham built the Kaba as the first house of prayer to God. So, it's much more than just a symbol to Muslims. They circle the Kaba to show that God is at the centre of their lives. Every ritual has a meaning and each is extremely important for Muslims. For example, after circling the Kaba, pilgrims run between the two hills near the mosque. They do this to re-enact the desperate search for water by Abraham's wife in the desert. Pilgrims take water from the Zam Zam well for the journey home. In the final stages of the Hajj, pilgrims stream back to Mecca for rituals at the Grand Mosque. They circle the Kaba seven times and fulfil the ritual of stoning the devil. The pilgrimage is an enormous journey — 30,000 buses are used to ferry pilgrims from Mecca to Mina and back. You have to be there to see it, experience it — and believe it. Mecca is a must-visit destination for all followers of Islam.

Yousef Ali Akbar, Birmingham, UK, speaking
about his pilgrimage to Mecca in 2030

Introduction

In 2007, Globus launched a separate religious division to develop and operate religious vacations because they predict religious tourism vacations will grow by 50% by 2010, both for Christian and Islamic faiths (see www.globusfaith.com). New religious vacations introduced by Globus include 'Christian England and the World of C.S. Lewis', 'A Journey through the Bible: Egypt and Jordan', 'The Grand Catholic Italy' vacation and a tour of Lourdes and the Shrines of France, all of which offer personal, in-depth visits to famous religious sites.

In 2006, Globus held regional Religious Travel Symposiums and Faith-Based Travel Showcases with presentations by pastors who run travel programs, providing education and sales strategies for travel agents interested in offering religious vacations to their clients. Additionally, the Globus Faith website acts as a resource for agents selling faith-based travel, as well as travellers interested in learning more about the world's great religious sites. Globus recently introduced a feature providing website visitors with the stories behind each religious site, giving them historical context for the offerings of each vacation.

So why is pilgrimage an important issue for the future? This chapter sets out to

• Explain the concept of pilgrimage and religious tourism
• Identify the trends shaping religious tourism and spirituality
• Discuss religions and world tourism
• Deliberate the phenomena of spirituality

History

One of the earliest motivations for travel was religious pilgrimage, whether this was to Mecca, Kumbh Mela or Jerusalem. Religion is still a major driver, and a clear example of this is travel to Israel, as are visits to Roman Catholic centres such as the Vatican City in Rome, Oberammergau in Bavaria and Lourdes in France. The visits include prominent houses of worship of all forms of religion, such as Notre Dame Cathedral, Saint Peter's Basilica and the renowned Sainte-Anne-de-Beauopre in Quebec.

In the Middle Ages, journeys to sacred places were undertaken because of religious motives. Travellers sought the blessing of their god and journeyed long distances to revere the deity. Rowling (1971) noted that in the Middle Ages revelry and feasting became important components of the journey of 'licentious living' amongst pilgrims. This legacy of the pilgrimage is significant for understanding the modern travellers' motivation. The pilgrimage elevated the importance of travel in life, whether visiting destinations or key sites (Goeldner & Brent Ritchie, 2006).

Whilst there is not a uniform definition of religious tourism, it can be loosely described as 'travelling to visit a place, a building or a shrine, which is sacred'. Religious tourism can be divided into four types: pilgrimages; religious tourism per se (visiting a religious site simply because it is sacred); travelling to a religious event (for example, Semena Santa in Seville); and church tourism. The last-named refers to simply visiting houses of worship and shrines because of their cultural, historical and architectural significance, rather than because of any form of religious motivation (Mintel, 2005f).

What is Pilgrimage?

The word 'pilgrim' comes from the Latin 'peregrinus', which translates as 'traveller' or 'stranger', although the combination of both of these words best describes a pilgrim, as defined by Chambers (2006). A pilgrimage, as far as religious trips are concerned, is essentially about travelling to a holy place to pay homage to a religious figure. Pilgrimages are motivated by a number of factors, including requests for help or blessing, a seeking of answers at a time of hardship, a search for comfort during a time of sorrow, or a search for a cure. Whatever the circumstances that lead to a decision to make a pilgrimage, they are generally underlined by religious faith.

In the wider context, religious tourism has associations with other tourism products, such as Chartreuse liqueur and the Chartreuse Order of cloistered monks, founded in 1084, making it — at more than 900 years old — one of the oldest orders in Christianity. The monastery is located in the French Alps and tourists can visit the longest liqueur cellar in the world, as well as the distillery of the Chartreuse Monks. Some would say that the only two things guaranteed in life are birth and death. From a religious tourism perspective, celebration and grief associated with birth and death are other reasons for visitation and travel. Many destinations promote wedding tourism as product.

The island of Iona (off the coast of Scotland), although a very busy tourist destination, is also a spiritual retreat, offering peace and tranquillity outside the peak visitor times. The church has always been associated with volunteerism through missionary work or community service. Tourism can well be regarded as a secondary product following religious belief, where the latter is the chief motivator, although sometimes a pilgrimage may not be religious. Even Elvis Presley is getting in on the act — pilgrimage tours to Graceland to commemorate the 30th anniversary of his death in 2007.

Drivers Shaping the Future of Religious Tourism

The World Tourism Organisation (UN WTO) has reported that the number of tourism arrivals in the Middle East and the Asia Pacific region has increased at a

Table 13.1: Drivers shaping religious and pilgrimage tourism.

Drivers
1 The changing face of world religions
2 It is not religion but spirituality from a Western perspective
3 The search for a more authentic experience through spiritual and cultural traditions
4 The emergence of niche markets
5 The well-travelled consumer and the increased frequency of short breaks
6 Trust and Religion
7 Self-actualisation and volunteerism

much faster rate over the last decade than in the rest of the world. The average annual increase in the Asia Pacific region was some 13%, whilst it was 10% in the Middle East. There are several factors behind this growth, including affordable flights and the increased focus on tourism. Religious tourism has played its part, especially when one considers that Buddhists and Hindus regard India as the most spiritual country on earth, that Saudi Arabia is home to the two holiest sites in Islam and that Israel and Palestine comprise the Holy Land, a destination of immense importance to Christians, Jews and Muslims throughout the world.

There are a number of forces or drivers, alongside faith itself, which drive the growth of religious and pilgrimage tourism and these are highlighted in Table 13.1.

Driver 1: The Changing Face of World Religions

The centre of any civilisation is its culture and the core of culture is religion. More than any other factor, religion infuses a culture with a perception of reality in the broadest sense of the term by offering explanations for the origins of the universe and giving a deeper meaning to historical events, as well as to humanity's place within history. At present, no single religion dominates among the 6.5 billion million people on Earth. Despite the hundreds of existing religions, nearly 75% of the planet's population belong to the five most influential religions in terms of global impact: Christianity (2.1 billion), Islam (1.3 billion), Hinduism (900 million), Buddhism (370 million) and Judaism (18 million). Christianity and Islam are found in more regions than all other religions. Together they encompass more than half the world's population. Add Hinduism, and two out of every three people belong to one of only three faiths. Clearly, religion is one of the major driving forces of the future (McFaul, 2006). Looking at the trends in detail, it is noted that Islam is the fastest-growing major religion in the world and the number of practising Muslims is forecast to overtake practising Christians by 2040 in the United Kingdom (see Figure 13.1).

Britain's churches could be redundant by 2040, with only just over 2% of the population attending Sunday services. By 2040, there will be nearly twice as many

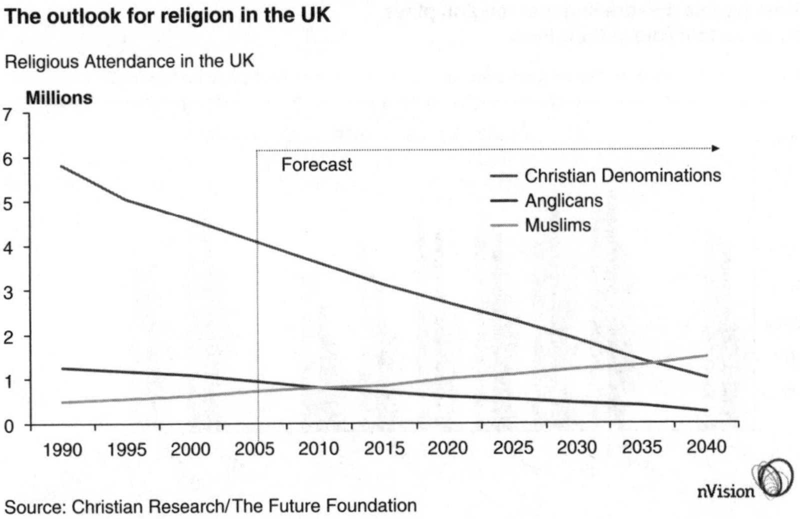

The outlook for religion in the UK

Religious Attendance in the UK

Source: Christian Research/The Future Foundation

Figure 13.1: The outlook for religion in the United Kingdom.

Muslims at prayer on a Friday compared with Christians on a Sunday (Petre, 2006). Professor Thomas McFaul (McFaul, 2006), writing in *The Futurist*, believes that most probably the direction of religion in the future is greater *Exclusiveness* and *Pluralism*. Between now and 2025, *Exclusiveness* will increase, whereas between 2025 and 2050 *Pluralism* will gradually replace it. *Exclusivist* is based on a global village disintegrating into an uncompromising clash of 'I'm right and you're wrong'; much of the blame for this is placed at the door of religion. Christianity and Islam will turn their backs on the quest for a common ground, which would transcend their differences, and this will create barriers between religions and block co-operation, whereas *Pluralism* will mean living together despite the differences. With the sprawling electronic communications, homogenous regions will become more heterogeneous which will drive the religious *Pluralism* to such an extent that religion and spirituality will become blurred.

Driver 2: It's Not Religion, but Spirituality from a Western Perspective

According to research by the Future Foundation (Bainbrigge, 2006), religion is playing less of a role in the lives of the British people, particularly the young, to the extent that one in five people consider themselves to be non-religious — nearly 9.1 million people. However, more people have a feeling of spirituality which may include an emotional experience of religious awe and reverence. Twenty per cent of the UK population have a desire for a more spiritual content in their lives and a sense of purpose. The word 'spirituality' is used in every areas of marketing — it is liberally used in the promotion of self-help, in inspirational literature and in

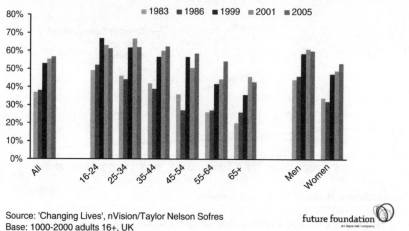

More people disagreeing that religion plays an important role in their lives

Proportion who disagree that religion is an important part of their life, by age and gender
Please say how much you agree or disagree with the following statement: "Religion is an important part of my life"

Source: 'Changing Lives', nVision/Taylor Nelson Sofres
Base: 1000-2000 adults 16+, UK

future foundation
An Experian company

5170:

Figure 13.2: The importance of religion in society.

holiday brochures. Spirituality appears to be less about attending formal ceremonies and more about incorporating a general sense of belief in daily lives (Figure 13.2).

Driver 3: The Search for a More Authentic Experience through Spiritual and Cultural Traditions

As the experience economy matures, consumers immerse themselves in more authentic experiences, such as the spiritual and cultural traditions associated with specific religions and pilgrimage sites. This, according to America's TV series Dr. Phil, defines authenticity and spirituality. The authentic self is the YOU which can be found at your absolute core. It's the part of you that is not defined by your job, or your function, or your role. It is the composite of all your unique gifts, skills, abilities, interests, talents, insights and wisdom. It's all your strengths and values which together are uniquely yours and need expression, versus what you have been programmed to believe that you are 'supposed to be and do' (Bainbrigge, 2006). Figure 13.3 shows that 50% of the UK population strives for a more authentic tourism experience; this finding is shown in a number of studies on future tourism (Yeoman et al., 2006; Yeoman, Brass, & McMahon-Beattie, 2007).

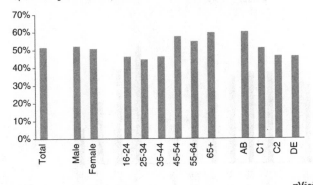

Authentic culture on holiday by gender, age and social grade

Proportion of people who agree that experiencing the authentic culture of a place is very important when they go on holiday

"How much do you agree with this statement ... When I go on holiday, the most important thing for me is to experience the authentic culture of a place... ?"

Source: 'Changing Lives'/nVision
Base: 1,414 adults aged 16+, UK, 2005

nVision

Figure 13.3: Authenticity.

Driver 4: The Emergence of Niche Markets

More diverse tourism products emerge as consumers take more holidays, especially short breaks, and as national tourist boards and providers seek to extend the traditional tourism season.

Over the last decade niche tourism has emerged to counteract 'mass tourism'. In a globalised world of sameness, niche tourism represents diversity and ways of making a difference to the consumer, to whom this kind of tourism appears to offer a more meaningful set of experiences; the- consumers are secure in the knowledge that their needs and wants are being met, whether they be cultural tourists or extreme-sports tourists. Tourists are now more sophisticated in their needs and preferences; thus, religion and spirituality have become a niche product (Novelli, 2005).

Driver 5: The Well-Travelled Consumer and the Increased Frequency of Short Breaks

UK consumers are more likely to have visited the Eiffel Tower than the Tate Modern gallery or Hadrian's Wall. There are approximately 220 countries in the world and the average UK traveller has visited 9.6 of them. One in ten of us have been as far afield as Australia, and today's pensioner has visited an average of 12.8 countries, compared to 5.8 countries visited by those under 25 (Voyager, 2003). Our propensity for travel has never been greater and more of us are taking short breaks than at any time in the past. According to the Future Foundation, 30% of the UK population

Taking short breaks abroad, by gender, age and social grade

Proportion who take a short break (1-3 nights) abroad at least once a year

"Please say (from this card) how often you take a short break"

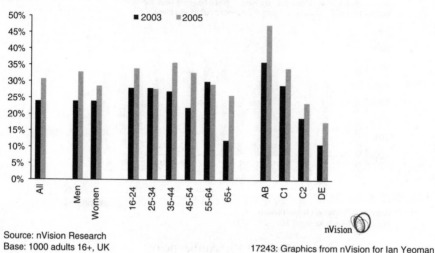

Source: nVision Research
Base: 1000 adults 16+, UK

nVision

17243: Graphics from nVision for Ian Yeoman

Figure 13.4: Short-break holidays abroad.

took a short break abroad in 2005, with this figure rising to 48% for those in the AB socio-economic group (Figure 13.4). For example, if consumers took four short breaks a year, religion and spirituality will become one of the main reasons for travel for one of those holidays.

Driver 6: Trust and Religion

The faith, which we, as consumers have, is a key driver which shapes religious tourism, whether a matter of faith and religion or a search for belief through spirituality. The combination of both these factors influences whom we trust in society. Consumers today have less trust in institutions and government, but are more likely to trust independent bodies — those organisations which campaign and speak out on issues of importance to society. Therefore, religion and spirituality have a high element of inner faith — which we trust and seek out.

Driver 7: Self-Actualisation and Volunteerism

In the early 1990s, the forecasting communities noticed a phenomenon of keeping 'away from the Joneses' (Yeoman et al., 2007), whereby consumers were not chasing materialism but rather seeking authenticity, uniqueness and a special experience. Consumers are searching for their inner self or self-actualisation. Today, virtually everyone in the United Kingdom agrees that it is important to put time and effort into personal development and this results in a movement away from conspicuous consumption to a less conspicuous form. One way of achieving self-actualisation is through volunteering and putting something back into the community, for example, by helping to save the planet or taking part in a volunteer project in Namibia, and there has been a rising interest in this. Volunteer tourism has become a mass niche market which focuses on the altruistic as participants 'do good' for society.

World Tourism and Religion

According to the UN World Tourism Organisation (2006), there were 38.4 million international arrivals in 2005, which is forecasted to rise to 158.9 million by 2030. The region of the world associated with religious tourism is the Middle East because this is the centre of pilgrimage for Islam, Christianity and Judaism. From Figure 13.5 we can see that the Middle East earned more than US $26 billion from international tourism in 2005. Egypt is the biggest earner in the region, with US $6.9 billion from

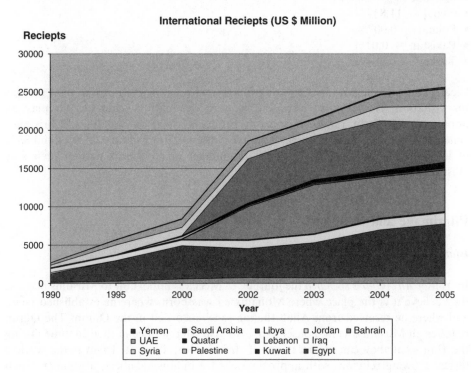

Figure 13.5: International receipts for tourism (*Source*: UN WTO).

international tourism, followed by Lebanon and Saudi Arabia. Leisure, recreation and holidays appear to be the most common purpose of travel. The second most important category of purpose of travel in 2005 was visiting friends and relatives (VFR), or for religion, health or other purposes — currently accounting for 34% of arrivals.

In 2004, 43% of international arrivals to Saudi Arabia were for pilgrimage or religious reasons, making pilgrimage the number-one reason for visits. Saudi Arabia is clearly out in front compared to other countries; even in Israel pilgrimage accounts for only 10% of international arrivals. As a result of the problems of collecting statistics in Palestine, year-on-year figures are not comparable. However, in 2000 there were 1 million international arrivals, 66% of which were for pilgrimage and religion. This number was reduced to 9453 in 2002 because of the ongoing geopolitical situation. Outside the Middle East — where statistics are available — the main reason for visits attributed to pilgrimage and religion as a percentage of all visitations was as follows (Glaesser, 2006):

- Bangladesh — 0.01%
- Bolivia — 0.01%
- Burkina Faso — 0.014%
- Ireland — 0.0005%
- Micronesia — 0.03%
- Nepal — 11.8%
- Poland — 0.007%
- Pakistan — 0.01%
- Turkey — 0.004%

Clearly, outside the Middle East, pilgrimage and religion are not the main reasons for visitation. However, in advanced western destinations churches do play an important role in a range of tourism products, such as weddings, Christmas, genealogy, interest in architecture or simple curiosity. For example, in Scotland 83% of international tourists visit a castle, monument or church as part of their stay (VisitScotland, 2006a).

Pilgrimage and Religion

Islam

In *Yousef Ali Akbar's scenario* the journey to Mecca is important to Muslims because they believe it is the place where Mohammed was born, where he established Islam and where he received from Allah the messages recorded in the Quran. The Quran requires all Muslims, as in Yousef's case, to visit Mecca once in their lifetime during the Hajj — if they can afford it and if their health allows it. Islam is the world's fastest growing religion, with approximately 1.2 billion members, a number which is forecast to grow to 2.0 billion by 2030. According to the 2001 (Mintel 2005f) census

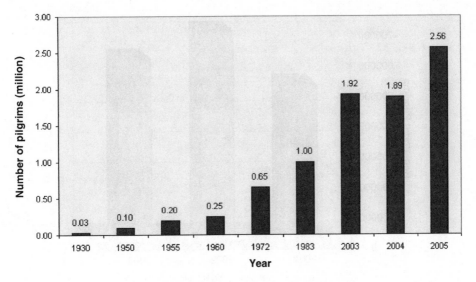

Figure 13.6: Visits to the Hajj.

there were 1.6 million Muslims in the United Kingdom, with 25% actively practising their faith (Figure 13.6).

In 2005, 2.56 million Muslims took part in the Hajj, an 8848% increase since 1930 or a 33% increase since 2004. Between 20,000 and 40,000 UK pilgrims travel to the Hajj every year, just like *Yousef Ali Akbar*. The number of pilgrims travelling to Mecca shows how the faith remains strong amongst followers, and specialist travel operators such as Umrah Travel and Afta Tours provide packages and escorted tours. This market can only grow.

Christianity

Christians comprise the biggest religious group in the world, with 2.1 billion followers. The Holy Land (Israel) is the cornerstone of Christianity because this is where Christians believe that their saviour Jesus Christ was born over 2000 years ago, and 25th December is the biggest Christian festival. Unlike the Quran, the Bible does not compel Christians to go on pilgrimages. This is because of the Christian belief that God is everywhere. However, Christians do embark on religious journeys to Palestine, Lourdes, the Camino De Santiago or Fatima.

In Fatima's case, the five reported apparitions of the Virgin Mary in 1917 catapulted this small village in Portugal on to the world stage (Mintel, 2005f). In the nine decades since then, Fatima has welcomed an increasing number of Christian pilgrims. These have included Pope John Paul II who travelled to the village in 1982 to give thanks to the Virgin Mary for sparing his life in an assassination attempt.

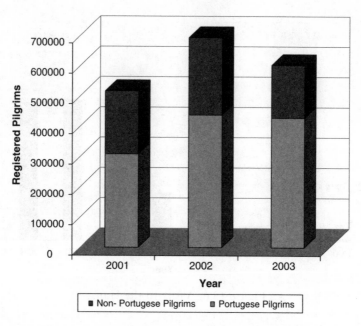

Figure 13.7: Pilgrimage to Santuario De Fatima.

Figure 13.7 shows that there has been an increase in the number of pilgrimages made to the Sanctuary of Fatima by Portuguese groups, with the number rising by 41% during 2001–2002. Other major destinations include the Sanctuary of Our Lady of Lourdes which has been associated with miracle cures since 1858. Lourdes attracts a large number of pilgrims, whose faith leads them to believe that they will find a cure for their ailments. Lourdes has developed into the second largest destination for Roman Catholics. Another main pilgrimage site is Czestochowa in Poland; Christians travel to this city principally to visit Jasna Gora Sanctuary, where they see the picture of Our Lady of Czestochowa, painted, they believe, by St Luke the Evangelist on a tabletop used by the Holy Family. An estimated 4–5 million people visit Jasna Gora every year, giving a daily average of 11,000–13,700 visitors (Mintel, 2005f). For Christians the most important sites in the Holy Land are the Church of Nativity in Bethlehem, which they believe stands on the place where Jesus Christ was born, and the Church of the Holy Sepulchre in Jerusalem, which is visited at Easter. Vatican City (the Holy See) is the Pope's residence and has attracted pilgrims for centuries. The busiest periods, in terms of tourism motivated by religion, are the Pope's traditional Easter address and his Christmas Day speech. It is estimated that up to 190,000 pilgrims converged on St Peter's Square in 2004 to listen to the pontiff's 'Urbi et Orbi' — Easter Address (Mintel, 2005f).

Hinduism

There are an estimated 900 million Hindus. As with Islam, religious pilgrimage is an important aspect of this faith, with Hindus travelling to sites associated with their deities, such as, in India, the River Ganges (where they bathe) and Varanasi, the home of Shiva.

Temples are the most popular destinations for pilgrimages. The Kumbh Mela is one of the most visited destination; here, the pilgrims bathe in the waters of rivers which Hindus consider holy. The story of Kumbh claims that Hindu deities fought over the nectar of immortality for 12 years; hence, the festival takes place in different locations on a 12-year cycle. Many Hindus believe that to bathe in the holy waters of these rivers will bring forgiveness for sinners, the blessing of the deities, immortality and even freedom from the cycle of rebirth. In 2005, over 70 million people visited the Kumbh Mela, compared to 4 million in 1954, an increase of 1600%.

Spirituality

From Figure 13.2 we can see that religion in Britain is playing an increasingly less important role in people's lives especially the younger generation. This, combined with the fact that one in five people do not assign to themselves any religion leads us to ask why is then there an interest in religious tourism per se. Religion is defined as a group of beliefs or attitudes concerning an object, person or system of thought considered to be supernatural, sacred or divine', whereas spirituality is a 'sense of connection to a much greater whole which includes an emotional experience of religious awe and reverence' (Bainbrigge, 2006).

From Figure 13.8, we can see that there is a growth in the number of people who wish that their lives had more spiritual content, more of a sense of higher purpose. We need to look only at the appearance of the word 'spirituality' in practically every area of self-help, inspirational literature and advertisements for many products, from deodorants to jewellery, fashion to holidays to see how the yearning for some kind of 'spirituality' has become ubiquitous. Spirituality appears to be less about attending formal ceremonies and services associated with religion and more about incorporating a generalised sense of belief into daily life. Spirituality is best exemplified in the *Chicken Soup* series of books (Cranfield & Hansen, 2006) which promote greater time for contemplation, whether an exploration of who you are, what goals you can achieve or how you 'connect' to other people. Spirituality manifests itself in terms of self-fulfilment, arguably the search for the quintessential authenticity in modern society and well-being, in which spirituality is an extension of our concern for longevity and health and fitness.

From a tourism perspective, spirituality manifests itself as the desire to get away from daily life, and holidays provide the avenue and the environment for mediated experiences. Whether this is 'it's just me and the mountain' or the enjoyment of the great outdoors which have a strong spiritual dimension (Reisinger, 2006).

The appetite for 'getting away from it all' or 'getting in touch with one's true self' is strong and is growing. Holidays certainly seem to provide the right environment

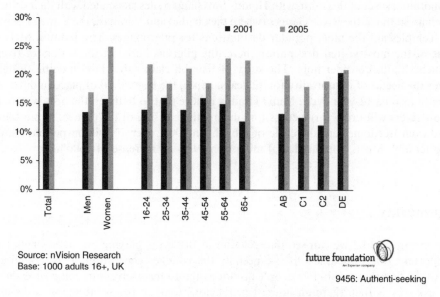

"I wish my life had more spiritual content"

Proportion who agree or strongly agree, by gender, age and social grade

Source: nVision Research
Base: 1000 adults 16+, UK

future foundation
An Experian company

9456: Authenti-seeking

Figure 13.8: The desire for spirituality.

for these kinds of 'unmediated' experiences, the idea that 'It's just me and the mountain' and, of course, for some people, the great outdoors has a strong spiritual dimension and satisfies some inner yearning. Hence the growing desire to find authenticity within ourselves, through rejecting fake destinations and attractions.

Figure 13.3 shows how 65% respondents from the Future Foundation's *Changing Lives* Survey agreed that when they go on holiday the most important thing to experience is the authentic culture of the destination. This finding cuts across all age, gender and socio-demographic profiles (Bainbrigge, 2006). The search for one's inner self is about a self-actualisation which focuses on the altruistic and self-development experiences. Volunteers can gain these experiences when working on projects. For example, the Church of Scotland supports a number of projects in several countries such as Malawi and Scotland. In these projects people volunteer their time and skills to help those who are less fortunate.

Spirituality is also connected to our participation in a cultured society driven by rising disposal income, which is illustrated by the consumer taking more short breaks and trying out new experiences. People in today's society participate in a wide variety of leisure activities, including a search for non-material, inner experiences, learning new skills or even going back to traditional activities and putting a modern, techno-friendly twist on them. This means that spirituality is becoming an important motive for travel and many destinations are promoted in connection with spiritual motivations. Religion spirituality and tourism are closely connected because religious sites become a haven for those seeking quiet and contemplation, such as Iona in Scotland or the sacred valleys of Bhutan.

And Finally, the Di Vinci Code Effect

In Scotland, churches and places of worship experienced a rise of 13.8% in the number of visitors over the course of 1 year, from 597,107 in 2004 to 679,794 in 2005. This is a significant recovery following a drop of 2.7% in the previous reporting year. Why? One reason was the phenomenon of the 'Da Vinci Code' novel and film. In 2005, Rosslyn Chapel saw an increase of 72% in the number of visitors against the 2004 figures. Other reasons for the increase include Scotland's history; many are drawn to trace their ancestral roots, leading to related attractions becoming popular. Visits to Glasgow Cathedral were up by 7.3%, and the Cathedral Church of St Paul in Dundee — which was celebrating its 100th year anniversary as a cathedral and 150 years as a church — had a massive rise of 314% from 1000 to 4147 visitors (Figure 13.9, VisitScotland, 2006a).

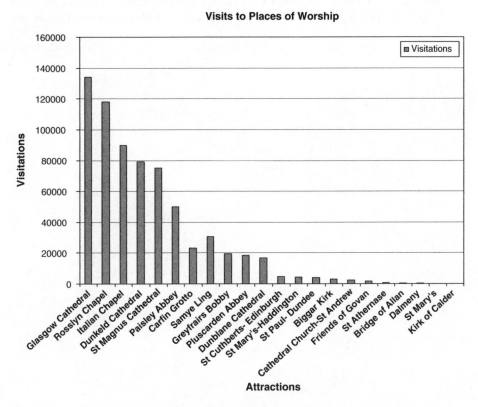

Figure 13.9: Visitations to places of worship in Scotland.

Conclusions

The outlook for religious tourism is good, especially for Islamic sites, given the strength of faith in that religion. Countries like Saudi Arabia will see a considerable growth. On the downside, the geopolitical environment in the Middle East is a barrier for development, especially for countries like Israel and Palestine. Religion whether we like it or not, is a consumer product. As the world becomes more accessible and niche products emerge, an interest in the rich culture which surrounds religion can be viewed only in a positive manner. Religion manifests itself at many stages of life, from birth to death, from marriage to times of tragedy, so it is very likely to be present in the tourism landscape for generations to come.

At present, pilgrimage per se is not a core driver for travel; this is evident in many countries such as Poland or Ireland where less than 0.001% of visits are made for purely religious reasons. However, places of worship or the function of religion in tourism activities, that is, weddings, means that religion is an important part of the product. Outside religion, the consumers' demand for a more authentic, spiritual and cultural experience will result in an increased number of itineraries, including religious sites and places of worship; these will become places of escapism, relaxation, meditation and well-being. Spirituality is just one element of the religious experience outside faith itself. Religion and spirituality have a part to play in future. That is only natural.

Chapter 14

Scotland's Food Tourist in 2015

The finest food in Europe, surpassing the best Michelin starred restaurants in France and Italy. The poached wild venison with a loganberry jelly, followed by the finest cheeses I have ever tasted. Scotland's cuisine is in a world of its own.

Michelin Food Guide (2015)

Introduction

Observers of Scotland's food have contrasting opinions. For some people, the Scots have the worst diet and the highest obesity rates in Europe; to others Scotland is regarded as producing the finest smoked salmon, game and shellfish in the world. Food is an important feature of Scotland's culinary landscape, whether it is fast food or slow food. Today's tourist is more cultured than visitors of even 20 years ago, is well travelled, is searching for new experiences, is concerned about the environment, is interested in taking part in a health/well-being lifestyle and wants to experience the local culture when he goes on holiday. Food is a significant aspect of the tourist's experience of a destination, driven by the growing trends of authenticity and the need to have a high-quality experience. Food tourism shapes gastro destinations such as France and Italy, but Scotland does not have that culinary heritage as a key driver of visitation. Scotland, amongst many other nations, falls into the category of a 'non-food' destination. According to the Scottish Tourism Attitudes Survey (VisitScotland, 2006b), Scottish cuisine is a key driver for only 4% of visitors, whereas 26% of visitors are very interested in Scottish food. On average, 21% of annual tourist expenditure in Scotland is spent on food and drink; this has fluctuated over the past 10 years, varying between 20% and 25%, depending on a number of factors, such as levels of disposal incomes, duration of stay and consumer preferences. So why today is there an interest in food tourism? This chapter sets out to:

- Identity the drivers shaping the food tourist's behaviour
- Food networks and destination cluster
- Future food tourist scenarios in Scotland in 2015

Drivers Shaping the Food Tourist

We all have to eat, whether at home or on holiday. However, the concept of food tourism is becoming the focal point of travel decision making and the hallmark attraction of destinations around the world. Eleven drivers are identified as shaping the importance of food and drink in society. These include:

1. Disposable income and spending patterns
2. Demographics and household change
3. Individualism
4. The multi-cultural consumer
5. The role of the celebrity chef and media
6. Well-being and food
7. Time pressures
8. Internet usage
9. The desire for new experiences and cultural capital
10. The science of food
11. However, the consumer is a hypochondriac

Driver 1: Disposable Income and Spending Patterns

All across world, growing affluence of the populations has a profound impact on consumer spending. In the past, much food expenditure was on stable items and tended to fall in price in real terms, resulting in an increase in discretionary income that was diverted to durable consumer goods such as consumer electronics and services. However, consumers also spent a higher proportion of their income on prepared food, gourmet products, eating out and food items with some form of health or ethical benefits. The key point is that according to Silverstein et al. (2005) writing in their book *Trading Up: The New American Luxury* the consumer has traded up where the product is aspiration or traded down when the product is only function. This is one reason why producers and retailers have focused on quality through products such as *Tesco's finest range* or ethical consumption, where the consumer will pay a premium for 'fair trade' product.

Driver 2: Demographics and Household Change

Families are also becoming increasingly democratic in food choice, as children get older they have more influence in what they eat and where the family eats. Children are also spending increasing amounts of time with their grandparents with over two-thirds of children born between 1978 and 1986 being looked after by their grandparents at least once a month, compared to one quarter of those born in 1937 or earlier. This increase indicates a demand for venues offering facilities that appeal to differing age groups and generations (Future Foundation, 2006d). By 2015, those aged between 45 and 59 will be part of the most populous age group in the United Kingdom. Households headed by those aged 50 plus will account for around 50% of all households, and this same age group will account for over 39% of all consumers spending on leisure goods and services. In 2004, the 50–64 age groups spent US $24.80 (£12.40) per household per week on restaurant meals, US $2.40 (£1.20) more than the national average — this will be a key market in the future. Another consequence of longevity is 'lifestyle fragmentation', the idea that life is increasingly being experienced as a series of non-linear events with no set pattern. As characteristics of different age groups becomes blurred and diverse, more people will expect the places they visit to be adaptable to different aspects of their daily lives. In other words, eating out opportunities suitable for whatever the situations requires — whether this is work, with children or simply eating alone (Future Foundation, 2006d). And finally, rising divorce rates are also good for food tourism, as Silverstein et al. (2005) observe that divorcees have to search for new partners and subsequently will take prospective partners out for dinner and away for romantic weekends.

Driver 3: Individualism

On the face of it, the ubiquity of fast food outlets and big brands is threatened by growing individuality within cultures across the world. However, this is not the end of mass customisation, as the power of brands in a complex world becomes even more important. For example, the success of Starbucks with its 6000 different coffee combinations (double tall, skinny latte, Soya milk, etc.) and McDonald's success in France are attributed to branding. Individualism allows global brands to tailor their products for local societies. For example, Centre Parcs offers regional specialities on their entire menu, driven by the consumers desire for regional and authentic dishes. Whereas Marks and Spencer promotes local produce such as Ayrshire milk, Scottish salmon and Islay scallops thus allowing individualism in a branded world.

Driver 4: The Multi-Cultured Consumer

The whole process of globalisation has significantly amplified the meaning of the term multi-culturalism within our social order. Access to an even wider range of ideas and interests has never been easier. The Internet boom, the expansion in specialist and minority TV channels, the relentless growth in international tourism, etc., combine to stretch perceptions and eliminate that what we might call mono-culturalism; seeing the world through only one set of pre-ordained, inherited notions. The consumer of today will watch the latest Bollywood film, consume a curry, purchase exotic spices for cooking and will read about Rajasthan in the latest edition of the *Lonely Planet*. Multi-culturalism has now become an everyday concept in the daily life of the consumer; today curry is the United Kingdom's favourite dish (Basi, 2003).

Driver 5: The Role of the Celebrity Chef and Media

The media has substantial influence in determining food product selection. The influence of celebrity chefs is often referred to as the 'the Delia effect' after the media chef Delia Smith, whose 1998 television programme 'How to Cook' resulted in an extra 1.3 million eggs being sold in Britain each day of the series (Hall & Mitchell, 2006). More recently, in the first week that Sainsbury supermarkets sold Jamie Oliver endorsed 21-day mature beef, 5000 packets left the shelves. The emergence of the niche food programmes, TV channels and magazines means the food celebrity and expert has been created. Today, that celebrity chef shapes tourism products, whether it is a cookery course with Nick Nairn or Padstow as a food destination that has being influenced by Rick Stein.

Driver 6: Well-Being and Food

Figure 14.1 tells us there is a higher awareness of health issues and food purchase decisions. Around 30% of adults say that they have been eating less fat and sugar compared to the previous year and 28% say they are eating less salt, whereas other food groups, notably vegetables, fruit and bread/cereal/pasta/potatoes are on the rise. These trends have transformed themselves into the food industry with Starbucks

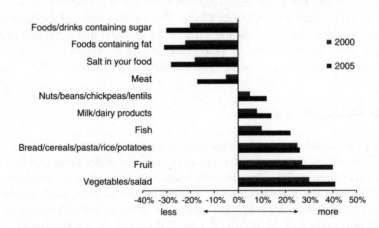

Proportion eating more or less of selected foods than in previous year

"Compared to a year ago, what food types have you been eating more of less of?"

Source: Food Standards Agency/nVision
Base: 3120+ adults aged 16+, UK

nVision

2275: Prospects for Restaurant, Cafe and Take-Away Sector

Figure 14.1: Proportion eating more or less of selected foods.

offering Soya milk, and McDonalds offering salads. In New York, the city council has banned certain types of fats.

The proportion of vegetarians has only increased slightly in the last 20 years, with just over 5% of UK adults reporting themselves to be vegetarian in 2004. However, the number of food venues offering vegetarian options due to its association with healthy eating has increased exponentially along with a perception that vegetarian food in restaurants is more than 'vegetable lasagne' or a 'cheese omelette'. Restaurants are also aware of specialist diets, whether it is catering for gluten free or the Atkins diet. Consumers will even visit a food nutritionalist or advisor of seek opinion about 'food balance' or 'sensitivity towards certain foods'. The specialist diet is becoming more mainstream with individuals avoiding certain foodstuffs like 'dairy products' or the promotion of detox diets to cleanse the body. Consumers are therefore becoming ever more demanding and cautious regarding the food they eat. These concerns and fears can be exploited in order to maximise potential marketing of certain products. However, due to the volatile nature of demands and trends, these requirements are hard to predict. Food providers need to have 'quick response' mechanisms in place to enable them to keep up with dietary fads and health scares.

Driver 7: Food as an Oasis

When on holiday, food becomes the social occasion when busy people create a 'time oasis', but also to connect with family members and friends who may in general be less time-impoverished. Food becomes a human-space within frequently much harried lives; the notion of the meal as a 'time oasis' seems to be a very powerful theme. As the consumer desire for new experiences increases, the 'authentic' restaurant experience becomes more important. Authenticity is about food that is simple, rooted in the region, natural, ethical, beautiful and human — all of the making for a food tourism destination.

Driver 8: Internet Usage

The world is online whether through your computer or mobile phone. Online restaurant reviews are the norm and companies like www.5pm.co.uk use the easyJet principles of yield management (Yeoman & McMahon-Beattie, 2004) allowing consumer's discounts, reviews, auctions for exclusive restaurants, reservations and for restaurants a distribution system for selling unused capacity.

Driver 9: The Desire for New Experiences and Cultural Capital

Food has an important position and role in the emerging experience economy whether in the preparation of it, knowledge of it or consuming it. As British sociologist Gershuny (2003) notes when discussing the whole concept of cultural capital:

> We have various skills in different sorts of consumption and organisational participation — we play football, we organise social events for the synagogue or church or mosque, we cook food and give dinner parties, we listen to music. All of these activities give us different sorts of satisfaction, and different degrees of social status, depending on how fully and effectively we are able to participate in them.

So, the growing importance of cultural issues, as a leisure activity and as a point of differentiation, means it is an important driver in food tourism as it is the tourist's knowledge of food that distinguishes them. This means the food tourist has a desire for new tastes, knowledge and concepts and therefore food creates its own cultural capital — which destinations need to capitalise on. As consumers become richer and more sophisticated, they are drawn to new tastes and more adventurous than previous generations.

Driver 10: The Science of Food

Food tourism is shaped by the geopolitical drivers. Today, we have rejected science from the food chain resulting in falling yields per hectare as we have rejected GM foods. Food inflation is rising all over the world, for example milk has doubled in price in the last 12 months (Anon, 2007). Farmers are planting crops for fuel rather than food in the rush for biofuels. Climate change is more disruptive and unpredictable. Rising temperatures mean less water in parts of the world. Land is becoming more expensive due to the increase in urbanisation, therefore less land for food production. Because of these reasons, will the world return to science in order to protect future food supplies and increase yields? Does this mean cuisine is going to return to Star trek pills and NASA vac packs? Who knows?

Driver 11: However, the Consumer is a Hypochondriac

Although there is evidence that healthy eating is on the rise, the importance of organic food and a desire to try local produce — the consumer can be viewed as a hypochondriac as what they say and actually do can be two different things. For example, obesity levels have trebled in the United Kingdom since 1980 and the amount of vegetables that people consume has steadily dropped since the 1970s. Figure 14.2 is an observation of France's love–hate relationship with the fast food company. On one hand, the French campaign against the company, saying it is a symbol of American imperialism and aggression in the world; promotes an unhealthy lifestyle and there is nothing good about its cuisine, whereas on the other hand, the French love the Big Mac, eating three times as many per head of population

The success of McDonald's

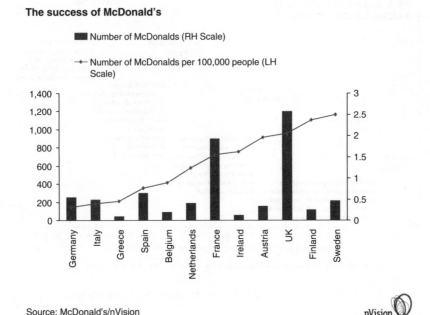

Source: McDonald's/nVision
2003

nVision

18601: Food and Eating Habits across Europe

Figure 14.2: McDonalds.

compared to Spain, Germany and Italy. The figures rise to five times compare to Sweden, Austria or 15 times compared to Ireland.

Developing Food Tourism Concept

Although it is an obvious statement that all tourists require food and drink, the sub-section of tourists who specifically visit a destination for the food are defined under 'gastronomic tourism'. Food tourism is defined by Hall and Mitchell (2005) as 'visitations to primary and secondary food producers, food festivals, restaurants and specific locations for which food-tasting and/or experiencing the attributes of specialist food production region are the primary motivating factor for travel'. Hall and Mitchell go on to segment the food tourist into different categories as shown in Figure 14.3.

As Figure 13.3 shows, the gastronomic tourism market represents a small number of the overall tourist visitors to a destination but these tourists are big spenders. Hall and Mitchell go onto classify food tourists on the basis of their interest in food, including rural tourism, where interest in food is low, although the tourist would visit a farmers market because 'it is something to do' to culinary tourism, where the

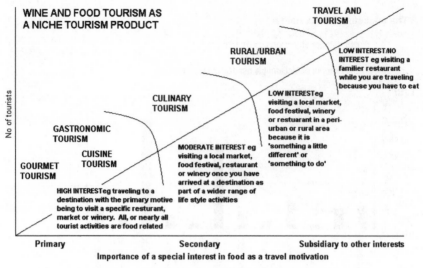

Food tourism as niche and special interest tourism. *Source.* After Hall & Sharples, 2003.

Figure 14.3: Food and wine niche tourism classification.

tourist is moderately interested in food, and would visit a winery or whiskey distillery as part of wider range of lifestyle activities. It is widely recognised that tourists provide a significant proportion of the market for restaurants and cafes around the world, with dining out often being cited as one of the main activities. However, food tourism is bigger than just cafes and restaurants, it is also the relationship to local suppliers and producers. According to research by the UK National Association of Farmers Markets (Hall & Mitchell, 2005), farmers markets contribute a core offering in any gastro destination as they become a living attraction for the tourist; they offer an authentic product that is rooted in the culture of the region. In addition, destinations wanting to set themselves up as food destinations must embrace the whole food chain, from production through to retail. One of the best examples of this proposition in Scotland is Arran, which supplies a range of local cheeses, produces its own beers and has a range of award winning restaurants.

Scotland has many positive factors which bolster its reputation as a food destination. In 2006, Scotland had eight 1-star and one 2-star Michelin restaurants, compared to the three 1-star Michelin star restaurants in the Republic of Ireland and Northern Ireland combined. The distribution of Scotland's Michelin-starred restaurants is also worthy of note, with two being in Edinburgh and the remaining seven in other parts of the country, from the Highlands to Dumfries and Galloway, from Argyll to North Ayrshire. This independent measure of the potential for the quality of the restaurant scene in Scotland stands testament to what can be achieved. VisitScotland's Quality Assurance scheme, 'EatScotland', has 400 restaurants graded, out of the 20,000 eating establishments in Scotland. With the other grading schemes and sources of information which exist, from motoring organisations to specialist guide books, the tourist should have little problem in determining the potential of an eatery prior to entering the establishment.

Food Tourism Destinations

Some destinations have begun to realise that there is great potential for food tourism to offer a sustainable tourism product, notably Victoria (Australia) and Niagara (Canada). VisitBritain (2003) recognised that food and drink had been neglected in terms of consistent and co-ordinated promotion and are working to address this, along with a number of Regional Tourism Organisations. One of the best examples of food tourism in the United Kingdom has been the rise in prominence of Ludlow as a food tourism destination, which now supposedly has the highest proportion ratio of Michelin star restaurants per capita in the United Kingdom. Ludlow from the early beginning of a farmers market has prospered into a major food tourism destination with a density of high-quality restaurants, an abundance of local food suppliers in the high street and food festivals and events to attract tourists (Kidd, 2006). Ludlow as a food destination illustrates its success through:

- Using food as a means to create cultural capital and social cachet
- Creating a density of food and drink suppliers which results in a tourism eating and shopping experience
- Creating a local authentic promise based on good quality and fair pricing
- Creating a unique product better than that found in other regional food destinations
- Producers seeing themselves as being involved in tourism
- Tourism providers focusing on food as a point of difference

---

Case Study — A Food Tourism Network

The Scottish Food and Drink Strategy devised by the key economic development bodies of Scottish Enterprise (SE) and Highlands and Island Enterprise (HIE) sets out its vision for the future as follows:

> Scottish Food and Drink industry is *thriving internationally*, with an unrivalled reputation for high quality, natural products which are completely in tune with international consumer tastes. Industry and supporting organisations operate in a climate of trust and mutual respect, with *strong linkages across the cluster* — between farmers, fishermen, processors and customers. The whole industry is pulling in one direction, with a *culture of innovation*, and investment in people, processes and marketing. These changes *attract ambitious young people* into a vibrant industry.

Creating vision statements is the easy part. The tough task is to translate it into a grass root level reality, engaging the farmers, fishermen, processors and customers in a sustainable manner. 'That's not so difficult', says Howard Wilkinson who is described as an influential, visionary and collaborative community entrepreneur. He goes on to explain that: 'if you view life in the form of the Olympic Games logo — a set of overlapping rings with soft edges, like pods letting you step from one to another — then you can achieve the vision'. Nice analogy that on the face of it appears tinged with a form of romanticism. Not so. Evidence of the translation of the SE/HIE vision into a grass root initiative can be seen embodied in the Ayrshire Food Network (AFN), an innovative idea that is championed by Howard who currently participates in it as a member and Chairman. It grew out of a Culture and Heritage Project set up by the regional tourism forum that had a sub-focus on Food/Gastronomy. AFN is described as: an informal network involving artisan food producers and fine food providers who use the best of Scottish produce from Ayrshire. Its purpose is to promote the creation and production within Ayrshire of artisan food and drink, its usage and consumption by way of a network of businesses in Ayrshire and surrounding environs.

AFN has 35 members, the majority of which are small- or micro-sized enterprises. The membership consists of restaurants, primary producers, coffee shops, specialist suppliers and shops, and hotels and bed and breakfast tourist accommodation. AFN could be described as an anti-response to globalisation believing in the need to preserve biodiversity, encourage food supply traceability and the reduction of food miles. It represents a geographic, business and tourism cluster that is concerned with sustainability across economic, social, environmental and tourism criteria. Cohesion and consolidation allows the coming together of food, culture and heritage — optimising the fact that Scotland's best-loved poet Robert Burns was born in Ayrshire, along with the beautiful natural environment, fertile farming and colourful historical legacy.

AFN is supported by private enterprises and public sector agencies at regional, local, national and European levels. In addition, it networks with:

- A local Further Education College (Kilmarnock) that has had access to Objective 3 European Funding — SME Learning Networks;
- An associated international network that share similar network aims and configurations in Finland and Sweden (www.skargardssmak.com);
- The Ayrshire Farmers Market, a co-operative of primary producers, some of the membership of which is shared with AFN;
- Lobbyist organisations, such as the Slow Food Movement established in Italy in 1986 with 83,000 members internationally that promotes food and wine culture, and defends food and agricultural biodiversity worldwide; and
- Involvement in an associated international business partnership organised under the European Funded DART programme (www.interreg-dart.com) involving Cork, Republic of Ireland and Hunsruck, Germany and the South Ayrshire council, building on the opportunities afforded by the 14 Ryanair

low-cost airline routes working out of Prestwick Airport, and the associated 2.6 million passengers moving through the airport and adjacent areas.

Started in 2003, AFN is primarily a distribution and marketing network. There is a commitment among members to deliver a total quality customer/tourist experience as manifested through their small- and micro-enterprises, their products and traditions. This has been enhanced through customer service training for members and other training initiatives. Joint marketing activity takes the form of the production of a multi-lingual brochure that is distributed at Prestwick Airport and to 4500 hotel bedrooms in Ayrshire. AFN participated and presented at the Slow Food's 2004 Terra Madre Conference in Turin that brought together 5000 food producers from approximately 130 different countries. The presentation focused on sustainable tourism and the use of local food produce.

A sophisticated e-business portal has been established that facilitates an online community, encouraging and maximising business-to-business opportunities and promotion to consumers (www.inandaroundayrshire.com and www.ayrshirefarmersmarket.co.uk). The portal also promotes inter-supplier trading arrangements, and the appearance of links to other AFN members on individual member's web pages. With the assistance of Scottish Enterprise/Highlands and Islands Enterprise's Tourism Innovation Toolkit (www.scottish-enterprise.com), which contains a range of practical tips, techniques and tool to enable businesses to be more creative, more innovative and more successful, AFN developed the Ayrshire Experience Box. It is made up of a selection of food, information about Robert Burns, a music CD, maps and details of Ayrshire food producers and the Food Trail. At a regional level, this enhanced business activity provides an attraction and employment opportunities for the young to remain in the locality rather than to migrate to the cities.

Thus, returning to the SE/HEI vision for the future statement, it is evident that at a regional level AFN can demonstrate that it is *thriving internationally*. Within only a few years, it has established a presence and awareness with international travellers arriving through Prestwick Airport, in the regional tourist accommodation, on the international stage of the Slow Food conference in Turin, and working in tandem with other similar networks in Finland, Sweden, Italy, Republic of Ireland and Germany. It has established strong *linkage across the cluster* through a diverse but cohesive membership that somehow have 'glued' together to enable the development and growth of a community of interest towards a sustainable, collective and common good for all stakeholders concerned. A *culture of innovation* appears to permeate the network drawing in the experience of members and the extended configuration of horizontal, vertical and diagonal networks. In turn, these innovatory and business performance optimising activities generate a greater industry cluster vibrancy that has improved potential to *attract ambitious young people*.

As the owner of a micro-business himself (Petrie Fine Foods that specialises in vegetarian and gluten-free produce which he runs in partnership with his wife Eileen), AFN's Chairman Howard Wilkinson concludes that: 'you don't have to be big to do something rather special. It's about thinking collaboratively. On our own we're nothing. Working with other people we are rather special'. This reinforces Howard's Olympic ring analogy where significant innovation and business performance achievement is secured for individual members and AFN collectively through the astute engineering of a composition of interlinked, overlapping, complementary networks of networks. *Source*: Morrison & Lynch (2008).

The Food Tourist in Scotland

Food tourism is not a driving force for international visitors according to a report prepared for the Ministry of Agricultural, Fisheries and Food (Enteleca Research and Consultancy, 2000) as only 3% of overseas visitors cited food and drink as the main purpose for their visit. This factor is supported by VisitScotland's Tourism Attitude Survey (VisitScotland, 2006b), which showed that only 2% of Italian and French visitors were influenced by Scotland's cuisine and only 1% of Swedish visitors. UK tourists to Scotland spent US $1.2 billion on food and drink,[1] representing 20% of all expenditure; this percentage has been constant for the past 10 years and there is no reason to believe that it will change in the future. Therefore, our base forecast for food and drink tourism in 2015 for UK domestic visitors is forecast to be US $1.8 billion, an increase of approximately 50% from 2005. In order to understand the potential of food tourism, visitors have been segmented according to the Enteleca Research and Consultancy (2000) study of regional food tourists and Hall's classification of Food and Wine Tourism (Hall & Mitchell, 2005).

In the benchmark scenario, the US $1.8 billion (£0.9 billion) has been distributed against the following profiles (see Figure 14.4):

Gastro Tourists

The gastro tourist represents 4% or US $72 million of food expenditure. This is the ultimate food expert, travelling to destinations because of the cultural heritage of its food and drink or its association with a particular chef. They are the early adopters when it comes to food, trying out a range of restaurant styles — as long as the food is of the highest quality. They are the champions and often most critical of food in destinations; they are predominately middle class, will enter cookery competitions and have always wanted to be a chef. They will often entertain at home and they worship Gordon Ramsay.

---

1. It is estimated that the total expenditure on food and drink by all tourist to Scotland is US $1.68 billion, however for segmentation reasons, the UK value is only used.

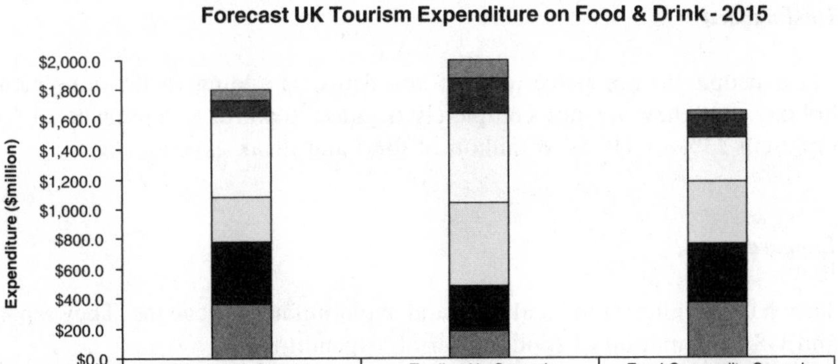

Forecast UK Tourism Expenditure on Food & Drink - 2015

	Benchmark Scenario	Trading Up Scenario	Food Commodity Scenario
▣ Gastro-Tourist ($m)	$72.2	$120.0	$33.2
■ The Foodie ($m)	$108.2	$240.0	$149.2
▢ Interested Purchaser ($m)	$541.2	$600.0	$298.4
▢ Un-Reached ($m)	$306.7	$560.0	$414.5
■ Un-Engaged ($m)	$414.9	$300.0	$397.9
▣ Laggards ($m)	$360.8	$180.0	$364.8

Source: Mintel/VisitScotland

Figure 14.4: Scotland's food tourist scenarios.

The Foodie

The food tourist or foodie represents 6% or US $108 million of expenditure. The foodie is a semi-dedicated food enthusiast who subscribes to the food channels, reads food-related magazines and chooses destinations based upon culture and cuisine. The foodie is sophisticated in his food choice, well informed and interested in good quality, locally sourced and seasonal food and drink.

Interested Purchaser

This group represents 30% or US $541 million of expenditure. People in this group believe that food in general can contribute to the enjoyment of their holiday and they purchase and/or eat local foods when the opportunity arises. These tourists do not pre-plan and are often the most active purchasers of local foods. They go to local farmers' markets as an alternative to something else to do, such as visiting castles.

Un-Reached

This group represents 17% or US $306 million of expenditure and believe that food and drink in general can contribute to their enjoyment on their holiday. They are happy to try local food if they come across it, but, at present, would not consciously go out of their way to do so.

Un-Engaged

These people do not perceive food and drink as adding to the enjoyment of their holiday, but they are not completely negative towards sampling local food. They represent 23% or US $414 million of food and drink expenditure.

Laggards

They have no interest in local food and avoid unfamiliar cuisine. They represent 20% and US $360 million of food and drink expenditure.

Today, food tourism provides a destination with a strong regional identity through the accumulation of cultural capital and social cachet. Local food and drink are an authentic experience as food is rooted in local produce, is simple, fresh, ethical in nature, good for the environment and community-based. The outlets for the produce are local shops and farmers' markets; shopping and local produce are clearly linked. However, in the benchmark scenario, over 60% of food purchasers are not really interested in local produce — rather food for them is functional. Only the gastro tourist or foodie can be counted as the 'true food tourist', where food is the main reason for the visit. This, combined, represents only 10% of all domestic visitors. Two alternative scenarios are presented which are variations of the benchmark scenario:

Scenario 1 — Trading Up. The consumer is trading up, as food acquires more cultural capital and social cachet than the benchmark scenario. Driving this scenario is an ageing population with disposable income who associate Scotland with a strong brand image, which is human, dramatic and enduring. Concerns about health regulation and a generally better educated population drive the growth in locally sourced, high-value, premium products. Scotland's open spaces, eco-friendly perception and strong local products which are quality assured, means an extra US $196 million in this scenario. The market segment changes are based upon the gastro tourist +2%, the foodie +6% and the un-reached +11%. The change in this scenario has meant that the disengaged and laggards groups have traded up.

Scenario 2 — Food Commodity. Although food and culture are important in society, prices have fallen as the product becomes more commoditised and homogeneous. Margins are squeezed and other destinations start to offer similar products. The standards of quality have risen, but profits have fallen. In this scenario, revenues from the foodie have increased by 3% but the uniqueness and commercial advantage of Scotland's food product has disappeared in the lower order categories. In this scenario, the value of food and expenditure drops to US $1.6 billion.

Implications for Scottish Tourism

By projecting in to the future and constructing scenarios VisitScotland has made a number of decisions about the future of food tourism.

The trading-up highlights the importance of driving up quality. In 2006, VisitScotland launched EatScotland, its national Quality Assurance Scheme for the food establishments. The scheme includes all sectors of the catering industry serving consumers, from fish and chip shops to pubs, takeaways and restaurants.

The trading-up scenario highlights the importance of creating cultural capital through food. This includes initiatives such as Taste of Arran with a focus on its cheeses, micro-breweries and local cuisine. The combined effect of this product development creates a sense of place for the island based upon an authentic product. Other initiatives include the addition of a food festival to Edinburgh's summer festival season, the development of new food trails, the use of the media and the cult of the celebrity chef to profile Scotland as food destination.

VisitScotland are promoting food as a central motivator for American visitors to explore the various regions of Scotland. As indicated earlier this is designed to appeal to the better travelled, more educated visitor from the east coast of the United States. In order to encourage the off-season domestic market, VisitScotland has combined with a number of city gastro associations to promote fine dining and encourage visitor numbers, for example the *Dine Around Campaign*.

Intimately, what VisitScotland is doing is creating a strategic conversation with the industry about the importance of food in Scottish tourism destination offering.

An Alternative — The Return of GM Food

What if the world returned to GM foods because of climate change, rising fuel prices and the need to guarantee food supply. In the last decade, GM foods have been rejected because of our concerns over the science. By 2030, the world will have to address these issues and increase efficiency. Image from North America to Argentina, from South Africa to China, farmers embracing new kinds of plants — for example soya bean plants engineered to survive chemical weed-killer, and maize and potatoes that secrete a pesticide in their leaves and stems. Companies such as Monsanto who have created GM crops in which the next generation of transgenic crops, such as vegetables and fruits that stay fresher for longer and crops enriched with nutrients, such as Vitamin A and iron, which are lacking in many diets. GM foodstuffs will return as the consumer wants low price and a guaranteed food chain. *Source*: BBC, 2001.

Conclusion

Today, the consumer is better educated, wealthy, has travelled more extensively, lives longer, and is concerned about his health and the environment. As a result food and drink has become more important and have a higher priority amongst certain social groupings. Observations have been made in this chapter about the changing nature of food in society which has been facilitated through attitudinal change regarding the prominence of individual health and well-being. Combined these trends are raising the importance of food tourism as living cultural experience. In the benchmark scenario, only 10% of revenue is associated with 'food tourism', with the scale of opportunity rising to 20% in the trading-up scenario. However, the number of tourists who may be interested in food ranges from 43% to 58%, whereas the uninterested ranges from only 24% to 44%. The threat imposed by driving up quality is highlighted in the food commodity scenario; first of all, other destinations will deliver a similar experience at a lower price and, secondly, authenticity becomes a homogenous trademark. One thing is clear; food must be a quality product, whether it is slow food or fast food. Scotland's food and restaurant industries have an opportunity to contribute towards the overall ambition to increase the value of Scottish tourism by 50% by the year 2015. Finally, if food is not for you, there is always the no-food movement which is all the rage in Japan where holiday-makers are flocking to the Arina Hotel in the idyllic Nagano Mountains for a fasting feast! (Spencer, 2003).

Chapter 15

The Sports Tourist: The Urban Rat Race

It is midnight and Chris, a 28-year-old corporate executive, is about to start off in London's urban rat race, a 24-h, extreme, endurance event, incorporating a full 24-mile marathon, swimming across the Thames, a 25-km cycle race, base-jumping from Canary Wharf, extreme ironing on Tower Bridge, a 100-m Nordic wife-carrying sprint and a 1000-m Parkour assault course across the skyline of the City of London. Chris is a veteran junkie of extreme sports, who has competed in a number of similar events across the world, including the Great Wallathon of China, Le Mans and the Dakar Survival Race. Chris is a member of Independent Riders, one of the best endurance sports teams in the United Kingdom, which raises over £1,000,000 for charity every year. This urban triathlon is scheduled to be part of the London Olympics in 2012.

Story in the Sunday Times, 20th August 2011

Introduction: Why Do Sport and Tourism Go Together?

Nowadays vast numbers of people are interested in sport and almost everyone aspires to a holiday (Buhalis & Costa, 2006). Sport is a key part of the tourism product whether people participate in a sporting activity or attend as spectators. Sport is now a global business, which includes sports magazines, sports TV channels, sports medicine, professional football and people going to the gym for exercise. A growing number of specialist travel companies, websites and brochures are promoting sports and adventure holidays. In travel and tourism magazines, advertising by resorts emphasises the availability of sporting facilities and opportunities. Spectator holidays are increasingly popular, with huge numbers of visitors attracted to sports events, whether major occasions such as the Olympics or international championships like the football World Cup. Every country in the world seems to have an events' strategy and sport is a key component. Sport and tourism are, therefore, closely linked and, as globalisation continues, new and innovative experiences emerge and countries once thought of as part of the Third World become mainstream sports tourism destinations; China is an example of this.

There are many examples across the world which highlight the importance of tourism and sport. Every year, 40–50 million visitors ski down the European Alps. It has 40,000 ski runs, 12,000 cable cars and a number of lifts which are part of the infrastructure of this popular sport, and it is capable of handling 1.5 million skiers an hour. Today, the ski market accounts for around 20% of the total European holiday market. Twenty per cent of Belgian tourists participate in sports when they holiday at home and this increases to 31% when holidays abroad are taken into account. Similar figures are found in the holiday market for New Zealand, the United States, France and the United Kingdom. The Tour de France, a 3-week, prestigious cycle race, claims to be the world's largest sporting event, attracting several million spectators along the 4000-km route. At the Athens Olympics in 2004, 11,000 athletes participated, accompanied by 10,000 coaches and members of national teams. The event attracted 20,000 journalists, 50,000 volunteers and 50,000 members of the organising committee whilst 5,400,000 tickets were sold and the events were watched by billions on television (Buhalis & Costa, 2006; McMahon-Beattie & Yeoman, 2004).

Some would say that sport and tourism are nothing new. Durie (2003) notes that Scotland has been a sporting destination for walking, golf and shooting since Victorian times. Today, adventure and active holidays are recognised as growing segments of the tourism industry. Sports training is acknowledged as an important sector. Wellness, healthcare and training of the body have boosted sport as a tourism product, and sport as a therapy is a growing market. Sport is a key driver in the hospitality category of tourism, such as corporate hospitality at Wimbledon or at Formula One motor racing events.

Sport contributes towards destinations' branding, influencing the consumers' perception of countries; for example, the All Blacks rugby team and New Zealand, the appearance of the Jamaican bobsleigh team in the winter Olympics, Bargo as Australia's cycling town, or Dubai as an indoor ski destination. As these examples show, events and places become associated with sport, with visible benefits, such as the emotional connection they establish between destinations and their markets, and their ability to attract tourists, investors, and residents. Sports–place branding capitalises on these attributes, in which sport drives or contributes towards destination marketing and location branding which allow countries to build capacity and to use sport as an economic benefit, to the extent that sport becomes a symbol, brand or extension of a country's character (Rein & Shields, 2007).

Extreme Sports and Tourism

Extreme sports, in particular, sports such as skateboarding, surfing, bugging, base-jumping and extreme ironing evoke a lifestyle choice involving a certain way of thinking associated with an adrenaline rush and an excitement which people seek in order to break through the boundaries of normality. Extreme sports have moved into mainstream, with consumers pushing their personal boundaries through the diversity of new experiences and a growth in affluence. Tourists go cage diving off Cape Town or zombing in Alaska. Leading specialist providers, such as Neilson's and Crystal (Mintel, 2005g), are gaining a strong foothold, with dedicated activities, and brochures featuring mountain biking and white-water rafting. Major leisure tour operators have purchased specialist activity-holiday operators, for example, Exodus is owned by First Choice, which can now offer a range of multi-activity holidays, with a fast-paced mix of up to 10 different pursuits in the mountains and on the snowfields, from canyoning to kayaking, and many other sports in between! Mark Warner now offers kite-surfing courses. Even Saga Holidays offer extreme sports for the over-fifties (Mintel, 2005g). Numerous extreme-sports competitions and festivals have grown in the United Kingdom; events range from local individual sports functions to those that cater for specialist events. Air O7 is a 3-day event held in Northampton with extreme-sports competitions such as BMX and skateboarding, and the Eastbourne Extreme Festival builds upon the former Skate Festival but with new, exciting additions such as wind surfing and jet skiing. As the interest in extreme sports grows, it is possible to buy gift vouchers called 'Do Something' which are sold on www.lastminute.com

So, let's look at Chris's adventure. What is the *Urban Rat Race* all about? The *Rat Race* (www.ratraceadventure.com) is a mental and physical adventure challenge that uses the cityscape as its playground over a whole weekend. Teams of three run, climb, mountain bike, abseil, Parkour and kayak the streets, structures, waterways and urban landscape as they navigate their way around a course that's revealed only hours before the race begins. The Rat Race is the creation of Jim Mee, who, whilst mountaineering in Peru, thought of making an adventure race as accessible for the amateur as it is challenging for the pro. The *Rat Race Urban Adventure* was born in 2004, with adventure sports being taken from the mountains and wilderness to where most people are — the city centres. Edinburgh hosted the first-ever *Rat Race Urban Adventure*. The city is a wonderland of great terrain, waterways, parkland and secret places, and, with an enthusiastic council, it proved an ideal venue for the first of the *Rat Race Urban Adventure* Series 2005.

In July 2005, the Edinburgh Rat Race returned with greater gusto, incorporating new, challenging experiences such as abseiling from Murrayfield rugby stadium, kayaking under the Forth Rail Bridge, and bouncing on the infamous space-hoppers at the Gyle Shopping Centre. Manchester City Council also wanted some urban action, so the Rat Race was incorporated into the Manchester Urban X, a festival of action sports, which also involved the inaugural Bruntwood Aerial Assault, where the top climbers from the United Kingdom took on the challenge of scaling 12 Manchester buildings and structures.

In 2006, the 'Rat' population continued to grow and invaded the cities of Bristol, Edinburgh and Manchester once more. All three cities were again up for the challenge of providing an epic race and that was matched by the enthusiasm and commitment of the racers and organisers alike. The Rats faced all kinds of bizarre challenges involving hairdressers, ninjas, gorillas and cows; zip slides across the Avon Gorge and Manchester's Piccadilly Gardens; aerial activities in, on or through stadiums, gap sites and viaducts; all negotiated on foot, bike and kayak. The Aerial

Assault also returned to challenge the top climbers with a variety of urban climbs on Manchester's array of interesting buildings. Watch out for the *Rat Race* as an Olympic sport in 2012!

Why Are We Interested in Sport?

Participation

The British appetite for sport is in a reasonably healthy condition, although more passive than participative. National sports participation is not just about gym membership, marathon training and 5-a-side football, but also about spectator — Wimbledon-inspired strawberries and cream, the inevitable penalty disaster of England's World Cup fixtures and the voyeuristic appeal of Celebrity Fit Club.[1] Sport appeals hugely to quasi-religious collective identities across the country. Britain, of course, has a strong historic and nostalgic relationship with sport, arguably stemming from the pioneering of many of the world's most popular sports — soccer, rugby, cricket and golf. *Therefore, why are Brits interested in sport and what's the connection with Chris's scenario?*

There seems to be a widely accepted view that *couch-potatoism* represents the norm of British sporting endeavour and that the most exercise that the majority of the British people take is either flicking through TV channels or playing fantasy league on the Internet. However, research identified by the Future Foundation's *Changing Lives* Survey (Figure 15.1) shows that more consumers than ever before are participating in sports at least once a month — or at least they are claiming to do so. There is a clear discrepancy between interest and participation: only about half of those who are concerned about keeping fit actually take any exercise. Whilst overall, sport participation has grown significantly over the past 25 years, participation has recently been stagnating or even declining in many sports. Unsurprisingly, it remains the case that men under the age of 40 are the sportiest people in the population but we note that it is amongst women where the largest increase in participation has occurred. If these rates of growth were to continue, by 2020 women would be taking part in as much sport as men. The over-forties generation is profoundly different from previous generations in terms of lifestyle and health. They are richer, they use sport to stave off the effects of ageing and there is a greater propensity to try new experiences; hence, Chris and the *Urban Rat Race*.

About a quarter of the UK adult population claim to take part in individual sports once a month. Clear demographic differences are apparent: men, young people and those in the higher social grades are the most likely to participate (Figure 15.2). Although this data is useful in providing insight into the extent of general participation in sports, it does not give us intelligence on any specific sports.

---

1. See http://www.weightlossresources.co.uk/logout/news_features/fitclub.htm

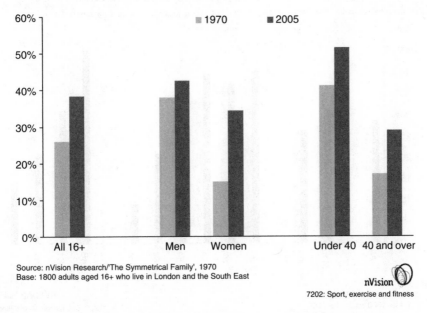

Sports participation, by gender and age
Proportion participating in sports at least once a month

Source: nVision Research/'The Symmetrical Family', 1970
Base: 1800 adults aged 16+ who live in London and the South East

nVision
7202: Sport, exercise and fitness

Figure 15.1: Sports participation in the United Kingdom.

Nonetheless, we know that individual sports are about twice as popular as team sports (which have been in decline for some time). The relative popularity of the former can be attributed to various factors:

- Edward Griffiths, Sports Minister in the Conservative Government of 1970–1974, believes that there has been a shift from collective to individual sports because as society has become wealthier, and the desire for new experiences means sport can be tailored to the individual. The desire for individualism has also driven people towards single-performance sports, in a bid to differentiate themselves from others. (Campbell, Mitchell, & Jackson, 2005)
- Individual sports are often perceived as less time-consuming than team sports because many such activities are easy to take part in and require little initial skill. They are also easier to drop as there is no bond with or dependence on other team members. Additionally, consumers' leisure portfolios have grown greatly over the past 25 years, although leisure time has increased by only 20 min per day in the same period. Clearly, people are trying out many activities, making it difficult to gain expertise in any specific sport.
- A significant proportion of the population have become time pressured. Alongside this phenomenon comes the demand for 'time-oasis' sports and exercise — activities which are meant to de-stress.

Playing individual sports, by gender, age and social grade

Proportion who play individual sports, e.g. jogging, tennis etc at least once a month

"Which of these best describes how often you play individual sports (e.g. jogging, tennis, golf, swimming etc)?"

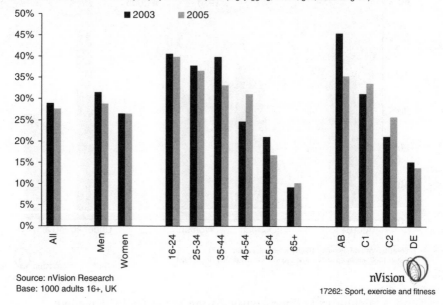

Source: nVision Research
Base: 1000 adults 16+, UK

nVision

17262: Sport, exercise and fitness

Figure 15.2: Participation in individual sports.

- Consumers are, more than ever, concerned about their appearance. Hence, the popularity of individual sports which focus specifically on improving certain body parts/toning.

It could be argued that the popularity of many new kinds of sport can be attributed to the rise of 'convenience fitness' where people like to look good while exercising. Certainly, for the image-conscious, participating in salsa is more graceful than becoming sweaty on the field!

The interest in individual sports will grow, alongside a demand for more variety. For example, dance exercise is one of the most phenomenal growth areas of sport in the twenty-first century Britain. Twenty years ago dance exercise was associated with a Jane Fonda workout, whereas today it includes everything from pole dancing to Ceroc to street dancing.

Participation in team sports is much lower than for individual sports and has been slowly declining over the years, particularly among young adults. As Figure 15.3 shows, team sports still remain the particular domain of youth and manhood. There is not as great a difference between social grades as there is with individual sports where there is a clear correlation. This is because there is more access throughout the country to free or low-cost team-sports facilities, whereas fees for activities such as dance classes and yoga can be much higher.

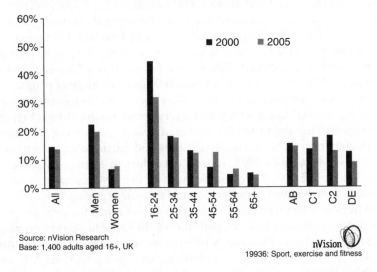

Participation in team sports, by gender, age and social grade

Proportion who play team sports at least once a month

"Which of these best describes how often you play team sports?" Once a month

Source: nVision Research
Base: 1,400 adults aged 16+, UK

nVision
19936: Sport, exercise and fitness

Figure 15.3: Participation in team sports.

The decline of team sports is a result of various factors:

- Whereas some 80% of school pupils in England enjoy 2 hours of timetabled sport per week (exceeding, in 2006, the government's target of 75%), often involving team competitions (virtually every school offers football and 85% offer cricket), there is some evidence that many young people are not maintaining an active engagement with sport when they leave school (Sport England, 2002).
- Team sports have become increasingly 'professionalised'. For example, cricket clubs have raised their standards over the years. Saturday league games are very competitive and Sunday social cricket is dying out. This phenomenon will invariably discourage the (more numerous) social rather than (less numerous) competitive players.
- As young people's commitment weakens, volunteer organisers of sport are harder to find. Hence, there is a lack of structural support for people who would like to participate in team sports.
- As society ages overall, team sports tend to become the domain of the young. Hence, the fall-off in team sports.
- Although the British seem to increasingly enjoy watching team sports on television, actually participating in them is another matter all together. Enthusiasm for team sports can be summarised by a finding in a survey conducted by 'The Observer'. While 100% of the 133 people polled said that the government should provide more money for sport, only 6% said that they preferred participating to being a spectator (Campbell et al., 2005).

Extreme Sports

In an era of unprecedented affluence, when the majority of people are middle class, many want more choice and seek new experiences, hence the boom in extreme sports, a phenomenon which is less than 30 years old. Before that the thought of jumping out of a plane for fun would have seemed completely foolhardy! However, in an age when a craving for artificial excitement seems natural, there is a corresponding market for manufactured danger. The Future Foundation's *Changing Lives* Survey shows that in the 20 years between 1983 and 2003 the proportion of people who agree with the statement '*Occasionally I like doing something dangerous solely for the sensation of risk taking*' has grown within every demographic group (Figure 15.4).

Extreme sports have converted the notion of 'living on the edge' into a consumer product. In 2005 over 25% of 16–24 year olds had participated in extreme sports, a growth of over 10% since 2003. Indeed, according to a study by Mintel (2005g) extreme sports are the fastest-growing segment of the leisure market. The variety is growing every year because consumers enjoy activities ranging from base-jumping to extreme ironing. The extreme-sports market is very much for younger people and growth is tied to demographics, so, with the 18–30-year-old market growing in the United Kingdom between 2005 and 2010, extreme sports are coming into their own. There is also a close correlation between extreme sports and the UK economy; if disposable income and consumer confidence are squeezed during the period 2008–2011, participation in extreme sports may fall. This is important, especially

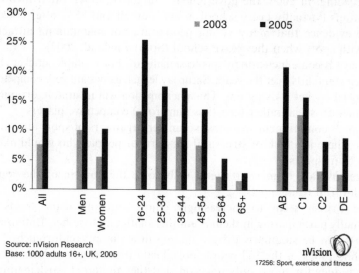

Figure 15.4: Extreme sports.

where extreme sports are part of a secondary break which people might forego should budget be an issue. Therefore, it is important for UK destinations to market extreme sports to international visitors because domestic tourism is expected to fall over the short term.

According to Mintel's (2005g) study on the extreme-sports market, less than 1% of the UK population participates in extreme sports, because it is considered expensive and specialised. However, some extreme sports are now mainstream, such as mountain biking and snow boarding, whereas the market prospects for some extreme sports such as extreme ironing and Nordic wife-sprinting are somewhat limited! To a certain extent extreme sports are becoming sanitised as they become mainstream. Organisers of *Urban Rat Races* need to continually innovate and rebel otherwise they will lose their social cachet, as participants have their own cultural dress and music. Extreme sports have their own cultural capital, with a younger audience checking out specialist sites on www.youtube.com and www.babo.com, often involving rebelling against the norm and promoting a certain kind of freedom.

The Gym as a Metaphor for Appearance

Since the initial boom in sports activities in the 1980s was kick-started by Jane Fonda, gym membership has steadily increased year on year — until very recently (Deloitte, 2006). What has also increased over the same period is the level of obesity in Britain. In 2005, nearly one-fifth of the population claimed that they went to the gym at least once a month (Figure 15.5) and there was a correlation between age and the propensity to exercise. Participation also tends to be more heavily dominated by ABC1s — this comes as no surprise because most gym memberships cost in excess of £200 a year. The government has been deliberating as whether or not to subsidise gym memberships for lower-income households. However, no concrete proposals have yet been put forward. It is uncertain whether any legislation will be instigated as critics have correctly pointed out that going to the gym once a month will do little for obesity unless lifestyles are also changed. Recently, consumer interest in gyms has been waning. A survey by Deloitte (2006) found that in the first quarter of 2006, within the gyms surveyed, membership levels had dropped significantly. Deloitte speculated that the drop was sparked by rising household bills and interest rates, which had resulted in an overall decline in spending by consumers. The strong suggestion is that gym membership is not a priority in the wake of any financial belt-tightening.

However, waning interest may also be caused by consumers looking for other means to keep fit. As Figure 15.5 shows, there has been a substantial fall within the 16–24-year-old age group between 2003 and 2005. This is perhaps because this age group is looking for newer, more exciting activities — indeed they are the ones driving the growth of dance classes and extreme sports. There will always be a demand for gym membership while concerns with health and fitness increase along with obesity levels, but there is no doubt that it is perhaps easily substituted by more innovative activities. At the same time, sport is about appearance and looking good.

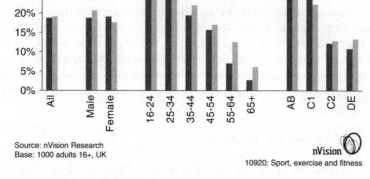

Going to the gym, by gender, age and social grade

Proportion who go to the gym at least once a month

"Which of these best describes how often you do each of the following activities...go to the gym?"

Source: nVision Research
Base: 1000 adults 16+, UK

nVision

10920: Sport, exercise and fitness

Figure 15.5: Going to the gym.

One of the key drivers for consumers going to a gym or participating in sport is to look good and healthy. Physical appearance is a focal point in many people's lives, especially amongst women and men under 34. Sports and exercise therefore benefit from this concern. Although gym memberships are falling, alternative sport and exercise classes seem to be on the rise, such as dance classes or Pilates (Campbell et al., 2005). In a time-pressured society, consumers are increasingly looking for outlets to keep fit, have fun and look good — all at the same time.

Sport as a Health Driver

Yoga is one of the individual activities which has experienced growth in recent years. Participation is dominated by people in the higher social grades and women. At the moment more than 10% of women practise yoga, Pilates or tai chi (Figure 15.6). Time-oasis activities and sports which provide an escape from everyday stress have all seen a steady expansion because

• Time pressure has resulted in consumers needing to de-stress, and activities which cater to this will inevitably prove popular. Currently over half the population, according to surveys by the Future Foundation, agree that they are 'often under time pressure in their everyday life'.

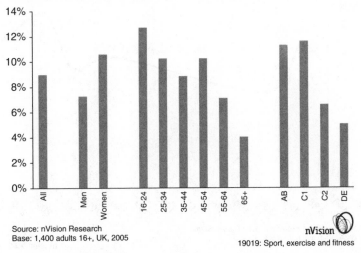

Doing yoga/pilates/tai chi, by gender, age and social grade

Proportion who do yoga, pilates, tai chi, at least once a month

"How often you do each of the following activities? Do yoga, pilates, tai chi"

Source: nVision Research
Base: 1,400 adults 16+, UK, 2005

nVision

19019: Sport, exercise and fitness

Figure 15.6: Time-oasis activities.

- Time-oasis activities are renowned for their holistic qualities. They improve not only the body but also the mind. Over recent years people have been particularly concerned with self-improvement.
- Yoga is practised predominantly by women. It is well known that the pattern of family building in Britain has been evolving over the years, freeing up much of women's time to participate in leisure activities because couples now have, in substantial numbers, their first child only when in their thirties. Such is the pressure of family care and the importance of the maintenance of dual incomes that it is inevitable that many women will feel that their access to sports participation is constricted — the very phenomenon which buttresses demand for time-oasis activity.

Being healthy has increasingly become a national pre-occupation. Figure 15.7 shows that since 1980, the proportion of consumers who are concerned about keeping fit and healthy has jumped by just under 20% to a majority of 75%. Since the mid-1980s, consumption of health foods has doubled. Yet we are to some extent less healthy than ever before; obesity levels have reached an all-time high. Indeed, our desire for well-being co-exists with a thirst for indulgence. We are taking steps to become healthier, but, at the same time, we are unwilling to sacrifice many aspects of our lifestyles which bring us pleasure. In addition, people are increasingly concerned with their appearance; hence, for many, the desire to look good acts as a catalyst for keeping fit, and this is more important than being mentally and emotionally healthy.

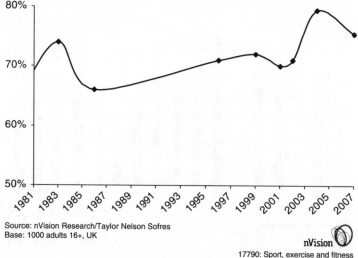

Concern with staying fit and healthy
Proportion of adults who say they are concerned about trying to stay fit and healthy
"Some of the things people have told us they are concerned about are listed here. For each item, please tell me whether you find you are concerned about it at all...Trying to stay fit and healthy"

Source: nVision Research/Taylor Nelson Sofres
Base: 1000 adults 16+, UK

nVision
17790: Sport, exercise and fitness

Figure 15.7: Concern for health.

Today, Britain is a nation pre-occupied with the notion of health but people are unwilling to do as much as they could about it.

Over the past 25 years levels of obesity have soared (Figure 15.8). In 1980 only 6% of men and 8% of women were obese, but by 2005 this figure had climbed to 21% and 25% respectively. In a worldwide study done by the International Association for the Study of Obesity (2004), it was found that there was no discrepancy between the proportion of British people who thought that they were obese and the proportion in reality. In contrast, in the United States and in Italy fewer people thought they were obese than actually were and in Japan less than half of people who thought they were obese actually were so. People are also aware of the need to be healthy and to take action whether by eating more fruit or reducing their intake of salt. Lately, obesity has achieved almost the same status as global warming as a target for public policy and promotional activity by the government. One of the problems lies in the lack of physical activity. The BBC (Newman, 2004) puts the cost of this inaction at 54,000 premature deaths each year and an extra £2 billion (US $4 billion) medical bill for the National Health Service. Manual labour is now rarely incorporated into work because manufacturing has been increasingly replaced by service industries.

Britain does not fare particularly well in the European league table of healthiness. The nation has the third-lowest proportion of ultra-healthy consumers in Europe (Figure 15.9). The country with the highest proportion of healthy consumers is Finland, which has over triple the proportion of ultra-healthy consumers as Britain.

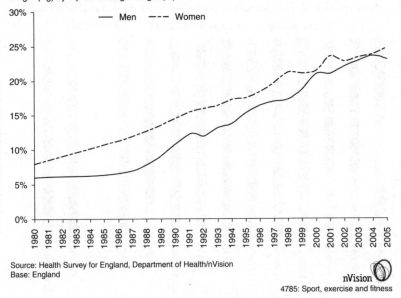

Prevalence of obesity, by gender

Obesity is defined as a body mass index (BMI) above 30 The BMI can be calculated by dividing weight (Kg) by square of length/height (m)

Source: Health Survey for England, Department of Health/nVision
Base: England

nVision
4785: Sport, exercise and fitness

Figure 15.8: The rise of obesity.

To understand the factors which differentiate the two countries, it is necessary to look more closely at each nation's behaviours which determine health. The United Kingdom and Finland have similar proportions of regular smokers (26% and 23% respectively). Consumers in both nations drink the same amount — approximately 11.3 L of pure alcohol per year. Diet is one indicator of the differentiation: 83% of Finns feel that they eat a good, balanced diet in comparison with only 64% of British. However, the clearest mark of differentiation is the government's sports policy and its effect on the nation's physical activity. The Finnish government invests far more in sport; their annual expenditure per head is £83.80 (US $167.60), whereas in England it is £36.10 (US $72.20).

The Finnish government also invests heavily in sport as a vehicle for social inclusion. In the United Kingdom there has been a professionalisation of sport which discourages many social players. There is an element of social exclusion in this because participation becomes more elite. In contrast, in Finland the Department for Social Affairs and Health invests heavily in community facilities. Every town has an outdoor municipal ice rink that converts to a tennis court in summer. There is also a focus on programmes that help people with limited physical mobility to exercise.

The result is that in Finland 53% of the population exercise at the minimum recommended levels — three half-hour sessions a week. In Britain the proportion is 21%. Undoubtedly, government expenditure and strategy are key factors in a nation's fitness.

Healthy lifestyle segmentation in Europe, by country
Proportion who combine different types of healthy and
unhealthy behaviours

"Now lets talk about your lifestyle do you or don't you..."Eat a balanced diet...Exercise at least twice a week....Regularly drink alcohol...Smoke?"

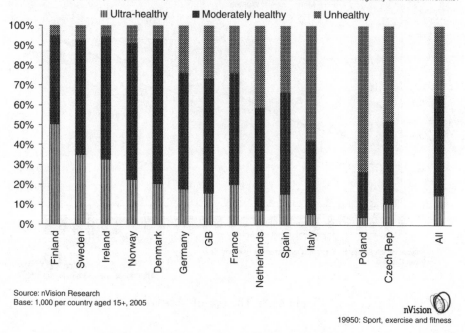

Source: nVision Research
Base: 1,000 per country aged 15+, 2005

nVision
19950: Sport, exercise and fitness

Figure 15.9: Healthy lifestyles in Europe.

Sport and the Media

As participation in sport stagnates, our interest in and passion for watching sports grows. Every year more people, globally, tune in to major sports events. Football players have become A-list celebrities. Even certain female segments of the population who have traditionally shunned sports have suddenly taken an extremely keen interest in both the games and the WAGS (football players' wives and girlfriends). Indeed, many sports, particularly football, have 'matured' into a cult of celebrity.

Viewing figures for sporting events are growing, whether the Olympic Games, Wimbledon or English Premier League. The amount of money invested in sport is also growing. In 1992, when BSkyB first bought the right to televise Premier League football live, it paid £180 million (US $360 million), but this rose to £1.1 billion (US $2.2 billion) in 2003. Today, each English premier club is guaranteed £100 million compared to £2 million (US $4 million) per football club in Scotland. News headlines about John Terry, the Chelsea captain, being paid £130,000 per week (US $260,000) in 2007 or Craig Gordon's transfer to Sunderland for £9 million (US $18 million) have turned footballers into the new superstars. The spin-off has been the phenomenon of 'footballers' wives', with Coleen McLoughlin, partner of Manchester United star, Wayne Rooney, a celebrity and a brand in her own right.

Sport, in particular football, has become a symbol of identity and nationalism. Football is bigger than religion, with more supporters attending football matches at weekends than attending church services on a Sunday. We could say that more people have faith in Manchester United's Cristiano Ronaldo or Liverpool's Steven Gerrard than in God, some would also say they are gods — but that is a different story!

The comparison of footballers with gods identifies sport as a major social narrative. Along with other facets of popular culture, such as music and films, it is a topic which can be discussed easily anywhere and at any time. Indeed, is it a form of social 'glue' — an aspect that links people's lives across any demographic divide. Football has cultural capital (Jenkins, 1992), especially amongst males: 60% of men — in contrast to 25% of women — talk about sport on a regular basis with their friends and family (Figure 15.10). It is among young males that interest is highest; there is then a sudden drop in the 35–44 age group, presumably because people are going through the stage of having young families and have less time to participate in or, far more likely, to watch sport on a regular basis. Consumers in the AB social grade converse about sport far more than those in any other social grade. In a study of topics of social currency, Future Foundation research asked people what they talk about with their friends and family, asking them to make a choice from a list of 16 items. The topics varied greatly-from cars to spirituality to music. AB's were far more likely to talk about every topic, with the exception of health and diet and clothes/fashion. Nearly 70% of AB's talked regularly about sport, probably

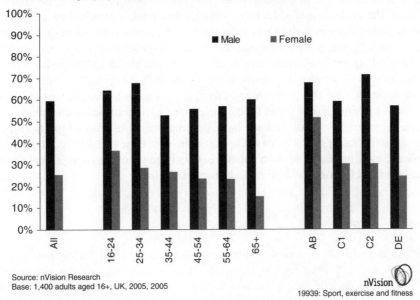

Sport as a topic of conversation, by gender
Proportion who personally talk about each topic with their friends and family
Which of the following do you personally talk about with your friends and family?

Source: nVision Research
Base: 1,400 adults aged 16+, UK, 2005, 2005

nVision
19939: Sport, exercise and fitness

Figure 15.10: Sport as a topic of conversation.

the nation's most dynamically viral theme. Few other subjects offer such vast communication possibilities, especially for the male and to the wealthier consumer.

Demographics

It is a well-known fact that Britain's population is ageing. In 30 years time, more than half the population will be aged over 40. Nearly a quarter of the population will be aged 65 or more, that is, almost as many as will be aged between 16 and 39. Sports participation by older people remains relatively low. Certainly, this is partly because they have lower levels of fitness than those enjoyed by their younger counterparts. However, participation is also greatly limited because of the lack of opportunity. Indeed, sports opportunities in Britain are greatly youth focused. While this phenomenon may not seem something particularly out of the ordinary, it again points to the ever-accelerating professionalisation of sport. As sport becomes increasingly competitive there is less room for those who are not highly physically fit, which includes the ageing population. Life expectancy in the United Kingdom is currently 76 for men and 80 for women. People are not only living longer, but are also living healthier lives than ever before, but there is little opportunity for older people to express their physical vitality. The problems of social isolation amongst the older generations are well known and sport could act as a vehicle for social inclusion initiatives. This is a market with an enormous amount of untapped potential. Can we expect more tournaments and championships for the over-sixties in the future, just as there are golf tournaments for seniors today?

A well-documented phenomenon of the twenty-first century is the inexorable decline of the nuclear family. In 1961, 48% of households consisted of a family with children; today this proportion has dropped to 27% and is forecast to decline further. Concurrently, single-person households of under pensionable age are increasing rapidly; by 2030, they will make up over 25% of all households in the United Kingdom.

The increased number of single households will drive the demand for more outside-home leisure (because individuals seek company as well as entertainment), but leisure providers must focus on offering more variety of non-competitive sports. As mentioned earlier, dance classes have become one of the most rapidly embraced physical activities within the past 20 years. In our increasingly sedentary society, people are looking less towards competitive sports and more towards social sports — a means to meet people as well as to become healthier.

Attitudinal Trends

Over the past 25 years, people have increasingly concerned themselves with self-expression and individualism. As Figure 15.11 shows, the proportion of people who feel that 'it is important to fit in' has fallen from about approximately half of the population to just over a third. Within the same time period, we have experienced the rise of consumer culture where people express many facets of their identity through

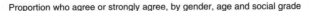

"It's more important to fit in than to be different from other people"

Proportion who agree or strongly agree, by gender, age and social grade

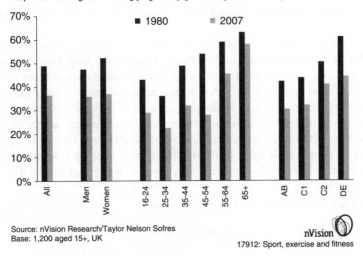

Source: nVision Research/Taylor Nelson Sofres
Base: 1,200 aged 15+, UK

nVision

17912: Sport, exercise and fitness

Figure 15.11: Individualism.

what they consume or do, rather than what they produce or feel. This has led to the fragmentation of the sports' market as consumers seek individual interests in sport in a bid to differentiate themselves from others. In the 1970s, according to the NHS General Health Survey (McMahon-Beattie & Yeoman, 2004) sports chosen for the survey were limited to walking, swimming, snooker/pool/billiards, cycling, darts, football, golf, weightlifting, running, keep fit/yoga, ten-pin bowls/skittle and badminton. This is, of course, not to say that these were the only sports that existed at the time. However, it was generally understood that there were certain core sports — and there was certainly far less choice than today. A quick check on www.wikipedia.com for sports shows that it lists almost 350 activities. Additionally, sports are broken down into categories such as team sports, opponent sports, achievement sports, extreme sports and the list continues. This expansion in the diversity of sports is also linked to the consumers' desire for new experiences in which, increasingly, differentiation is important.

The growth of self-expression will continue to play a dominant role in the years to come and the sports world will respond to demand by offering more unique/exciting experiences, leading to even greater market fragmentation.

Sport and Self-Improvement

In our era of affluence, people approach life with a voracious appetite to 'have it all'. However, the connotations of this have changed since the 1980s and 1990s, when 'having it all' conjured up images of a high-powered woman executive successfully juggling career, family and social life. Now, 'having it all' refers to individual choice, to living life as one wants to rather than adhering to traditional notions of success, and not denying oneself any value-laden experience in spite of stress and shortage of time.

As an intrinsic facet of 'having it all', many consumers are constantly on the lookout for self-improvement, to be better in whatever way they choose. This is evident in a variety of areas of life, for example, adult education courses which do not lead to an official qualification, that is learning for leisure, have never been as popular as they are now. There is also a relationship between those who participate in certain types of sport and their strong self-improvement ethic, showing that participation is often inherent to the notion of betterment. Figure 15.12 shows the proportion of people who work hard at self-improvement by frequently taking part in various sports. The conclusion is broadly clear — sport is considered to be closely

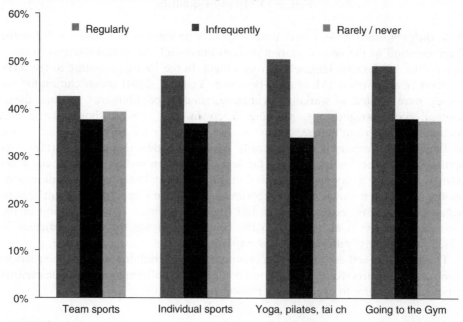

Sports and exercise participation, by self improvement ethic

Proportion of people who work hard at self improvement and participate in the following activities, by frequency*

"Which of these statements comes closest to your own feelings? Self improvement..?"

Source: nVision Research
Base: 1,400 adults aged 16+, UK, 2005

nVision
19944: Sport, exercise and fitness

Figure 15.12: Sport and self-improvement.

associated with self-improvement, a term which suggests something far more than simply exercising, having fun or losing weight. The most pronounced drop in participation is in yoga, Pilates and tai chi. The reason for this is obvious — benefits from these sports are known to go beyond the physical and the self-aggrandising. It is unclear how this trend towards self-improvement will affect the entire sports market. Although there will always be a core of consumers using sports as means for self-improvement, others may adopt a more passive approach to enhancing their lives.

Nonetheless, research by the Future Foundation shows that the market for seeking self-improvement through sports is likely to grow. Sport providers who offer opportunities for consumers to improve in a variety of ways, not just physically, should enjoy success. This does not always have to lead down the well-trodden path of yoga and Pilates, but could be as innovative as dance classes coupled with optional classes on dance history.

Two of the beneficiaries of sport and self-improvement are charity and volunteering. As society has become wealthier, sporting events have leveraged charity giving as a reason for participation, whether marathon-running or extreme-sporting events (see Figure 15.13). For example, in 2006 more than 36,000 athletes participated in the London Marathon, with over £41.5 million (US $83 million) raised for charity. The Marathon has grown exponentially since 1981 when 7747 runners took part and the runners have cumulatively raised over £315 million (US $630 million) for charity over the years. Today, most capital cities in the world have a marathon, such as Beijing, Olso, New York and Boston. Year on year, these marathons have seen growth both in the number of participants and in the amount raised for charities.

Sport and Nationhood

Tessa Jowell (2004), the UK Olympics Minister, was quoted as saying 'sports define us as a nation'. Indeed, sport has always acted as much more than a means to an end or just a leisure activity. It is central to defining our national identity. In particular, football's role as a signifier of English culture and Englishness has long been recognised. McKibbin (2000) in his book, *Classes and Cultures*, observed that football was 'one of the most powerful of England's civic cultures'. Unlike some other sports, football in the United Kingdom can be played in the international arena by the four countries as separate, individual, national teams only. However, until recent years English fans have nonetheless used the Union Jack interchangeably with the St. George's Cross when supporting England. In 2002, however, this changed, when, at the World Cup the St. George's Cross predominated over the Union Jack (Polley, 2004). This happened within the context of the Labour government's proactive policy towards devolution in the United Kingdom. True, England fans may not have been consciously thinking about this, but it was still an overt show of nationalism in a context of confusion over the true notion of Britishness.

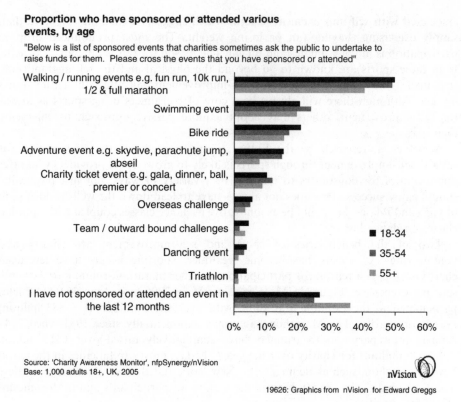

Proportion who have sponsored or attended various events, by age

"Below is a list of sponsored events that charities sometimes ask the public to undertake to raise funds for them. Please cross the events that you have sponsored or attended"

Source: 'Charity Awareness Monitor', nfpSynergy/nVision
Base: 1,000 adults 18+, UK, 2005

nVision

19626: Graphics from nVision for Edward Greggs

Figure 15.13: Sport sponsorship.

Hume (2002) noted that many people hope that sports fixtures can re-create a sense of community and togetherness. Such hopes are high at this time; yet, never have they been more likely to be dashed. In an era of globalisation, national identities are becoming increasingly fragmented and difficult to define. Necessary for any national identity are grand narratives storylines which define a nation and a culture. In the United Kingdom, sport has always been one of them and in football in particular overtly display of nationalism has become even more central to defining nationality in a world where identities are becoming more fluid every day.

Sport and Events

There seems no doubting the effect that major sporting events can have on the nation's psyche but what are the lasting effects? Do they play any role in increasing participation or are they simply emotive and economic? These are the questions that governments of host countries ask themselves in the run-up to major international sporting events in an attempt to make the benefits long term and sustainable.

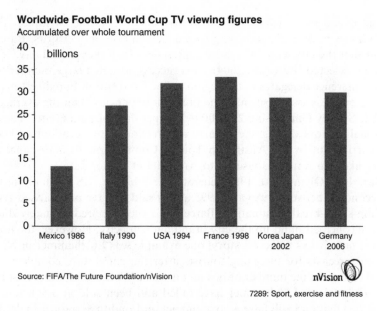

Worldwide Football World Cup TV viewing figures
Accumulated over whole tournament

Figure 15.14: FIFA world cup viewing figures.

The significance of major events such as the World Cup or the Olympics can hardly be understated. As Figure 15.14 shows, they attract millions of viewers worldwide. Britain has had relative success in recent years in a number of different sports — swimming at the 2005 Olympics, the Rugby World Cup in 2004 and the Ashes in 2005. While this has brought strong emotions at home, these achievements have not really affected the consumers' long-term attitudes towards sport or their behaviour. People's levels of physical activity remain as low as ever.

There are no doubts over the short-term economic benefits of sporting events. For example, the increase in tourism can be phenomenal for major events, but in terms of economics, poor planning can lead to problems in the long term. For instance, mismatched supply and demand conditions can result in bankruptcies, foreclosures and other negative economic conditions that can undermine the stability of the host region. Citizens are generally positive about hosting major events. A recent ICM poll (BBC, 2006c) showed that 77% of UK citizens were pleased that the Olympics are to be held in London in 2012.

The Olympics may cost the taxpayer a great deal of money but it is generally felt that it will be worth it for national prestige, the feel-good factor and possible encouragement of sports. Indeed, the population of the United Kingdom is positive about the Olympics.

The moment on 6th July 2006 when cheers erupted from the Trafalgar Square crowds as it was announced that London would hold the Olympic Games 2012 is already a nostalgic euphoria in the national memory. The challenge now is to turn this mega event into one which will result in long-term sustainable benefits rather than a short-lived time of economic windfalls for a small part of the country.

Tourism is one sector which will obviously benefit from the Olympics. The 2004 Olympic Games in Sydney, according to the Convention and Visitors' Bureau, had the benefit that the city won 34% more conferences than they would have if Sydney had not been selected (Edwards, 2004). This success attracted large numbers of high-spending conference delegates to the region — the Convention Bureau estimated that the average business visitor spends nine times more per day than the average leisure tourist. The Sydney Games sold 250,000 tickets per day for paid events. The number of additional visitors during the Games was reckoned to be about 110,000, and research carried out by the Australian Tourist Commission estimated that 88% of these were likely to return as visitors to Australia at a later date.

The Barcelona Olympics of 1992 generated £8.8 billion (US $16.6 billion) for the Spanish economy between 1986 and 1993 and is said to have popularised Barcelona as a leading short-break destination. Barcelona's success, predominately due to the Olympics, has helped build up the city brand and capacity. However, the hosting of Olympics is not always a success story; one example was Lillehammer in Norway in 1994, when forecasts for incoming tourists after the game were completely wrong. The actual change in the number of bed nights was 67% less than the lowest forecast, and 40% of hotels in Lillehammer have failed and been sold at a substantial loss. Therefore the Olympics will have a large impact on London as a tourism destination, in terms of destination brand, capacity building and social narrative.

Concluding Thoughts

Sport is both a product (extreme sports) and a place (Olympic Games). As the British economy has moved from a manufacturing to a service-based economy, sport has emerged as an important sector of tourism. Politicians, especially in Western economies, no longer talk about inward investment in terms of shipbuilding, coalmining or even technology but in terms of sports events and tourism. The sports events are part of the product mix in which countries promote themselves as places to visit, work, live and play. At the same time, consumers are pushing out their personal boundaries, wanting more individuality and diversity of experiences, and being concerned about their health and image, leading to the emergence of extreme sports. Eventually, extreme sports will evolve into mainstream, just like mountain biking and snow sports. Looking into the future, the competition to host extreme and mainstream sporting events will be intensive, so that's why the *Urban Rat Race* may become an Olympic event in future, maybe not in 2012 … but perhaps in 2032.

Chapter 16

The Space Tourist: A Metaphor for Understanding the Changing Meaning of Luxury and the Desire for New Experiences

> In 2030 Gleneagles Space Station will be the worlds most exclusive resort, catching the Virgin Galactic from Auchterarder, space tourists will fasten there seat belts and hear the rockets roar. As the spaceship reaches the stratosphere, they will gaze down to Planet Earth for the most exclusive view in the world, all for the exclusive price of US $50,000.
>
> Report in the Sunday Times Travel Supplement on the 29th June 2030

Introduction

In 2030, the Gleneagles Lunar Space Station will be the world's most exclusive resort. Catching the Virgin Galactic from Auchterarder, space tourists will fasten their seat belt, hear the rockets roar and feel a sudden power acceleration of 4G. As the spaceship reaches the stratosphere, tourists will gaze down on the Planet Earth for the most exclusive view in the world. During their stay at the Gleneagles Space Station tourists will take in a round of golf, take the lunar buggy out for a spin and float around the leisure complex. They will enjoy the best of Scottish cuisine — vacuum packed.

Sound a bit far fetched? Well it is not. The Virgin Galactic is a real proposition, starting a regular passenger service in 2009 from New Mexico. It is an exclusive travel experience, with celebrities and the mega-rich initially paying US $200,000 (£100,000) for the privilege. However, by 2012, this price should fall to US $75,000 (£37,500).

But in real terms this is far cheaper than the first scheduled flight to cross the Atlantic in 1939. Then, passengers paid US $75,000 in today's money. Today the average fare across the Atlantic is over US $600 (£300). So by 2030 space tourism should be affordable for us all. The space tourism phenomenon is driven by the consumers' desire for new experiences and luxury markets. For Scottish tourism, it is about understanding now tourism and the tourist is changing, as expectations and desires will be different tomorrow. In this chapter, space tourism is used as a metaphor to understand that change.

Space Tourism

In the words of Captain James T Kirk the final frontier refers to transcending the boundaries of the universe, and into the realm of God, truly where no man has gone before. Space tourism is the ultimate tourism adventure. According to Duval (2005) the desire and market is there. With advances in science and technology space tourism in 2030 may have opened up to the masses. The desire for travel into space is not new. Since the first organised tours under the guidance of Thomas Cook, curiosity about travel to space has being relentless, given that over half a million people in the United States formally apply each year to become astronauts (Tito, 2003) and is best represented in Stanley Kubrick's movie *2001: A Space Odyssey* which saw tourists travelling to the moon on Pan AM SST (Morgan, 2001) The first space tourist was Dennis Tito. Tito spent US $20 million for the opportunity to ride a Russian Soyuz rocket and capsule that eventually docked with the international space station. Mark Shuttleworth was the second space tourist, spending 1 week abroad the same station as Tito. Today, Space Adventures, a company based in the United States has entered into a relationship with Rosaviakosmos, the Russian space agency to fly at least two more individuals to the International Space Station within the next couple of years. Although in 2008, space tourism is limited to the mega-rich who want the most exclusive experience — however by 2030, space travel could become a mass tourism experience when the cost of air travel in 1939 is compared to the present. Flying to Australia or to a far away place is now within the reach of most middle classes of the world. So given a similar time period, space tourism becomes affordable and reachable for most of us. However, space tourism is only the metaphor for the underlining core drivers of the desire for new experiences and the changing definition of luxury.

The Desire for New Experiences

With rising affluence, consumer values have changed, with a lessening emphasis upon material possessions and an increasing concern for experiential and quality of life issues. The tourist in 2030 will be keen to spend money in new ways that grant them access to new experiences or awareness of new ways of living. As goods and services are no longer enough, in today's society an increasingly competitive environment means tourism providers must learn to stage experiences, this is what Pine and Gilmore (1999) called the *Experience Economy*. In 2005, according to the Future Foundation, the UK consumer spent £101 billion (US $202 billion) on enrichment compared to £61 billion (US $122 billion) on material goods. Only about one-third of

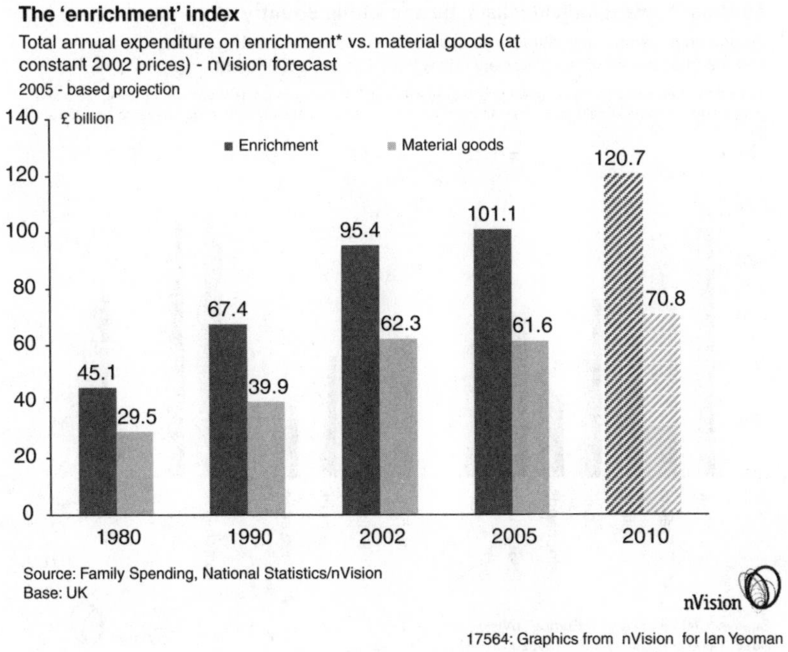
The 'enrichment' index
Total annual expenditure on enrichment* vs. material goods (at constant 2002 prices) - nVision forecast
2005 - based projection
£ billion
Enrichment
Material goods
140
120
100
80
60
40
20
0
45.1
29.5
67.4
39.9
95.4
62.3
101.1
61.6
120.7
70.8
1980
1990
2002
2005
2010
Source: Family Spending, National Statistics/nVision
Base: UK
nVision
17564: Graphics from nVision for Ian Yeoman

Figure 16.1: The enrichment index.

all household spending is now devoted to what economists call tangibles — the author estimates that by 2030, enrichment expenditure will have reached 70% (Figure 16.1).

The biggest beneficiary of this rise has been the tourism and leisure industries. As affluence has increased over the past 30 years there has been a corresponding rise in the repertoire of activities that consumers 'try-out' in any given time period. Today, consumers differentiate themselves with what they do rather than what they buy; they are more individualistic than any other generation. This is particular stronger in countries with higher GDP per capita such as Norway and Sweden (Figure 16.2).

The best example of this has been the rise of niche tourism products, especially adventure tourism, whether this is bugging (white water rafting without the raft) or recreating a Tour De France cycling holiday.

As we see in Figure 16.3, there is a desired exposure to a broader range of activities than was available in the past and that certain activities are no longer regarded as 'special'. For example, most people do not feel that going out for a meal is any longer something out of the ordinary. This is not to say that they do not enjoy going out for a meal or that a meal cannot be a special occasion — but simply that eating out is now regarded as a more everyday activity than in the past. There is a profound yearning for new experiences — which has resulted in a 'checklist mentality' when it comes to trying new things. Consumers increasingly try out something once so they have had the experience but will not necessarily do it again — a one-off experience that does not have to enter their regular portfolio of activities. In doing this they will

Attitudes toward individualism, by age within country

Proportion of people who 'agree' with the statement "people should go along
with the mainstream views of society rather than trying to be different"

"Please indicate how much you agree or disagree with each of the statements I read out by using the scale
on the card...People should go along with the mainstream views of society rather than trying to be different"

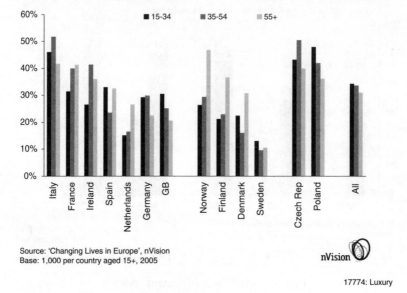

Source: 'Changing Lives in Europe', nVision
Base: 1,000 per country aged 15+, 2005

nVision

17774: Luxury

Figure 16.2: The rise of individualism.

also often take a risk and try something adventurous. The consumer wants to be
challenged, is seeking a thrill and wants to avoid boredom.

Another significant beneficiary of the desire for new experience is the hobby
tourist or what Silverstein et al. (2005) call *questering*. This could mean the
experience of becoming engrossed in a sport and playing at club level, or the
experience of becoming an art, wine or food connoisseur, in short, new experiences
are defined by becoming passionate about a specific activity. Take the example of
Jake, who is a recreational golfer who will pay US $4000 for a complete set of
Callaway clubs, when a similar set of clubs can be purchased for US $300. Why?

> He does not fit the bill of a typical golfer (Jake) — the well heeled,
> executive duffer. He is a thirty four year old construction worker who
> earns US $18 per hour, paid in cash at the end of the shift — less that
> US $50,000 a year. Throughout the eight-month golf season, Jake
> works the early shift, starting at 6 am, so he can be on the golf course
> by 2 pm. He plays eighteen holes Monday through Friday and thirty-
> six holes — on Saturday and Sunday, He is a three-index golfer, which
> means he is expected to shoot just three holes over par. Jake is single
> and lives alone in a one bedroom apartment he rents for US $600 a

Trying lots of different leisure activities

% who agree strongly / agree

"Please indicate how much you agree or disagree with each of the statements that I read out...
I like to try lots of different leisure activities, rather than concentrating on a few"

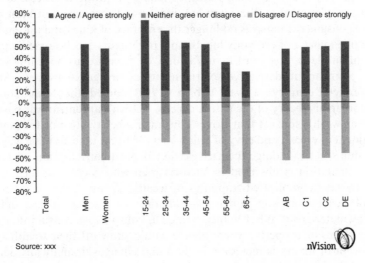

Source: xxx   nVision

Figure 16.3: Trying lots of leisure activities.

month. He has dated many women but has never found who will tolerate his 'addiction' to golf. ... (Jake says) "these are the best clubs money can buy". ... "they cost me a pretty penny, and I have to save money for a whole year to buy them, but they've worth it." He described in detail the technical differences: the titanium face, the expanded sweet spot, the balances weight and the other features. To afford them, Jack told us that he has to distort his spending — he was a true golf rocketer. "Forty cents for every dollar I make goes on golf fees, equipment, golf clothes and golf trips," he said "Golf is my life."

Technical differences and performance improvements were only part of the attraction Jake felt for Callaway. "The real reason I bought them" he says, "is that they make me feel rich. You can run the biggest company in the world and be one of the richest guys in the world, but you can't buy better clubs than these" ... "I can match up with guys like you all the time. You are tight, stressed and don't practice very much. When I kick your butt on the course, I feel good. I feel equal. I may make a lot less than you, but I think I have a better time.

(Silverstein et al., 2005, pp. 226–227)

Jakes story is about that recreational golfer who is passionate and emotional about golf. To him golf is his luxury; nothing comes before it (including girlfriends).

Defining Luxury

Luxury is no longer reserved for the selected few; it is now within the reach of middle classes of the world due to rising affluence based on property prices, low interest rates, stable employment markets and low inflation. Times have not been better for the average consumer. Luxury is no longer the embrace of kings and queens but mass marketing phenomena of everyday life. Simply put, luxury has become luxurification of the common place. The word luxury is derived from Luxus, meaning sensuality, splendour, pomp and its derivative luxuria, means extravagance, riot, etc. At the turn of the twentieth century, it was Veblen (1994) coined the term 'conspicuous consumption' in his theory of the leisure classes. Veblen's argument was based on the belief that as wealth spreads that drives consumer's behaviour not for comfort but the 'attainment of esteem and envy of fellow men.' At that time, as male wage earners are too circumspect to indulge themselves, they deposit consumption on surrogates. Vicarious ostentation is observed in Victoria men who encourage their wives and daughters to wear complicated trappings of wealth. What Veblen thought that the purpose of acquisition was public consumption of esteem, status and anxiety displayed by materialism. What Veblen termed as conspicuous consumption were the trophies as slaves or property, where people would show off their wealth.

The concept of luxury is incredibility fluid and changes dramatically across time and culture. In the past it was associated with champagne, caviar, designer clothes and sports cars. Nowadays with increased affluence, luxury is a blurred genre which is no longer the preserve of the elite. More and more consumers have traded up as the old values of tradition and nobility have become less important. People are enjoying much more material comfort in comparison to previous generations, resulting in a trend of a cultural shift for personal fulfilment and aspiration through experience. Therefore, it could be argued that luxury is increasingly about enrichment and time, as well as materialism (Figure 16.4).

This focus on enrichment and time means increasing emphasis on personal transformation through, for example well-being and travel. This means that consumers want to improve their life. This is what Danziger (2005), Israel (2003) and Gamber (1997) defined as the feminisation of luxury, where luxury has moved on from its male trophies and status symbols towards experience and indulgence. Therefore, luxury is becoming a lot more difficult to define, as the language has changed. Luxury today is not a necessity or necessarily expensive. It can be mass market, not traditional, but personal, authentic and experiential. Although, the old world luxury of consumption and elitism still prevails.

In the Western world, there has actually been a decrease in paid work-time during the last decade — although there is a misconception that the opposite is happening. Still, people's perception that they live under increased time-pressure is growing, perhaps because after time has been allocated to both paid and unpaid chores like housework, the left-over time for leisure is crammed with an ever growing desire for doing more stuff, go on more holidays, regularly seeing friends and family, etc. — but there still only remains 24 h in the day. Women as well as people in the family stage/career-stage are more likely to report stress. In effect free time has become an

Redefining Luxury: Materialism, enrichment
and Time

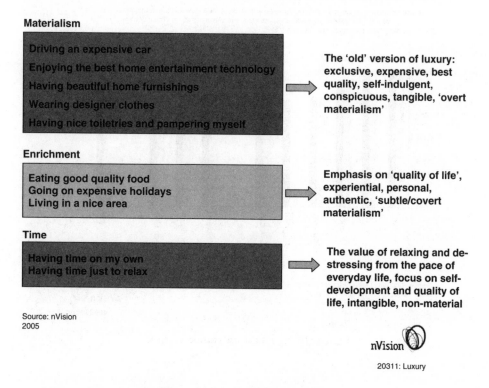

Materialism

Driving an expensive car

Enjoying the best home entertainment technology

Having beautiful home furnishings

Wearing designer clothes

Having nice toiletries and pampering myself

The 'old' version of luxury:
exclusive, expensive, best
quality, self-indulgent,
conspicuous, tangible, 'overt
materialism'

Enrichment

Eating good quality food
Going on expensive holidays
Living in a nice area

Emphasis on 'quality of life',
experiential, personal,
authentic, 'subtle/covert
materialism'

Time

Having time on my own
Having time just to relax

The value of relaxing and de-
stressing from the pace of
everyday life, focus on self-
development and quality of
life, intangible, non-material

Source: nVision
2005

nVision

20311: Luxury

Figure 16.4: Defining luxury.

ever more sought after resource and so has the understanding of 'quality-time'
changed (See Figure 16.5).

This means that luxury for more people translates into the simple pleasure of
having time on their own to relax. This can mean legs up reading a book or, as many
leisure providers have already spotted, taking a liking to recreational therapies such
as spa-treatments or yoga-classes. This is about striking the balance and combining
the desire for leisure, self-development, new experiences, and, creating a time-oasis
for all those busy, stressed out people.

Enrichment is all about improving the quality of your life through experimental
and less subtle material — not the 'bling' but the wow. As discussed earlier, this
drives the desire for new experiences — the constant search for novelty and change.
From a tourism perspective, destinations offer diversity and activity. Whether this
searching for ancestors or painting a landscape. These activities are both mind and
body for tomorrow's tourist (Figure 16.6).

As luxurification becomes commonplace, due to the rises in disposal income of the
middle classes, consumers start to trade up. Silverstein et al. (2005) work on trading

Perception of time pressure, by country and gender

Proportion who agree or strongly agree that they are under time pressure in their everyday life

"Please indicate how much you agree or disagree with each of the following statements that I read out.
Remember, we are interested in your attitudes, opinions and views alone, not those of others. Firstly...
I'm often under time pressure in my everyday life"

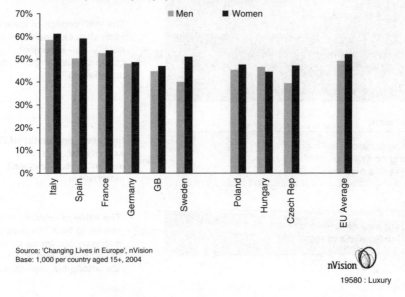

Source: 'Changing Lives in Europe', nVision
Base: 1,000 per country aged 15+, 2004

nVision

19580 : Luxury

Figure 16.5: The importance of time.

up explores the US phenomena of middle-market, middle-income earners who are willing to pay premium prices for products and services that possess higher levels of quality, taste and aspiration than other goods in the same category. These 'new luxury' goods have flouted conventional wisdom that suggest the higher the price the lower the volume. These new luxury goods sell at higher prices and at higher volumes than traditional luxury goods. The washing machine, once a luxury for the very rich was transformed to an everyday household item in the 1960s. It is no longer a luxury item, as society has become more affluent. Silverstein et al. highlight how the middle-market consumer selectively trades up to better products and services and trades down in others to pay for his or her premium purchases. This is a person who travels with a budget carrier but stays in a five-star hotel. Much of this change on the demand side has come about due to a rise in real incomes and home equity, the cash windfall delivered by mass retailers, the changing role of women and the family structure, the rise in divorce, the increasing worldliness and sophistication of the consumer and the increased focus on emotions and growing cultural permission to spend have been drivers of luxury.

On the supply side we have witnessed the impact of the role of the entrepreneur, shifts in the dynamics of retailing and the increased access to flexible supply-chain networks and global resources. As consumers trade up, they spend 20–200% above

Attitudes towards novelty and change

Proportion who agree or strongly agree that they would welcome
more novelty and change in their life, by gender and social grade

"Please indicate how much you agree or disagree with each of thestatements that I read out.
Remember that we are interested in your attitudes, opinions and views - yours alone, not those of others.
Firstly ... I would welcome more novelty and change in my life."

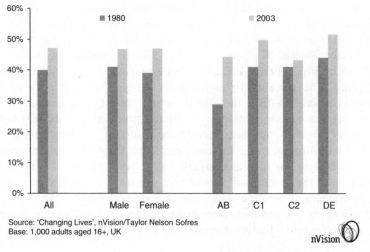

Source: 'Changing Lives', nVision/Taylor Nelson Sofres
Base: 1,000 adults aged 16+, UK

nVision

16952: Graphics from nVision for Jamie Allsopp

Figure 16.6: Novelty and change.

the norm for the product or the service. Consumers have woken up to appreciate
better quality wines or how they have a desire for faraway exotic holidays. Everyday
goods and services such as cosmetics, sandwiches, white goods and pet foods are now
traded up. The basis of trading up is access and aspiration. Examples would include
the Mercedes-Benz C-class that constituted the affordable version of a product that
has traditionally been bought only by more wealthy consumers. Such goods offer an
emotional engagement whether it is premium vodka or an environmentally sensitive
cosmetic range such as Veda.

What is also interesting is how consumers are trading up to aspirational new
luxury goods and trading down to products and services that are less important to
them. This type of product and service mixing (disharmony of consumption) is
occurring in retail as consumers shop at Wal-Mart or ASDA but drive a Mercedes.
The analogy in the tourism sector is apparent in the use of budget air travel and the
purchase of quality accommodation and food in the host destination.

In terms of consumer drivers the demand for luxury is affected by demographics
and cultural shifts. In addition the degree and amount of disposable income has
increased significantly. This has been catalysed by the growth in consumer credit and
the contribution to consumer wealth made by large discount retailers. In recent years,
they have reduced the costs of living substantially for middle-market consumers.
Furthermore, the increasingly active role of female consumers has helped catalyse

luxury demand at a range of levels. The fact that couples are getting married later in life (if at all) and are having fewer children (often later in life) means that the amount of disposable income for luxuries has grown substantially. The increasing number of singles and the growing divorce rate means that the amount of money spent on the individual has increased. Such expenditure is often used to help rebuild lives, confidence and provide a panacea for emotional distress. In such cases the propensity of the consumer to spend on luxury products and services will increase.

A further influence on the luxury spend profile is the relative sophistication of the consumer. In the United Kingdom and the United States, the middle-market consumer is increasingly better educated, better travelled, more adventurous and more discerning. The pressure to increase the amount of graduates in the UK workforce will continue to drive the growth of the sophisticated consumer.

Other key impacts include availability of luxury products and services not just in traditional retail contexts but also in electronic format via the Internet. Travel buying, data on destinations and the continual emergence of new locations means that luxury availability has increased significantly. Furthermore, the disinflation of travel supply and the continued downward pressure on prices has served to 'democratise' travel and in some senses this has democratised 'luxury.' Previously exclusive destinations and products from cruises to resorts have become more widely available and their relative badge of exclusivity has become more main stream.

Conclusion

In the future, space will not be the final frontier, with the advent of vessels such as the Virgin Galactic, the desire of new experiences and luxury will become more mainstream by 2030. Space travel means the ultimate adventure is here as the technologies and science makes it affordable and accessible. The creation of space travellers is the ultimate dream of glory, adventure and something to tell the grand children. This phenomena means luxury is more experimental and individualistic than ever before. The future tourist is looking for newness and adventure which is fulfilling and distinguishes them from the crowd. Luxury has now definitely moved from the physical to the more emotive appeal. Space tourism maybe the ultimate luxury experience, but it is only a metaphor for understanding that change.

Chapter 17

The Gambler in Macao: Las Vegas of the Orient

Your future is decided by the spin of the roulette wheel. Macao is a place where the poor feel rich and the rich lose thousands on the throw of a dice. Euphoria is Macao's defining mood, where you play the penny slot machines or drop a bankroll every night. A place where Playboy bunnies offer complimentary drinks — whether you are a novice or a high-roller. Careering from one opulent casino to the next, looking for the next red-hot table, downing martinis, smoking stogies and devouring sizzling, Peking-style fillet steak with noodles — you'll pinch yourself and ask, does this ever have to end? Time is irrelevant as there are no clocks, just never-ending buffets and ever-flowing drinks. Acrobats spiral above the blackjack tables in the MGM Grand and fountains play musical masterpieces in the Harrah's Deluxe. Macao is the ultimate in conspicuous consumption for the Chinese tourist. You can indulge in a spa after midnight, slip past a nightclub's velvet ropes after hopping out of a stretch limo and taste the seven-star offerings of Asia's top chef's. Emptying your wallet never felt so damn good. Macao is the Las Vegas of the Orient, where anything happens and anything goes — well away from those dull days of Communist rule in a bygone era.

Report in the China Times, 24th September 2030.

By 2030, Macao will outstrip Las Vegas as the world's most important gambling and entertainment resort. Tourism receipts will rise exponentially from US $7.7 billion in 2005 to US $28 billion (£28 billion) in 2030 (Yeoman & The Future Foundation, 2008). Much of the growth is being driven by the Chinese people's love of gambling and the lack of opportunity to indulge in this passion on mainland China. Macao, from its humble origins as a Portuguese colony, is undergoing a huge transformation and is rapidly becoming the 'Las Vegas of the Orient'. Gambling has been legal in Macao since the 1850s when the Portuguese government legalised it. In 2005, Macao had 24 casinos in operation, plus a dozen under construction, and Playboy organisation has announced that it will open a casino and bunny club by 2009. In 2005, there were 9 million overnight international arrivals, staying in 36,000 hotel bedrooms, plus about 31 million day-trippers — and another 13,000 bedrooms are under construction.

Macao is a gambling state, with 95% of the gamblers from mainland China or Hong Kong. However, this will slowly change as the Western-managed casinos open up and new international visitors from Asia and further afield visit the destination. According to a report by Deutsche Bank (Falcone, 2005), revenue to the Macao casino market will grow by 25% a year over the next 5 years. The average casino win per table per day in Macao is $22,000, compared with $2600 in New Jersey's Atlantic City and $2200 in Las Vegas. As the Chinese economy expands and travel and visa restrictions are relaxed, more and more people are expected to make the trek to Macao. There are more than 100 million people living within a 3-h drive and more than 1 billion within a short plane journey (McCartney, 2006).

China's Rising Middle Class

The rising economy in China will lift hundreds of millions of households out of poverty. In 1985, 99% of Chinese consumers could be classified as poor, but by 2025 only 10% will be, according to forecasts by McKinsey. McKinsey (Farrel, Gersch, & Stephenson, 2006) has established that urban households will make up one of the largest consumer markets in the world, spending about RMB 20 trillion (0.12 RMB: US $1) — almost as much as all Japanese households spend today. Over the next 20 years an increasing number of rural Chinese will migrate to the cities to seek higher-paying jobs. These working consumers, once the country's poorest, will steadily climb the income ladder, creating a massive new middle class. Rapid economic growth will continue to transform the impoverished but largely egalitarian society of China's past into one with distinct income classes. This evolution is already widening the gap between rich and poor, and tackling the resulting social and economic tension has become a focus of government policy. McKinsey's projections indicate, however, that China will avoid the 'barbell economy' that plagues much of the developing world and which results in large numbers of poor, a small group of the very wealthy, and only a few in the middle. Even as the absolute difference between the richest and poorest continues to widen, incomes will increase across all urban segments (Figure 17.1).

As this economic tide rises, McKinsey anticipates two phases of steep growth in the middle class, with waves of consumers in distinct income brackets emerging and receding at specific points. The first wave, predicted to happen in 2010, will be the lower middle class, defined as households with annual incomes of RMB 25,001–40,000. A decade later, the upper middle class, with annual household incomes of RMB 40,001–100,000, will follow. These numbers may seem low compared with consumer incomes in the world's richest countries — current exchange rates and relative prices tend to understate China's buying power — but such people are solidly middle class by global standards. When accounting for purchasing power parity, a household income of RMB 100,000 for instance buys a lifestyle in China similar to that of a household earning $40,000 in the United States. By about 2010 the lower middle class will number some 290 million people, representing the largest segment in

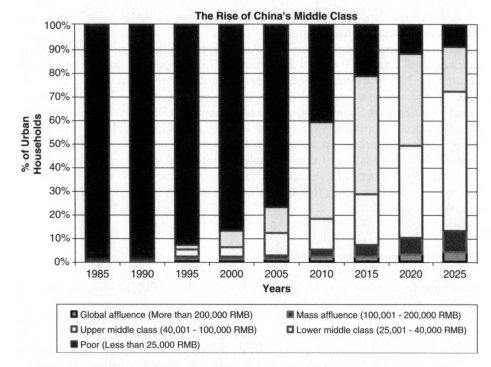

Figure 17.1: China's emerging urban middle classes (*Source*: Farrel et al., 2006).

urban China and accounting for about 44% of the urban population, according to *McKinsey's* model. Growth in this group should peak around 2015, when they will have a total spending power of RMB 4.8 trillion. A second transition is projected to occur in the following decade, when hundreds of millions will join the upper middle class. By 2025 this segment will comprise a staggering 520 million people — more than half of the expected urban population of China — with a combined total disposable income of RMB 13.3 trillion.

Two features of China's emerging middle class are already particularly notable. First, it will be unusually young compared with that of most developed markets, whose highest earners tend to be middle-aged. In the United States, for example, income generally peaks between the ages of 45 and 54. Since higher-paying jobs, on average, require a higher level of education and training than what the older generations have obtained, the Chinese government is currently making substantial investment in higher education for younger people, which means that the country's wealthiest consumers will be between 25 and 44 years old (Farrel et al., 2006).

Second, the urban middle class will dwarf the current urban-affluent segment in both size and total spending power. From 2010 onwards some distinct sub-segments will evolve among the affluent, including the mass- and global-affluent categories, but they will still total only 40 million households by 2025 and account for just 11%

of all urban dwellers. Their total consumption will equal RMB 5.7 trillion — just 41% of middle-class consumption.

While total spending by the middle class will exceed that of affluent consumers, the latter will remain of critical importance. These upper-tier households already account for 25% of Chinese household savings and they will continue to control the bulk of the nation's accumulated wealth — 60% by 2025. These consumers, especially those from Shanghai, Beijing and Guangzhou (Penhirin, 2007), are looking for experiences and products very similar to those found in Hong Kong and in most other developed markets. In addition, government measures to stimulate spending through the consolidation of national holidays into week-long breaks have brought about the development of a leisure class. Consequently, a middle class–leisure class will emerge, so where better to spend this newly gained wealth but in Macao — the Las Vegas of the Orient!

Why Do the Chinese Love Gambling?

According to research by Access Asia Limited (Lam, 2007), keno (a form of gambling) was first played in China about 3000 years ago. The concept of many of today's favourite card games, such as blackjack and poker, is thought to have also been invented here. Gambling, which started as a kind of entertainment, was very popular in ancient China and throughout its history, despite the fact that gambling was under strict regulatory controls and banned. Historically, gambling has always been very popular among the rich as well as the poor and, indeed, throughout Chinese society. According to numerous accounts, the concept of games of chance was introduced during the Xia (2000–1500 B.C.) and Shang (1700–1027 B.C.) dynasties. In fact, gaming had already become very popular among high-class Chinese by the time of the Shang era (Lam, 2007). Today, 'social' gambling in the form of mahjong[1] is common and public lottery games have proliferated (Lam, 2007).

According to Chong (2007) gambling is an acceptable form of social activity in the homes of friends or relatives and is accepted by Chinese society. Gambling is how friends meet to discuss life, engage in business transactions and sign deals. But it must also be remembered that the Chinese visit casinos for financial reasons; they seek instant wealth and material possessions. They also have a hunger for financial

---

1. Mahjong (traditional Chinese pinyin: Májiàng; Cantonese: Màhjeung; other common English spellings include mahjongg, hyphenated forms such as mah-jong or mah-jongg, non-hyphenated forms such as mah jongg or mah jong, and the Pinyin spelling of majiang) is a game for four players, which originated in China. Also known as Chinese: pinyin: Máquè; Cantonese: Màhjeuk; Japanese: Mājan.

Mahjong involves skill, strategy and calculation, as well as a certain degree of luck. Depending on the variation which is played, luck can be anything from a minor to a dominant factor in success. In Asia, mahjong is also popular as gambling or computer games.

The object of the game is to build complete suits — or melds — usually of threes, from either 13 or 16 tiles. The first person to achieve this goal wins the game. The winning tile completes the player's set of either 14 or 17 tiles (Wikipedia, 2007b).

stability and gambling provides one way to achieve this. Daily life is still relatively poor and mundane (especially for the rural population) so gambling is a source of pleasure and excitement as well as a hobby. It is just like going to the pub in England and playing dominoes — a form of social engagement. Gambling is also an escape from life's difficulties. It is also, however, about skill rather than luck, which is why card games like blackjack are popular.

A study by the Hong Kong government into gambling (Centre for Policy Studies, 2002) highlighted the fact that a high proportion of gamblers are exposed to recreational gambling at a very young age, often in childhood, usually at home or in a family environment. They pick up gambling skills (e.g. playing mahjong, cards, etc) from parents, relatives and neighbours. The study also highlighted that gambling is the number-one social activity and is regarded as a socially and culturally acceptable behaviour (Table 17.1).

The Dark Side

The casino industry is viewed by some as harmful to society. A high crime rate was one of the biggest problems that Macao's colonial Portuguese government had to face. Since Macao's return to China's rule in 1999, the public security situation has markedly improved. With the growth of the casino industry, a business called 'bate-ficha' developed, usually run by triad societies. Bate-ficha involves selling customers 'dead chips' that cannot be exchanged for cash in the casinos, but only by bate-ficha men or women, officially known as 'gaming promoters' or 'middlemen', who take a commission.

Triad involvement in Macao casinos makes a serious social impact on the local area, because it attracts the attention of Chinese gangsters, whose deadly battles over the fortunes to be made from racketeering and extortion in Macao are a continuing problem. As different triad societies compete for control of the casinos and the streets, disputes between societies occur from time to time and these are often settled in violent ways. Even worse, triad societies have grown so powerful in Macao that people seek help from them rather than from the police. Although the situation has improved dramatically, where there is gambling there is crime (Wikipedia, 2007a).

Turning Macao into the Las Vegas of Orient

There are no legal gambling resorts in mainland China, but as consumers become wealthier, they want to have fun and, because the Chinese love to gamble, it is guaranteed that gambling in Macao will always be a winner. The potential growth in future demand is nothing short of stratospheric. Macao's key catchment area is southern China, incorporating some of the country's most affluent provinces, with over 90 million people living within a 4-h drive of the gaming tables. While many inhabitants of the southern mainland remain poor, the Chinese love of gambling, the rapidly growing middle class and the improving road infrastructure should result in a

Table 17.1: Reasons for social gambling in Hong Kong.

Group	Years of social gambling	Psychological characteristics	Reasons	Forms of gambling	Amount of wages (HK$ per week)
1	10–20	Gambling was acceptable	To socialise with friends	Cards	200–500
		Winning money was not important	To kill time	Mahjong	
		No strong lust for material possessions	To seek fun and pleasure	Mark six	
		Good control of gambling	To get some money	Horse racing	
		No problem in finance management			
2	30–40	Money was important but not the most important	To kill time	Mahjong	300
		Losses were expected	To seek entertainment	Horse racing	
		To seek entertainment with friends	Habitual leisure activity	Cards	
		Would not gamble alone		Macao casino	
		Refused to borrow to chase after losses		Mark six	
		Health was wealth			
		Life goal: fulfilling mother's role			
3	25–35	To seek entertainment	To seek pleasure	Cards	1000–2000
		To socialise with friends and colleagues	To relax	Mahjong	
		Could accept losing money	To socialise with friends and relatives	Casino ship	
		Can stop gambling at pre-determined level			
		Money fostered a sense of security			
		Family was a source of satisfaction			
		Planned to budget and save up			

steadily increasing target audience. With tourism arrivals to the Macao area[2] forecast to grow from 9 million to 45 million by 2030, so will the demand grow?

---

2. Because of capacity constraints it is envisaged that the Macau casino peninsula (*a peninsula can't expand. How about '…envisaged that the casinos will expand beyond the Macau peninsula and into mainland…'*) will have to expand into mainland China in order to cope with the number of international arrivals forecast by 2030.

A survey by Deloitte (MacCharles & Oaten, 2006) reveals that two-thirds of their respondents had not previously gambled in a casino. However, over 40% of this huge, untapped market is interested in doing so in the future. Large-scale demand clearly exists in volume terms, but once through the casino door, how much are these mass-market customers prepared to spend? The survey suggests that over three-quarters of the Chinese mass-market visitors are likely to spend under US $65 (RMB 500) per hand on average, with only a small proportion betting over US $260 (RMB 2000) per hand (Figure 17.2). To put this into context, many of Macao's VIP gaming tables currently impose a minimum bet of US $1300 (RMB 10,000) per hand.

Deloitte's analysis suggests a probable average casino win of US $90–150 per person for mass-market players, versus an estimated Las Vegas average win of US $275 across the whole market. Although these figures seem relatively modest, the huge potential volume of players should ensure that the mass market becomes an extremely important source of revenue for Macao.

Chinese gamblers may spend less than their American counterparts, but the Deliotte data suggest that they are prepared to wager a higher percentage of their income and gamble more intensively. Despite the widespread enjoyment of gambling amongst the mainland Chinese, lack of knowledge of casino gaming appears to be a key impediment for many potential punters. About 40% of the survey respondents who had previous gambling experience and about 90% of those without previous experience showed an interest in learning how to play casino games. Like Las Vegas, Macao will have to provide training and demonstration classes for their wannabe gamblers.

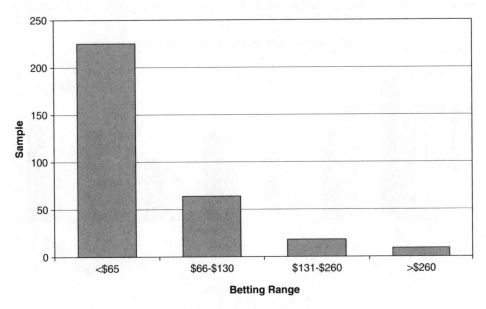

Figure 17.2: Average bet.

The Deloitte survey shows that inexperienced mass-market customers have a particular interest in slot machines, which historically have had a low acceptance rate in Asian gaming markets. The new electronic terminals used by the fast-growing Chinese lottery are increasingly widespread in mainland China and are likely to foster a growth in the number of slot machines in casinos. Greater provision of slot machines appears likely to be the key factor in winning over inexperienced gamblers, particularly women. While baccarat is currently the overwhelming favourite game in Macao as a whole, blackjack is the winner for male gamblers in the casinos.

The evident popularity of slot machines appears to justify current projections for the escalation in their use in Macao casinos, from around 5000 in 2006 to a possible 18,000 machines by the end of the decade.

If Macao Wants to be Las Vegas of the Orient, What Will Have to Change?

Deloitte's survey reveals that the way to the heart of the Chinese mass market is through its stomach, with the largest percentages of both men and women selecting restaurants as the most important facility influencing their decision to visit Macao (Figure 17.3).

Shopping is rated as a major priority, especially by women, many of whom seek retail outlets for both super-premium brands and the everyday items which carry import taxes in Mainland China. Health and beauty products have a very strong appeal for both sexes, with men apparently happy to skip the shopping for an invigorating sauna or a relaxing massage. The survey also shows that women are just as likely to enjoy arcade games as men. The majority of respondents were willing to

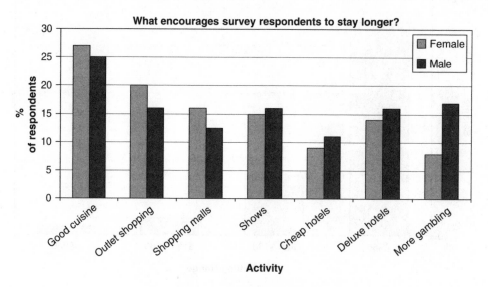

Figure 17.3: Encouraging visitors to stay longer.

stay in Macao for 1 or 2 days and to gamble in casinos for up to 5 h per day. A major challenge for tourism operators is to convert a significant proportion of these short-stay and day-trippers into longer-stay visitors.

The anticipated growth in visitors arriving by air from other major cities in China will also swell demand for a wide range of leisure experiences. Again, the Deloitte survey underlines the importance of gourmet cuisine as the overriding factor likely to encourage longer visits to Macao by both sexes, followed by luxury and discount shopping facilities, particularly amongst women.

Entertainment will also be a crucial part of the Macao mix. Importing the Vegas experience into Macao is likely to be a recipe for success. However, an understanding of where Chinese tastes do appear to differ could provide an important extra ingredient. The Deliotte survey suggests that musicals and superstar concerts are the shows most likely to attract Chinese mass-market visitors, who are known for their passion for music. The survey also indicated that between US \$13 and US \$65 (RMB 100–500) appeared to be the accepted price range for show tickets. Over 85% of the respondents would pay US \$65 (RMB 500) or less for a performance ticket. The vibrant and colourful atmosphere of the carnival also has an extremely strong appeal to mainland tourists (Figure 17.4). However, the large-scale dance and circus-style extravaganzas such as Cirque Du Soleil, popular in Las Vegas, do not appear to have the same resonance with Chinese visitors.

According to the HotelBenchmark™ Survey by Deloitte, average room rates in Macao have risen by 66.8% since 2002, reaching US \$100 per night per room for the first time in 2006. The trend looks set to continue in 2007; an average room rate of US \$104 for the first quarter of the year, including the lucrative Chinese New Year period in February, has resulted in revenue per available room (revPAR) rising to US \$78 — an incredible 74.3% increase from 2002.

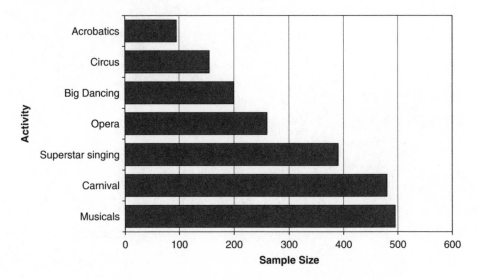

Figure 17.4: Type of performance preferred.

Conclusion

As world tourism moves eastwards, Macao will become the symbol of lavishness, fun and self-indulgence. The number-one leisure activity in China is gambling and Macao will become the honeypot for tourism in the region, just like Las Vegas is in the Mid West of the United States. However, the peninsula will also have to develop into an entertainment destination with retail outlets, musical and cabaret shows and nightlife (just like Las Vegas) in order to meet the demands and desires of the thrill-seeking, experience-seeking Chinese tourist in 2030.

Chapter 18

The New Cultural 'Capitalist' — The Rio Carnival

Dear Ian

Rio is the world's best and biggest party! I have now been in Rio for three weeks; in the first week of the holiday I was learning how to do the samba at the Asa Branca School, which has some of the very best mangueria musicians and dancers. The School organised my costume and provided a really authentic experience. Last week, the Carnival Parade was awesome, with spectacular floats and colourful women dressed up like peacocks and strutting their stuff. The costumes ranged from flowing dresses and African robes to just glitter on naked bodies. The Rio Carnival was a sambodromo extravaganza. Everyone was writhing and wriggling from dawn to dusk. Throughout the week, there were parties, but the real action was at the blocos and bandas (street carnivals) which were a lot cheaper and where I met the real people of Brazil. Anyway, it is now week three and I am just chilling out on the beach.

See you soon

Fiona

A postcard, 2030

The globalisation of festivals and events has evolved in the twenty-first century. This phenomenal evolution, coupled with increased consumer awareness, has resulted in the tourism world 'doing' festivals, including such major and diverse ones as the Edinburgh International Arts Festival, Scotland and the Whole Enchilada Festival in Las Cruces, New Mexico. Many festivals are at a mature stage of their lives such as the Oktoberfest, Germany, whereas others are still in their teenager years such as the Reggae Sumfest, Jamaica. On a global basis, there is unprecedented interest in festivals and events, at national and international level, in cities, towns and villages, and even in rural and coastal areas (Yeoman, Robertson, Ali-Knight, Drummond, & McMahon-Beattie, 2004). Tourists are now travelling to all corners of the Earth and are more sophisticated and interested in different cultures, and festivals often provide an authentic insight into the life of communities.

Many communities want to celebrate their particular form of culture, tradition, difference or uniqueness. Festivals and events help promote destinations and many tourism leaders have formulated their destination development plans based on a calendar of festivals as one of the drivers to attract tourists. Across the developed world, consumers are spending more of their out-of-home expenditure on culture; it is, however, the living, creative cultural sector which is benefiting, rather than museums and heritage centres. Consumers' consumption of culture is no longer limited to the highbrow performing arts or the lowbrow comedy circuit, but could be described rather as 'no brow' because consumers are comfortable with a diversity of festival experiences, from opera to rock music, from comedy to Shakespeare and from books to films.

The term 'festival tourism' is used to encompass a vast array of events, from Country and Western music concerts to devout, religious festivals, from glitzy sports contests to events celebrating natural phenomena. The world has embraced the festivalisation phenomenon and the Carnival in Rio de Janeiro is the biggest and most famous of them all, according to the *Rough Guide to World Party* (Anon., 2007, p. 244)

> The Rio Carnival exists in everyone's imagination. When foreigners think of it, the images that usually spring to mind are of a colourful parade, loud music and pounding drums, the extravagant costumes, lots of near-naked flesh and the unbridled hedonism.

The World of Festivals

The exponential growth in the number of festivals and events highlights unique leisure and cultural experiences, because they provide authenticity and uniqueness associated with a destination's sense of place (Douglas, Douglas, & Derrett, 2001). Getz (1997) identifies festivals as 'attractions, image-makers, animators of static attractions and catalysts for further development'. They can be seen to minimise the negative impacts of mass visitation and foster better host–guest relations. The word 'festival' derives from *feast* and implies *a time to celebrate*. The use of festivals as celebrations can extent tourist seasons, and introduce 'new seasons' into the tourism year for places.

A development of festivals across the world can be described as 'festivalisation', which has been linked to the economic development of destinations' competitiveness and the use of tourism and culture as drivers to attract visitors, business and communities. Festivals act as drivers to develop destinations as large-scale platforms for the creation of and consumption of cultural experiences. Although the key period of the development of international cultural festivals in Europe was in the period following the Second World War, that is the Edinburgh International Festival, a large number of destinations around the world continue to create international festivals and events as important catalysts for regeneration of urban landscapes and image-making, linked with an increasing pre-occupation with the realisable impact of festivals in hard economic terms, and, in certain cities, also in relation to softer social inclusion and objectives in the world of education.

Festivals often define destinations, for example the Rio Carnival, the Calgary Stampede in Canada, Mardi Gras in New Orleans, Oktoberfest in Munich, the Country Music Festival in Tamworth, Australia, and London's Thames Festivals all define their home town or city in terms of a festival brand. Some of these festivals have been sustained over many years and seek to satisfy the needs of the residents as well as of visitors. Munich's Oktoberfest was launched in 1810 as an occasion to allow the people to celebrate a royal marriage, whereas other festivals have been started to take advantage of an opportunity or even by accident (Douglas et al., 2001). Edinburgh's International Festival began in 1947 because an international arts festival could not be staged in Vienna after World War II and the Edinburgh Fringe came about because the organisers of the International Festival turned away certain shows as not being 'highbrow' enough, hence the emergence of what is now an extensive and successful festival.

The Rio Carnival

The roots of Rio Carnival can be traced to the celebration of spring by the ancient Romans and Greeks. In several European countries, including France, Spain and Portugal, people gave thanks annually for the return of spring by throwing parties, wearing masks and dancing in the streets. The Portuguese first brought the concept of 'celebration or carnival' to Rio about 1850 and the idea of holding balls and masquerade parties was imported from Paris by the city's bourgeoisie. However, in Brazil the traditions soon evolved over time, acquiring unique elements derived from the African and Amerindian cultures. Groups of people would parade through the streets playing music and dancing and during Carnival it was usual for aristocrats to dress up as commoners, men to dress as women and the poor to dress up as princes and princesses. It was expected that social roles and class differences would be forgotten once a year — but only for the duration of the festival. The Rio Carnival takes place during the height of summer in a 4-day celebration, which draws in thousands of people from all over the world. The Carnival begins on the Saturday and ends on Fat Tuesday or Mardi Gras, with Carnival Sunday always falling 7 weeks before Easter Sunday.

The Cultural Consumption of Festivals

In the 1970s, the French sociologist Pierre Bourdieu championed the concept of cultural capital (Jenkins, 2002). Culture brings distinction to the image and profile of destinations; it enriches the experience for the consumer and creates a sense of place.

The cultural capital of consumers represents the 'stock' of their knowledge, attitudes, skills, education and tastes. Bourdieu regarded cultural capital as taking three forms: *embodied* (long-lasting dispositions of mind and body which must be constantly maintained and updated), *objectified* (the goods and services chosen by different consumers) and *institutionalised* (a measure of the qualifications bestowed on individuals by academic institutions). As consumers become more affluent, they differentiate themselves less by their material trappings and more by their use of cultural and social knowledge and individual identity. Increasingly, it is not what you own, but what you do and whom you know. As affluence grows, so also do cultural and social knowledge and people's expectations (and the way in which this informs consumption) become more important considerations. The cultural capital of festivals is how tourists talk about their experience of festivals and their participation in them, hence the cultural consumption of festivals.

How can one define the cultural capital of tourists? Looking at the different words associated with life stages and holidays we can see that age appears to be a quite a strong predictor of what consumers feel to be a 'good' holiday (Figure 18.1).

However, not as much difference is displayed in the ranking of adjectives as one might expect. For example, among younger consumers, the three most popular factors are 'fun/amusing', 'relaxed/informal' and 'value for money' — which are the same three chosen first by the oldest age group, albeit in a different order.

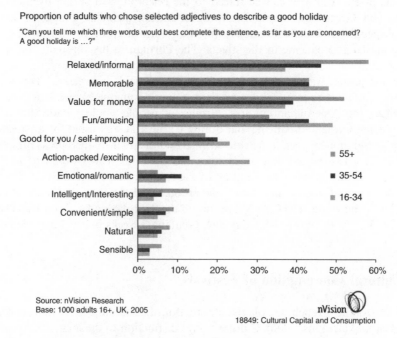

Figure 18.1: Adjectives associated with good holidays.

This is indicative of the broader finding that demographics, in general, appear not to be a particularly good predictor of tastes in markets.

What this means is that, in general, because all consumers in similar markets tend to associate similar adjectives, it is more insightful to examine the adjectives chosen by specific demographic groups, compared to those chosen by other groups. For example, for 'good' holidays younger consumers are more likely to pick 'action-packed/exciting', 'good for you/self-improving', 'fun/amusing' than other groups. Middle-aged consumers are more likely to pick 'emotional/romantic' than other groups, and the 55+ group are more likely to pick 'sensible', 'convenient/ simple', 'intelligent/interesting' than their younger counterparts. From the perspective of festivals and events we can draw many conclusions. The interest in book festivals or intellectual tourism has, to a certain extent, been driven by the 55+ age group; as Figure 18.1 highlights 'intelligent/interesting' is a key attribute. Whereas younger consumers interested in 'action-packed/exciting' holidays are drawn to music festivals and comedy, middle-aged consumers linked with 'emotion/romance' are more interested in historical enactment. The Rio Carnival encapsulates the concept of many of those adjectives. For the younger consumer it is 'fun and action-packed', whereas for all age groups it is 'memorable'.

Learning about a leisure activity will lead to the acquisition of social and cultural capital. As Gershuny (2003), Professor of Sociology at the University of Essex, discusses the specific knowledge about consumption contributes to individual satisfaction and pleasure. Having the knowledge and ability necessary to participate in an activity is closely correlated with the desire to do so. That's why the Rio Carnival is all about participation — tourists are encouraged to learn the samba at one of the samba schools so that they can participate in a truly authentic experience.

Festivals have become a way to express oneself and the Rio Carnival provides just such an experience. Gidden's (2006) encouraged us to believe that we can be 'the authors of our own life' and this is the notion that is increasingly gaining currency in contemporary society. If consumers regard their personal development as a project — 'Project Me' — then the Rio Carnival and other festivals become both an expression and an aspiration of 'Project Me'. Participation in the Carnival becomes something new, a means to enjoy hedonistic behaviour, an experience that is both naughty and fun. According to the Future Foundation's *Changing Lives* Survey, the proportion of consumers wanting to learn more, the proportion seeking 'self-fulfilment' and the proportion feeling the need 'to be a creative person' are all on the rise, resulting in a growth of the experience economy, and the Rio Carnival and other such festivals offer a new experience through participation.

The largest increase in the desire for new experiences is found in the 55–64 age group and this tallies well with their heavy spending on travel. A third of this age group claims to be somewhere each year where they have never been before. In addition, tourists have a tick-list mentality when it comes to destinations, that is they want to visit new places so they can say that they have been there — and the Rio Carnival can be perceived as just that, a 'must see-must visit' destination.

The Rio Carnival is a spectacular extravaganza of costumes and parades; each costume is hand-made and is an expression of the individual wearing it. There is nothing conformist about participating in the Carnival — it is a parade of expression and creativity that encourages non-conformity. The reference point for the tourist who takes part is the individuality and innovation of being different as being at the Carnival is a self-expression of escapism from the norm and being the kind of person one cannot be at home — that is the beauty of the Rio Carnival.

Societies have always wanted to have fun — and music and dancing are expressions of fun, sex and indulgence. In recent years, there has been a renaissance of the BBC television programme, 'Strictly Come Dancing', and between 2001–2005 Scotland's National Dance Centre had a 450% increase in customers. Eurovision's 'Dance4life', a live, pop-dance charity show, runs international, simultaneously broadcast dance extravaganzas. Dance has also become an even more important part of films, including Richard Gere in 'Shall We Dance' and Antonio Banderas in 'Take the Lead'. Dance has become a participatory activity, a visual art and an entertainment form. Even pole-dancing, has become a form of fitness-enhancing exercise, with pole-dancing lessons available in many cities (as seen at www. poledancing.co.uk). In Cardiff, pole-dancing lessons have become another visitor activity (see http://www.chillisauce.co.uk/). According to Fieldman (2007)

> seeing if someone is a good dancer is a good way to judge if they have promise as a mate. Dancing is the new flirting, whether it is the rumba, which relies on the age-old premise of the lady trying to dominate the gentleman by the means of her womanly charms or the samba, ... there should be a lot of wiggly bums.

Music has a global perspective and appeals to a range of consumers, whether they are fans of Beethoven or Elvis Presley, of heavy rock or sentimental ballads. The first musical tourists were associated with classical music, when young, well-to-do men and women visited 'festival' cities as part of their Grand Tours of Europe (Gibson & Connell, 2004). Today, music plays an ever-more important part in the event-driven world of tourism, with fans flocking to events which re-create the Woodstock festival of the 1960s or taking part in a pilgrimage to Elvis Presley's Graceland. Music festivals of all kinds are events that encourage tourists to visit destinations 'to do something'. Music and dance provide a purpose for their visit.

The over-arching attribute of the Rio Carnival, however, is pleasure, based on the philosophy that pleasure is the most important pursuit of mankind, a proposition that holds that pleasure seeking is not what people *ought to be*; it is the way people actually are — they naturally seek pleasure. According to Gibson and Connell (2004), the actual meaning of participation and the pleasure gained as a result is the most significant dimension of festivals. The Rio Carnival is all about hedonistic pleasure and people want to be there.

Concluding Remarks

The Rio Carnival is an expression of consumption and the 'festivalisation' of the world; festivals have become the embodiment of individuality and of hedonistic behaviour and that is what Fiona is exhibiting on her holiday. The Rio Carnival could be described as the world's best party, and pleasure-seeking tourists want to be there. Tourism is about pleasure and enjoying oneself — which is exactly what the tourist wants to do. In 2030, the new cultural capitalist will be the hedonistic tourist.

Chapter 19

Life on Mars — How Different Generations Perceive the Future of Holidays in Scotland

Introduction: Life in 1973

In 2006/07, there was a popular BBC television programme titled 'Life on Mars' in which a police detective from 2006 finds himself back in 1973. As his 2006 values clashes with the culture of 1973, many conflicts are produced. So what would happen the opposite way, what if tourists from 2007 were to be transported to the future, say to 2025, what would they find strange. This concept of projecting people through time (but to the future, not the past) is explored through the eyes of what the Henley Centre (2007) describes as 'global clans', that is groups of like-minded people; the three clans chosen are: Freedom Fighters (those 65 and older in 2025), the Millennial Sophisticates (those 40–45 in 2005) and the Shanghai Virtual Social Network (those 20–25 in 2025).

To help us understand what they may face and how much the world has already changed, let's first paint a picture of what the world looked like in 1973. To do so, it is important to recall the following events that happened in 1973:

- The United Kingdom, Ireland and Denmark all joined the European Economic Community (EU)
- Peace accord in Vietnam, and the last US soldier left Vietnam
- First call was made on a mobile phone
- Patent for first ATM is granted
- FedEx is formed
- National work stoppage in the United Kingdom — 1.6 million workers stopped work
- First space station (Skylab) is launched
- The United States halts its bombing of Cambodia
- East Germany and West Germany are formally admitted to the UN
- The Yon Kippur War begins
- Arab Oil embargo begins — triggers the 1973 Energy crisis, oil prices quadrupled
- Coal shortages in the United Kingdom, and the start of 3-day working week

Despite these events, it was an exciting time within tourism, the UK National Tourist Boards were only established some 4 years earlier, and they developed their first strategic development plans. This was the time when there was still a strong belief in centralised planning and regionalism, and eight new regional local authorities were established in Scotland, but there were still over 30 area tourist boards. The Hotel Development Scheme had just come to an end, which resulted in the biggest increase in hotels in Scotland, since the building of the great railway hotels of Victorian time. This scheme resulted in some 70,000 new hotel rooms in the United Kingdom, and the Scottish Tourist Board (STB) established its first set of minimum standards for accommodation. In terms of tourism, 1973 was the year when 'the British seaside holidays probably reached its high point in volume' (Middleton, 2007).

Outside Scotland, the following events impacted the development of tourism:

- PanAm and TWA cancelled plans to buy 13 Concordes
- US $ devalued by 10%
- First IRA bombs explode at the Old Bailey and in Whitehall
- Queen opened the New London Bridge
- Greek Military proclaims Greece a republic
- Fire at the Summerland amusement complex in the Isle of Man kills 51 people
- Five international airlines experienced major plane crashes

But it was all not bad news, because 1973 also saw the opening of some of the world's iconic tourism attractions — Sydney Opera House, Singapore Zoo, World Trade Centre and the Bosporus Bridge linking Europe to Asia.

Life in the United Kingdom in 1973 was tough; it was marked by increasing trade union militancy activities, which through fuel shortages led to the introduction of the 3-day working week, high employment and high inflation (Scottish Abstract of Statistics, 1975). Street lights were dark, and most homes experienced 'brown-outs' as power was reduced. Offices and factories only worked limited hours, so production fell. The Internet was unknown, the BBC's Ceefax service was at the cutting edge of information technology and the hand-held calculators were all the rage. Marriage was the norm and people were generally happy with life. Alf Garnet and the Six Million Dollar Man made their debut on TV; Elton John released 'Crocodile Rock'; 'Dr Atkins Diet Revolution' was one of the best selling books; the 'Exorcist' and the 'Battle of the Planet of the Apes' were amongst the most popular movies; and Pink Floyds' 'Dark Side of the Moon' was a global hit!

On the negative side, there was real industrial strife in the United Kingdom and there was a real threat that the Government would be unable to control the strikes; nationalism in Scotland was on the rise; and oil and gas exploration rigs were actively seeking new sources in the North Sea. There was a very strong feeling both for and against the United Kingdom joining European Community, as the country experienced its first national referendum.

Scenarios

So what will the tourists look like in 2025, as they certainly will be different from 1973? This can be determined taking into account three main variables: life stages;

life history; and the wider environment and personal circumstances — 'Freedom Fighters' and the 'Millennial Sophisticates' and one overseas clan, the 'Shanghai Virtual Social Network' (Future Foundation, 2007).

Freedom Fighters — 65 Years Old in 2025, Born in 1960

In a sense, this is the group that never had it so good, they came of age in the Thatcher years in the 1980s, and to them work was at the centre of their lives. Of the three clans investigated, they were by far the most materialistic, and were under constant pressure to show their wealth to the world. However, as they are now likely to be in, or moving into retirement, they might be seeking a greater work/life balance — but still wealth and status will be important to them. They have also experienced a number of major changes at both the workplace and the home, but perhaps the move towards gender equality was the greatest change, though even in 2025, true equality has not been achieved. Both the men and women in this group have a deep-seated fear that having been busy all their lives, they will have nothing to do in retirement. This offers great opportunities for Scotland, to help them fill their lives meaningfully. They will be high spenders because their pensions will be secure, as they will have tried to avert any shortfalls in their pension funds.

They are an unusual generation, because they will remember the time when much of the technology that others take for granted did not exist, and it will not be integrated fully into their lives. They see technology as a functional activity — it is there to do things, such as booking holidays, transfer money into bank account, etc. They will not use it to the same extent as other younger groups, for social networking or for entertainment.

Two key factors important to them:

- Careers. This is core to their lives; they see a good job as an absolute necessity, and this is likely to impact on their holiday needs in two ways — a desire to keep busy and use time productively, and a focus on material goods and materialism. They also like to have 'stuff', as they see this as a physical manifestation of their success.
- Holidays. As part of this accumulation of wealth, holidays are a key expression of luxury and status and are seen as key status symbol for this group. They really do believe that where they go on holiday and what they do on holiday defines them as people. Given this, it is not surprising they are likely to focus on luxury holidays in high-status destinations.

It is tempting to classify these older travellers with many of the age-based stereotypes. This is a mistake today and will certainly be a much bigger mistake in the future. This new type of 'Freedom Fighter' tourist will be very different from today's older tourists; for a start, they will be much healthier and certainly wealthier, but the biggest difference will be in their expectations, they will exhibit lifestyles we associate with today's younger tourist.

Their interests in holidays are likely to be in

- International destinations
- Range of cultural activities
- Newer and authentic experiences

So what will they look like, and what types of holidays will go on in Scotland? Freedom Fighter Holiday Profile: Golf and Whisky Tour

> James and Melanie live in London, where James has recently retried from a long career in the financial services sector. His partner gave up work when their first child was born, and since the kids have left home, she has focused on creative purists and the theatre. They are visiting Scotland as a celebration trip for James' retirement; this is an ideal destination for them, as it caters for James' passions — whisky and golf. The trip has been designed to meet their needs, it is not a standard packaged tour, and although they are based in Grantown, they will be travelling around the area. In terms of planning the trip, James made heavy use of the Internet, to find a place of the beaten track, away from other tourists.

> He thought it was a great holiday and they did experience some real Scottish culture, but they had to run the gauntlet of the environmental demonstrators at Inverness airport, and this was a bit of a sour note. Melanie, however, was overall a bit disappointed; she found few places where she could indulge in her passion for theatre and culture, for after living in London with its rich culture and the arts, she thought Scotland was disappointing and a bit inward looking.

Millennial Sophisticates — 40–45 Year Olds in 2025, Born in 1980–1985

Like the previous group, which was defined by the Thatcher years, this group came of age during the New Labour Governments of Blair/Brown. Their early years before 9/11 were defined by a period of new hope, prosperity and optimism about the future. However, with the growth in international terrorism, some of this optimism was tempered by real world events, such as SARs, Blue Tongue and Foot and Mouth and this led to a great deal of cynicism about accepting the promises and motivations of leaders and others in authority. This lack of faith in what they are told extends to businesses, brands and marketing, for they increasingly use other sources of information, such as their friends, especially their online friends (Hay, 2007).

A key characteristic of this generation is their desire 'to have it all'. They want and expect success in everything they do — in their personal relationships, friendships, hobbies and careers. What drives this group is individualism and self-fulfilment, and they are wealthy and self-oriented enough to regard their own lives as one of their 'projects' — something to be researched, invested in with milestones and goals, with clear options and to be indulged in, for its own sake. Despite this somewhat cynical focus, they are also the first generation to embrace a range of environmental and ethical concerns in their personal consumption behaviour. They see themselves as the generation that has to deal with the dual and sometimes conflicting issues of climate change and international development issues. These issues are important to them, and will have a direct impact on their holiday's decisions — they will want all the companies they deal with, including holiday companies, to make it easy for them to consume their products ethically — they want their share of the cake and they want to eat it!

Unlike the previous generation (Freedom Fighters 65+), for them work/life balance is the norm, not an idealised impossibility. Though they have all the appearance of being wealthy, they are squeezed financially — struggling to support their kids through higher education, increasingly worried about their pension funds and retirement, and acting as carers for their parents, who are living longer than any previous generation. They are also the generation that is much more dependent on technology, and see technology as a time-saving product that helps to solve problems in their busy lives. What they are expecting from technology is simplicity and efficiency; when travelling they like to have access to all the technology, so that they can access their office and keep in contact with their social networks.

Four key factors important to them:

- Variety. This is truly the spice of life, they have grown up in the experience economy, where new experiences have become the norm. They are also the generation which has seen an unprecedented growth in consumer choice, and this has made them less loyal to companies and to destinations. Because of increasing choice, if they are disappointed with a tourism product, not only will they tell their friends, but also will not use that product again.
- Network. Technology will be deeply embedded into this generation's activities. They will be dependent on technology as it has always been there and will feel lost if they cannot access technology. Being contactable 24/7/365 is very important to them, even when on holiday; they would not consider a destination without wi-fi and mobile phone access.
- Environmental Awareness. This is the generation that will have grown up when environmental issues were at the core of much public policy debate. They will have seen images of environmental disasters through TV and the Internet, and such concerns will have an impact on their choice of holidays.
- Family. This group will also experience both the benefits and the drawbacks of the 'vertical' family tree — that is one with three or even four generations. As we all live longer and longer and as fertility rates continue to fall, families will form strong relationships both up and down this tree, unlike in previous generations where many of the relations were horizontal, with the same generation, such as cousins. A benefit of the longer vertical family is that parents will seek help from grandparents in terms of childcare, but a drawback is that this generation may have increased responsibilities as carers for their parents. A clear trend of this

could be the development of multi-generation (or at least two generation) family holidays. The impact of this trend on destinations will be to provide activities, attractions and entertainment for a much wider range of ages.

Their interests in holidays are likely to be in

- Short-haul (including the United Kingdom) over long-haul flights, but also fewer flights overall
- Destinations that can show their sustainability, in terms of their local impacts on the environment
- Carbon 'off-setting' schemes
- Multi-generation holidays

Millennial Sophisticates Holiday Profile: A Multi-Generation Family Holiday in Skye

> Oliver and Carolyn live in Darlington with their two kids, Oliver works as an IT consultant and Carolyn works as a part time office manager, and will be holidaying in Skye with Carolyn's parents. Last year they went to Goa, and even with carbon off-setting they were appalled by the damage already done to the Goa's coastline by mass tourism, and this only increased their concerns about the impact of their tourism choices.
>
> They were looking for a holiday destination which offered a wide variety of activities for all the family members, had a minimal impact on the environment, but also one which enabled Oliver to keep in contact with his office. Indeed, constant access to interactive technologies was important to all members of the family. They travelled from Darlington to Kyle of Lochalsh by train, where they hired an electronic people carrier. Carolyn used the Internet to book the whole trip, and although she had been there before she made extensive use of her online friends travel blogs, and was particularly pleased at the high praise that Skye received as an eco-resort that offered a carbon-free holiday.
>
> They knew the holiday would be expensive, but they did not mind, as family holidays were a high priority for them. The kids experienced a real 'retro holiday' as both they and the adults went swimming in the sea, built sandcastles and went rock pooling, but what they liked the most was the chance to learn new activities, such as wind surfing. Sometimes they took part in activities together, and sometimes separately. Carolyn's parents took part in a 3-day cookery course, making use of local grown and picked ingredients, while the rest of the family went on a guided wilderness trek.

The whole family enjoyed the holiday and felt they were entertained and stimulated by the experience. They always knew it would be difficult to find a holiday destination that could cater for three generations, and the only issue they had was the limited choice of things to do in the evening, but this was only a small issue and it did not spoil their holiday.

Shanghai Virtual Social Network — 20–25 Years Old, Born in 2000–2025

This cohort of people is about to enter primary school, and of all the three groups, they are the most difficult to predict, as their working and life environment has still to be developed. They are truly the Internet generation, for they will have grown up with technology and will continue to absorb any new developments in technology. They will be a generation of technophiles, and technology will fit seamlessly into their lives, and will not be a source of concern, which perhaps was seen in the previous two generations. For this generation the 'screen' will be their primary source for learning, both in education and about the wider world. They will be the 'second-life generation', with a blurring between the 'real world' and their 'online world', to them both worlds are interchangeable.

They will use technology for work, play, entertainment and developing friendships. They expect everything will be downloaded, and will no longer 'read' for a degree, but 'download' for a degree. Technology will help shape them as persons and will help in forming their identities, allowing them to adopt different identities in different situations, in work and play.

There is no doubt that globalisation will continue to play a key role in economic development, and that this generation will truly be citizens of the world, even if they hold a Chinese passport. In this world, the development of worldwide integrated trading will have a positive impact on visitors to Scotland. Because countries such as China are at an emerging stage in terms of their consumer culture, the visitors from these countries are likely to display behaviours similar to the Western tourists in the 1990s — including a focus on indulgence, materialism and conspicuous wealth — rather like the 65+ Freedom Fighters did in their tourism activities. However, this phase in their development will be much quicker than that happened in the West, with global media coverage accelerating such markets into the contemporised developed consumer culture.

There is no doubt that increased global competition will have a greater influence on the lives of this group. They will be expected to work hard at school, and as national economies will become more competitive, a rather serious and focussed generation will be created. However, as with the young across the world, they want to have fun and enjoy their life — let their hair down. These twin forces of seriousness and fun may lead to swings of extremes of hedonism and back again — and future tourism destinations will need to cater for such swings.

Five key factors important to them:

- Technology. This young generation will grow up with technology and will be highly adept at seeking out information via the Internet, and seeking it fast. It will be three or four clicks and you are out — as a holiday destination. They must be able to find you, and find information about you, very quickly. This empowerment will enable this group to build their own holidays — for example, automatic checks will be made by the technology to ensure they have enough insurance for the whole trip.
- Implanted Technologies. This will be the first generation to embrace and feel comfortable enough to wear or even have implanted technology in their bodies. They will be able to download information to themselves when on a trip, such as instant guided tours at attractions in any language, special offers from restaurants they walk by, and even when the next bus is due. To paraphrase Scotty in Star Trek 'It is tourism Jim, but not as we know it'!
- Fluid Identities. We know that globalisation will bring increased mobility, and it is rare for a person to live all their lives in one place — the world is moving, and the United Nations (2006) estimates that 190 million of us live in a different country from where we were born and this will increase to 250 million in 2020. This along with the growing internationalism of multi-media news channels adds to the growing fluidity of identity and complexity of consumer individuality. We have many ways to express ourselves, and often adopt different personalities for different situations. We all have to play these multiple roles, and by 2025 the 'who am I' question will not be relevant because we will define ourselves in different ways to suit the task — at work, speaking with friends or playing online games. These multi-identity roles will have a profound impact on marketing brands — who is your consumer? The segmenting of consumers will be very difficult, so building one-to-one marketing must become the norm, for any tourism destination.
- Bloggers Rule. The reality is that individuals will and can create their own content, and this will create a whole new set of realities, and make communications with the Shanghai Virtual Social Network even more difficult. Bloggers will more readily speak to other bloggers about your product than speak to you, and so reputation marketing will become more and more difficult. You will also no longer be alone in making decisions, as you can now draw on the knowledge of your online friends — the citizen consumer will become much more powerful, at the expense of the brand.
- Green to Ethical. This will be the generation that takes a wide view of consumerism, by embracing a much wider set of values than just green issues. The concept of ethical consumption will be a core value of this group. Issues pioneered by the green movement will have moved on, and may now include wage rates, treatment of workers, their living conditions, etc. These issues will be very important for this generation, and they will want to ensure that their holiday destination complies with a wide range of ethical issues so that they can genuinely feel good about themselves. This may seem to be in conflict with their desire for

indulgence and conspicuous consumption, but this tract will be short lived; therefore, the potential conflict will be resolved. Also by 2025, the conditions of many of the workers in their home country will be much improved, raising their awareness of such issues, and so expect this awareness to be reflected in their destination decisions.

Their interests in holidays likely to be in

- Fairness in the treatment of tourism workers
- Places for short, but intensive busts of fun
- Holidays with friends
- Destinations bookable through the Internet

Shanghai Virtual Social Network Holiday Profile — Edinburgh Festival

Fan Li Pin is a 23 year old from Shanghai, and has just completed an MA on the History on Interactive Technology — he is, as he admits an IT freak. He owns all the latest label gadgets and is particularly proud of his new interactive glasses that at a flick give him access to the Net Generation 3 voice activated tools. The right designer brand is also important to him, hence his interest in brands.

However, he is not all IT focussed, he also loves plays and has developed a real interest in the works of a new playwright, and is travelling to Edinburgh to meet up with a group of people who share his passion; they all want to see the premier of a new work by this playwright. He has never met the group before in real life, only over the web, and is a bit nervous as he has described himself as a 30-year-old novelist.

He flies direct from Shanghai to London, but takes the fast 3-h train connection to Edinburgh. He would fly, but the environmental taxes on UK domestic flights no longer makes such flights affordable to the ordinary tourist. He booked his accommodation on the net, looking at the hotel through virtual tour. He would never book any accommodation that does not offer a virtual tour. Given the conspicuous designer side of his personality, he would love to stay in one of the new 'mega boutique' hotels in Edinburgh, but the cost is too high. He loves the iconic development of Princess Street and the brave new architecture of the city, and dictates notes and takes photos of what he sees through his glasses, as he walks around the city. He really enjoyed the trip, and coming clean about his background was not a problem because most members of his group had elaborated to some extent.

Key Implications for Scottish Tourism

The Freedom Fighters will be looking for

- Outdoor activities that convey a sense of adventure, but are also safe — hill walking, wildlife watching
- Variation by incorporating multiple destinations/activities on the same trip — walking in the day, spa treatment at night
- 'Real and authentic experiences' of Scotland — golf, whisky and fishing — which could be built around learning a new skill
- Green issues, which are a concern, but not enough to allow them to compromise on pleasure
- Accommodation for large groups of friends or extended family — historic houses, castles

Millennial Sophisticates will be looking for

- A variety of destinations and options, and expectation to get what they want — island hoping, helicopter tours, sport-based or adventure holidays — intensive experiences, all in a short time
- Personalised holidays — they want continuous Internet contact — 24 h/day
- Destinations chosen based on consumer reviews and advice from friends
- Socially responsible activities, green, ethical, rewarding and satisfying — a liberal outlook on life
- Fashionable and must-see destinations — also keeps abreast of trends by reading the latest travel writing news
- Flexible accommodation arrangements, to suit diverse family groupings
- Affordable costs, but will pay if they want something

Shanghai Virtual Social Network will be looking for

- A new spin on established ideas, themed holidays, new sports
- Single holidays with real world and online friends
- Interactive or viral advertising — providers will need to respond to booking/enquiries very quickly, could be last minute bookings.
- Adventure holidays/extreme sport
- Holidays based around technology — making movie and then editing it at the hotel, making pod casts, creating online holiday shows for their friends.
- Separate activities/accommodation for different generations, opportunity to interact with similar holidaymakers when on holiday

Conclusions

There is no doubt that the future will be different from the past, we only have to think how much the world has changed, from 1973 to today, to know that 2025 will be very different from 1973. Although there are a number of known critical uncertainties (oil prices, the environment, etc.) which the tourism industry can manage, if it chooses, there are also unknown uncertainties (diseases, terrorism, etc.) over which the tourism industry has no control, but both will impact on the development of tourism in Scotland.

This chapter has looked at the tourist from the perspective of three different, but typical 'clans'. As the scenarios highlight, it is worth reminding ourselves that the quality of our home life is rising, as more and more discretionary spending is done on making our lives easier. Tourists are no longer prepared to accept a lower quality of facilities and services on holiday compared to their home — they want and expect quality when they travel, such as wi-fi and broadband. It is also important to recall that tourists do not leave their 'values baggage and experiences' at home when they go on holiday. For example, as shown in the 'Freedom Fighters' clan holiday, if they have experienced high quality arts and culture at home, they expect this experience when on holiday, and if not, we can be sure that they will be attracted to other destinations that highlight this factor.

However, this quality has to be delivered within a changing societal framework, one that cares about the environmental impact of its activities. There is no doubt that tourists are increasingly aware of the impact of their activities on the environment, and each generation struggles to find a solution. Some believe it can be achieved through voluntary actions (individual decisions, driven by their consciousness) or can be delivered through regulation (Green Business Tourism Scheme), while some put their faith in market forces (businesses/destinations marketing their eco-friendly credentials). This concern about the environment needs to be balanced against the desire for some market segments to display their hedonism and materialism. This dilemma of wanting to both show care for the environment and display hedonism (they want to have their cake, and to eat it) is one that is difficult to resolve, but one which we must, if we want to maintain the product that attracts the tourists.

This chapter also noted the widening of the green debate, including other issues such as workers conditions of employment. It is clear that by 2025, the green debate will have moved to one that incorporates ethical employment standards, and this is where Scotland has the opportunity to develop. The best employers already know that in a service industry such as tourism, contented employees deliver the best. By 2025, with increased globalisation will come commoditisation and equality of product standards across the world; however, on a holiday quality of experiences delivered through a contented workforce will make Scotland standout from other destinations.

Tourists from newer countries, such as China and Eastern Europe, will have different values from our traditional markets. These tourists will probably have a strong emphasis on conspicuous consumption, and they will want to display their holiday experiences as 'trophies' to their friends. This could lead to a conflict between consumerism and what Scotland offers as a product, and this will need to be resolved. However, it may only be a short-term issue because these markets will mature relatively quickly, by absorbing Western values, which downplay displays of wealth and place more emphasis on environmental concerns.

We also need to recognise that many destinations (including Scotland) are facing many newer competitors, all hungry for the tourism pound, dollar, franc, rouble, yen, and with the rise of the 'consumer citizen' if we fail to deliver, we will not see them again! As consumers adopt different and newer lifestyles, traditional marketing techniques and tools will become more irrelevant, mass marketing will not work, new marketing techniques such as viral marketing and relationship marketing, focused on 'me as a person' and delivered in a way that appeals to you, will need to become the norm.

Chapter 20

The Asian Tigress: The Feminisation of the Business and Travel in China

Wendi Zhang, the thirty-year-old CEO of Air China, is typical of the business world in China today; she is entrepreneurial, female, an MBA graduate of Peking University Business School, and a visionary, whose parents moved from rural China in 1985 to start a new life in Shanghai. The business world in China has been through a social transformation of feminisation.

China Daily, 1st August 2030

Introduction

China's economic engine has been in overdrive for much of the past two decades, as a result of the decision by Chairman Deng Xiaoping in 1978 to move away from running the country by state planning to a market-driven economy. China's GDP is growing by an average of almost 10% per annum. The expansion of the economy is regarded by many respected commentators as one of the major factors which will affect the world's geopolitical environment over the next decades (Scase, 2000). The consequences are of major significance, from the need to feed the exponential demand in growth in the consumer population and the alteration in world economic power from west to east. Such is China's concern about this growth and its requirement for a steady and expanding energy supply in the future that it is now the most active nation in helping certain African countries to develop their economies, in return for their oil and minerals. China has 20% of the world's population and currently holds the largest currency reserve, having overtaken Japan in February 2006 (Anon, 2006). Extensive purchasing of resources outstrips the consumption of many other nations as China's growth accelerates. As the economy grows so too does the consumers' prosperity, a change which is transforming the lifestyle of the Chinese people. And from within China's Asian Tiger is emerging the Asian Tigress.

By 2030, international arrivals to China will grow to 167 million, an annual growth rate of 5.1%, and receipts will rise to US $114 billion by 2030. China will be the world's number-one destination in terms of international arrivals, with an 8.8%

market share, and third in terms of receipts, representing a 5.7% market share, respectively.

The Business Travel Market in China

China's sustained and rapid economic transformation is responsible for the extremely strong momentum in growth of the business travel market in that country.

- According to the American Express Business Travel's second survey of corporate travel management service in China in 2006, within 5 years the country will become the world's third-largest market for corporate travel (Davidson, 2007).
- The same source indicated that the healthy growth of China's GDP is likely to secure a two-digit rise in the business travel market by 2010. It is estimated that by 2020, the number of Chinese business travellers will be five times as many as that in 2007. International travel service providers and global giants such as American Express, Kar Shun Travel and Rosenbluth have noticed the potential of Chinese market for business travel and have made inroads into the market. American Express's third China Business Travel Survey estimated that corporations in China spent US $7.41 billion on air travel in 2005, making China the fourth biggest business travel market in the world after the United States, Japan and Germany. The growth of Chinese spend on business travel is largely driven by the domestic market — 87% of the travel expenditure of those surveyed for the American Express report was in mainland China and in Hong Kong (Davidson, 2007).
- Business travel in the Asia Pacific region is still dominated by men. According to MasterCard,© travel is split 66:33 between the sexes (Hedrick-Wong, 2005), but with increased urbanisation growth in educational attainment by females, and the transformation of the role of women in a modern China, this ratio will change.

The Feminisation of Doing Business in China

Women have always been important to the Chinese economy; to a certain extent they have been the 'working warriors' who work for the motherland. The Chinese woman is strong and ambitious and is devoted to achieving both professional and national recognition. She is willing to forfeit femininity and even neglect the family (Doctoroff, 2006). Such an interpretation is based on women's individual need to be approved by society and this characteristic has been shaped by the Cultural Revolution of the 1970s. Chairman Mao decreed that women *must*, not *can* achieve. Mao was, however, very specific regarding what achievements would be condoned, that is only those accomplishments that contributed to the wealth of the nation and to man's hold on power. Real individualism implies a strong sense of self, even in the face of public scorn. According to Doctoroff, the Chinese admire the singer Madonna because she writes her own rules and controls her own image; she is, however, admired but never emulated.

A survey by Cranfield University (Singh & Vinnicombe, 2006) has shown that of the total number of entrepreneurs in China, women account for 20% and, more significantly, that they represent 41% of the private sector. The proportion of female members of the boards of Chinese companies is 10.73% — higher than the proportion of female board directors in the UK's FTSE 100 top companies, which stands at 10% of directorships, according to the 2006 Female FTSE report (Singh & Vinnicombe, 2006). The important role played by women in business means that the scene is set for the feminisation of business travel in China.

Business by consensus is an absolute priority in China; reaching an overall agreement is crucial and the key to successful co-operation is to address each party's wishes in the decision-making process. Business decisions are considered successful only if all stakeholders are signed up to them. There is no question of one party triumphing over another. This attitude fits in perfectly with the way in which most negotiations are conducted within the industry, where a 'win-win' agreement is usually the preferred option and one which ensures effective long-term business relationships between buyers, suppliers and intermediaries. A scenario that requires diplomacy and softer skills that many writers attribute to the feminisation of business rather than male behaviour (Davidson, 2007).

The Feminisation of the Chinese Consumer

China's consumer market, given its size, the evident momentum in growth and the emerging segments of sophistication and high-spend, has become more alluring than ever before. China's consumer market is growing exponentially and women are emerging as the 'Asian Tigresses' of the consumer marketplace (Hedrick-Wong, 2005). Below is a story from the 'Herald Tribune' (2007) which reflects the feminisation power of the Chinese consumer:

> Waiting for a friend in Shenzhen's plush Kingglory Plaza, Chen Jing, 25, admires her new Nokia mobile phone. Complete with MP3 and third-generation network capability, the red phone cost just over 3,000 yuan — Chen's entire monthly wage.
>
> Extravagant spending perhaps, but female consumers like Chen are spurring much-needed growth in Chinese consumption and helping offset the country's high savings rate, a source of tension with its trading partners.
>
> Retail sales in China climbed 15.7% in the first eight months of this year reflecting rising incomes and urbanisation. Household consumption, however, is the lowest of any major economy. It fell to 36.4% of gross domestic product in 2006 from 37.7% in 2005, when the comparable figures for the United States and India were 70% and 61%, respectively. The downward trend is not new — in 1990 the ratio was 4%.

Donis Zhao, 26, a beauty consultant, says that her mother, a doctor, kept telling her to start saving, but she saw no need to do so. 'I want to focus on my job. If I work very hard and learn a lot, I can earn more', she said. 'It's not like when my mother was young twenty years ago and China was poor'.

Gen Tang, who lives in Hong Kong and whose wife is from Shenzhen, says that young Chinese women are too susceptible to advertising by foreign brands like Louis Vuitton. 'They're buying for status', he says. 'LV tells them "this is good", and they buy it'.

His wife, May Yang, sporting a pink Abercrombie & Fitch baseball cap, admits to a weakness for Versace cosmetics and said she spent up to 1,000 yuan on a new Dior perfume every few months. 'I've got friends who'll save ten months' wages to buy a 20,000 yuan scarf, easily'. she said.

Fenton (2007)

The role of women in Chinese society and economy cannot be understood without taking account of the dramatic swings in the government's policies on population in the past 50 years. In the 1950s, the government aggressively promoted large families as the keystone to faster industrialisation and as a means of enhancing China's geopolitical clout. The birth-rate rose dramatically and a huge demographic bulge appeared in the late 1960s. People in 2007 entering retirement come from this generation of runaway population growth. Women in this age group have suffered low living standards and poor education because of political turmoil and upheaval.

Runaway population growth was followed by a firm brake on fertility in the 1970s. The one-child policy was introduced in 1997 and the fertility rate plummeted from 5.27 per 1000 in 1971 to 2.78 in 1978. Since then, the consequences of the one-child policy has led to the birth-rate declining to below the replacement rate; it was at 1.71 in 2005 and will continue to decline in the coming decades.

The result of this change means that the number of births will decline from 11.2 in 2005 to 6.2 in 2030, because of the traditional preference of parents for male rather than female children, which is aided by technology-facilitated sex-selection. The male-to-female birth ratio has been estimated at around 118 male per 100 female births (Hedrick-Wong, 2005).

China's population will, therefore, peak in 2015 at 1.3 billion and then undergo a slow but steady decline. Along with the peaking of the population growth will be the rapid trend of an ageing population. By 2030, China will move from being a middle-aged nation to an older one. In 2005, the average age was 35 years, but by 2030 it will be 47 years. By then, the only country in Asia with a population older than China's will be Japan. To put it in perspective, in 2000 there were 600 million people worldwide aged over 60 and 130 million (or 21.7%) live in China. By 2030, 23% of China's population will be over the age of 60, compared to 11% in 2005 and, because, increasingly women outlive men, this 60+ group will be dominated by the former.

The trend of declining population growth also means that more and more people are opting to stay single and childless, or, if they marry, to postpone having children. In 2005, young singles, (under 35 years and not married), and young marrieds with no children (childless couples under 35 years old) accounted for 75% of adults. By 2030, these households will have declined to 40% of adults. On the other hand, the working age empty nesters will account for 46% of the population. These trends will mean changes in consumption, family structures and patterns of expenditure. As a result, China is following a similar path to that which has taking place in the Western world.

Social Transformation of Women

Women account for 45% of the workforce and their average income is about 80% of men's income (Davidson, 2007); around 36% of senior government officials are women, and women held 25% of the seats in the People's Congress in 2005. The overall social and economic power of women in China is being shaped by three critical trends: urbanisation, education and economic well-being. China's economy has expanded rapidly over the past decade, and the manufacturing sector has been particularly important. Young women have flooded the workforce, meeting the rising demand for labour in a wide range of manufacturing industries.

At the same time, in cities like Shanghai demand is for highly educated, skilled professional and knowledgeable workers, with educated women securing their share of employment and business opportunities. Urbanisation and wealth-creation are the fastest growing trends in China, a fact highlighted by the forecast that by 2025, 90% of the urban population will be classified as middle-class or higher whereas in 1985 the figure was only 1% — how times are changing (Farrel et al., 2006)! Urbanisation has had a profound impact on the purchasing power of consumers; for example in 2005, the provincial capitals accounted for 10% of the population but 34% of the total household earnings. In a rural economy, the main wage earners are male, whereas in an urban economy wealth is more evenly distributed between the sexes. An urban culture results in a more liberated environment for women, both socially and economically.

MasterCard (Hedrick-Wong, 2005) estimated that 85% of women of working age in urban China had their own sources of income, even if they were married and their husbands earned enough to support the whole family. In the same survey, it was found that women were assuming a more proactive role in planning and managing family finance, and households were becoming more accustomed to the concept of credit. As the trend of delayed marriage/no marriage continues, the size of the household is shrinking, with the number of households with two persons or under rising rapidly, from 106 million in 2005 to 225 million in 2030. These transformations will result in a rise in the number of urban singletons, who will be health-conscious and will enjoy travelling. In addition, urban youth will spend almost all their disposable income on themselves because they will not need to support their parents.

Table 20.1: Estimates of China's urban population.

	2008 (million)	2015 (estimate)
Young single (under 35, not married)	27.5	26.8
Young married (one child aged under 10)	42.5	31.0
Married (child aged 10 to 20)	67.0	62.0
Empty nester	63.0	80.0
Old single	21.5	28.0

Young singles, especially females, can now be classified as DINK (double income, no kids). A survey conducted by Horizon Key (Hedrick-Wong, 2005) found that the number of couples in Beijing, Shanghai and Wuhan opting for a DINK lifestyle has been on the increase. Preference for the DINK lifestyle also correlates with income, with over 14% aspiring to live the DINK lifestyle amongst those earning more than 5000 yuan per month; these DINKS are hedonists who value individuality and the quality of married life more than parenthood.

In contrast to the young and single lifestyles of urban women are the older segments. These can be grouped into 'empty nesters' and the 'old singles'. The empty nesters are people over 45 years old, still married, but without any economically dependent children living at home. In a strange mirror image of the young singles and the DINKs, the empty nesters and old singles are increasingly living independent, healthier and active lives, and are living longer.

Estimates of the urban female population by Asian Demographics (2007) are shown in Table 20.1. The relative size of the different groups reflects the lifestyle stages between 2008 and 2015. The young, female, singles' segment has more of lifestyle choice, despite the decrease in the size of the group. It is estimated that by 2015, urban females in China will be spending US $460 billion, compared to US $330 billion in 2008, with the fastest rising expenditure items being education, culture, recreation, transport, communication, dining out and shopping — hence the arrival of the Asian Tigress.

The Feminisation of Travel in Asia

With an economic growth rate of around 5.6% per annum to 2030, the Asia/Pacific region is experiencing one of the world's fastest growths in travel. In the terms of travel volume, Asia is second only to Europe, where growth is slowing. The much-analysed and discussed statistic, that China is the main reason for growth in Asia needs further comment. It is the women in the region who comprise the fastest growing segment. UN World Tourism Organisation statistics provide very little detail on genders with countries but regional data is available from travel surveys provided by AMEX and MasterCard. In 1990, the male-to-female ratio for travel was 90:10, whereas in 2005 it was 60:40. Korea's visitor arrivals reflect that pattern. In 1975, the ratio was 98:11 (males to females). In 2005, the figure had shifted 58:42. Thus, not only has the number of women visitors to the Asia/Pacific increased but women's market share of travel has also increased.

Male-to-female ratios in developed regions such as North America and Europe are 50:50, and Asia/Pacific will most probably follow that trend. A good indication of this trend can be found in Japan, where the ratio in 55:45 and in Singapore the ratio is 56:44. In order to understand this trend, MasterCard's Asian Lifestyle Survey (Hedrick-Wong, 2005) provides some answers. Travel for women has become a way of life, with 77.5% of women considering travel important for their lifestyles and 36.7% reporting that they had taken at least one international flight for personal reasons in the previous 12 months. One interesting fact is, that shopping does not appear to be a primary reason for travel — but rather it is adventure, new experiences, family and leisure time.

From a business travel perspective, if women's entry and rise in the workforce follows that of men (which it will no doubt do!) then Asia's female business travellers will be the fastest growing segment in the future. This is reflected in the MasterCard survey when asked about intentions to travel in the next 12 months, more women than men (but only marginally) replied yes.

Concluding Remarks

Chinese women have enjoyed much progress and many benefits in the past two decades as China's economy and society have been liberalised. The economic status of modern Chinese women has been greatly influenced by the rapidly changing environment they live in and are exposed to, as well as by their educational background and the career opportunities that are available to them. Education has been a key factor in the progression of Chinese women, and education levels and opportunities for women to be educated are at an all time high. As a result, more and more Chinese women are receiving higher education and embarking on a professional career path, especially amongst the younger generation. The impact of these changes is especially visible in China's key urban cities where growing numbers of women have been able to secure well-paying jobs and advance up the career ladder with their skills and qualifications; hence the feminisation of business in China and its impact on travel in the country.

Futureproofing

Are your strategies, products and services fit for the future?

Futureproofing is a technique designed to answer questions such as:

"Will our organisation be affected by trends like the ageing of society. And how significant will that impact be?"

"Are our core brand attributes going to be as resonant in the future as they are now?"

"Will my offer still be appropriate in the future or are current trends undermining its appeal?"

"How are trends likely to affect the size and needs of current market segments?"

"Are the dynamics of society working for or against my market?"

This technique starts from the premise that too many business decisions, and the market research strategies they are based on, are conducted without sufficient orientation to the future. The future is often seen as indecipherable or unpredictable.

Ironically, the one thing we can guarantee is that our world is changing and the future is certain to bring with it different business conditions, market opportunities, competitive threats and consumer desires. Understanding the past is not enough. Decisions need to be 'futureproofed' — that is, made with an understanding of key trends and how they might impact going forward.

Futureproofing is a process designed to interpret how our society is changing and to forecast the likely impact of those changes on key strategic decisions. The process is quite simple, yet powerful.

• Taking the management issue that is being considered — customer segments, your core offer, the markets you operate in, your brand attributes — we assess how social, economic, cultural, political and technological trends might affect it.

• Interrogating nVision — our unique and comprehensive pool of consumer insight— enables us to identify and prioritise those trends that are most important for the issue in hand.

• We then use a special workshop process to rate and rank these trends in terms of their likelihood of occurring and their importance should they occur. Sometimes this is done just by our own experienced analysts but often, and preferably, we involve the client organisation too.

• The outcome is a map of trends on the two dimensions of importance and likelihood. This allows us to highlight the potential pressure points and opportunities of the future — is your current strategy the right one for the emerging environment? Have you made the right decision?

Many organisations including Asda, Electrolux and McDonalds have found this technique invaluable in developing new products, services, marketing programmes and location strategies.

For a full guide to this technique and selection of case-studies please contact
E: info@futurefoundation.net
W: www.futurefoundation.net
T: + 44 (0) 203 042 4747

future foundation
An Experian company

The Future Foundation 6th Floor, Cardinal Place, 80 Victoria Street, London, SW1E 5JL, UK

SECTION III

SECTION III

Chapter 21

What If, the World No Longer Wanted to Holiday in the US by 2030?

The United States no longer trusts the world and world is uncomfortable in the presence of Americans to the extent that the worldwide boycott of Brand America is now having an impact on tourism in the United States. Last week, Disneyland in Florida filed for Chapter 11 and McDonald's Restaurants decided to drop the Big Mac for the Little Mac instead. In fact, many American corporations are no more or have changed their name. Pizza Hut promotes itself as an authentic Italian restaurant chain. Paris Hilton, the CEO of Hilton Inc., has re-branded the hotel chain 'Paris' to reflect a more 'European contemporary style', whilst Marriott is owned by the Chinese First National Bank. It seems no one wants to be an American!

Report in USA Today, 21st November 2030

Introduction

In 2005, the United States is the third most popular destination for international arrivals and the highest in the terms of tourism receipts. Despite this, the United States is losing market share. According to the World Travel and Tourism Council (Mintel, 2007a), share of global travel and tourism market in the United States has declined by 36% in the last 15 years, if the United States had kept pace with world growth, another 9 million visitors would have arrived in 2005. According to analysis by Mintel (2007a), there is no question that the growth of inbound tourism is being held back presently by a combination of a negative image of the country, following the Iraq war, foreign policy and entry restrictions.

International arrivals are down from 51.2 million in 2000 to 49.2 million in 2005, a loss of 3.6%. This figure disguises the disparity of loses for countries such as Argentina at −27% or the slow rate of growth from UK markets at 3%. Why? Is the product perceived as old fashioned, the destination historically has not invested in the brand and or does the world simply not like America's attitude to the world. Is the US holiday industry is in turmoil and decline? Much is attributed to America's attitude towards the world, whether it is rejection of the Kyoto protocol or it is unilateral foreign policy stance. Some would say the world no longer wants Mickey Mouse, Donald Duck and John Wayne. If this stance continues, the United States could see continued decline in international arrivals over the next decades. This chapter explores the consolidation of anti-American feeling in traditional allies such as Britain and Australia, continued security restrictions, the perception in the world of America as mono cultural imperialistic power and concluding with scenarios forecasts for inbound tourism to the United States by 2030.

Context: The Low Trust Globalisation Scenario

The dual crisis of security and trust has fundamentally challenged the visions of the world (Shell International, 2005) as companies and individuals are seriously concerned for their physical security and anxious about the future. Combined with consumers' lack of trust in companies and concerns for security of welfare, jobs, assets and pensions means security and trust are prominent driving forces post-9/11. In Shell's Global Scenarios of 2025, the *low trust globalisation* scenario presumes a world without trust in which individuals and companies have to 'prove it' — this is a world of insecurity and distrust. Here, transparency, a *leitmotif of* this scenario is equated with disclosure procedures that are mandatory, complex and costly. Barriers to entry are high, as companies are now accountable for suppliers and consumers. The state plays a major role in providing security to the nation and overseeing the process whereby trust in the market is preserved through market abuses or dysfunctions. This involves a stronger coercive and discretionary power for the state and independent regulatory agencies. Regulators themselves are not trusted and they must demonstrate they take the interests of investors, consumers and other stakeholders into proper consideration. Agencies must use metrics to gauge severity of problems in an increasingly quantitative and data intensive world. The media tends to focus on scandals and breaches of faith. Altogether, dealing with regulatory and compliance risks has become a part of corporate business. Communities have become isolated and are not as tolerant of other values and religions; in fact the unknown is a driver of fear in society.

It is against this background that the post-9/11 world has emerged in which tourism in the United States is a symptom. In this scenario, tourists have to prove themselves to the authorities. Tourists are either preferred or regulated visitors. Preferred visitors have secured entrance requirements through a Visa Waiver Program whereas regulated visitors have to require visas from embassies undergoing lengthy interview and intrusive processes. There is a sense that regulated visitors are not trusted as their values and religions are not the same as same as America's. The creation of barriers to entry means the loss of business due to the lengthy time process and costs associated with entry. In a world where time is precious *visitors from emerging economies* feel the hassle is not worth it, therefore do not want to do business with the United States. In retaliation they have created their own regulations for US businesses in their market. The *low trust globalisation* scenario is the scenario that is shaping US tourism, leading to a crisis of confidence in the industry.

US Tourism — A Crisis of Confidence

In 2005, tourism receipts in the United States where US $81 billion according to the US Office of Travel & Tourism Industries (2006) and is projected to grow to US $223 billion by 2030. Making the United States, the world's largest tourism economy. However, a report on www.travelmole.com (Davies, 2006) highlights the crisis of confidence in the US travel industry. The Discover America Partnership involves top executives from Walt Disney Parks and Resorts, Inter-Continental Hotels, Marriott and Anheuser-Busch issued a national challenge to attract an extra 10 million travellers a year to the United States from 2007. In 2005, there were 4.3 million UK arrivals in the United States, 8% below the record high of 4.7 million achieved in 2000 — prior to the 9/11 terrorist attacks. At the same time the Travel Industry Association of America revealed at the World Travel Market in London that its marketing campaign is to revert back to the slogan 'Discover America' from 'See America'. Travel Industry Association of America CEO Roger Dow described 'See America' as too arrogant while Discover America was also better suited to a dotcom environment through a new website.

Dow blamed the decline in UK visitors to the United States in 2006 on a combination of factors including the perceived hassle of entering the country, world events, global competition for tourists and the impact of the World Cup. The partnership admits its target of 10 million more international visitors will be a tough one to achieve. Dow states that

> achieving 10 million new visitors will not happen easily. Our nation does little to encourage international travellers to the US. And those who choose to do are often greeted by an increasingly difficult entry process. At a time when America needs 'people-to-people communications' like never before, the US share of the global travel and tourism market is declining — down 36% in the past 15 years. To improve our global standing and ensure our future vitality, we must address the obstacles to visiting the US and recapture our place among the world's destinations of choice.
>
> Davies (cf. Dow, 2006)

The 9/11 security concerns have tightened travel restrictions to the United States slowing inbound tourism into the country. President Bush's 'War on Terror' led to a global scrutiny of Americanism outside the US borders, signalling that the United States is not friendly to foreign visitors. Central to the crisis are visas'. Many Western countries that are considered safe, such as Britain, France, Iceland and New Zealand are part of the Visa Waiver Program, which allows residents of 27 countries to freely enter the United States for less than 90 days as long as they have a machine-readable passport. However, countries that fall outside of this program have the hassle of obtaining visas'. This means:

- Tourists must attend an interview at an embassy or consulate and require special 'e-passports' containing biometric finger or iris scans.
- An interagency review of applicants from 'high risk' countries.

These measures have strained the resources of the Department of State and created hassles for foreign visitors. For example, in November 2006, tourists applying for visa in Recife, Brazil had to wait 100 days; in Mumbai, India it was worse — 184 days. The time it takes to process visa is impacting upon high yielding business travel. The United States is losing substantial numbers of business travellers to Europe because of the stringent security measures it imposes on international visitors. Research conducted by Euro monitor International — found that total business arrivals to the United States fell by 10% to 7 million over the 2004–2005 period, while the number of the business visitors to Europe grew by 8% to 84 million over the same period (Associated Press, 2006).

The US Travel and Tourism Advisory Board (2006) report *Restoring America's Travel Brand: National Strategy to Compete for International Visitors* assessment of the present situation is seen in Table 21.1.

In 1996, the US Travel and Tourism Administration[1] were dismantled due to a lack of funding from Congress. At the same time, other countries across the world have exponentially grown spending on marketing and promotion. For example, Scotland spends US $40 million compared to US $6.1 million in the United States. Even countries like Albania, Poland and Greece outstrip the United States.

Basically the report states that although world tourism is growing and the United States is losing market share. In the *low trust globalisation* scenario, the world's perception of United States is affecting inbound travel and tourism markets. Let's find how?

Anti-Americanism

In 1945, the United States was the founding impulse behind the cornerstones of the International Community: the World Bank, International Monetary Fund and most of all the United Nations. Untainted by colonialism or fascism, heroic in warfare and idealistic at home, the United States presented itself as a paragon to inspire a less noble and divided world. Sixty years later as the low trust globalisation scenario prevails, that perception had been almost completely reversed. Today, the world and America seem to view the world differently, whether this environment, culture or commerce leading to polarisation and disconnection with the United States.

---

1. A new Office of Travel and Tourism Industries (see http://tinet.ita.doc.gov/) was formed with a research and statistics function rather than destination marketing. At the time of writing a bill was passing through the US Congress advocating a new destination marketing organisation for the US funded by a US $10 international departure tax.

Table 21.1: Environmental assessment of America's travel brand.

The good	The bad
In 2006, the US is projected to return to — and — possibly surpass — the levels of international arrivals last reached in 2000.	The US has captured 0% of nearly 20% growth in country-to-country travel since 2000. By the end of 2005, North America was the only sub region of the world to have recorded a decline in arrivals since 2000.
The US captured 6.1% of 808 million international travellers in 2005 — ranking third behind France and Spain. This represents a second year increase in market share.	US share of international travel has fallen 35% since 1992 — from a high of 9.4% to the current 6.1%. Had the US maintained its share of the world travel market, 27 million more travellers would have visited the US in 2005.
The US captured 12% of the US $622 billion in revenue that was spent by country-to-country travellers in 2004 — by far the highest ranking among countries in the world.	US share of revenue from international travel has fallen 29% since 1992 — costing the US an estimated US $43 billion in 2005 alone. The cumulative cost since 1992 is estimated at US $286 billion in economic growth and millions of jobs.
The US leads the world in international travel and tourism receipts. The US gained 65% more revenue from international visitors than Spain and 83% more revenue than Spain.	In 2004 — the US took in US $8 billion less from foreign visitors than it did in 2000, at the same time that total world receipts were US $149 billion higher.
The travel and tourism surplus rose to US $7.4 billion in 2005, an increase of 84% over 2004 and the second year in a row the surplus has nearly doubled.	Compared to 10 years ago, the US international tourism balance of trade has declined nearly 72% — from US $26.3 billion in 1996 to US $7.4 billion in 2005.
The US benefits from perhaps the widest, richest array of tourist attractions in the world, as well as a world class level of service, infrastructure and hospitality facilities.	According the Anholt-GMI National Brands Index, the US has fallen from 1st to 6th among dream destinations for international travellers. And a survey of travel buyers showed that 77% believed that the US is more difficult to visit than any other destinations.

Criticism of the United States today is found in:

- US foreign policy was perceived as unilateralism and imperialism
- Refusal to sign up to various international treaties, such as Kyoto protocol
- Perception that the United States is the main proponent of globalisation/ neo-liberal trade policy
- Criticism of the ethical behaviour of certain American corporations
- Claims of excessive nationalism and religiosity
- Perceived ignorance of peoples and places outside the United States

This anti-Americanism is ascribed by many as a reaction to the foreign policy of the current President Bush administration in Washington, however there is a history of anti-Americanism in the world. The concept of anti-Americanism dates back almost to the discovery of the New World and has undergone many changes to reach throughout history to reach its current form. Ceaser (2003) in his paper titled *A genealogy of anti-Americanism* identifies five major historical areas of anti-Americanism, all of which still have some relevance today:

- *The degeneracy thesis*: The idea that America degraded everything it touched. Hamilton (1797) noted that ' ... even men admired as profound philosophers gravely asserted that all animals, and with them the human species, degenerate in America'.
- A romantic rejection of the rationalism of which the United States was founded. The alleged *rootlessness* of American society meant that there was no real sense of community, just a 'dull materialism'.
- *The spectre of racial impurity*: Racialist theorists such as Gobineau (1999) found the mixing and levelling of the races abhorrent. America was, at one time, seen as a 'Great White Hope', where 'Aryans' would re-assert their rightful dominance in the world.
- *The empire of technology*: Many European thinkers deplored the industrialisation of America, although it mirrored that of Britain, as a repulsive move towards the gargantuan. The development of techniques of mass productions (and their spread to Europe) was lamented by Nietzsche (Caesar, 2003) as 'spreading a spiritual emptiness over the Continent'.
- *Soullessness and rampant consumerism*: German philosopher Martin Heidegger (Smith, 2006) described America as a 'catastrophe site', a place of 'indifference' and 'sameness', and all this bound up in 'an atmosphere that lacks completely any sense of history'. This is perhaps the version of anti-Americanism that has the most currency today.

What Is the World Saying about the US Today?

Perceptions of America

According to the Pew Global Attitudes survey of 110,000 people across the world shows a negative shift in opinions towards the United States, including in traditionally 'Atlanticist' countries, namely Great Britain and Germany (Figure 21.1). The 'special

Favourable opinion of the US, by country

% who have an overall favourable opinion of the US

"Please tell me if you have a very favourable, somewhat favourable, somewhat unfavourable, or very unfavourable opinion of…The United States?"

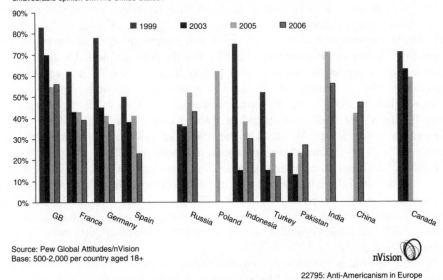

Source: Pew Global Attitudes/nVision
Base: 500-2,000 per country aged 18+

nVision

22795: Anti-Americanism in Europe

Figure 21.1: Favourable (or unfavourable) opinions of the US by selected countries.

relationship' between the United States and United Kingdom may still exist at a governmental level, but there is now only a slight majority of people in the United Kingdom that have an overall favourable opinion of the United States as a country.

Germany (especially the former West) has enjoyed excellent relations with the United States stretching as far back as the end of the Second World War when American loans helped to rebuild the country's shattered infrastructure. Relations suffered greatly during the build up to the Iraq war, to which the German people were strongly opposed. By contrast, feelings towards the United States in the Eastern European countries tend to be more positive, where America is seen (especially by the young) as an aspirational place, following the demise of communism.

This build up of anti-Americanism has built up a head of steam over the last 5 years, with the headlines of the Pew survey reporting:

- December 2002 — America's image slips, although goodwill towards the United States remains
- June 2003 — US image plunges in the wake of the Iraq war
- March 2004 — No improvement in US image, some worsening in Europe
- June 2005 — US image improves slightly, although still negative in most places and anti-Americanism is becoming increasingly entrenched
- June 2006 — Show little further progress — in fact some back sliding. Even as the publics of the world concurred with the Americans on many global problems

It is important to remember that Figure 21.1 only shows the overall opinion of the United States. The 2006 Pew survey (Pew Research Center, 2006) asked all those with an unfavourable opinion of the United States whether their feelings were mainly due to President Bush or a more general problem with America. The response 'mainly Bush' constituted a majority in every country (nearly 3/4 in France and Germany). This data is consistent with the increase in anti-American sentiment between 1999 (when Bill Clinton was President) and 2003 (after the Iraq conflict). The level of anti-Bush sentiment across the world cannot be understated. A BBC poll conducted in September 2004, 2 months before the US presidential election, showed that an overwhelming majority in the European countries surveyed (with the exception of Poland) wanted the Democrat candidate, John Kerry, to be elected. Only 10% of Germans wanted George W. Bush to be re-elected (74% Kerry) and just 5% in France (64% Kerry). American's opinion in the world is falling.

Figure 21.1 shows us although opinion plummeted in 2003, the year the United States invaded Iraq there has been a gain in public opinion towards the United States in Indonesia, which dropped to 15% in 2003 only to rebound to 38% in 2005, notably because of the US aid effort to that country's tsunami disaster but then fall again to 30% in 2006. A similar picture is found in India in 2005, when opinion reached 71% then fell to 56% in 2006.

Negative attitudes towards the United States in many Muslim countries have intensified. After Iraq, many in Muslim countries began to see the United States as a threat to Islam, and what had perhaps been loathing for the United States turned into both fear and loathing. A 2006 Pew study (Figure 21.2) found that in all five majority Muslim countries surveyed, solid majorities said they worried that the United States might become a military threat to their country. At 46%, nearly half of Turks have an unfavourable opinion of the United States and a staggering 77% of Pakistan citizens have an unfavourable perception of the United States. Both of these countries are supposedly close American allies with Turkey being a member of NATO.

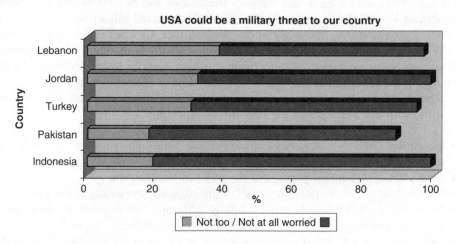

Figure 21.2: US could be a military threat to our country. *Source*: Pew Research Center, 2006.

Although US and European policymakers report that official relations have improved in the past year, most observers argue that the image of the United States and President Bush among the European publics has not improved since their strong opposition to the war in Iraq in 2003. New German Chancellor Angela Merkel changed.

The tenor of US–German relations, but her warm visits to Washington and welcome of President Bush to Germany were accompanied by persistent concerns about the alleged CIA rendition of a German citizen and the treatment of prisoners in Guantanamo Bay. Only three European countries currently view US leadership more positively than negatively: the Netherlands (51% to 44%), Romania (47% to 35%) and the United Kingdom (48% to 45%). Similarly, when asked to evaluate their feelings of warmth toward the United States on a 100-point thermometer scale, Europeans ratings declined from 64 degrees in 2002 to 51 in 2006 (See Figure 21.3).

The percentage of Europeans who agree that NATO is essential for their country's security has declined each year since 2002, from 69% that year to 55% in 2006 (Figure 21.4). The largest declines have come in countries traditionally perceived as strong supporters of NATO; in Germany, support fell from 74% in 2002 to 56% in 2006, and in Italy, support dropped from 68% in 2002 to 52% in 2006. In Poland, support fell from 64% in 2002 to 48% in 2006, and in Turkey, support dropped from 53% in 2004 to 44% in 2000s In the United States, support for NATO rose from 56% in 2002 to 61% in 2006. The most important point from this trend is that for the first time France gave NATO a higher rating when compared to Germany. The steady fall of the importance of NATO amongst the German population represents a shift from those that where born before the Second World War to those that where

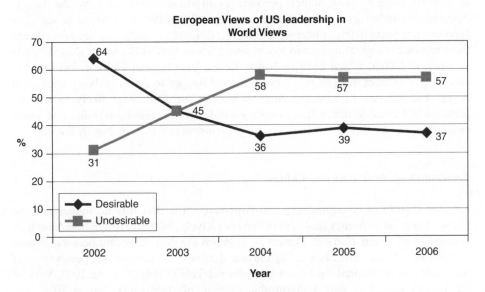

Figure 21.3: European views of US leadership in world affairs.
Source: Transatlantic trends.

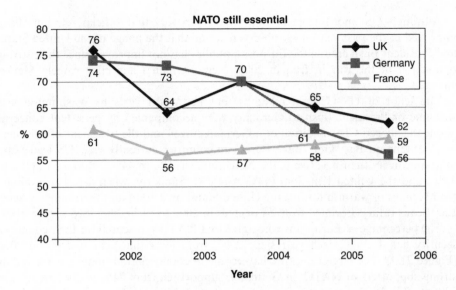

Figure 21.4: Is NATO still essential? *Source*: Transatlantic trends.

born after the war based on an understanding that Germany owes United States something for the cold war and saving it from the Soviet Union (Yeoman, 2007).

Figure 21.5 highlights opinions about threats to global peace also reflect regional concerns. While solid majorities in Jordan and Egypt see America's presence in Iraq as a great danger, even higher percentages in these countries view the Israel–Palestinian conflict as a great danger to regional stability and world peace. The Japanese are particularly concerned about North Korea — 46% say the government there represents a great danger to world peace. Those concerns are not shared nearly as much in China, which borders North Korea; just 11% of Chinese feel that the current government in Pyongyang poses a great danger to Asian stability and world peace. The British, French and Spanish publics were all more likely to say the presence of United States in Iraq poses a great danger to regional stability and world peace than to say this about the current governments of Iran or North Korea.

Perceptions of Americans and Culture

Another feature of contemporary anti-Americanism is that it is no longer just the United States as a country that is perceived negatively, but increasingly the American people as well, a sign that anti-American opinions are deepening and becoming more entrenched. There has been a significant decrease in favourable perception of Americans in traditional European inbound markets (Table 21.2). In 2002, 83% of the United Kingdom had a favourable opinion of Americans, but in 2006, this number was 69. However, in Asian countries, US perception has risen, from 73% to

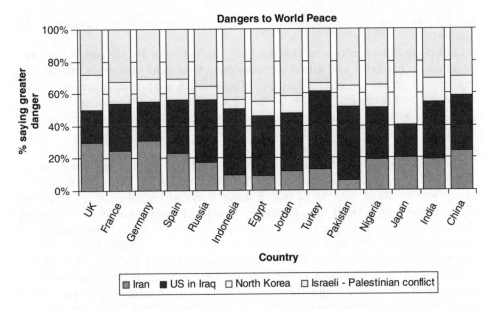

Figure 21.5: Dangers to the world. *Source*: Pew Research Center, 2006.

Table 21.2: Favourable opinion of Americans (PEW, 2006).

	Favourable opinion of Americans				
	Very/somewhat favourable (%)				
	2002	**2003**	**2004**	**2005**	**2006**
UK	83	80	73	70	69
France	71	58	53	64	65
Germany	70	67	68	65	66
Spain		47		55	37
Russia	67	65	64	61	57
Japan	73				82
India	58			71	67
China				43	49

82% in Japan and from 58% to 67% in India. So why has the perception of Americans fallen amongst Europeans. In 2005, the Pew Global Attitudes survey asked what adjectives you associate with Americans. On the positive side, Americans are widely seen as hardworking and inventive. On the negative side, in most of the countries surveyed, fewer than half said Americans are honest, while majorities said they are greedy and violent. Significant numbers also considered Americans rude and immoral.

Looking at this country-wise (Figure 21.6), we find more French people associate the adjective 'hardworking' with Americans than Americans themselves and this is a view echoed across the rest of Europe. Inventiveness is also an American quality recognised by Europeans, with more than 3/4 of French and Germans associating those terms with Americans. Americans also recognise the more negative parts of their character, with 70% of US citizens describing Americans as 'greedy', a higher proportion than any other country.

The importance of the distinction between the US government and the American people within European reactions is given further weight by Pew Global Attitude survey which asked people in six European countries whether they trusted the American people, with the same question asked for the American government. Those trusting the American people exceeded 55% in each of the countries covered (ranging between 56% in France and 81% in Denmark) whilst trust in the US government did not pass 40% in any country, with a low of just 17% in France.

Another difference between Europe and the United States is the secularisation of Europe is firmly at odds with the trend towards greater religiosity in the United States. This is best exemplified in the United Kingdom, where Islam is expected to overtake Christian Denominations by 2040. Christian religion and the church have found themselves increasingly sidelined in their importance to everyday life in Europe (Figure 21.7).

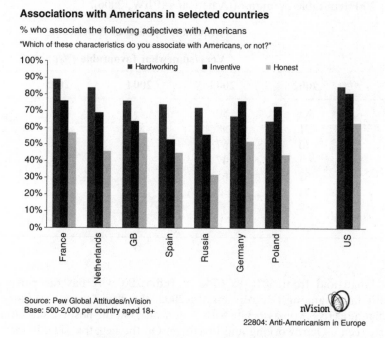

Figure 21.6: Associations with Americans.

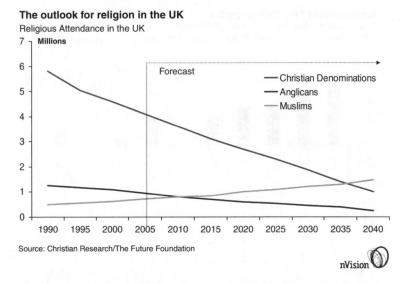

The outlook for religion in the UK

Religious Attendance in the UK

Figure 21.7: Forecasts of UK religion in society.

From Figure 21.8, just 41% of Europeans state that they have trust in the church, compared to 50% in 1997, whilst the drop in attending religious services has been even sharper in Europe. Contrast this with the situation on the other side of the Atlantic. Despite the importance of religion in the United States (59% described it as 'very important' in their lives, compared to 33% in Great Britain, 27% in Italy, 21% in Germany and just 11% in France), the majority of Americans feel their country is not religious enough. Indeed, according to an IPSOS (Future Foundation, 2006e) survey in June 2005, 40% of Americans feel religious leaders should influence public policy. Only 20% in the United Kingdom and Germany expressed similar sentiment, with that number falling to 12% in France.

What divides Europe and the United States even further in this respect, though, is the level of their belief in God. 70% of Americans agreed with the statement 'I know God really exists and have no doubts about it' (23% in the United Kingdom, 24% in France, 22% in Germany and 32% in Spain). This divergence has provoked scorn from Europe and the United States towards one another. American commentators have written of an "aggressive secularism sweeping Europe" and "Christianophobia", whilst some of their European counterparts describe America as an excessively religious society, led by an overtly religious leader under the thumb of religious institutions. The sharp divide in attitudes to religion can only exacerbate differences in areas such as foreign policy, as has proved to be the case over recent years.

Figure 21.9 identifies that European attitudes to American culture are anything but straightforward. A majority of those surveyed in all countries bar Russia stated that they liked American culture, with nearly 2/3 of French respondents stating this. However, in France and Germany this proportion is outweighed by the number

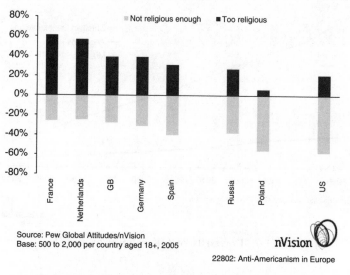

Figure 21.8: Feelings about American's religiosity.

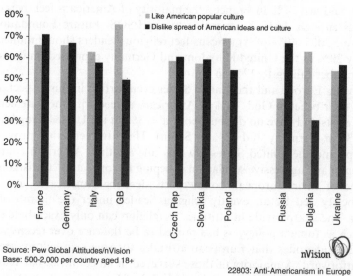

Figure 21.9: Attitudes towards America.

stating that they dislike the spread of American ideas and culture. France in particular has been pro-active in seeking to promote the growth of home-grown talent in the musical and film arenas, even passing a law which obliges 40% of radio output to be in French. Despite these attempts, the influence of American culture remains strong. In 2003, just 3 of the top 10 films in France were home-produced.

The example of McDonalds in France is cited often to highlight the contradictory nature of feelings towards American culture. Since its entry into the French market it has been much maligned in a political and social sense. The destruction of a half-built McDonalds franchise in the town of Millau by Jose Bové, a French farmer, in protest at American import duties on Roquefort cheese, received widespread public support. Ex French President Chirac (Freeze, 2002) stated that 'It would be in nobody's interests to allow one single power, albeit a respectable and friendly one, to rule undivided over the planet's food markets'. Yet despite this, France remains McDonalds most profitable European market, with its former CEO even invited to head up European operations recently. Unsurprisingly, a greater sense of shared heritage makes Britain the least negative of Western European countries towards American culture, although 50% of British people dislike the spread of American ideas and culture. The attitudes in the Eastern European countries are also revealing. Despite being relatively uncritical of US policy, levels of dislike for American culture are in line with the Western European average.

Perceptions of Trust

Figure 21.10 tells us that current low levels of trust in the US government appear to have had an effect on American standing in the business arena. Trust in American brands is currently at a very low ebb, with iconic American brands such as Coca-Cola, McDonalds and Starbucks recording low levels of trust in France and Germany (and, to a lesser extent, in the United Kingdom). Just 20% of French people give Starbucks a trust rating of 6 or more and only 26% in Germany. Starbucks records the lowest level of any business in any country by this measure. The invasion of an American company into a commercial-cultural territory (coffee preparation), which must be regarded by many as nationalistically French may have generated a certain hostility amongst French consumers. Nevertheless, Starbucks has now made its entry into the French market and has 22 branches in the Paris area, with plans to open more across the whole country. Judging by Starbucks' expansion (and sales figures) it would appear that low levels of trust do not translate into poor sales. The differences between countries and business sectors are obviously a key factor in the levels of trust a business enjoys. UK consumers tend to be more trusting than their French and German counterparts, in line with their lower levels of anti-American sentiment. Exxon-Mobil has the lowest levels of trust across the board in all four countries surveyed, which we can attribute perhaps in part to general image issues affecting the oil industry. It is also interesting to note universal high levels of trust in Nissan (the only Japanese brand listed). It is clear that perception of a brand's provenance is key

Trust in leading corporate brands, by country

% who on a 9 point scale, where 0 means no trust at all and 9 means
trust them a great deal, gave each company a score of 6 or more

I am going to read you a list of organizations and companies. For each one, please tell me how much you
TRUST that company or organization to do what is right. This time, please use a 9-point scale where one
means that you "do not trust them at all" and nine means that you "trust them a great deal".
The higher the number the more you trust them to do what is right".

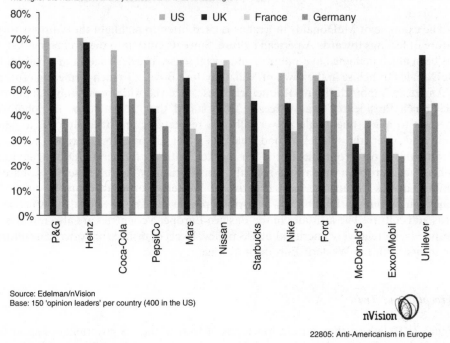

Source: Edelman/nVision
Base: 150 'opinion leaders' per country (400 in the US)

nVision

22805: Anti-Americanism in Europe

Figure 21.10: Trust of American brands.

to its level of trust amongst consumers. Many UK consumers associate Heinz brands
with being quintessentially British, belying their parent company's American status.
Nike is another example of a brand that has managed to establish itself as a global
brand in Europe and manages to enjoy relatively high levels of trust.

We earlier alluded to the realisation in America that its popularity abroad is at a
particularly low level at the moment. Figure 21.11 provides the most concise example
of this feeling. Just 26% of Americans feel that their country is generally liked by
other countries, in stark contrast to its northern neighbour, Canada (94%). This is
the lowest of any of the 13 countries surveyed. Germany was the least positive EU15
member in its estimation of its standing abroad, but even in this case over 50%
replied in the positive. It is clear that there is bi-partisan agreement in America that
events of recent years, such as the war in Iraq, withdrawal from the Kyoto treaty and
disputes over trade tariffs have seriously affected America's standing abroad. It is
this that has led to Americans seeking a rapprochement with their European
counterparts.

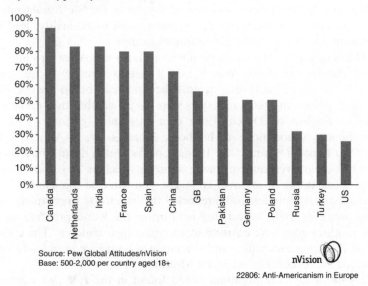

Perception of how much respondent's country is liked by other nationalities

% who feel that their country is generally liked by those of other nationalities

"How do you think people in other countries of the world feel about your country? Is your country generally liked or disliked?"

Source: Pew Global Attitudes/nVision
Base: 500-2,000 per country aged 18+

nVision

22806: Anti-Americanism in Europe

Figure 21.11: Americans perception of how others think of them.

The findings highlighted so far have illustrated the lack of trust in United States and its citizens. With these feelings seemingly so widespread, the possible implications for American businesses are obvious. Elements of American business have been active in seeking to promote a more positive image abroad. This is clearly illustrated in the creation of 'Business for Diplomatic Action', a private sector organisation set up to counter act anti-Americanism. Counting McDonalds, UPS and PepsiCo as members, it seeks to build bridges to other parts of the world through various programs as well as commissioning research into the root causes of anti-Americanism. One the programmes that the Business for Diplomatic Action has initiated includes a guide for Americans travelling abroad on how to act, which can be found at www.worldcitizensguide.org

So, What Does All This Mean for Brand America?

Does this all mean that American brand is tarnished with the wrong images and has lost faith in products such as Nike, Hilton or Disney? It could be argued that these American icons as lacking cultural capital and social cachet which are important drivers for tomorrow's tourist if we follow the anti-American scenario to a logical conclusion. Harris (2005) argues the Disneyfication image of tourism product in the United States strips away the human and cultural elements of the product leaving a cold and manufactured tourism experience, which middle-class consumers are turning away from. Bourdieu (1993) theory on cultural capital is quick to explain the blandness of the American tourism experience, whether it is mass cruising or retail malls as sophisticated consumers sees no added value in the McDonaldization of the US tourism experience in the terms of uniqueness and individuality, leading to the disenchantment and dislike amongst consumer groups.

So, what has changed? The world no longer feels it owes America something. The gratitude of the Second World War is now a distant memory to the generations X and Y's. Examples of backlashes against the American brand are everywhere. In 1992 and 1998, groups of Dutch teenagers were asked whether they preferred Nike's advertising in English or Dutch. Even over this short period, opinion shifted noticeably. Simon Anholt notes in his book *Brand America* (Anholt & Hildreth, 2004) in 1992 a typical response was 'If Nike speaks Dutch it can't be a cool brand', whereas in 1998, many respondents made comments such as 'If you can't even figure out how to speak to me in my own language, you can't be too smart'. The World Health Organisation (Foulkes, 2004) reported that its efforts to complete the task of eradicating police by 2005 were being held up in the Kano province in northern Nigeria by mothers who were refusing to vaccinate their children. The culprit was a rumour that the American made vaccine contained oestrogen in order to make their children sterile and eventually eradicate Muslims.

Does this mean that the premium brand found in the *I ♥ NY* campaign, will disappear. The relentless communications of American values, cultures and lifestyles through mass communications leads to familiarity and breeds contempt. America is no longer a mysterious, idealized and magical land. The uniqueness and individuality of its cultural capital has disappeared due to the accessibility of other cultures and destinations through travel, media and business. 'Made in America' has lost its social cachet and economic advantage as even American consumers buy Japanese rather than Ford cars. The world's love affair with America is over, as that lover has found another partner, whether it is *Exotic India, Cultured China or the New Brazil*. In 2030, other countries can provide the same or better experiences and products in the terms of quality and consistency but at a cheaper price.

Consumers no longer trust *Brand America,* for example a survey in August 2002 found that 68% of people were less likely to trust everyday brands as a result of unscrupulous actions of Enron and WorldCom (Zawoody, 2004). The United States has always promoted itself as the land of hope and opportunity, but if dishonesty prevails *Brand America* is tarnished by the constant presentation of scandals in the world's media.

Klein (2002) in her book *No Logo* criticises the Bush administration's talk of re-branding America on the grounds that 'America's problem is not with its brand — which could scarcely be stronger — but with its product'. According to Klein, what make people angry about America is its false promises, the fact that it says one thing and does another. Therefore, drawing the conclusion, can we really trust America? President Bush's ascertain that Iraq held weapons of mass destruction, then committing the cardinal sin of taking a country to war — is perceived as the ultimate breach of trust. If the world cannot trust the President of the United States they will certainly not trust *Brand America*.

America's uneasiness with Islam taints the multi-cultural image of *Brand America*, resulting in Muslims across the world being convinced that the United States is intolerant to their religion based on the presence that all Muslims must be terrorists as they all look the same (Buchanan, 2002). The United States went to war with Iraq and at the same time gave Al-Queada a play ground in its own backyard resulting in a constant stream of suicide bombers and a war that cannot be won (Yeoman et al., 2005).

In fact anti-Americanism is becoming so strong, that Cox (2006), a US citizen living in London, wrote on the BBC news website to express her concern about the amount of abuse she receives because of her nationality. She says the level of anti-Americanism she has experienced 'feels like a kind of racism....I don't want anyone to feel sorry for Americans, or me, I just want people to realise that we are dealing with hatred too'.

In a survey of 1259 high school students in countries such as Saudi Arabia, Spain, Italy and China, teenagers said that Americans are violent, materialistic, want to dominate and are disrespectful of people unlike them, not generous and lack strong family values. At the same time, male respondents said they would like to have a relationship with an American female so they could go to bed with her on the first date (Taffe, 2002).

The real issue for the United States is trust. The challenge is how to reverse the impact of images of Abu Ghraib and Guantanamo that now shape the views of young people all around the world, as favourable depictions of America as defender of freedom in the twentieth century did then. Because if it does not, *Brand America* will be so tainted it will be thought of by consumers as unethical. Tomorrow's consumers are concerned with how they live, what they eat and how the world behaves. Therefore, is an international boycott of America a feasible scenario?

What Are the Prospects?

There is a difference between what people say and what people do (Eden & Ackerman, 1998). For example, for every 100 people that say they will shop ethically only 3% of UK consumers do (Yeoman & The Future Foundation, 2008). Will all this talk of anti-Americanism translate itself into a boycott in which we see the end of US tourism? One way to put into perspective is to use scenario forecasts, which present different growth rates. However, before we condemn US tourism there are a number of important factors that need to be considered.

The United States is the largest inbound destination in the world, offering a vast range of attractions to visitors, whether it is national parks like Yellowstone and Yosemite, Disney theme parks, vibrant cities such as New York and San Francisco and the beaches of Florida, California and Hawaii. Furthermore, with Hollywood, being its advertising agent and with favourable exchange rates, the prospects must be

Table 21.3: Baseline forecasts for inbound US tourism assuming a growth rate of 3.5% per annum.

	1990	2000	2005	2015	2030
Arrivals (millions)	39.4	51.2	49.2	69.7	116.7

good. In the long run, it is reasonable to assume growth will get back on track for the United States. Whether it is facilitated by a change in foreign policy or the present restrictions become better managed. It can be assumed that the international arrivals to the United States will grow by 3.4% by 2030. Thus by 2030, arrivals should have reached 116.7 million, more than doubling the market compared to the 2005 base (Table 21.3).

The terrorist events of 9/11 fractured the steady upward flow of inbound tourism to the United States. In 2000, 1 year before the attacks, tourism reached an all time high of over 51 million visitors and dropped to 41.2 million in 2003 as consequence of the attacks. However, like any other terrorism incident, destinations bounce back and international arrivals have grown year-on-year ever since. A number of factors are facilitating this growth, including the desire for international travel, low interests in Europe, the United States as the world's largest economy and trading nation and in particular currency markets.

International tourism is influenced by currency markets. In 2003, the British £ to the US $ was 1.63, in 2007 it had crossed the US $2.00 stretch hold — a stacking 23.3% change in 4 years. The US $ has weakened against key currencies across the world, including the Euro, Australian Dollar, Mexican Peso and Venezuelan Bolivar. In the short term, continued US fiscal deficit will mean that US $ remains weak against other currencies.

This means, tourists will be attracted to the United States for retail bargains. According to Mintel (2007b), the exchange rate is appealing to tourists with dispensable incomes interested in luxury goods, which translates into good news high end retailers like Saks and Tiffany.

The US government will facilitate a number of major advertising campaigns in Europe with the support of industry and a national web presence will be enabled. This government — private sector partnership will ensure tourism is better organised in attracting inbound overseas markets. In the future, it would not be Europe that will be America's prime market but Japan, South Korea, China and India. The growing middles classes of India and China in particular will be the driving forces of future growth. These markets will also grow because of open skies. Canada and Mexico will continue to remain the top two inbound markets for the United States.

However, if America see its future in the terms of international isolation, continued security checks, problems acquiring visas and a perception of an unwelcoming nation. The rate of growth will be less than the competition. In this scenario US inbound tourism will only grow at 1.9% per annum (Table 21.4).

The difference between the forecasts is a cumulative loss of nearly 400 million international arrivals of tourists to the US economy, a number not to be taken lightly!

Table 21.4: Alternative forecasts for inbound US tourism assuming a growth rate of 1.9% per annum.

	1990	**2000**	**2005**	**2015**	**2030**
Arrivals (millions)	39.4	51.2	49.2	59.4	78.7

Concluding Remarks

So far we have discussed the low trust globalisation scenario and the rise of anti-American. However, at the same time Shell's *Open Doors* scenario (Shell International, 2005) and the power of the United States as the world's largest economy in 2030 overcomes many of the barriers of the *low trust globalisation* scenario. This is why Harvard Business School professor John Quelch has found that only small minority of overseas customers, between 10% and 15%, would not buy global brands. But he attributes that behaviour to the anti-global movement that arose in the late 1990s, not to more recent anti-American sentiment. 'I'm skeptical that the average consumer in the world is going to let their views of American foreign policy affect their brand-choice behaviour', he says (Gumber, 2005). People outside the United States, and especially in Europe, are increasingly telling pollsters that they no longer like or feel good about familiar US brands, including Coca-Cola, McDonald's, Marlboro and Heinz. A poll of 8000 consumers in eight nations taken last December by GMI Inc., based in Seattle, shows that 61% of French consumers and 58% of Germans feel negatively toward US firms. Another poll by the Edelman public relations firm, based in New York City, found that the image of brands including Merck, Procter & Gamble and Kraft has taken a substantial hit in the past year. However, Jan Lindemann, Global Brand-Valuation Director at New York-based consultancy, Interbrand, being interviewed in *Business Week*.

> Despite a deluge of images showing outraged protesters and headlines calling for boycotts, the activists are a minority, Lindemann says. He points out that consumers abroad act much like their US counterparts: Most don't take their political views to the cash register. Ultimately, any backlash should be a "blip" that doesn't cause lasting damage to US companies or brands. There's little historic proof that war and antiwar sentiments have had massive impact. This [anti-American] debate is waged by ... groups that don't reflect most consumers. He also points out that globalization has changed the way people view products and brands, observing that the strongest brands — often from the larger, richer companies — are likely to continue winning share in foreign markets.
>
> Tsa (2003) Business Week

According to Erdmann (2006) of the US Office of Travel and Tourism Industries:

> The US's visitors are primarily repeat travellers. We know that for the overseas market, which excludes Canada and Mexico that 79% of the visitors have been to the US before. Furthermore, in 2005, the US set arrival records for 7 of the top 25 arrival markets for the country. And, the top 25 countries account for 91% of all arrivals to the US. Australia was one of the countries that set an arrival record. But, I remember seeing some quoted research that said Australians would not visit the US. Then, if you look at 2006, through August 2006, Australia is up 5% and poised to set another new record for visitation to the country.

However, the tourist is still coming to the United States to see Mickey Mouse, Donald Duck and John Wayne as war, boycotts and anti-Americanism seems to fade away. However, the danger for American brands is that 1-day consumer behaviour could follow the anti-American attitude, not trust the brand and think that a holiday in the United States is unethical.

Chapter 22

What If Global Warming and Climate Change Were to Change Our Holiday Plans

Looks like the beach holiday in the Maldives and skiing in the French Alps are out of the question for the rest of eternity.

Tourist choosing a holiday in 2030

Introduction

In 2030 world tourism will be the world's largest industry, representing 1.9 billion international arrivals and US $2 trillion receipts (Yeoman & The Future Foundation, 2008), but can the world cope with a rapidly growing carbon footprint, much of which will be caused by the consequences of travel, and, in any case, does the tourist really care? Today, the majority of opinion polls show that consumers are more concerned about the environment now than before, but few travellers actually change their plans in order to minimise CO_2 emissions. It seems that going on holiday is more important than the environment. Many destinations are struggling to become carbon neutral, including Scotland, the Caribbean and Costa Rica. Even Richard Branson is promoting the 'green' credentials of space travel, and five-star 'green' resorts are being opened in Colonel Gaddafi's Libya. The majority of consumers are aware that they need to do something to reduce their carbon footprint, but very few translate this awareness into action. Today, global warming and climate change are 'hot' topics, so what if the threat of climate change and global warming were to change consumers' holiday intentions.

Climate Change and Global Warming

Climate change refers to the changes in temperature, precipitation, wind and humidity for a given region. It defines the average state of the atmosphere over timescales ranging from short term (decades) to long term (millions of years) (Gore, 2006). Recently, the term climate change has often been used to describe only increased temperatures in today's climate. Climate change can, however, involve both cooling and heating. The term global warming defines an increase in average global temperatures, which in turn causes climate change. Temperature readings taken over recent decades based on derived sources, for example, ice cores, tree rings, etc., show that average global temperatures have risen since the Industrial Revolution in the eighteenth and nineteenth centuries, and the rate of increase has accelerated over the past few decades.

The 2006 Stern report concluded that 'the scientific evidence is now overwhelming: climate change presents very serious global risks, and it demands an urgent global response'. The business community must also consider these risks and determine its response, and the tourism industry is likely to be impacted on more than the most. As the temperatures rise there will be winners as well as losers in global tourism; this will vary according to location, type of holiday and the target consumer market. For many destinations the future will depend on the decisions they take today. The full extent of climate change is still uncertain and the outcome will be affected by how quickly the world acts to reduce its carbon footprint. However, whatever action may be taken in the future to minimise carbon emissions, many changes appear to be already locked in. The Intergovernmental Panel on Climate Change (Houghton, Ding, Noguer, Linden van der, & Xiaosu, 2001) has 'very high confidence that the global average net effect of human activities since 1750 has been one of warming'. Temperature increases are not, however, taking place evenly across the world. While many countries will become warmer, others will remain stable or in some cases even experience a decline in temperature (see Figure 22.1 for a possible scenario on global warming).

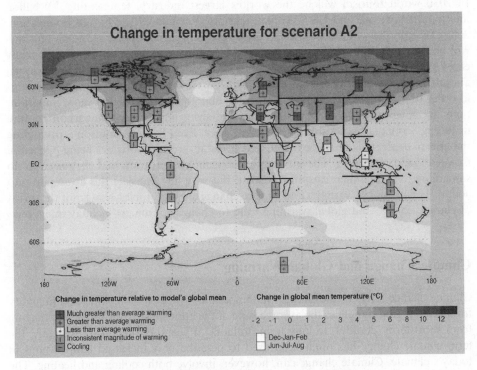

Figure 22.1: Climate change. *Source*: IPCC.

What Will This Mean for World Tourism in 2030?

In 2030 the global average temperatures are likely to have risen by between 1°C and 2°C (Figure 22.1) and global sea-levels could be 72 mm higher, but the accelerated melting of the Greenland and the West Antarctic ice sheets could lead to levels reaching 25 cm higher (McGuire, 2006). Every 1-mm rise in sea-level translates into a 1.5-m retreat of the shoreline. This means that it could be expected that by 2030 shorelines in many areas will have retreated by at least 108 m, and possibly by up to 375 m. This would wipe out beaches across the world and threaten coastal amenities such as hotels, golf courses and retail facilities.

Global warming is expected to have most impact on the Northern Hemisphere, leading to more temperate climates in Canada, the United Kingdom, Scandinavia and Russia. These destinations could benefit from an increased appeal for travellers seeking to escape the sweltering temperatures forecast for parts of continental Europe and the United States.

Warmer ocean temperatures and melting polar ice caps will cause sea-levels to rise in many parts of the world, impacting on those destinations which rely economically on tourism. Florida and the Caribbean are likely to suffer from more frequent and severe hurricanes, such as Hurricane Katrina which devastated New Orleans in 2005. Elsewhere, retreating shorelines and coastal flooding could lead to the subsidence of seaside property and erosion in tourism honeypots such as Venice, which already faces uncertainty about its future. The Maldives will not exist as a country because it will have been submerged by the sea. By 2030, according to McGuire (2006), the number of ski resorts with good-quality skiing and snow-boarding slopes will have been reduced by 40% and in Europe the Alps will have 30% less snow.

Country Focus — Summer and Winter Seasons

Spain

For the Mediterranean countries, higher temperatures by 2030 are likely to make much of the region excessively hot for summer beach holidays, although conditions will be more bearable during the winter months. The impact of these changes means that Spain's peak tourist season is likely to shift. Whilst Spain is at present one of Europe's leading summer destinations, in 2030 the very hot summers, but cooler autumn and winter months will mean that the country will attract far more tourists during these months than it does at present. A 2°C rise in average global temperatures could result in up to 21 more extremely hot days and stifling nights in the summer, and the over-development of resorts, second homes and golf courses in Southern Spain will be curtailed because of the shortage of water and stricter regulations as to its use.

In the Canary Islands more frequent Atlantic storms may bring flash floods, damaging winds and landslides. Without the construction of sea defences, a combination of increased wave height, bigger storm surges and rises in sea-level will cause major erosion. Storm activity and higher waves can also be expected to threaten beach-front property more frequently.

France: Provence and the Côte d'Azur

In France, tourism is likely to prosper in the shoulder months, as the warmer weather continues for longer into the autumn. Wildfires are going to be a major problem, particularly away from the coast and in the months of August and September as the vegetation becomes tinder dry. Rising sea-levels will require authorities to address the problem of beach erosion and also put in place plans to move threatened buildings a good distance back from the shoreline. Wetlands that are at present popular with visitors will suffer, either because of drying out or infiltration by saltwater or even complete inundation by the sea.

France: The Alps

The French Alps could experience a 30% reduction in snow, with resorts such as Flaine and Mourzine becoming unsustainable, whereas other resorts such as Val Thorens and Chamonix, which have access to glacier skiing and are at a higher altitude, are the least likely to be affected.

Greece: The Islands

The principal threat from climate change to tourism in the Greek islands, including Crete, is likely to come from a combination of soaring temperatures and increasingly scarce water supplies. Inevitably, water is going to become a major problem on the islands, many of which must rely on wells because of minimal river flow. Crete appears to be particularly vulnerable and within a decade could face serious water shortages. Increasing aridity is also resulting in creeping desertification, which may severely affect the landscape by 2030.

Italy: The Amalfi Coast and Tuscany

The number of heatwaves in Tuscany is also predicted to rise dramatically. The Amalfi area will also endure many more unbearably hot and humid nights, with another 35–42 tropical nights each year, when temperatures are not likely to fall below 20°C. Both regions are likely to have at least 20 more dry days per year, contributing to an increased risk of fires. However, more extreme precipitation events are also predicted, which will bring the prospect of more frequent flash floods. Longer dry spells, particularly in southern Italy, will also increase the potential for water shortages and drought. With sea-levels anything up to 20 cm or more higher by 2030, all the beach resorts of both Tuscany and the Amalfi coast will be badly affected by the erosion caused by higher tides, storm surges and bigger waves. We can also expect malaria and other tropical diseases such as West Nile Fever to be prevalent in Italy by 2030.

Italy: The Dolomites

Half of Italy's winter-sports villages are located at less than 1300 m and by 2030 they will no longer be viable as snow-sports destinations. Cortina d'Ampezzo and Canazei will suffer badly because the snow could well be unreliable, especially early and late in the season. In the Dolomites, Madonna di Campiglio and Selva will fare better because their base stations are above 1500 m.

United States: Florida

The state of Florida is low lying, with much of the south in particular close to sea-level. Without the construction of coastal defences, a sea-level rise of between 7 and 25 cm could result in the sea making inroads of between 100 and 400 m inland. This would ensure the loss of Florida's typically low-gradient beaches along both coasts and also seriously affect the coastal ecosystems of the Florida Keys. The Everglades would suffer as a result of seawater infiltration, higher tides and bigger storm surges, especially if the protective mangrove barrier is lost as the sea-level rises.

With Atlantic sea-surface temperatures set to climb upwards in the run-up to 2030 and beyond, the Florida coastline may well face a battering from ever-more powerful hurricanes. Serious coastal flooding will become far more frequent as a result of a combination of sea-level rise and storm surges of 5 m or more that will accompany the more powerful hurricanes.

The Caribbean Islands

The Small Island Developing States (SIDS) of the Caribbean, including Barbados, Antigua, St Lucia and others, are especially vulnerable to climate change. The islands have poorly developed infrastructures, limited natural resources, economies that are sensitive to external shocks and high exposure to natural hazards. The main threats are likely to come from an increase in the number of more powerful hurricanes, coastal inundation and erosion, saltwater penetration of freshwater aquifers, damage to coral reefs and other ecosystems, and the emergence of vector-borne disease, that is, West Nile Fever. A number of factors are likely to lead to the Caribbean Islands becoming less attractive to visitors. Energy and water resources will be strained as a result of higher temperatures (and therefore increased demand for air conditioning), aquifer contamination and a predicted drying of the climate, perhaps leading to water shortages and power cuts. Bleaching of the coral reefs will lead to falling demand for dive tourism, while beach erosion and inundation resulting from hurricane-related storm surges and rising sea-levels are likely to make beach holidays less attractive.

Australia: Queensland

Queensland is also expected to become drier as a consequence of decreased rainfall and increased evaporation, leading to the likelihood of drought and water shortages. The most devastating impact of climate change on the Queensland is reserved for the jewel in its crown — the Great Barrier Reef. If the water around the Reef becomes too warm, the corals will expel the tiny, symbiotic algae living within them, leading to bleaching of the coral and ultimately to the death of the Reef. An average rise of just 2°C in the global temperature may be sufficient to kill off 90% of the world's coral reefs.

North Africa: Morocco and Tunisia

A combination of heat and humidity already makes places like Marrakech extremely uncomfortable and this situation will be far worse in 2030 and beyond. The beaches of both Morocco and Tunisia will suffer increasing erosion as sea-levels rise, while the threat of desertification is also significant.

In Tunisia, 75% of the countryside is under the threat of desertification and every year more communities vanish beneath the advancing sand dunes. In the future this will be compounded by higher temperatures and by a significant reduction in rainfall.

India and the Indian Ocean: Goa and Kerala

The main impact of climate change on Goa will result from rising sea-levels, with this very flat, low-lying area extremely susceptible to even the smallest rise. By 2030, beach erosion and inundation of shoreline properties is likely to be a real problem. Kerala is also low lying and vulnerable to rising sea-levels and is likely to encounter similar problems, although because it is a small state, fewer people will be affected. Nevertheless, the coastal zones that benefit from much of the tourist trade will suffer increasingly from beach erosion and inundation in the run-up to 2030 and beyond. Both Goa and Kerala are within the Indian Ocean's cyclone belt and will be affected by an increase in the number of more powerful cyclones predicted to occur as a result of climate change; a trend that may already be apparent. This will increase the probability of wind damage and coastal flooding due to storm surges, exacerbating further the problems caused by rising sea-levels. Climate change may also result in a more unpredictable monsoon period, leading, on the one hand, to severe flooding and, on the other, to periods of extended drought, causing water shortages.

Maldives and Seychelles

The big problem for the Maldives will undoubtedly be rising sea-levels, with most of the 200 or so inhabited islands rarely more than 1 or 2 m above sea-level. By 2030, the rise in sea-level will certainly have caused major beach erosion and at worst may have begun to submerge substantial areas of the islands. Saltwater intrusion of aquifers is likely to make individual islands uninhabitable, while the loss of coral reefs because of rising sea temperatures will mean the annihilation of dive tourism. By the end of the century, the Maldives could be almost totally submerged. Loss of its beaches and coral reefs will also take a serious toll on tourism in the Seychelles, but the higher topography — up to 900 m in places — will at least ensure that the country does not completely vanish beneath the waves.

Can Tourism Destinations Afford to Ignore the Risk?

As McGuire (2006) points out, if the IPCC climate change scientific research is correct, then tourism will be reshaped, the French Alps will no longer be a winter-sports destination for the majority of enthusiasts, and in many parts of Europe winter sports will be restricted and expensive. The growth in Mediterranean tourism will slow down because the climate will be too hot, and desertification will increase, leading to unattractive landscapes and water shortages.

But What About the Tourists — Do They Really Care About the Environment?

Over the past 20 years the Henley Centre (Harrison, 2006) has been asking people in the United Kingdom on an annual basis whether they believe that the quality of life in Britain is better improved by looking after the community's interests 'rather than simply their own', or looking after themselves 'which ultimately raises the standards for everyone' (Figure 22.2). According to Michelle Harrison of the Henley Centre, for the first time in decades, their survey has recorded a majority of people suggesting that looking after themselves is the best way to improve the quality of life in Britain.

This apparent rise in people's belief in individualism manifests itself in a number of ways. British people, for instance, accept their role in and responsibility for climate change. Harrison goes on to deduce that individual consumers are more 'at fault' for causing climate change than the service sector industries and more 'responsible for tackling it' than any companies in the corporate sectors. Harrison suggests that consumers are starting to feel guilty about the damage being caused to the environment and want to do something about it. Therefore, companies' brand may be at risk if they don't do something about it! (Johnson, 2006).

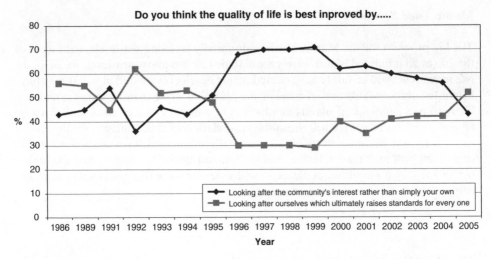

Figure 22.2: It's all about me or all about us! *Source*: Harrison, 2006.

Research by the Carbon Trust (Johnson 2006) suggests that society is at a tipping point in terms of climate change because the consequences are highly visible to consumers, including

- Severe weather changes happening more frequently
- Regulatory impact on people's daily lives
- Increased discussion on the topic in politics and current affairs
- Commercial anticipation

There are frequent reports in the UK media relating to climate change and global warming. In 1994 there were 150 stories per quarter and this rose to 2750 by 2004.

What implications do these findings have? Johnson suggests that companies' brands are at risk if they don't take climate change seriously and engage in the process of adaptation and mitigation. For example, the airlines and the food and beverage industries are perceived to be most at risk (Figure 22.3), with values of US $3 billion (£1.5 billion) and US $13.2 billion (£6.6 billion) respectively.

Will Whitehorn (2006) of Virgin Galactic recently said that if a business is not green and clean in the future then it will be penalised by higher taxes. It is probable that regulation will drive the agenda over the issue of the environment. In the future governments will encourage good behaviour and discourage or even prohibit bad behaviour. Government regulation and incentives will change the behaviour of both consumers and companies. All over the world governments are already introducing legislation, with examples of this being the Californian legislature and the UK Government's Climate Change Bill (BBC, 2006b). Even China is taking action (Shukman, 2006).

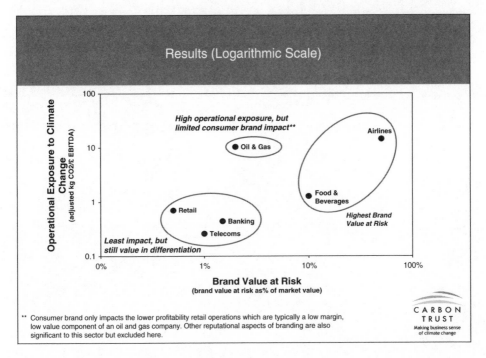

Figure 22.3: Is your brand at risk.

Conclusion

Tomorrow's tourist will be wealthier and better educated, and will travel further afield. Tourists will be more aware of and more interested in the environment, but they will also visit casinos in Las Vegas and travel thousands of miles to sunbathe on the tranquil beaches of Hawaii. However, by 2030 where tourists can go and what they can do may be shaped by global warming and climate change. The Maldives will not exist as a country, let alone as a holiday destination; much of the French Alps will no longer provide skiing and in many other European winter-sports destinations the availability of skiing will be restricted and expensive. All in all, destinations cannot afford to ignore the threat imposed by climate change because if they do, their brand image will be spoiled.

Chapter 23

What If Governments Banned Tourism in 2030 Because It Was Deemed Immoral, Dangerous and Bad for the Environment?

In 2050, 80-year-old Walter McDonald is reminiscing about world tourism. Once upon a time, he said, tourism had been a US $677.5 billion industry, with the prospect of the value reaching US $2016 billion in 2030. However, in 2029 the UN World Health Organisation deemed tourism to be bad for people's health and for the environment and this led to the World Prohibition of Tourism Act. How did this happen? It all started when the do-gooders in society decided that tourism should be a sustainable industry. The subsequent restrictions and regulations meant that it became difficult for people to go where they wanted and to enjoy themselves on holiday. In fact, going on holiday was regarded politically incorrect. In Germany, drinking of alcohol was frowned upon because of health and moral reasons and in 2030 it became a criminal offence for pregnant women to drink alcohol in public, with on-the-spot fines of US $1000. In France, hotel swimming pools were closed because, after a number of landmark personal-injury cases, swimming was considered too dangerous, with the backstroke style being considered the most reckless of all. In the United States, riding stables went bankrupt as a result of escalating insurance premiums and the burdensome red-tape culture. New Zealand, once known as the adventure tourism capital of the world, was no longer promoted as such, because, under the country's Trades Descriptions Act there was no adventure in the country's tourism product. It became extremely difficult to visit China because many of the airports were closed because of foreign consumers' perception that flying damages the environment. In addition, Africa's hopes of becoming an eco-tourism continent disappeared overnight with the introduction in 2021 of personal carbon allowances. Buckingham Palace closed its doors to tourists in 2022 because of the increasing amount of red tape which was associated with risk assessment and children. For example, when children were accompanied to the Palace by non-parents, that is, friends or grandparents, the latter had to undergo a full background security check to prove that they were responsible adults. In the United Kingdom, trainspotting, once a national pastime, was banned because of the perceived threat that trainspotters are in fact potential terrorists searching for their next target.

The Melbourne Comedy Festival was banned in 2023 because comedians were no longer allowed to tell jokes. Their material was constantly censored in case it might contain incitement to terrorism or racial or religious overtones. In 2027, all food in Italy was banned and replaced by a single nutritional tablet, because of the government's concerns about the traceability of food, health scares and obesity.

Today, tourism is a virtual world. The only way for people to experience what was previously called 'going on holiday' is by joining Captain Picard's holiday world through their Nano PS25.

Walter McDonald, 1st August 2050

Introduction

In 2007, there is hardly any aspect of the modern world that does not attract some form of moral or political debate — today one of the debates revolves around the relationship between the state and the individual, where the former is increasingly regulating the social order and restricting the individual's choice of lifestyle. In a free society where the individual should have choices, the range of options is declining. Authorities are increasingly intervening to restrict options and to prohibit activities, including smoking, gambling and even eating certain foodstuffs. From a consumer's perspective political correctness has reached the point at which they always have to worry about what they do and how they behave.

Society appears to be worrying about all sorts of things and debating issues such as how much people drink, what gifts children should receive, whether flying should be allowed, what products should be advertised and the extent of our carbon footprint. To a certain extent this phenomenon of excessive worrying is actually taking the fun out of pleasure! A society that worries to excess results in a sclerosis in commercial activity as a result of regulations and the extent to which red tape and rising insurance premiums impact on choice — resulting in tourism businesses being unable to operate viably. These issues lead to the new puritanical society and a trend which the Future Foundation refers to as the *Assault on Pleasure*, which — if followed to its natural conclusion — will result in the banning of tourism by 2030, because it will be deemed bad for the health of both consumers and the world.

Drivers Shaping the Assault on Pleasure

The Culture of Fear

The two key drivers shaping the *Assault on Pleasure* are 'the culture of fear' and 'the myth of decline'. The culture of fear was first illustrated by Frank Furedi in 1997 in his book of the same title, and in 2007, just 10 years later, the culture of fear has matured into one of the baffling trends in the Western world, where there exists a culture which dictates people's everyday lives, from parental concerns over the safety of their children, to going on holiday, and to how best to take care of their health.

The culture of fear can be characterised as follows:

- An increasingly dominant assumption by consumers is that they are faced by deterioration in all aspects of society, whatever the reality of the issue. This relates to concerns about pollution, terrorism, public service and children's safety.
- An easily triggered conviction that formal authority — corporate or political — is simply not to be trusted, whatever expert opinion it says it can provide.
- A general belief that caution is a stronger virtue than acceptance or optimism, whatever the restrictions that might be placed upon experimentation, risk-taking and having fun.

This phenomenon of the culture of fear has the characteristics of a 'Da Vinci Code Society' where conspirators, plotting to disguise the new depths of risks threatening society, walk the corridors of big government and corporate business, seeking to restrict choice in everyday life. This is a society where an accident cannot and must not be allowed to happen! The realisation that this culture of fear has gone too far led Tony Blair (UK Prime Minister) in 2005 (BBC, 2005) to make a speech about what he saw as the excessively interfering policy-making in the whole field of risk management. Citing the case of a local authority removing hanging baskets from the streets (because of the danger of one inadvertently crushing a passing head), he said

> We cannot respond to every accident by trying to guarantee ever-more tiny margins of safety. We cannot, in other words, eliminate risk. We have to live with it, manage it and sometimes we have to accept that no one is to blame.
>
> (BBC, 2005)

According to Paul Flatters, Chief Executive of the Future Foundation (Flatters, 2005), society realises that 'accidents' do not happen any more to the extent that the *British Medical Journal* no longer uses nor approves the use of the word 'accident' in its columns. Consumers have sued McDonalds because their coffee was too hot or because of super size meals. Product labelling for the sake of perceived possible risk is now commonplace to an illogical extent, for example, peanut products carry a warning on the packet 'this product may contain nuts' — such is the extent of the culture of fear.

Soldiers have sued the Ministry of Defence because they contracted malaria during a military mission in Sierra Leone and ex-servicemen have taken class actions based on their suffering from post-traumatic stress disorder. In 2005, the Association of British Travel Agents had to respond to suggestions from the University of Cardiff that holidaymakers might soon be suing travel operators if they contracted skin cancer via the over-exposure to foreign sunlight (Vilella, Yeoman, Page, Greenwood, & McMahon-Beattie, 2007).

The culture of fear is synonymous with the New Puritans who engender irrational tendencies which politicians, campaigners and the media cannot resist. As shown in Figure 23.1, the New Puritans create issues for society to become concerned about, which in turn promotes a reactionary approach to change and a dysfunctional use of resources in which billions of dollars are spent on combating minor changes, and real problems are neglected (Vilella et al., 2007). The New Puritans are a generation of young, educated and opinionated people determined to sidestep the consumerist perils of modern life. If you own a 4 × 4, spend all your time shopping or are simply overweight — watch your back, the New Puritans are after you!

Siege (2005) writing in *The Observer* said

'Something very interesting, indeed radical, is happening to Britain', confirms Jim Murphy, Associate Director of the Future Foundation,

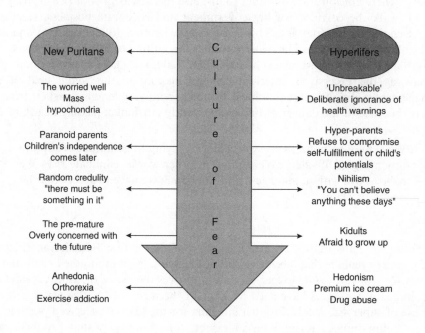

Figure 23.1: The New Puritans.

the trends forecaster which coined the term 'New Puritan'. If you look at the way our lives are filled with different kinds of social opprobrium, a lot of people are increasingly under ethical.

According to the Future Foundation, people are increasingly curbing their enthusiasm for profligate consumption and health-damaging and environment-threatening behaviour. Gone is the guilt-free pleasure-seeker, to be replaced by the model, well-meaning citizen, the New Puritans — a tag which is interchangeable with neo-Cromwellian, harking back to an era when self-important righteousness was the mark of a society in revolt against royalist self-indulgence. The New Puritans consider the consequences of activities previously regarded as pleasurable, and invariably elect to live without them. Think of it as the dietician's favourite adage, 'a moment on the lips, a lifetime on the hips' being given a socio-economic resonance.

Arguably, these personal codes of conduct would provide an arresting enough story on their own, but the New Puritans believe that the curbs must also be extended to other people's behaviour, and, wherever possible, should be enshrined by legislation — for the New Puritans do not fear the nanny state. According to Murphy, 'In common with all important movements, this one has a silent march. It's under-noticed and under-observed'.

Such stealth might suit elements of the New Puritan movement very well, especially when it comes to tackling an issue such as the menace of the Sports Utility Vehicle. Part of the New Puritans' brief is to penalise those who make choices in their lives which will have a negative impact on the rest of society — in this case the gas-guzzling, emissions-generating Montessori wagons that choke town centre streets and pollute the atmosphere to the detriment of their fellow citizens. In Paris, the well-supported rage against this particular vehicle is demonstrated by Les Degonfles (The Deflated), a clandestine team who, in the dead of night, patrol the streets and deflate the tyres of SUVs, also splattering them with mud. Les Degonfles aim to puncture the tyres of about forty SUVs every week.

In the United Kingdom, the task of deterring SUVs has fallen to Sian Berry, a rational and reasonable young woman who runs the Alliance Against Urban 4 × 4s and posts fake fixed-penalty notices on offending vehicles. Although this is low-intensity warfare; New Puritans believe that if governments will not legislate, then they have the right to take matters into their own hands. To date only in Sweden has the government introduced plans to ban non-registered 4 × 4s, so if other

governments do not pass similar legislation, then the New Puritans will
go it alone, with only their principles for company.

Admittedly, these principles vary. You can assume that New Puritans
do not binge drink, smoke, buy products from international
companies, take cheap flights, eat junk food, have multiple sexual
partners, waste money on designer clothes, grow fat beyond their
optimum weight, subscribe to 'celebrity' magazines, drive a flash car,
or live to watch television. The list of 'don't dos' is likely to grow
longer: research by the Future Foundation found that 80%of people
whom they surveyed agreed that alcohol should not be consumed at
work; 25% said that snack-type products should not be offered at
business meetings; more than a third agreed that people should think
twice before giving sweets and chocolates as gifts; and a further 2%
thought that 'the government should start a campaign to discourage
people from drinking alcohol on their own at home (this rises to 41%
in Scotland).

The culture of fear creates a risk-adverse and safety-conscious society, where people
are concerned with protecting their wealth, their power as a consumer, and their
lifestyles. The culture also influences the way in which consumers purchase goods and
spend their leisure time. In a risk-adverse society everything becomes a hazard. As
Furedi (1997) notes

hazards are not merely such obvious threats as poison, bacteria, toxic
wastes or hurricanes. At various times, tampons, automobiles and the
contraceptive pill have been represented as hazards.

This is the central feature of the risk-adverse culture, where some people's concerns
are legitimate, whilst others are hyped by the media, and consumers become over-
sensitised to a fear of the harmless. In other words, irrationality becomes
fundamental to the risk-adverse society. Living in such a society results in people
searching for ways to safeguard their rights in all spheres of their lives, and they seek
to protect themselves also from external risks, hence the popularity of gated
communities for the wealthier and the increasing demand for burglar alarms and
personal security devices. As affluence in society grows, so also do people's concerns
for safety and this results in more rules and regulations. This is what Furedi (1997)
calls the 'audit culture' — the world of meaningless happy bunnies. Citing an
example in the travel industry, he states

Returning from our summer holiday, we were cornered by an angry
travel rep(resentative). "You haven't filled out your feedback form",
she said, before explaining that her job depended on positive comments
and a high response rate.

Propensity to sue companies for compensation

Proportion who would be likely to sue a company for compensation in various situations

These days people are much more aware of the possibility of getting compensation when accidents happen. In each of the situations I read out, can you tell me if you would be LIKELY, or UNLIKELY to try and sue a company for compensation if it happened to you?

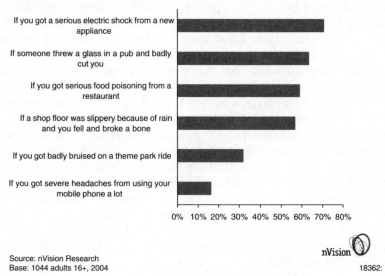

Source: nVision Research
Base: 1044 adults 16+, 2004

nVision

18362:

Figure 23.2: Propensity to sue.

In the scenario in this chapter we refer to the closure of hotel swimming pools and soaring insurance premiums, both of which have been facilitated by the rise of the litigation culture. Figure 23.2 identifies the scope of individuals' propensity to sue. There are concerns about corporate responsibility and negligence, both of which rate highly on the list of people's concerns; they would, therefore, consider suing companies. Now, there seems to be a culture of litigation reinforced by advertisements on television, urging people to contact legal firms in order to sue on a no-win no-fee basis. This culture of litigation is further illustrated in a survey by the US law firm Fulbright & Jaworski (Anon, 2005), according to which two-thirds of UK businesses had faced court action in the previous 12 months and almost half of UK corporations expected to face litigation within the following year.

What does a compensation culture prove? Either we have developed into a self-confident generation of consumer citizens or the lawyers are winning! The compensation culture will continue as long as the regulatory environment gives impetus to people's new-found propensity to sue.

In the scenario at the beginning of this chapter, Buckingham Palace is used as an example; it had to close because of the risk assessment associated with non-parents being in charge of children, presumably leading to the belief that the world is a dangerous place. On the contrary, however, the United Kingdom is said to be one of the safest countries in the world. According to a report by the United Nations

Children's Fund (UNICEF), the United Kingdom has one of the world's lowest rates of child death caused by accidents or abuse. In a survey of the 26 most industrialised countries, only Sweden was ranked lower (Duffy, 2001). In the aftermath of high-profile child murderers such as Ian Huntley (BBC, 2001) and the abduction of Madeleine McCann (BBC, 2007b), newspapers have routinely carried lurid stories about children being in mortal danger. Yet, in the United Kingdom, a child is no more likely to be abducted and killed than they were 30 years ago, when children were given much more freedom to roam. One of the unintended consequences of this trend is the fear amongst adults that they could be branded as a paedophile when working with children and this concern has led to a sharp fall in the number of adults volunteering to work with playgroups, junior sports clubs, etc, according to a report by Scotland's Commissioner for Children and Young People (BBC, 2007a).

The culture of fear has reshaped the political agenda, and this is demonstrated by the power of the Homeland Security Department and the Patriot Act in the United States. Terrorism and the war on terror are frequently headline news in newspapers, on television news and on Internet sites and form the topic of many daily conversations. This trend drives a feeling of insecurity which leads society to surround its people with protectionist measures — to the extent that trainspotters have been banned from certain railway stations in the United Kingdom because they are perceived as potential terrorists searching for their next target like the Madrid train bombers (Wilson, 2003).

The Myth of Decline

Running concurrently with the culture of fear is the 'myth of decline' which insists that although society progresses and people become better-off there is a perception that families and communities are not as strong and close-knit as before, that the neurosis of competitive individualism makes people incapable of consuming wisely, and that the boom in alternative therapies of all kinds shows how much we have lost our way in society. The myth of decline matters because

- It can translate into widespread assumptions and even urban myths and become the cultural prism through which consumers view the world
- It shapes public perceptions of what businesses and organisations really ought to be saying and doing and what issues they should be addressing
- It appears, perversely, to become stronger rather than to disappear in times of relative prosperity, making it a sturdy piece of cultural furniture for companies to negotiate.

The myth of decline is driven by collective individualism; today's consumer appreciates the power of joining forces with others, of seeking out the best sources of intelligence, of pursuing economies of scale, and of sharing experiences with fellow consumers. Nowhere is this trend better demonstrated than in the use of the Internet as a focus of collective individualism. The advent of broadband has given rise to the phenomenon of blogging, vlogging, tagging and pod-casting and such innovations are multiplying the amount of information, opinion and advice available to consumers in search of enhanced choices.

In the scenario, the myth of decline is captured by the perception of the danger of excessive alcohol consumption. Today's media is full of stories about how the misuse of alcohol causes major social and physical damage. The British Medical Association has stated that binge-drinking by the young results in acute and chronic health problems. In response, the drinks companies, fearing a return to prohibition, have launched a campaign to urge all consumers to be more balanced in their consumption — a 'drink sensibly' approach. But the fact is that our consumption of alcohol per capita has hardly changed over the past 20 years in the United Kingdom. This is what Office of National Statistics said about alcohol consumption in 2004 (Vilella et al., 2007):

> Between 1998 and 2003/4 there was little change in the proportions of men and women exceeding the daily benchmark (for alcohol consumption). Heavy drinking among men changed little between 1998 and 2002/3, but rose from 21% to 23% in 2003/4. Among women, the proportion of heavy drinkers stayed at 10% from 2000/1 to 2002/3, following a rise from 8% in 1998. In 2003/4, among women the proportion of heavy drinkers was 9%.

Additionally, according to the World Health Organisation (Vilella et al., 2007), alcohol consumption per capita per annum in the United Kingdom is less than that in France, Germany, Spain, Denmark, Portugal and Austria. The United Kingdom also has a lower incidence of cirrhosis of the liver than any of these European neighbours.

During the last outbreak of Foot and Mouth Disease (FMD) in Scotland (in 2001), there were a number of myths that impacted negatively on Scottish tourism, including one which said that Scotland was closed and also that if visitors came they could catch foot and mouth. The point of all this, of course, is that actual facts have little to do with what is portrayed in discourses, in the media and in marketing messages. The truth often gets lost in outer space, orbiting like an MIR spacecraft waiting to land, but often ignored.

Let's Ban It — An Assault on Pleasure

The Institute of Public Policy has called upon the UK government to introduce environmental health warnings on airline tickets, and campaigning groups such as Greenpeace are telling people how they should conduct their lives, advocating the use of public transport instead of cars and telling people to opt for a shower instead of a bath (Vilella et al., 2007). In 2004, a health lobby group asked if it were appropriate for children to go on school trips to venues such as Cadbury World, one of the most successful visitor attractions in the United Kingdom (Vilella et al., 2007).

Holidays as an indulgent experience for the consumer is at the centre of the debate. This debate may centre on the development of golf courses in hot climates and their excessive use of water or individuals buying second homes in rural communities and pricing local people out of the market. Governments and public bodies are urged by pressure groups and by public opinion to intervene in the marketplace, and to restrict choice and prohibit activities, which barely a generation ago were considered ordinary and harmless. The liberal presumption that people should be free to make choices, whether the products concerned are objectively beneficial or not, is now as culturally prevalent as shoulder pads or punk rock were in the 1970s. Subsequently, tourism as an industry supplying indulgent experiences when exposed to the environmental agenda comes under pressure to justify its existence, and holiday providers are asked to alter their products and to make radical changes. People often ask how tourism can be a sustainable industry when tourists usually have to fly should they opt for a holiday overseas, thus impacting negatively on the environment.

In many countries in the developed world, smoking in public places has been banned for very good reasons of health, but at the same time there appears to be a trend in which authorities are using creeping *regulation by stealth* to tell us what we cannot do — it's a movement that Professor David Littlejohn (2007) of Glasgow Caledonian University calls the 'freedom to' too 'freedom from', where society is increasingly telling people what they can or cannot indulge in. For example, in New York authorities are advocating the banning of mineral water because of the impact of bottles on landfill sites. Crisps, chocolate and carbonated drinks have been banned from school in Germany, Sweden and the United Kingdom because of the increased risk of obesity in children.

Tomato ketchup has been prohibited by Calderdale District Council in schools because of its salt and sugar content. Children in Shropshire are no longer allowed to bring birthday cakes into school because of the drive for healthy eating (Vilella et al., 2007). Invariably, such measures are about improving the environment or invoking the goal of children being better nourished. The significance of this is that there is a sense of moral authority where the political elite knows best rather than the individual.

It is not disputed that climate change is taking place. (Greenwood & Yeoman, 2007); the consensus among scientists, politicians and environmentalists is unequivocal. The issue that is overlooked is that climate change has been taking place since the dawn of time. Within today's politicised environment, messages become blurred and issues which should be based on observation and evidence are presented to the public in a distorted manner which may not represent the actual truth. The strength of the lobby for protection of the environment could present the biggest assault on the enjoyment of holidays to the extent that it will be the major factor to affect the future of the tourism industry.

Within the context of this predicted assault on pleasure, lines are increasingly being drawn to restrict individuals' right to travel for leisure, with political parties talking of flight taxes, restriction on the number of flights taken by individuals, and where one can go and what one can do. From a tourism perspective the response of the industry has been to move towards carbon neutrality and to promote sustainability, both of which actions will minimise damage to the environment. If, however, restrictions on travel limit the freedom to visit foreign countries and tourism providers have to charge consumers more because of increasing energy costs and environmental taxation, then will this move impede the ability to sustain the economic viability of the tourism industry in some countries? For example, restrictions on flying would impact on the long-term viability of tourism in Africa because the markets for African countries are in Europe and North America from where travel is viable only by air.

Conclusions

If this scenario is followed to its natural conclusion, tomorrow's tourist will have the choice of holidays only in a virtual world and even then the New Puritans will complain that consumers are playing too many video games. An assault on pleasure is a dilemma that threatens tourism. On the one hand regulation is about developing a better society, but, on the other hand, if destinations continue to dictate to their visitors what they can or cannot do on holiday, then the tourist will simply go elsewhere.

SECTION IV

Chapter 24

How to? Futureproofing the Future

Introduction: Using Research to Futureproof Strategies

Too many business decisions and the market research strategies they are based on are conducted without sufficient orientation to the future. Too often, the future is seen as indecipherable or unpredictable, so decisions are based on a tacit assumption that the conditions of the future will be the same as the past. Ironically, the one thing we can *guarantee* is that our world is changing and the future is certain to bring with it different business conditions, market opportunities, competitive threats and consumer desires. Being able to interpret how our society is changing and to forecast the likely impact of these trends is vital to making strategic decisions that will remain relevant in our dynamic, changing world. Currently, much market research thinking and practice is focused on the detailed examination of a particular sector or consumer behaviour within a sector, without a sufficient understanding of the broader context surrounding the sector and without an understanding of the factors that might drive future change. Furthermore, all too often the market research industry enforces decisions based on snapshot data — without the benefit of an understanding of the trend and the direction in which it may be heading.

The Future Foundation argues that a rigorous, research-based approach to strategic decisions is *not enough*. Unless such decisions are 'futureproof' — that is made with an understanding of key trends and how they might impact in the future-organisations remain vulnerable to the changes the future will bring.

The Importance of the Future View

The Future Foundation's 'futureproofing' technique presents a field of possibilities, not a 'linear' future. This is an 'open-ended' attitude to the future. It is about using forecasting to sharpen awareness of choices and opportunities. Thus, the Future Foundations 'futureproofing' methodology aims at generating open-ended (though not entirely anarchical) perspectives on future developments. It is also about seeing how a business can proactively re-shape a market, not merely react to inevitable changing conditions. 'Back-casting' is another technique used to encourage a proactive approach to the future — essentially, it asks the question, 'to end up in this situation, which intermediate steps must we take?'

Framing Time

If getting the right kind of 'future-focus' is ever more important for businesses, one of the primary functions of good forecasting is to help to get a sense of when, as well as what may take place. To do this requires an accurate sense of the rate and magnitude of change in different areas, rather than merely accumulating a mass of insights located in an undifferentiated future.

As Dyson (1998, p. 142) points out, in his 'imagined worlds':

> Our history is dominated by different processes ... (Occurring) at different time-scales. When we think about the future, we must first understand that the future, like the past, comes with all these different time-scales. It is important, in any discussion of the future, to distinguish carefully the time-scales on which various things may happen.

Some areas, for example technology and its impact on social networks, are changing relatively rapidly while others such as demographics are shifting slowly but nonetheless dramatically.

Figure 24.1 above illustrates what is essentially a simple point — that change in the commercial environment tends to take place on a somewhat longer timescale than popular culture or many other 'social' trends. That is to say, businesses can gain advantage by anticipating such changes, but tend to be 'playing catch up' all the time.

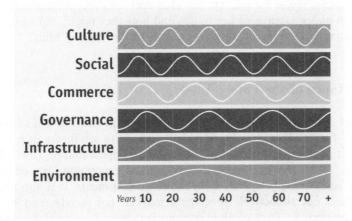

Figure 24.1: Envisioning the future (*Source*: Future Foundation).

Conversely, other kinds of change, such as change in demography, infrastructure, politics and environmental change, tend to happen slowly, and often change more slowly than the commercial environment. In principle, this means that businesses will not have to worry about being 'taken by surprise' by such trends. In practice, however, business strategy is equally likely to 'miss' long-term changes, for their impact lies beyond the horizons of employees and shareholders.

Futureproofing

Futureproofing is the Future Foundation's multi-disciplinary, multi-methodological approach which helps drive future orientation within client organisations. This process unites elements of the entire spectrum of approaches to exploring the future and therefore has broad relevance to many questions, sectors and organisations.

Futureproofing takes the management issue that is being considered (customer segments, the organisation's core offer, relevant markets/sectors, brand attributes, etc.) and assesses how social, economic, cultural, political and technological trends might impact on it. Futureproofing provides the analytical rigour of long-term trends analysis combined with more qualitative methodologies which often take the form of collaborative workshop processes to rate and rank the most relevant and important trends, those most likely to have an impact on the future of a market and/or organisation and those most likely to be future drivers.

Questions which have been explored using this approach in the past include:

- Are the dynamics of society working for or against my market, product or service?
- How are trends likely to affect the size and needs of current market segments?
- Are our core brand attributes going to be as resonant in the future as they are now?
- Has our long-term strategic plan been informed by a 'real' understanding of the key trends affecting our organisation (and how they might alter in the future)?

Futureproofing starts with a comprehensive interrogation of nVision — the Future Foundation's unique source of information, trends and forecasts about the UK economy, markets and society. This enables identification and prioritisation of those trends that are most important for the question being explored. After an initial interrogation of nVision, an exercise to identify a list of the trends of highest relevance to the particular question/client is carried out.

The Future Foundation then use a special workshop process to rate and rank trends in terms of their likelihood of occurring and their importance to the question in hand. This often involves visual tools that allow internal clients who may not be accustomed to working with insight to quickly familiarise themselves, research findings and examples. The workshop process is designed as a collaborative exercise and therefore should involve participation from key client (and possibly agency) personnel. The outcome is a map of trends on the two dimensions of importance (to the key question) and likelihood. This highlights the potential pressure points and opportunities for the future.

Futureproofing Scottish Tourism

VisitScotland engaged the Future Foundation to construct a number of scenarios about the future of Scottish Tourism. These scenarios can be seen at www. tomorrowstourist.com.

The core question for the project was:

> What actions does VisitScotland and its stakeholders need to take to ensure tourism is the *First and Everlasting* industry of Scotland by 2025?

In addressing this core question the groups explored the following, more detailed questions:

- Which markets will thrive and which will decline by 2025?
- Which product offers will thrive and which will decline by 2025?
- How will consumer needs and wants change by 2025?
- How will supply-side and structural issues assist or hinder the development of Scottish tourism by 2025?

Futureproofing was used at the beginning of the project to make sense of all the possible trends that could impact on the future. Figure 24.2 is an example of a Futureproof exercise undertaken during the project.

The Futureproofing workshop identified four focal points for the future of Scottish tourism as the following:

- *New experiences* — With rising affluence-citizen, the consumer values have changed, with a lessening emphasis upon material well-being and an increasing concern for experiential and quality-of-life issues. Consumers in the future will be keener to spend money in ways that grant them access to new experiences or awareness of new ways of living.
- *Cultural capital* — As they become more sophisticated, people increasingly differentiate themselves less on the material trappings they have accumulated and more on the cultural and social knowledge that resides in their brains. Tourism in the future will revolve more around increasing cultural capital. This allows self-enrichment but also gives people social cachet — different forms of cultural capital will become a key status symbol in the future. It will not necessarily be highbrow culture, cultural capital will include categories from knowledge of sport and celebrities to creative writing and knowledge of Scotland's built heritage.
- *Authenticity* — More affluent, sophisticated consumers are not looking for imitation — they will not be satisfied with the ersatz. They want to have a real experience that can add to their cultural capital — increasingly they are looking for authenticity. This concept should not be confused with tradition. An authentic experience may involve a new phenomenon, for example an authentic theme park experience or it could be centred around existing built heritage, for example — it is not age dependent. The challenge for the Scottish tourism industry is to combine

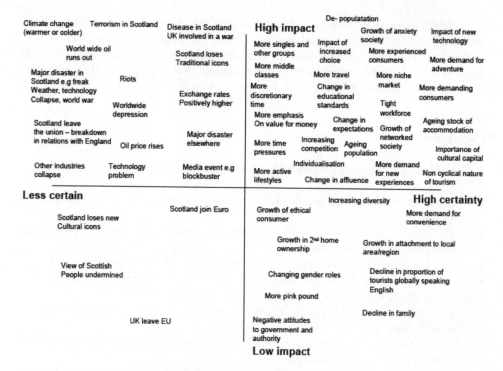

Figure 24.2: Futureproofing Scottish tourism.

these three focal points providing new experiences in an authentic way that is aspirational too so that it adds to people's cultural capital.

• *Business tourism* — Business travellers are inextricably linked to the economic success of a destination. In the future, however, it will become increasingly hard to distinguish between business and leisure travellers. Non-discretionary business travel will decline as technological solutions become more commonplace but discretionary business travel, 'business tourism', will grow as business people travel to improve relationships, build networks, incentivise teams and so on. Business travellers will have the same demands as leisure travellers such as new experiences and authenticity. Similarly, a growing proportion of leisure travellers will want to access interactive solutions while on holiday (even if it is just to check on their pets as opposed to keeping up with their workplace). Many leisure travellers will also demand the services accessed by business travellers currently such as executive lounges and faster checking times at airports or low-cost luxury accommodation in their final destination. Overall, we expect the differences between these two groups to become less marked and the types of offer and the methods of communication for each to become more similar.

By focusing on these areas Scottish tourism plays to its strengths and also meets the emergent trends of increasingly affluent and sophisticated consumers. These clusters of authenticity, new experiences, cultural capital and business tourism became the distinguishing features of a set of scenarios about Scottish tourism by 2025.

Readers will find further 'how to' techniques at www.tomorrowstourist.com whether it is a beginners guide to scenario-planning; using cause and effect diagrams to structure scenarios or prioritising drivers and trends.

Conclusion

To conclude, we summarise a few of the benefits of the Futureproofing approach.

- It eases consensus making among senior strategy teams, particularly when active input has taken place
- It facilitates communication of outputs to senior stakeholders within an organisation and its partners
- It is a transparent methodology for driving strategic planning process
- Its evidence-based approach makes it particularly appropriate for quality standards/review processes and public sector organisations
- It is relatively fast — as it can be applied to maximising an organisation's existing knowledge and data
- It is collaborative and demands close interaction between clients and market research providers
- It combines quantitative and qualitative methodologies, and encourages holistic thinking
- It demands a dynamic approach to research, calling for trend data rather than mere 'snapshot' market research
- It is a highly flexible approach — adaptable to different timescales and markets
- It ensures that consumer insight is closely aligned with other business processes and promotes understanding of research findings

Finally then, to echo our introduction, the primary and fundamental benefit of the method is in ensuring that businesses' strategies will remain relevant in a fast-changing environment — to ensure that strategy is 'futureproof'.

References

Albert, A. (2001). *Brothel: Mustang ranch and its women*. New York: Random House.

Allsopp, J. (2004). Premium pricing. Paper presented at the Future Foundation Changing Lives Conference. 2nd December, Queen Elizabeth Conference Centre, London.

Anderson, C. (2007). *The long tail: How endless choice is creating unlimited demand*. London: Random House.

Anholt, S. (2006). *Competitive identity: The new brand management for nations, cities and regions*. Basingstoke: Palgrave Macmillan.

Anholt, S., & Hildreth, J. (2004). *Brand America: The mother of all brands*. London: Cyan Press.

Anon. (2002). *Future world population growth to be concentrated in urban areas of world*. UN Population Division, accessed on 06/04/2006 at www.un.org/esa/population/publications/wup2001/wup2001-pressrelease.pdf

Anon. (2005). *UK companies expect to face more lawsuits*, accessed on 24th April 2006 at www.out-law.com/page-6222

Anon. (2006). *China currency reserves top Japan's*, accessed on 4th April 2006 at http://www.bloomberg.com/apps/news?pid = 10000087&sid = aIJ7mKLQ01rg&refer = top_world_news

Anon. (2007). *The world party*. London: Rough Guide.

Ashcroft, A. (2004). *Efforts to combat trafficking in Persons, Washington, D.C.: US Department of Justice*, accessed on 17th January 2007 at http://www.state.gov/documents/organization/23598.pd

Asian Demographics. (2007). Accessed on 10th November at www.asiandemographics.com

Asimov, A. (1968). *I, Robot*. New York: Voyager.

Associated Press. (2006). *US losing business travellers to Europe*, accessed on 12th November 2006 at http://www.msnbc.msn.com/id/15590942/

Bainbrigge, N. (2006). Religious tourism and the consumer. Presentation to VisitScotland's/ Tourism Society Seminar on 'Religion, Pilgrimage and Spirituality — A Scottish Tourism Perspective', Edinburgh.

Baker, N. (1984). *The beauty trap: Exploring woman's greatest obsession*. New York: Frank Watts.

Barbel, K. (2006). *Dubai: A sustainable tourism proposition*. VisitScotland Futures Lecture Series, 5th September, Edinburgh.

Basi, S. (2003). *Curry: The story of the nation's favourite dish*. Birmingham: Sutton Publishing.

Baudrillard, J. (1983). *Simulations*. New York: Semiotext.

Bauer, T. G., & McKercher, B. (2003). *Sex and tourism: Journeys of romance, love and lust*. London: Haworth Press.

BBC. (2001). *Bugler statement in full*, 22nd June, accessed on 10th April 2006 at http://news.bbc.co.uk/1/hi/uk/1402798.stm

BBC. (2005). *End compensation culture*, 26th May, accessed on 10th April 2006 at http://news.bbc.co.uk/1/hi/uk_politics/4584009.stm

BBC. (2006a). *Backing for Severn barrage power*, accessed on 18th April 2006 at http://news.bbc.co.uk/1/hi/wales/south_east/4927744.stm

BBC. (2006b). *Britain and California make climate change pact*, accessed on 8th April 2007 at http://news.bbc.co.uk/1/hi/world/5233466.stm

BBC. (2006c). *Home nations fans back England*, 30th March, accessed on 7th August 2007 at http://news.bbc.co.uk/sport1/hi/front_page/4857268.stm

BBC. (2007a). *Adults to 'afraid of' youth work*, 26th October, accessed on 1st November 2007 at http://news.bbc.co.uk/1/hi/scotland/7045544.stm

BBC. (2007b). *McCanns mark six months of search*, 4th November, accessed on 4th November 2007 at http://news.bbc.co.uk/1/hi/uk/7076089.stm

BBC. (2007c). *Are We Having Fun Yet*, accessed on the 8th March 2008, available at: www.news.bbc.co.uk/1/hi/programmes/6431045.stm

Beck, U., & Beck-Gernsheim, E. (2002). *Reinventing the family: In search of lifestyles*. London: Polity Press.

Bloom, D., Canning, D., & Chan, K. (2006). *Higher education and economic development in Africa*, accessed on 10/04/2006 at http://www.worldbank.org/afr/teia/pdfs/Higher_Education_Econ_Dev.pdf

Bohlin, M. (1982). *The spatial and economic impact of recreational expenditures and sales in the Pigeon Lake Area of Alberta. Forskningsrapporter fran Kulturgegrafiska instutionen vid Uppsala universitet 77.* Uppsala: Kulturgeografiska institutionen.

Bourdieu, P. (1993). *Sociology in question*. London: Sage.

Boyle, D. (2004). *Authenticity: Brands, fakes, spin and the lust for real life*. London: Harper Perennial.

Brass, D. (2005). Authentic seeking. Presentation at the Futures Foundation, Changing Lives Conference, London, 7th December.

Brass, D. (2006). *Authenti-seeking: The search for the real*. Research paper accessed on 24th January 2006 at www.nvisiononline.net

Brents, B. (2000). Inside Nevada's Brothel Industry. In: R. Weitzer (Ed.), *Sex for sale: Prostitution, pornography, and the sex industry* (pp. 217–241). New York: Routledge.

Briggs, A. (2001). *Michael Yooung: Social entrepreneur*. London: Palgrave MacMillan.

Brodie, S. J., & Biley, F. C. (1999). An exploration of the potential benefits of pet-facilitated therapy. *Journal of Clinical Nursing, 8*(4), 329–337.

Buchanan, P. J. (2002). *The death of the west*. New York: Thomas Dunne Books.

Buhalis, D., & Costa, C. (2006). *Tourism business frontiers: Consumers, products and industry*. Oxford: Elsevier.

Burgess, K. (2004). Country study: China. In: *Financial Times*, 20/11/2004.

Burns, L. (1993). *Busy bodies: Why our time obsessed society keeps us running in place*. New York: W.W. Norton.

Caesar, J. (2003). *A Genealogy of anti-Americanism*, accessed on 10th March 2008, available at: www.travelbrochuregraphics.com/extra/a_genealogy_of_antiamericanism.htm

Campbell, D., Mitchell, D., & Jackson, J. (2005). Hang up your boots and dance. *The Observer*, accessed on 7th August 2007 at http://observer.guardian.co.uk/sport/story/0,,1461614,00.html

Carey, B. (2006). *The importance of sustainable tourism*, accessed on 30th January 2006 at http://www.scotexchange.net/know_your_market/scenarios/scenarioplanning_policies.htm

Carter, T., & Dunston, L. (2006). *Dubai*. Melbourne: Lonely Planet.

Casado-Diaz, M. A. (2004). Second homes in Spain. In: C. M. Hall & D. K. Muller (Eds), *Tourism, mobility and second homes*. Clevedon: Channel View.

Casson, L. (1974). *Travel in the ancient world*. London: Allen & Unwin.

Castells, M. (1996). *The rise of the network society. The information age: Economy, society and culture*((Vol. 1). London: Blackwell.

Ceaser, J. W. (2003). A genealogy of anti-Americanism. *Public Interest, 152*, 3–18.

Cederwell, W. (2004). Should we be worried by a dropping dollar? *The Guardian*, 11th November, p. 14.

Centre for Social Policy Studies of The Department of Applied Social Sciences & the General Education Centre of The Hong Kong Polytechnic University. (2002). *A Study of Hong Kong People's Participation in Gambling Activities*. Hong Kong: The Hong Kong Polytechnic University.

Chong, C. (2007). *Gambling, casino's and the Chinese*, accessed on 1st September 2007 at http://chinese-school.netfirms.com/casinos.html

Clift, S., & Carter, S. (2000). *Tourism and sex: Culture, commerce and coercion*. Oxford: Pinter.

Cohen, D. (2002). The Economic impact of the HIV Epidemic, Issue Paper No 2. UNDP HIV and Development Programme, accessed on 19/04/2006 at http://www.undp.org/hiv/publications/issues/english/issue02.htm

Condon, R. (2004). *The manchurian candidate*. New York: Orion Books.

Connell, J. (2006). Medical tourism: Sea, sun, sand and …… surgery. *Tourism Management, 27*(6), 1093–1100.

Coppocks, J. T. (1977). *Second homes: Curse or blessing?* Oxford: Pergamon.

Corrigan, P. (1997). *The sociology of consumption*. London: Sage.

Coughlan, S. (2005). *The discomfort of stranger*, 26th July, accessed on 28th August 2006 at http://news.bbc.co.uk/1/hi/magazine/4717251.stm

Cox, C. (2006). *Anti-Americanism feels like racism*, 16th April, accessed on 18th November 2006 at http://news.bbc.co.uk/1/hi/uk/4881474.stm

Cranfield, J., & Hansen, M. V. (2006). *Chicken soup for the soul: Stories that restore your faith in human nature*. London: Vermillion.

Curry, S. R. (2000). Grandtravel catches on. *Advertising Age, 1*(29), 2.

Danziger, P. (2004). *Why people buy things they don't need: Understanding and predicting consumer behaviour*. New York: Dearborn.

Danziger, P. N. (2005). *Let them eat cake: Marketing luxury to the masses — as well as the classes*. New York: Dearborn Trading Publishing.

Davidson, D. (2007). China's Meeting Industry in 2030. Working Paper, VisitScotland, Edinburgh.

Davies, P. (2006). *US business leaders call for tourism action*, accessed on 12th November 2006 at http://www.travelmole.com/stories/1113871.php

deGrandpre, R. (2000). *Ritalin nation: Rapid-fire culture and the transformation of human consciousness*. New York: W.W. Norton.

Deloitte. (2006). *Steep drop in membership of health clubs*. 25th August. Healthclubbenchmark, accessed on 7th August 2007 at http://www.healthclubbenchmark.com/Content/PressRoom/Articles/20060825UK-EN.aspx

Denzin, N. K., & Lincoln, Y. S. (2002). *Handbook of qualitative research*. London: Sage.

Dixon, M., & Margo, J. (2006). *Population politics*, 22nd February, accessed on 25th September 2007 at http://www.ippr.org/articles/?id = 1959

Doctoroff, T. (2006). *Billions: Selling to the New Chinese consumer*. Basingstoke: Palgrave.

Douglas, N., Douglas, N., & Derrett, R. (2001). *Special interest tourism*. Chichester: Wiley.

Dudley, J., Roughton, M., Fidler, J., & Woollacot, S. (2006). *Control of immigration: Statisitics.* Home Office, 14/05, accessed on 7th September 2007 at http://www.homeoffice. gov.uk/rds/pdfs05/hosb1405.pdf

Duffy, J. (2001). *The child safety catch*, 7th February, accessed on 10th April 2007 at http:// news.bbc.co.uk/1/hi/uk/1156063.stm

Durex. (2005). *Global Sex Survey*, accessed on 1st March 2007, available at: www.durwx.com

Durie, A. (2006). *Water is best: Hydros and health tourism in Scotland 1840–1939.* Edinburgh: John Donald Publishers.

Durie, A. J. (2000). *Scotland for holidays? A history of tourism in Scotland 1780–1939.* East Linton: Tuckwell Press.

Durie, A. J. (2003). *Scotland for the holidays? Tourism in Scotland ca. 1780–1939.* Edinburgh: Tuckwell Press.

Duval, D. T. (2005). Space tourism — small steps, gaint leaps: Space as a destination of the future. In: M. Novelli (Ed.), *Niche tourism: Contemporary issues, trends and cases* (pp. 213–222). Oxford: Butterworth-Heinemann.

Dyson, F. (1998). *Imagined worlds* (142 pp). Boston: Harvard Business Press.

Eden, C., & Ackerman, F. (1998). *Making Strategy.* London: Sage.

Edwards, D. (2004). *Foresight. London's olympic bid*, accessed on 7th August 2007 at http:// www.tourismtrade.org.uk/Images/2004%2010%20Norway%20Sweden%20Denmark%20% 26%20Finland_tcm12-11888.doc

EHRIC. (2004). *Medical statistics at a glance*, accessed on 19th October 2006 at http:// www.ehirc.com/individuals/statistics.html#

Enteleca Research and Consultancy. (2000). *Tourist attitudes towards regional and local foods.* London: Ministry of Agriculture, Fisheries and Food and the Countryside Agency.

Erdman, R. (2006). *America's perception of the world.* Ron Erdman's reply posted on STATE_PROVINCIAL_RESEARCHNETWORK@PEACH.EASE.LSOFT.COM

Estes, R. J., & Weiner, N. J. (2002). *The commercial sexual exploitation of children in the US, Canada, and Mexico*, accessed on 1st November, 2006 at http://www.sp2.upenn.edu/~restes/ CSEC_Files/Complete_CSEC_020220.pdf

Etcoft, N., Orbach, S., Scott, J., & D'Agostino, H. (2004). *The real truth about beauty — A global report.* Commissioned by Dove — A Unilver Beauty Brand, accessed on 2nd October 2006 at http://www.campaignforrealbeauty.com/uploadedfiles/dove_white_paper_final.pdf

Euromonitor. (2006). *World travel market — Global trends report*, accessed on 4th September 2007 at http://www.wtmlondon.com/images/100487/SHOWARTICLES/WTMReportfinal4.pdf

Everest, L. (2004). *Oil, power and empire: Iraq and the US global agenda.* Monroe, Maine: Common Courage Press.

Falcone, M. (2005). *Gaming industry additional insights on Macau gaming and MGG/MBG, Deutsche Bank Securities Inc*, accessed on 1st September 2007 at http://web7.infotrac. galegroup.com/itw/infomark/529/95/72573139w7/

Farley, M. (2007). *Nevada prostitution*, accessed on 7th September 2007 at http://www. prostitutionresearch.com

Farrel, D., Gersch, U., & Stephenson, E. (2006). *The value of China's emerging middle classes*, accessed on 27th September 2007 at http://www.mckinseyquarterly.com/Economic_Studies/ Productivity_Performance/The_value_of_Chinas_emerging_middle_class_1798

Fenton, S. (2007). *Women at forefront of consumer spending in China. International Tribune*, 17th September, accessed on 10th November 2007 at http://www.iht.com/articles/2007/09/ 17/business/yuan.php

Fieldman, G. (2007). *Self expression*, accessed on 10th October at http://www.george-fieldman.co.uk

Flatters, P. (2005). The UK's Top Twenty Trends. Presentation to VisitScotland, 19th November, Edinburgh.

Foulkes, I. (2004). *Nigeria polio drive can resume*, 30th June, accessed on 18th November 2006 at http://news.bbc.co.uk/1/hi/health/3854533.stm

Freeze, R. (2002). *French food vs. fast food. Jose Bove take on McDonalds*. Masters Thesis, Ohio University, accessed on 31st May 2007 at http://www.ohiolink.edu/etd/send-pdf.cgi?ohiou1029182528

Frommer's. (2007). *Las Vegas*, accessed on 1st September 2007 at http://www.frommers.com/destinations/lasvegas/0013021105.html

Furedi, F. (1997). *The culture of fear*. London: Continuum Books.

Future Foundation. (2006a). *Changing Lives Survey*, accessed on 14th September 2006 at www.nvisiononline.co.uk

Future Foundation. (2006b). *Health care and the key issues in Europe*, accessed on 1st October 2006 at www.nvisiononline.co.uk

Future Foundation. (2006c). *The cult of the home*, accessed on 1st September 2006 at www.nvisiononline.co.uk

Future Foundation. (2006d). *Eating habits across Europe*, accessed on 1st November 2006 at www.nvisiononline.co.uk

Future Foundation. (2006e). *Anti-Americanism in Europe*, accessed on 31st May 2007 at www.nvisiononline.co.uk

Future Foundation. (2007). *'The future tourists': A report for VisitScotland & Partners scenario planning group*. London: Future Foundation.

Future Foundation. (2008). *The Future of UK Tourism*, accessed on 20th March 2008, available at: www.nvisiononline.co.uk

Future Foundation and VisitScotland. (2005). *Our ambitions for Scottish tourism: A journey to 2025*. Edinburgh: VisitScotland, accessed on 7th November 2005 at www.scotexchange.net/spg

Gamber, P. (1997). *Female economy*. Illinois: University of Illinois Press.

Gardyn, R. (2001). The new American vacation. *American Demographics*, *23*(8), 42–47.

Gershuny, J. (2003). *Changing times: Work and leisure in postindustrial society*. Oxford: Oxford University Press.

Gertner, S. (2000). *Philosophy 304 — Paper 2*, 28th February, accessed on 26th January 2006 at http://www.williams.edu/philosophy/faculty/jsawicki/previous_sawicki_page/s_gertner_022800.html

Getz, D. (1997). *Event management and event tourism*. London: Cognizant Communication.

Gibson, C., & Connell, J. (2004). *Music and tourism*. London: Channel View Publications.

Giddens, A. (2006). *Sociology*. London: Polity Press.

Glaesser, D. (2006). Private Correspondence with Dr Dirk Glaesser, Head of Publication and Education, UN — World Tourism Organisation, Madrid.

Glover, A. (2004). *Sun, sand, sea and cinema: Why Hollywood stars are the new travel agents*, accessed on 25th June 2005 at www.lexispr.com/thomsom/

GMI. (2006). *New poll reveals that internet dating is no longer the preserve of geeks, freaks and the plain desperate*, accessed on 5th June 2007 at http://www.gmi-mr.com/gmipoll/release.php?p=20060131-uk

Gobineau, A. (1999). *The inequality of human races*. New York: Howard Fertiq.

Godwin, S. (2005). *All marketers are liars: The power of telling authentic stories in a low-trust world*. New York: Penguin Books.

Goeldner, C. R., & Brent Ritchie, J. R. (2006). *Tourism: Principles, practices and philosophies*. Chichester/New Jersey: Wiley.

Gore, A. (2006). *An inconvenient truth*. New York: Bloomsbury Books.

Greenfield, S. (2003). *Tomorrows people: How technology is changing the way we think*. New York: Allen Lane.

Greenwood, C., & Yeoman, I. (2007). *Analysis of the Polemical responses to climate change and its impact on tourism*. Working Paper Series, VisitScotland, Edinburgh.

Gumber, P. (2005). *Brand America*, 20th February, accessed on 19th November 2006 at http://www.time.com/time/globalbusiness/printout/0,8816,1029838,00.html

Guthrie, W. K. C. (1987). *A history of Greek philosophy* ((Vol. 4). Cambridge: Cambridge University Press.

Hall, C. M., & Mitchell, R. (2005). Gastronomic tourism, comparing food and wine tourism experiences. In: M. Novelli (Ed.), *Niche tourism: Contemporary issues, trends and cases* (p. 74). Oxford: Butterworth-Heinemann.

Hall, C. M., & Mitchell, R. (2006). Gastronomy, food and wine tourism. In: D. Buhalis & C. Costa (Eds), *Tourism business frontiers: Consumers, products and industry*. Oxford: Elsevier.

Hall, C. M., & Muller, D. K. (2004). *Tourism, mobility and second homes*. Clevedon: Channel View.

Hamilton, A. (1797). *November 2006 The Founders Constitution*, Chapter 7, pp. 65–77, accessed on 27th May 2007 at http://presspubs.uchicago.edu/founders/documents/v1ch7s13.html

Harris, D. (2005). *Key concepts in leisure studies*. London/Thousand Oaks: Sage.

Harrison, M. (2006). Learning lessons from the future. In: T. Hampson (Ed.), *2025: What next for the make poverty history generation*. London: Fabian Society.

Hay. B. (2007). *Fantasy Tourism*. In: Proceedings of the 2008 CAUTHE Conference, Queensland University, Griffith University, Queensland.

Hedrick-Wong, Y. (2005). Women consumer of China — The powerhouse with a powerhouse. *Insights*, 5(4), 1–9.

Henley Centre Headlight Vision. (2007). *Future Traveller Tribes; 2020*. A Report for the Air Travel Industry, Amadeus.

Hindle, C., Bindloss, J., Hargreaves, C., Kirby, J., & Nystrom, A. (2006). *The career break book*. Melbourne: Lonely Planet.

Houghton, J. T., Ding, Y., Noguer, P., Linden van der, J., & Xiaosu, D. (2001). *Climate change 2001: The scientific basis*. Cambridge: Cambridge University Press.

Hume, M. (2002). Brazilian artistry, English fighting spirit, Henman grit. Oh, and avian pigs. *The Times*, 1 July, 2002.

Hutchings, R. (2004). Mapping the global future. *Report of the National Intelligence Councils 2020 Project*, accessed on 26th January 2006, available at: www.foia.cia.gov/2020/2020.pdf

International Association for the Study of Obesity. (2004). *Global obesity epidemic putting brakes on economic development*, 28th October, accessed on 7th August 2007 at http://www.iotf.org/media/releaseoct28.htm

Israel, B. (2003). *Bachelor girl: The secret history of single women in the 20th century*. London: William Morrow.

James, P. D. (2006). *Children of men*. London: Faber & Faber.

Jeffrey, N., & Collins, S. (2001). Family: The grandparent industry. *The Wall Street Journal (Eastern Edition)*, 2nd November, p. 2.

Jenkins, R. (1992). *Pierre Bourdieu*. London: Routledge.

Jenkins, R. (2002). *Pierre Bourdieu*. London: Routledge.

Johnson, E. (2006). *Is Your Brand at Risk?* Presentation at Climate Change and Scottish Tourism Seminar, 6th February, VisitScotland, Edinburgh, accessed on 5th May 2007 at http://www.visitscotland.org/brand_value_at_risk_from_climate_change.ppt#258,1, Slide 1.

Johnstone, I. (2006). *Men, you have 30 seconds to impress women, Scotsman*, 14th April, accessed on 7th September 2007 at http://news.scotsman.com/scitech.cfm?id = 567952006

Jordan, J. W. (1980). The summer people and the natives: Some effects of tourism in a vermont vacation village. *Annals of Tourism Research, 7*(1), 34–55.

Jowell, T. (2004). *Game plan: A strategy for delivering sport and physical activity objectives*, Department of Media, Culture & Sport, accessed on 10th August 2007 at http://www.isrm.co.uk/reference/documents/gameplanpart1_000.pdf

Kidd, G. (2006). *Ludlow food town's success*. Paper presented at Castle Douglas Food town conference, 14 November, [Online] accessed at http://www.cd-foodtown.org/news_detail.asp?newsID = 80

Klein, N. (2002). *No logo: No space, no choice, no Jobs*. New York: Picador.

Koenig, H. (2004). *Very special vacations exclusively for grandparents and grandchildren*, accessed on 11th May 2004 at http://www.grandtrvl.com

Kuhlmann, R. (2004). Why revenue management is not working? *Journal of Revenue & Pricing Management, 2*(4), 378–387.

Kuhn, K. (2006). *Moscow hotels hit October Revpar high*, accessed on 17th August 2007 at http://www.caterersearch.com/Articles/2006/12/07/310413/moscow-hotels-hit-october-revpar-high.html

Kuntze, J., Lindstaedt, N., & Lehmann, K. (2007). *Retail opportunities in the middle east*, accessed on 20th August 2007 at www.occstrategy.com

Lam, D. (2007). *The brief Chinese history of gambling*, accessed on 27th September 2007 at http://www.umac.mo/iscg/Publications/InternalResources/Desmond_article3.pdf

Leco, M. (2006). *Sex in Las Vegas*, accessed on 1st September 2007 at http://www.usatourist.com/english/places/lasvegas/sex.html

Lederer, P. (2003). *Future of Scottish tourism*. Research Seminar on Family Markets, 3rd September, VisitScotland, Edinburgh.

Levi-Strauss, C. (1996). *The savage mind*. Chicago: University of Chicago Press.

Lister, G. (1999). *Hopes and fears for the future of health: A European scenario for health and care in 2022*, accessed on 2nd October 2006 at http://www.jbs.cam.ac.uk/research/health/polfutures/pdf/hopes.pdf

Littlejohn, D. (2007). *Transport and tourism seminar*. Glasgow Caledonian University, 20th April.

Lutz, W. (2001). The end of world population growth. *Nature, 412*, 543–545.

MacCharles, A., & Oaten, S. (2006). *Macau's Great Gamble*, accessed on 25th September 2007 at http://www.deloitte.comwww.deloitte.com

Mandeville, J. (1375). *The travels of Sir John Mandeville*. Republished by Kessinger Publishing, London, 2004.

Marcouiller, D. W., Green, G. P., Deller, S. C., Sumathi, N. R., & Erikkila, D. C. (1998). *Recreational homes and regional development: A case study from the Upper Great Lakes states*. Madison: Co-operative Extension Publications.

Marwick, A. (1998). *Beauty in history*. London: Thames & Hudson.

Masciandaro, D. (2004). Global financial crime: Terrorism, money laundering and offshore centres, Aldershot, Burlington, VT, USA.

Maslow, A., & Lowry, R. (1999). *Toward a psychology of being*. Chichester: Wiley.

Mathers, C. D., & Loncar, D. (2005). *Updated projections of global mortality and burden of disease, 2002–2030: Data sources, methods and results*, World Health Organisation, accessed on 19th April 2007 at http://www.who.int/healthinfo/statistics/bodprojectionspaper.pdf

Mathews, J. (2004). *Who will be beautiful in the future*, accessed on 14th October 2006 at http://news.bbc.co.uk/1/hi/uk/4003049.stm

Maxwell, N. (1998). Have grandkids, will travel: Grandparents and grandchildren are the latest in touring companions. *The Wall Street Journal*, 14th September, p. 18.

McCartney, G. (2006). Casinos as a tourism redevelopment strategy. The Case of Macau. *Journal of Macau Gaming Research Association, 1*(2), 40–52.

McFaul, T. R. (2006). Religion in the future global civilization. *The Futurist*, September–October, Bol 40, No 5, pp. 30–38.

McGraw, P. C. (2004). *Self matters: Creating your life from the inside out*. New York: Pocket Books.

McGuire, B. (2030). *Holiday 2030*, accessed on 8th March 2008, available at: www.benfieldhrc.org/activities/misc_papers/Holiday.2030.pdf

McKibbin, R. (2000). *Classes and cultures: England 1918–1951*. Oxford: Oxford University Press.

McMahon-Beattie, U., & Yeoman, I. (2004). *Sport and leisure operations management*. London: Thomson.

Middleton, V. T. C. (2007). *British tourism: The remarkable story of growth*. Netherlands: Butterworth-Heinemann.

Mintel. (2001). *Singles on holiday*. Leisure Intelligence. London: Mintel.

Mintel. (2004a) *Morocco*. Travel and Tourism. November. London: Mintel.

Mintel. (2004b). *Health and wellness tourism*. Global Travel and Tourism Analyst, August. London: Mintel.

Mintel. (2004c). *Round the world travel*. Leisure Intelligence. February. London: Mintel International.

Mintel. (2005a). *What the Brits do on holiday*. Leisure Intelligence. November. London: Mintel International Group.

Mintel. (2005b). *Saudi Arabia*. Travel and Tourism. August. London: Mintel.

Mintel. (2005c). *Spa holidays*. Leisure Intelligence. January. London: Mintel.

Mintel. (2005d). *Holiday resorts*, accessed on 14th September 2006 at http://premier.mintel.com/sinatra/premier/search_results/show&/display/id = 151359

Mintel. (2005e). *Gap year travel*. International, Travel & Tourism Analyst. No. 12, July. London: Mintel International.

Mintel. (2005f). *Religious tourism*. Travel and Tourism Analyst. Accessed on 16th September 2006 at http://premier.mintel.com/sinatra/premier/search_results/show&/display/id = 149120

Mintel. (2005g). *Extreme sports*. Leisure Intelligence. October. London: Mintel.

Mintel. (2005h). *Festival tourism — International*. Travel & Tourism Analyst. No 13, August. London: Mintel International. Accessed on the 1st September 2007 at www.mintel.com

Mintel. (2006a). *International tourism forecasts*. December. London: Mintel.

Mintel. (2006b). *Uganda*. Travel and Tourism. May. London: Mintel.

Mintel. (2006c). *Brazil*. Travel and Tourism. November. London: Mintel.

Mintel. (2006d). *Argentina*. Travel and Tourism. November. London: Mintel.

Mintel. (2006e). *South Africa*. Travel and Tourism. May. London: Mintel.

Mintel. (2006f). *What Brits do on overseas holidays*, accessed on 1st September 2006 at http://premier.mintel.com/sinatra/premier/search_results/display/id = 155763/display/id = 190121/display/id = 155763

Mintel. (2006g). *Golf tourism International*, accessed on 14th September 2006 at http://premier.mintel.com/sinatra/premier/search_results/display/id = 187835&cover/display/id = 211448&section?select_section = 211449

Mintel. (2006h). *Luxury goods retail — Global.* July. Mintel International, accessed on 5th September 2007 at www.mintel.com

Mintel. (2007a). *US Inbound.* March. London: Mintel International.

Mintel. (2007b). *Luxury travel — International.* Travel and Tourism Analyst. No 12, July, accessed on 1st August 2007 at www.mintel.com

Morgan, D. (2001). *The Legacy of 2001: The visionary film will turn 33 years old — but is it dated?* Accessed on 1st April 2007 at http://www.abcnews.go.com/sections/sections/scittech/DailyNews/2001_001223.hmtl

Morgan, P. (2007). *Prospects for 2007.* Presentation at the Travel and Tourism Research Association Conference, Las Vegas, 19th June.

Morris, D. (1994). *The human animal.* London: BBC Books.

Morrison, A., & Lynch, P. (2008). *Tourism entrepreneurial innovation: The case of Howard Wilkinson and the Ayrshire Food Network.* Working Paper. Strathclyde University Business School.

Moss, C. (2005). *The new seekers*, accessed on 21st June 2005 at www.travel.guardian.co.uk/saturdaysection/story/0,8922,1410768,00.html

Mullur. (1999). Tomorrow's Clifton and Plet. *Finance Week*, 14th May, p. 52.

Nadon, S., Koverola, C., & Schludermann, E. (1998). Antecedents to prostitution: Childhood victimization. *Journal of Interpersonal Violence*, *13*(4), p. 234.

Naisbitt, J. (1982). *Megatrends: Ten new directions transforming our lives.* London: Warner Books.

National Intelligence Council. (2004). *Mapping the global future*, accessed on 21st July 2007 at http://www.cia.gov/nic/PDF_GIF_2020_Support/2020.pdf

Newman, N. (2004). *London olympic bid*, accessed on 10th August 2007 at http://www.bbc.co.uk/dna/actionnetwork/A2683578

Nordin, U. (1993). Second-homes. In: H. Aldskogius (Ed.), *Cultural life, recreation and tourism: National Atlas of Sweden.* Stockholm: Royal Swedish Academy of Science.

Novelli, M. (2005). Niche tourism: An introduction. In: M. Novelli (Ed.), *Niche tourism: Contemporary issues, trends and cases.* Oxford: Elsevier.

Nozick, R. (1989). *Examined life.* New York: Touchstone.

O'Brien, S. (2007). *Grand travel: Ideas for travel with grandchildren*, accessed on 20th September 2007 at http://seniorliving.about.com/od/travelsmart/a/grandtravel.htm

OECD. (2006). *OECD Health Data 2006*, accessed on 14th October 2006 at http://www.oecd.org/document/30/0,2340,en_2825_495642_12968734_1_1_1_1,00.html

Office of Travel & Tourism Industries. (2006). *US Commerce Department Forecasts record arrivals and spending from travellers to the United States*, accessed on 12th November 2006 at http://www.tinet.ita.doc.gov/tinews/archive/tinews2006/20061106.html

Opperman, M. (1999). Sex tourism. *Annals of Tourism Research*, *26*, 251–266.

Orlando/Orange County Convention and Visitors Bureau. (2001). Research shows Orlando is #1 grandtravel destination, (online) retrieved 6th May, 2004, from www.familytravelnetwork.com/articles/grand_14.asp, Cited in Palmieri (2006).

Oxford Forecasting. (2006). *Forecasts for world growth.* Research Prepared for VisitScotland, Edinburgh.

Page, S., Bentley, T. A., & Walker, L. (2005). Scoping the nature and extent of adventure tourism. Operations in Scotland: How safe are they? *Tourism Management*, *26*(3), 381–387.

Palmieri, C. (2006). *Intergenerational solidarity as a way of understanding grandtravel.* MSc Thesis. University of Florida. Privileged access through Dr Lori Pennington-Gray, Dissertation supervisor.

Pearson, I. (2004). *NBIC by 2030*, accessed on 20th April 2006 at www.btinternet.com/~ian.pearson/web/future/nbicby2030.htm

Pedro, A. (2006). Urbanization and second-home tourism. In: C. Buhalis & S. Costa (Eds), *Tourism business frontiers: Consumers, products and industry.* Oxford: Elsevier.

Pender, J. (2004). Slow dollar exit. *Financial Times*, 25th November 2006, p. 6.

Penhirin, J. (2007). *Understanding Chinese consumers*, accessed on 27th September 2007 at http://www.mckinseyquarterly.com/Economic_Studies/Productivity_Performance/Understanding_the_Chinese_consumer_1468

Peters, T. (2001). *Women roar: The new economys (either economy's or economies') hidden imperative*, accessed on 1st September 2007 at http://wowstore.tompeters.com/store/women-roar

Petre, J. (2006). *Churches 'on road to doom if trend'*, accessed on 15th September 2006 at http://www.telegraph.co.uk/news/main.jhtml?xml=/news/2005/09/03/nchurch03.xml

Pew Research Center. (2006). *Percentage very happy by marital status*, accessed on 26th September at http://pewresearch.org/pubs/?ChartID=17

Pickard, J., & Mulligan, M. (2007). Second homes face price fall. *Financial Times*, accessed on 10th October 2007 at http://www.ft.com/cms/s/0/f29aeeb8-6de8-11dc-b8ab-0000779fd2ac.html

Pine, B. J., II., & Gilmore, J. H. (1999). *The experience economy: The work is theatre and every business a stage.* Boston: Harvard Business School Press.

Pine, J. (2004). *The authentic experience.* Travel and Tourism Research Association Conference, Montreal, Canada, 19 June.

Pole, G. (1991). *The Canadian rockies: A history in photograph.* Vancouver: Altitude Publishing.

Polley, M. (2004). Sport and national identity in contemporary England. In: D. Porter & A. Smith (Eds), *Sport and national identity in the post-war world* (pp. 10–30). London: Routledge.

Porter, M. (1985). *Competitive advantage.* New York: Free Press.

Prahalad, C., & Ramaswamy, V. (2000). Co-opting customer competence. *Harvard Business Review.* January, accessed on 1st September 2007 at http://harvardbusinessonline.hbsp.harvard.edu/b02/en/search/searchResults.jhtml?Ntx=mode%2Bmatchallpartial&Ntt=pradhalad+ramaswamy&N=105&Ntk=main_search

Press Association (2006). *McConnell on vow of binge drinking*, accessed on 13th October 2006 at http://news.scotsman.com/latest_scotland.cfm?id=15102006

Putman, R. (2001). *Bowling alone: The collapse and revival of American community.* New York: Simon & Schuster.

Rein, I., & Shields, B. (2007). Place branding sports: Strategies for differentiating emerging, transitional, negatively viewed and newly industrialised nations. *Place Branding & Public Diplomacy*, *3*(1), 73–85.

Reisinger, Y. (2006). Travel/tourism: Spiritual experiences. In: D. Buhalis & C. Costa (Eds), *Tourism business frontiers: Consumers, products and industry.* Oxford: Elsevier.

Roberts, D. (2004). US Icons. *Financial Times*, 25th October, p. 6.

Rowling, M. (1971). *Everyday life of medieval travellers.* London: B. T. Batsford.

Saga Holidays. (2007). *One in seven of us take a solo holiday to escape the other half*, accessed on 5th June 2007 at http://www.saga.co.uk/corporate/press_releases/press_release.asp?id=1732

Sawhney, M. (2002). *An interview with Dr Monanbir Sawhney*, accessed on 1st September 2007 at http://www.capitalideasonline.com/articles/index.php?id=549

Scase, R. (2000). *Britain in 2010: The New business landscape*. London: Capstone.

Schlesinger, V. (2006). *Kawaza Village Tourism Project: Authentic village visits*, accessed on 26th January 2006 at http://www.gonomad.com/helps/0103/schlesinger_kawazavillage.html

Schlosberg, J. (1990). Demographics of grandparents. *American Demographics*, *12*, 7 and 33.

Schwartz, B. (2004). *The paradox of choice*. New York: Harper Collins.

Schwartz, P. (1991). *The art of the long view: Planning for the future in an uncertain world*. New York: Currency Doubleday.

Scott, W. (1810). *The lady on the lake: A poem*. Edinburgh: James Ballantyne.

Shapner, S. (2007). *Demographics of the United States*. New York: Nova Science Publishers.

Shared Hope International. (2007). *Demand*, accessed on 1st September 2007 at http://www.sharedhope.org/files/demand_us.pdf

Sheehan, J. (2006). *Skin city*. London: Harper.

Shell International. (2005). *The Shell Global Scenarios to 2025*. London: Shell International.

Shucksmith, D. M. (1983). Second-homes. *Town Planning Review*, *54*, 174–193.

Shukman. D. (2006). *Addresssing China's climate change*, 8th August, accessed on 25th April 2007 at http://news.bbc.co.uk/1/hi/sci/tech/6111528.stm

Siege, L. (2005). Just say no. *The Observer*, 23rd October, accessed on 5th November at http://observer.guardian.co.uk/magazine/story/0,11913,1596540,00.html

Silverstein, M., Fiske, N., & Butman, J. (2005). *Trading up: The New American luxury* (2nd edition). New York: Portfolio.

Singh, V., & Vinnicombe, D. (2006). *Identifying the new generation of women directors*. The Female FTSE Report, accessed on 7th November 2007 at http://www.som.cranfield.ac.uk/som/research/centres/cdwbl/downloads/FTSE2006full.pdf

Smith, F. E. (2006). *Martin Heidegger (1889–1976)*, accessed on 27th May 2007 at http://www.fsmitha.com/thinkers/heidegger.htm

Smith, J. L. (2005). *Standalone, strip mall massage parlours scrutinized for prostitution*, accessed on 1st September 2007 at http://www.reviewjournal.com/lvrj_home/2005/May-11-Wed-2005/news/26491311.html

Spencer, M. (2003). *I've already eaten ... days ago*, 13th July, accessed at http://observer.guardian.co.uk/foodmonthly/story/0,,995235,00.html

Sport England. (2002). Physical activity plan. *Sport England*, accessed on 7th August 2007 at http://www.sportengland.org/regional_physical_activity_plan.pdf

Strauss-Khan, D. (2004). A sense of common interest for the eurozone. *Financial Times*, 14/10/2004, p. 8.

Stuchebrukhov, O. (2004). The subaltern syndrome and Dostoevsky's quest for authenticity of being. *Dostoevsky Journal*, 4pages unspecified.

Taffe, R. (2002). *Boston University study shows global teens attitudes about U.S society set stage for next generation terrorism*, accessed on 30th May 2007 at http://www.bu.edu/phpbin/news/releases/display.php?id=215

Timothy, D. J. (2005). *Shopping tourism, retailing and leisure*. Clevedon: Channel View.

Tisdall, S. (2004). Ganging up on the global policeman. *The Guardian*, 01/10/2004, p. 3.

Tito, D. (2003). Why I won't invest in rockets for space tourism ... yet. *Aviation Week and Space Technology*, *159*(4), 66, 28th July.

Travis, K. (2004). Editorial — Growing strains of Hostility to the US amongst British voters. *The Guardian*, 15/10/2004, p. 5.

Tsa, A. (2003). Wars and boycotts fade away. *Business Week*, 8th April, accessed on 17th November 2006 at http://www.businessweek.com/bwdaily/dnflash/apr2003/nf2003048_2414_db053.htm

Ulrich, R. S. (1983). Aesthetic and affective response to natural environment. In: I. Altman & J. F. Wohlwill (Eds), *Human behaviour and environment: Advances in theory and research* (Vol. 6, pp. 85–125). New York: Plenum Press.

UN World Tourism Organisation. (2001). *Tourism 2020 vision, Vol. 7: Global forecasts and profiles of market segments.* Madrid: UN World Tourism Organisation.

UN World Tourism Organisation. (2006). *UNWTO World Tourism Barometer, 4*(3), October.

US Travel and Tourism Advisory Board. (2006). *Restoring America's travel brand: National strategy to compete for international visitors*, accessed on 12th November at http://www.tinet.ita.doc.gov/TTAB/docs/2006_FINALTTAB_National_Tourism_Strategy.pdf

Veblen, T. (1994). *The theory of the leisure class.* New York: Dover Publications.

Vilella, M., Yeoman, I., Page, S., Greenwood, C., & McMahon-Beattie, U. (2007). A risk adverse society — What it could mean for Scotland's tourism industry. *Tomorrow's World, Consumer & Tourist, 3*(1), accessed on 2nd November 2007 at http://www.visitscotland.org/research_and_statistics/scenarios/scenarioplanning_newsletter/scenario_planning_newsletter_7_risk_adverse.htm

VisitBritain. (2003). *Food and drink in Britain.* London: British Tourist Authority.

VisitScotland. (2004). *Luxury markets.* Edinburgh: Ledbury Consulting.

VisitScotland. (2006a). Visitor Attractions Monitor, 2005.

VisitScotland. (2006b). *Tourism Attitudes Survey*, accessed on 1st October 2006 at www.scotexchange.net/research

Voyager. (2003). *How well travelled are you*, accessed on 14th September 2006 at www.world666.com

Wacker, W., & Taylor, J. (2000). *The visionary's handbook: Nine paradoxes that will shape the future of your business.* London: Harper Collins.

Wagstyl, S. (2004). Surprise rise in exports economy. *Financial Times*, 21/09/2004, p. 2.

Walt Disney World. (2005). *Magical gatherings*, accessed on 10th September 2007.

Watters, E. (2004). *Urban tribes: Are friends the new family.* London: Bloomsbury.

Weissman, M. M., Bland, R. C., Canino, G. J., Faravelli, C., Greenwald, S., Hwu, H. G., Joyce, P. R., Karam, E. G., Lee, C. K., Lellouch, J., Lepine, J. P., Newman, S. C., Rubio-Stipec, M., Wells, J. E., Wickramaratne, P. J., Wittchen, H., & Yeh, E. K. (1996). Cross-national epidemiology of major depression and bipolar disorder. *Journal of American Medical Association, 276*, 293–299.

Whitehorn, W. (2006). *Space: The final frontier.* VisitScotland Futures Lecture Series, 11th October, Stirling University.

Wikipedia. (2007a). *Gambling in Macau*, accessed on 1st September 2007 at http://en.wikipedia.org/wiki/Gambling_in_Macau

Wikipedia. (2007b). *Mahjong*, accessed on 20th September 2007 at http://en.wikipedia.org/wiki/Mahjong

Wilmott, M. (2003). *Citizen brands.* Chichester: Wiley.

Wilmott, M., & Nelson, W. (2003). *Complicated lives: Sophisticated consumers, intricate lifestyles and simple solutions.* Chichester: Wiley.

Wilson, G. (2003). *Terrorism fear derails train-spotters*, 28th May, accessed on 1st November 2007 at http://news.bbc.co.uk/1/hi/uk/2943304.stm

Woestendiek, J. (2002). The dog who rescued Richard Nixon. *Baltimore Sun*, 22nd September, accessed on 1st September 2007 at http://www.baltimoresun.com/entertainment/custom/altoday/bal-pets092202,0,4073811.story?coll = bal_entertainment_custom_altoday_xpromo

World Travel Market. (2005). *UK & European Travel Report*, accessed on 24th May 2006 at www.hospitalitynet.org

Wright, B. (2004). *Maharastra woos medical tourists*, accessed on 14th October 2006 at http://news.bbc.co.uk/1/hi/world/south_asia/3467105.stm

Yeoman, I. (2004a). *The development of conceptual map of soft operational research*. PhD Thesis, Napier University, Edinburgh.

Yeoman, I. (2004b). What will Scottish tourism look like in 2015? *Quarterly Economic Commentary*, *29*(2), 31–47.

Yeoman, I. (2007). Why the world no longer wants to holiday in the US? Presentation at Travel and Tourism Research Association Annual Conference, 18th June, Las Vegas.

Yeoman, I., & McMahon-Beattie, U. (2004). *Revenue management and pricing: Case studies and applications*. London: Thompson Publications.

Yeoman, I., & McMahon-Beattie, U. (2005). *An information society*, accessed on 23rd July 2007 at www.visitscotland.org/scenarios

Yeoman, I., & McMahon-Beattie, U. (2006). Luxury markets and premium pricing. *Journal of Revenue Management & Pricing*, *4*(4), 319–328.

Yeoman, I., & The Future Foundation. (2008). *Tomorrow's tourist: Trends and scenarios*. Oxford: Elsevier.

Yeoman, I., Brass, D., & McMahon-Beattie, U. (2007). The authentic tourist. *Tourism Management*, *28*(4), 1128–1138.

Yeoman, I., Galt, M., & McMahon-Beattie, U. (2005). A case study of how VisitScotland prepared for war. *Journal of Travel Research*, *44*(1), 6–20.

Yeoman, I., Munro, C., & McMahon-Beattie, U. (2006). Tomorrow's world, consumer and tourist. *Journal of Vacation Marketing*, *12*(2), 174–190.

Yeoman, I., Robertson, M., Ali-Knight, J., Drummond, S., & McMahon-Beattie, U. (2004). *Festivals and events management: An international arts and cultural perspective*. Oxford: Elsevier.

YouGov. (2007). *Dating Survey*, accessed on 7th September 2007 at http://www.yougov.com/archives/pdf/datingsurvey.pdf

Zawoody, J. (2004). *Discriminating trust and corporate leadership blog*, accessed on 18th November 2006 at http://jeremy.zawodny.com/blog/archives/006355.html

Subject Index